"A path-breaking set of essays that exai
consequences of the transnationalization
policy, with reference to criminalizing glc
impunity for serious international crimes, and efforts to build human
rights penal standards. The work is guided by a coherent theory of the
varying roles of states in transnational legal orders. No student of contemporary criminal justice should miss the chance to learn from the
theory and case studies."

David Nelken, King's College London

"Norms of criminal justice, no less than crime itself, refuse to remain
neatly contained within national jurisdictions. Gregory Shaffer and Ely
Aaronson's collection of essays illustrates the ways in which a reasonably
distinct transnational order has developed, become elaborated, and in
some cases encountered contradiction and resistance. One of the book's
great insights is that the transnational legal ordering of criminal law has
in some ways empowered the state to reclaim its own legal authority.
Read this book, and you will appreciate the impossibility of dichotomiz-
ing the study of modern 'national' and 'international' criminal law."

**Beth A. Simmons, Andrea Mitchell University
Professor of Law, Political Science
and Business Ethics, University of Pennsylvania**

"The norms, institutions, and practices of criminal justice systems
around the world have been deeply transformed in the last few decades
by globalization and many new international and transnational legal
regimes. Criminal justice, comparative law, and international law
scholars are still grappling with these changes. By applying the illuminating theory of transnational legal ordering to criminal justice, this
impressive group of top scholars gathered in this book provides crucial
insights to make sense of these changes. This book is an essential tool for
anyone interested in them."

**Máximo Langer, Professor of Law and Director
of the Transnational Program on Criminal Justice,
UCLA School of Law**

TRANSNATIONAL LEGAL ORDERING OF CRIMINAL JUSTICE

Hard and soft law developed by international and regional organizations, transgovernmental networks, and international courts increasingly shape rules, procedures, and practices governing criminalization, policing, prosecution, and punishment. This dynamic calls into question traditional approaches that study criminal justice from a predominantly national perspective or that dichotomize the study of international from national criminal law. Building on socio-legal theories of transnational legal ordering, this book develops a new approach for studying the interaction between international and domestic criminal law and practice. Distinguished scholars from different disciplines apply this approach in ten case studies of transnational legal ordering that address transnational crimes such as money laundering, corruption, and human trafficking; international crimes such as mass atrocities; and human rights abuses in law enforcement. The book provides a comprehensive treatment of the changing transnational nature of criminal justice policy making and practice in today's globalized world.

GREGORY SHAFFER is Chancellor's Professor at the University of California, Irvine. His publications include seven books and more than one hundred articles and book chapters, including *Constitution-Making and Transnational Legal Order* (with Ginsburg and Halliday, 2019), *Transnational Legal Orders* (with Halliday, 2015), and *Transnational Legal Ordering and State Change* (2013).

ELY AARONSON is Associate Professor at the University of Haifa, Faculty of Law. His main areas of scholarship include legal history, socio-legal theory, criminal justice, and comparative and transnational legal theory. He is the author of *From Slave Abuse to Hate Crime: The Criminalization of Racial Violence in American History* (2014).

CAMBRIDGE STUDIES IN LAW AND SOCIETY

Founded in 1997, Cambridge Studies in Law and Society is a hub for leading scholarship in socio-legal studies. Located at the intersection of law, the humanities, and the social sciences, it publishes empirically innovative and theoretically sophisticated work on law's manifestations in everyday life: from discourses to practices, and from institutions to cultures. The series editors have longstanding expertise in the interdisciplinary study of law, and welcome contributions that place legal phenomena in national, comparative, or international perspective. Series authors come from a range of disciplines, including anthropology, history, law, literature, political science, and sociology.

Series Editors

Mark Fathi Massoud, *University of California, Santa Cruz*

Jens Meierhenrich, *London School of Economics and Political Science*

Rachel E. Stern, *University of California, Berkeley*

A list of books in the series can be found at the back of this book.

TRANSNATIONAL LEGAL ORDERING OF CRIMINAL JUSTICE

Edited by

Gregory Shaffer
University of California, Irvine

Ely Aaronson
University of Haifa

CAMBRIDGE UNIVERSITY PRESS

CAMBRIDGE
UNIVERSITY PRESS

University Printing House, Cambridge CB2 8BS, United Kingdom

One Liberty Plaza, 20th Floor, New York, NY 10006, USA

477 Williamstown Road, Port Melbourne, VIC 3207, Australia

314-321, 3rd Floor, Plot 3, Splendor Forum, Jasola District Centre, New Delhi - 110025, India

103 Penang Road, #05-06/07, Visioncrest Commercial, Singapore 238467

Cambridge University Press is part of the University of Cambridge.

It furthers the University's mission by disseminating knowledge in the pursuit of
education, learning and research at the highest international levels of excellence.

www.cambridge.org
Information on this title: www.cambridge.org/9781108812603
DOI: 10.1017/9781108873994

First published 2020
First paperback edition 2021

A catalogue record for this publication is available from the British Library

Library of Congress Cataloging in Publication data
Names: Shaffer, Gregory C., 1958– editor. | Aaronson, Ely, 1973– editor.
Title: Transnational legal ordering of criminal justice / edited by Gregory Shaffer, University
of California, Irvine [and] Ely Aaronson, University of Haifa, Israel.
Description: Cambridge, United Kingdom ; New York, NY, USA : Cambridge University
Press, 2020. | "This book arose out of a series of workshops we held on the topic at the
annual meeting of the Law and Society Association in Toronto and a two-day exchange at
the University of California, Irvine, in 2018" – ECIP acknowledgements. | Includes
bibliographical references and index.
Identifiers: LCCN 2019060069 (print) | LCCN 2019060070 (ebook) | ISBN
9781108836586 (hardback) | ISBN 9781108873994 (ebook)
Subjects: LCSH: Transnational crime – Law and legislation – Congresses.
Classification: LCC K5014.8 . T73 2020 (print) | LCC K5014.8 (ebook) |
DDC 345/.0235–dc23
LC record available at https://lccn.loc.gov/2019060069
LC ebook record available at https://lccn.loc.gov/2019060070

ISBN 978-1-108-83658-6 Hardback
ISBN 978-1-108-81260-3 Paperback

Gregory Shaffer would like to dedicate this book to Michele, Brooks, and Sage

Ely Aaronson would like to dedicate this book to Karin, Daniel, and Yahli

CONTENTS

FIGURES

TABLES

CONTRIBUTORS

The Editors

Gregory Shaffer is Chancellor's Professor at the University of California, Irvine, School of Law.

Ely Aaronson is Associate Professor at the University of Haifa, Faculty of Law.

The Authors

Vanessa Barker is Professor of Sociology at Stockholm University.

Terence Halliday is Research Professor, American Bar Foundation, and Honorary Professor, School of Regulation and Global Governance, the Australian National University.

Manuel Iturralde is Associate Professor at the Law Department, University of Los Andes (Colombia).

Radha Ivory is Senior Lecturer at the TC Beirne School of Law, University of Queensland, Australia.

Prabha Kotiswaran is Professor of Law and Social Justice at King's College London.

Michael Levi is Professor of Criminology at Cardiff University.

Ron Levi is Associate Professor and the holder of the George Ignatieff Chair of Peace and Conflict Studies at the Munk School of Global Affairs and the Department of Sociology, with cross-appointments in Law and in Political Science, at the University of Toronto.

Sally Engle Merry is Silver Professor and Professor of Anthropology at New York University.

Stefanie Neumeier is a PhD student in Political Science and International Relations at the University of Southern California.

Peter Reuter is Professor in the School of Public Policy and in the Department of Criminology at the University of Maryland.

Wayne Sandholtz is the John A. McCone Chair in International Relations and Professor in the School of International Relations and Gould School of Law at the University of Southern California.

Joachim J. Savelsberg is Professor of Sociology and Law and holder of the Arsham and Charlotte Ohanessian Chair, University of Minnesota.

Ioana Sendroiu is a doctoral student in the Department of Sociology at the University of Toronto.

Dirk van Zyl Smit is Professor of Comparative and International Penal Law and Head of the School of Law at the University of Nottingham.

ACKNOWLEDGMENTS

The moment of saying "thank you" is always a pleasure. We are delighted to express our appreciation and gratitude to the outstanding group of scholars who joined us in this collaborative project. The opportunity to exchange ideas and learn from each other's work has been deeply enlightening and enjoyable. The substantial effort each of the contributors devoted to this project has helped sharpen the arguments that run through this book and develop new ways of thinking about the larger theoretical questions concerning the globalization of criminal law.

This book arose out of a series of workshops we held on the topic at the annual meeting of the Law and Society Association in Toronto and a two-day exchange at the University of California, Irvine, in 2018. We thank the participants in these events for the rich and stimulating discussions, including the commentators for the different papers: Eve Darian-Smith, Terence Halliday, Manuel Iturralde, Prabha Kotiswaran, Maximo Langer, Ron Levi, Felix Lüth, Mona Lynch, Sally Merry, Keramet Reiter, Wayne Sandholtz, and Joachim Savelsberg.

For funding for the two-day workshop at the University of California, Irvine, we thank the Center on Globalization, Law, and Society (GLAS). We also thank the Israeli Science Foundation for the support received under the terms of Ely Aaronson's research grant on the globalized dimensions of criminalization processes (grant no. 1281/14).

We are grateful to Finola O'Sullivan, Marianne Nield, and the editorial team at Cambridge University Press for their support and guidance through the editorial and publishing process. We also thank the series editors of Cambridge Studies in Law and Society (Mark Fathi Massoud, Jens Meierhenrich, and Rachel Stern) and two anonymous reviewers for their valuable suggestions.

Finally, we take great pleasure in thanking our families – Michele, Brooks, and Sage (for Greg), and Karin, Daniel, and Yahli (for Ely) – for their support. It is with love and gratitude that we dedicate this book to them.

PART I

INTRODUCTION

CHAPTER ONE

THE TRANSNATIONAL LEGAL ORDERING OF CRIMINAL JUSTICE

Ely Aaronson and Gregory Shaffer

1.1 INTRODUCTION

Criminal justice, conventionally understood, is a system of legal norms and institutions that govern the exercise of the state's monopoly over the legitimate use of violence (Weber 1948: 78). This claim to monopoly is grounded in an assumption that nation-states are the ultimate providers of the public goods criminal law is to deliver – the maintenance of civic order, the protection of individuals against violence, the reinforcement of society's fundamental values, and the meting out of "just deserts" to culpable offenders (du-Bois, Ulvang, and Asp 2017). It also resonates with the Westphalian principle that restricts other states from intervening in matters that are essentially within a state's domestic jurisdiction.[1] As David Nelken (2011: 194) writes, "criminal law continues to be a powerful icon of sovereign statehood."

The tendency to view the criminal justice system as a state-based system has long shaped theory and empirical analysis (Zedner 2003: 3). The development and institutionalization of international criminal law since the 1990s has provided an opportunity to transcend the conventional state-centered approach, but the opportunity remained underutilized in light of conventional understandings of the distinction between the domestic and international law planes (Christensen and Levi 2017). Following the conflicts in the Balkans in the 1990s,

---

[1] In parallel, under private international law, states are not to apply foreign penal law or recognize or enforce foreign penal judgments out of sovereign respect for each other's criminal law systems – known as the "public law taboo" (Dodge 2002).

scholars in diverse disciplines, including law, political science, international relations, sociology, and history, attended to the distinctive aspects of criminal justice developed by ad hoc international criminal tribunals addressing war crimes in former Yugoslavia, Rwanda, Sierra Leone, Lebanon, and Cambodia, followed by the creation of the International Criminal Court (ICC) and complemented by the United Nations (UN) Commissions of Inquiry (Baas 2000; Hagan 2003; Hagan, Levi, and Ferrales 2006; Meierhenrich 2014; Minow, True-Frost, and Whiting 2014). Yet the development of international criminal tribunals did not meaningfully challenge methodologically nationalist approaches to criminal justice. Although some of the literature addresses the complementary role played by domestic courts under the Rome Statute of the International Criminal Court (Houwen 2013), there remains little socio-legal work on the interaction between domestic and international criminal justice systems, much less regarding broader transnational influences on national and local criminal justice. Indeed, most criminal justice scholarship continues to assume that the forces driving criminalization, policing, prosecution, and punishment are effectively domestic, as if they lie in splendid isolation from foreign and international influences (Aas 2017: 354).

This book, in contrast, examines how processes of transnational legal ordering catalyze the construction and flow of legal norms (Shaffer 2013) that reconfigure the relationship among international, regional, national, and local sites of criminal justice norm making and practice. To start, national criminal justice policy has developed collaborative interstate procedures to address crime. Such procedures hark back at least to the early twentieth century when anxieties about "white slavery," "anarchist terrorism," and cross-border liquor smuggling spurred growing concern about illicit actors' ability to defy national borders (Deflem 2002; Knepper 2010; Limoncelli 2010; Nadelmann 1993). As the world became more economically, technologically, and socially interconnected, international and regional organizations, supranational courts, and transnational nongovernmental organizations (NGOs) addressing criminal justice issues proliferated, and domestic processes of criminal lawmaking and enforcement became increasingly enmeshed within transnational frameworks that elaborate norms and practices. International treaties increasingly define criminal law norms and create duties on states to implement them. In complement, international organizations develop soft law instruments to help enforce these norms (Kotiswaran and Palmer 2015). Judges and prosecutors within the ICC and regional human rights systems participate in interpretive dialogues with domestic judicial and political actors implementing international norms attributing responsibility to perpetrators of grave human rights violations. The development of these norms and mechanisms calls into question the traditional framing of crime as an inherently territorial phenomenon defined by states (Cotterrell 2015). The accelerated institutionalization of policing and security bodies with a global or regional reach (such as Interpol, Europol, the World Customs Organization, and the Association of Caribbean Police Commissioners) facilitates the transnational diffusion of rationalities of crime governance and technologies of crime control across diverse areas, including organized crime, drug trafficking, terrorism, cyber-crime, and borders (Bigo 2013; Bowling 2010; Bowling and Sheptycki 2012). Distinct criminal justice initiatives now aim to motivate states to tighten the regulation of cross-border financial flows (Sharman 2011), save endangered species from extinction (Felbab-Brown 2017), combat cartel price-fixing (Shaffer, Nesbit, and Waller 2015), stop the plunder of antiquities (Cuno 2010), safeguard intellectual property (Haber 2018), and protect individuals from forced labor and sexual exploitation (Kotiswaran 2017), among other matters.

International institutions and NGOs, in parallel, use international instruments to call into question the legitimacy of state penal practices from a rights perspective (Clark 2001; Van Zyl Smit and Snacken 2009). In Europe, international institutions such as the European Court of Human Rights and the European Committee for the Prevention of Torture influence constitutional and administrative law principles concerning prison governance and prisoners' rights (Easton 2011; Van Zyl Smit 2006; Van Zyl Smit and Weatherby 2014). In Colombia, prosecutors from the International Criminal Court shaped the state's and rebel group's positions in negotiating a peace settlement (Hillebrecht and Huneeus 2018; Iturralde, Chapter 8). There and elsewhere, nongovernmental organizations have pressed the Inter-American Commission to bring claims under the American Convention on Human Rights to ensure accountability of those accused of gross human rights violations, creating a quasi-criminal jurisdiction of a human rights court (Huneeus 2013).

The intensity, complexity, and salience of these efforts call into question conventional theorizing of criminal justice from an analytic perspective that dichotomizes the study of national and international criminal law. Although many criminal justice scholars increasingly recognize the need to move beyond state-centric approaches, little progress has been made in developing a systematic analytic framework that addresses the relationship between international and domestic processes of criminal justice policy (Christensen and Levi 2018: 2). This book takes up the challenge by applying the conceptual tools of the theory of transnational legal orders (TLOs) to analyze the dynamic and recursive interactions between the international, regional, national, and local levels in shaping criminal justice law and policy.

Halliday and Shaffer (2015) define a transnational legal order as "a collection of formalized legal norms and associated organizations and actors that authoritatively order the understanding and practice of law across national jurisdictions" (Halliday and Shaffer 2015: 3). Drawing on the theoretical tools and empirical insights developed in earlier work on transnational legal ordering (Halliday and Shaffer 2015; Shaffer 2013, 2016; Shaffer, Ginsburg, and Halliday 2019; Shaffer and Halliday, 2020), the studies in this book examine the complex processes through which transnational norms governing criminal justice practices migrate across jurisdictions and shape the norms and practices of national and local actors. They assess the driving forces – bottom-up and top-down – behind the emergence of new mechanisms of transnational legal ordering in criminal law and policy, analyze their limits and their effects, and evaluate their implications for our understanding of the nature of criminal justice as a social and political institution. By linking empirical insights drawn from a wide variety of substantive areas, this volume facilitates theorization of the changing nature of the relationship between domestic and international forms of criminal justice policy making. In particular, we are concerned with the following questions:

- Can we identify distinct transnational legal orders in the field of criminal justice?
- If so, how do these criminal justice transnational legal orders form? Why do certain practices of criminalization, policing, procedure, and penalization exercised by nation-states become subject to transnational regulation?
- How do criminal justice transnational legal orders institutionalize? What processes and mechanisms drive institutionalization?
- How do criminal justice transnational legal orders align and compete with TLOs operating in other fields, such as human rights and constitutional law, administrative law, and business and labor law?

- What explains the variation in how transnational criminal justice norms are implemented in national and local contexts? Under what conditions do criminal justice TLOs facilitate concordance of the settled meanings of criminal justice norms across international, national, and local levels?
- What are the social, political, and cultural impacts of criminal justice TLOs?
- Under what conditions do criminal justice TLOs decline?
- What is distinctive about transnational legal orders in the field of criminal justice compared to other legal fields?

The ten case studies were carefully selected to capture the variability of the phenomenon of transnational legal ordering across different substantive areas of criminal justice policy. In particular, they highlight the commonalities and differences between three types of criminal justice TLOs. The first type consists of transnational legal orders aimed at improving the capacities of states to address crimes that have transboundary impacts. These TLOs define certain categories of conduct as transnational crimes and induce national governments to establish effective domestic mechanisms of policing, prosecuting, and punishing offenders who commit such crimes. The second type consists of transnational legal orders that govern the interactions between international and domestic legal institutions addressing "core" international crimes such as genocide, crimes against humanity, war crimes, and the crime of aggression. The third type consists of transnational legal orders aimed at abolishing or restraining the use of repressive penal and policing practices. With respect to each category of criminal justice TLO, we selected case studies that illustrate broader patterns of transnational legal ordering coupled with variation to apply, assess, and develop different dimensions of TLO theory.

This introductory chapter sets the analytic framework for the ensuing case studies. The chapter presents the key theoretical concepts of TLO theory and frames the book's inquiry within broader scholarly debates regarding the impact of globalization on criminal justice policies. Drawing on the book's case studies, it applies the TLO theoretical framework to the criminal justice field, presents the book's findings, and identifies future avenues of research. It is organized around three aspects of criminal justice transnational legal orders – their formation (Part II), their institutionalization (Part III), and their consequences (Part IV). These sections address competition among and resistance within transnational legal ordering processes that shape and constrain a TLO's formation, institutionalization, and consequences. This introduction highlights the book's contributions to the broader project of developing socio-legal theory on transnational legal ordering. Part V concludes by summarizing the case studies and their findings.

1.2   THE FORMATION OF CRIMINAL JUSTICE TLOS

We begin with the question of why certain state practices of criminalization, policing, trial procedure, and penalization become transnationalized. We aim to develop theoretical and empirical understanding of the processes through which social and institutional behaviors become defined as transnational and international crimes, on the one hand, and as illegitimate crime control and penal practices, on the other. Our approach is premised on predominantly constructivist rather than functionalist premises. We posit that the emergence of new transnational criminal justice norms is primarily driven by political and professional actors' success in shaping the dominant frames through which a social problem is defined and acted upon. In this vein, we employ the sociological concept of *framing* (Benford and Snow 2000; Goffman 1974) to investigate how social and institutional behaviors become defined as problems that necessitate legal intervention. We assess the strategies of political mobilization shaping the formation of cultural scripts, hard and soft law norms, and institutional practices in light of facilitating historical circumstances and precipitating conditions that give rise to a TLO (Halliday and Shaffer 2015). In parallel, we emphasize the role of political and social resistance in shaping the normative architecture and institutional design of TLOs. As we will see, the construction of transnational criminal justice norms is fraught with political controversy, reflecting the conflicting interests, values, and experiences of actors that differ in their capacity to influence the norms' content and their implementation.

TLO theory carves a middle ground between theoretical approaches that emphasize macrostructural explanations of legal change and those that focus on bottom-up processes involving agency in the construction of issues as social problems. The chapters in this book examine how a range of structural changes in the last decades, following the end of the Cold War, the impact of a neoliberal American-led world order (Andreas and Nadelmann 2006; Ikenberry 2011), and the growth of global markets, encouraged norm entrepreneurs to develop new crime-governance frames and how the construction of these frames, in turn, catalyzed changes in legal consciousness and legal practice. The changing nature of illegal markets in a globalizing economy spurred the formation of new mechanisms of national crime governance. In a world characterized by unprecedented levels of cross-border mobility of people, goods, capital, information, and technology, criminal organizations and groups sought to take advantage of new opportunities to establish transnational networks for the production, financing, and trafficking of illicit goods and services (Castells 1998: 172). Technological advances in transportation and communication sharply reduced the cost of smuggling banned commodities, such as drugs, guns, and counterfeit goods (Efrat 2012). Electronic banking and offshore financial centers facilitated the "laundering" of illegally obtained profits and the cross-border financing of terrorist and other criminal activities (Palan 2006). Networks diffusing information on opportunities in the Global North, combined with civil conflict, economic shocks, climate change, and other pressures, intensified the scale of clandestine border crossings of migrants vulnerable to human trafficking. Along with these large-scale social transformations, the formation of new criminal justice TLOs was also precipitated by specific historical events. The Asian Financial Crisis spurred large-scale regulatory reforms that extended the application of criminal law to activities such as tax evasion and money laundering (Sharman 2011). The September 11 attacks triggered the creation of extensive counterterrorism surveillance, policing, and detention (Ali 2018; Murphy 2012).

These broad social transformations and historical events facilitate and precipitate the development of new frames highlighting the transnational dimensions of criminal behaviors and crime governance. The ideational content of these frames and the strategies through which they are disseminated reflect the interests, values, choices, and practices of the actors who produce them (Kotiswaran and Palmer 2015).[2] The studies in this book identify the range of actors who shape the normative and institutional structures of criminal justice TLOs, analyze their legal mobilization strategies, and assess the factors that explain the success and failure of these endeavors. Collectively, they develop a more nuanced understanding of the relationship between state and

---

[2] For a range of other cases involving the construction of transnational legal orders, see Dezalay and Garth 1996; Halliday and Shaffer 2015; Seabrooke and Henriksen 2017.

non-state actors in constructing criminal justice policy and practice transnationally.

Much of the current scholarship on the formation of international and regional crime-governance frameworks tends to characterize states as unified entities that dominate the policy-making agenda, and it focuses on the role of powerful states such as the United States. TLO theory, in contrast, rejects the conceptualization of the state as a unified actor (Shaffer and Halliday 2020), and it posits that officials operating within the constituent branches and agencies of the state develop their positions and practices through interactions with non-state actors and administrative officials working for international organizations and foreign governments. As an alternative to theoretical approaches that reify the state as autonomous in its ability to set domestic policy agendas, TLO theory emphasizes the interactions that take place between state and non-state actors both within and outside of national boundaries in functionally differentiated domains. These interactions provide platforms for the development of new policy frames, engaging intergovernmental networks and broader knowledge and practice communities (Haas 1992; Keck and Sikkink 1998; Slaughter 2004). In an era in which international organizations and transnational networks acquire more resources, expertise, legitimacy, and policy autonomy, states face increasing pressure to enhance their de facto public policy-making authority and to implement the criminal justice norms developed under their auspices (Alvarez 2005; Barnett and Finnemore 2004). By viewing state actors within this wider ecology of national and global lawmaking (Block-Lieb and Halliday 2017), this project moves beyond the state-centric approach that has long dominated criminal justice scholarship and opens new avenues for theoretical development and empirical research.

Existing literature tends to portray the United States as the major driving force behind the formation of new transnational criminal justice frameworks (Andreas and Nadelmann 2006; Chuang 2006; McLeod 2010; Nadelmann 1990). In this book, we seek to develop a more nuanced understanding of the role played by the United States in transnational criminal justice governance. By juxtaposing case studies dealing with three different categories of criminal justice TLOs – respectively focusing on the governance of transnational crimes, the implementation of international norms criminalizing atrocities, and the establishment of human rights safeguards against repressive policing and penal practices – we illuminate the different postures taken by the United States toward TLO-formation projects in differing contexts. The United States often operates as a fervent supporter of the establishment of transnational rules and institutions dealing with cross-border illicit flows. However, it has been reluctant to embrace initiatives to strengthen the enforcement of "core" international crimes and to establish more effective instruments that address international human rights violations by prison authorities, police, and administrative officials, including the imposition of the death penalty. In this context, this book sheds important light on how criminal justice TLOs develop in regulatory contexts in which the United States deliberately refrains from assuming a norm-making role.

From a methodological perspective, our critique of conventional discussions of US hegemony rests on a more general proposition in TLO theory that transnational legal orders are formed through recursive interactions between bottom-up and top-down norm-making processes and institutional interactions (Halliday 2009). In some issue areas, the impact of bottom-up practices of norm-making is particularly notable. For example, Kathryn Sikkink (2011) traced in her genealogy of the anti-impunity movement how the triumph of a new frame attributing criminal liability to perpetrators of human rights violations was the product of a long process establishing anti-impunity norms in various national contexts (including Greece, Portugal, Spain, and Argentina). However, the construction of key features of this TLO – including the language of its constitutive documents, the institutional design of international tribunals, and the role of prosecutors – also relied upon hierarchical forms of international lawmaking (Rudolph 2017). In other issue areas, top-down norm-making processes play a more central role – for example, following the September 11 attacks, the UN Security Council issued Resolution 1373, which rendered some of the provisions of the Terrorist Financing Convention mandatory for all UN member states.

Due to the close attention it pays to empirical questions concerning the implementation of transnational norms in national and local settings, TLO theory helps identify and explain the recursive interactions between bottom-up and top-down norm-making processes. This focus allows us to develop a richer account of the different forms of power at play in constructing transnational crime-governance frames. In contrast with approaches that tend to privilege a single macro concept of power (such as the capacity of powerful countries to coerce weaker ones to join treaties and comply with them), we emphasize the polymorphous nature of power and the complex interactions that take place between distinct forms of power (Barnett and Duvall 2005; Lukes 1974). The case studies examine the interactions among the coercive techniques used by powerful countries, the symbolic authority of epistemic communities and international organizations, and the power of legalized norms to shape cultural meanings and individual attitudes and behavior. This multifaceted assessment of the role of power enables the authors to consider the interests and values of the range of actors who participate in the complex processes of TLO formation.

Framing processes always involve wider diagnostic struggles over the ways in which social problems should be understood and regulated (Halliday and Carruthers 2007: 1150–1151). At times, these struggles drive processes of *domain expansion* through which new conceptualizations of a social problem gain traction and extend the definitional boundaries of the targeted phenomenon (Jenness 1995). For example, as Prabha Kotiswaran (Chapter 4) shows, the dominant frame for conceptualizing the problem of trafficking long focused on the recruitment of women and children for purposes of sexual exploitation. The extensive institutionalization of this frame during the first decade of the twentieth century generated growing criticism of its neglect of other forms of human exploitation, which spurred the inclusion of new types of behaviors within the definition of trafficking (including involuntary child labor, forced marriage, and debt bondage). In turn, this process of domain expansion enabled new actors, such as the International Labor Organization, the International Labor Affairs Bureau in the US Labor Department, and labor rights' organizations, to participate in shaping the meaning of anti-trafficking norms in transnational and national contexts. As this case study demonstrates, processes of domain expansion in the area of criminal justice rely on the willingness of norm entrepreneurs to accept the individualistic assumptions underpinning criminal law (Norrie 2000) and to abandon structuralist frames for understanding the targeted problem (Simon 2006). Proponents of the labor approach to trafficking argue that the focus of the criminal justice frame on overtly violent and egregious forms of trafficking diverts attention from the need to address economic root causes that make migrants vulnerable to exploitative labor conditions in the global economy. Instead of demanding further expansion of the definitional scope of the offense of trafficking, these critics call for more radical steps to restructure labor markets, such as by guaranteeing migrant workers' rights to unionize and extending their access to employment protections (Shamir 2012). In such settings of diagnostic struggle, criminal justice frames often triumph over their competitors because they appeal to the interests of national lawmakers and law enforcement bureaucracies, which can appropriate them for political ends and to enhance their organizational resources (Lloyd and Simmons 2015: 430). For example, in his discussion of the impact of international criminal law on the Colombian peace process, Manuel Iturralde (Chapter 8) shows how opponents of the peace agreement deployed the anti-impunity norms developed by the International Criminal Court and the Inter-American Court of Human Rights to mobilize popular sentiment of indignation and vengeance and to justify a particular vision of post-conflict justice.

One of the salient features of criminal justice TLOs is that they seek to transform the social meanings of the behaviors they regulate and to subject these behaviors to public condemnation (Lessig 1995). This feature takes different forms in different domains of criminal justice. On the one hand, TLOs propagating norms of criminal prohibition aspire to utilize the stigmatizing force and the distinctive "moral voice" of criminal law to highlight the negative characteristics of the behavior in question (Duff 2001: 60). The strategies of legal diffusion resonate with a Durkheimian view that conceptualizes criminal law as "a conventional device for the expression of attitudes of resentment and indignation, and of judgments of disapproval and reprobation" (Feinberg 1974: 98). On the other hand, TLOs aiming at restraining the use of repressive policing and penal practices usually draw on the broader ideological and institutional infrastructures of international human rights. The case studies identify the advantages and disadvantages of the strategic reliance of norm entrepreneurs on these distinct modes of framing. These processes of meaning-making serve as important vehicles for the transnational diffusion of liberal values (Simmons, Dobbin, and Garrett 2006). They also spur domestic challenges to the implicit claims of moral superiority that such norm-diffusion campaigns symbolize.

The uneasy relationship between criminal law and human rights raises distinctive normative challenges (Boister 2018). As Herbert Packer (1968: 366) famously observed, "the criminal sanction is at once prime guarantor and prime threatener of human freedom. ... The tensions that inhere in the criminal sanction can never be wholly resolved in favor of guaranty and against threat." The Janus-faced character of criminal law – its operation, simultaneously, as "a law which protects" and "a law from which protection is required" (Tulkens 2011: 578) – creates ideological tensions that deeply affect the legitimacy of transnational legal orders in this field. TLOs dealing with transnational crimes produce the most evident patterns of conflict with transnational human rights norms (Boister 2002; Gammeltoft-Hansen and Vedsted-Hansen 2017). But the tensions between human rights principles and crime-governance frames also become apparent in TLOs that aim to restrain the forms of institutionalized violence that criminal justice systems inflict. Because they develop in a political climate that constitutes and reinforces public fears about crime (Simon 2006), TLOs that establish minimum standards of due process and penal moderation are often coopted to serve crime control purposes. As Dirk van Zyl Smit (Chapter 9) notes, along with the benevolent impacts of the establishment of minimum standards of prison conditions, the mutual recognition of common standards facilitates the extradition of accused persons and sentenced prisoners among states and can thereby support the punitive aims of the global "war on crime." In this context, the relationship among different types of criminal justice TLOs reveals patterns of differentiation as well as hidden forms of symbiosis.

1.3   THE INSTITUTIONALIZATION OF CRIMINAL JUSTICE TLOS

Actors participating in the formation of transnational legal orders use a variety of legal and institutional tools. They devise soft-law instruments and draft treaties (Abbott and Snidal 2000; Merry 2015; Shaffer and Pollack 2010). They develop peer-review mechanisms and devise other formal and informal means to name and shame non-complying states (Friman 2015; Kelley and Simmons 2015; Merry 2016; Merry et al. 2015; Nelken 2015). They create international fora where individuals and civil society groups can challenge the legitimacy of domestic laws and policies (Levi and Sendroiu, Chapter 11). They establish methods to incentivize and to socialize domestic governmental and private actors to incorporate these norms into their organizational structures (Bartley 2007; Koh 1996). The degree to which these efforts succeed in institutionalizing effective transnational legal orders varies. To explain these variations, TLO theory investigates the processes that shape the degree of *normative settlement* within a transnational legal order across levels of social organization and the *alignment* of that legal order with the issues it addresses, including in relation to other TLOs.

The socio-legal concept of *normative settlement* concerns the processes through which particular understandings of a legal norm come to be shared, taken for granted, and routinely practiced by actors across institutional contexts, reflecting "a high level of normative consensus" (Grattet et al. 1998). The institutionalization of TLOs is highly dependent on the degree to which their underlying normative frameworks become settled at the international, national, and local levels, and shape practice (Halliday and Shaffer 2015: 42–43). The accompanying concept of *concordance* addresses the extent to which the settled meanings of a norm at the international, national, and local levels converge with one another. In other words, one can have normative settlement at the international level, but that settlement may not concord with what settles at either the national level in terms of legal enactment or at the local level in terms of legal practice. A TLO is fully institutionalized only when normative settlement concords to a significant extent across all three levels.

The studies in this book apply these concepts to assess the processes that lead to the institutionalization of transnational legal orders in different areas of criminal justice. They analyze the conditions under which criminal justice norms settle at the international, regional, national, and local levels, and the factors that facilitate or hinder normative concordance across these levels. The ratification of multilateral treaties provides one pathway for settling the meaning of legal norms at the international level. The scope and range of international treaties have expanded since the 1970s. A growing number of them focus on crime-governance issues, while numerous others incorporate provisions that require criminalization (Boister 2003). International conventions codifying standards of criminalization, due process, and law enforcement cooperation facilitate the development of common interpretations in different crime-governance contexts. As Beth Simmons (2009: 121) writes in the context of human rights treaties, the process of negotiating, signing, and ratifying treaty obligations can reduce the scope of disagreement across nations regarding the status and meaning of legal norms and narrow "the scope for plausible deniability of violation."

However, treaties can be difficult and time-consuming to negotiate. Because of their binding nature, they may give rise to compromises that leave obligations ambiguous. As a result, transnational actors seek to overcome these constraints by developing "informal" lawmaking techniques to produce more precise legal rules having regional or global reach (Krisch 2014; Pauwelyn, Wessel, and Wouters 2012). For example, UN bodies like the UN Office on Drugs and Crime issue legislative guides that provide common models for implementing crime suppression treaties (Romaniuk 2009). Specialist organizations, such as the International Narcotics Control Board and the Financial Action Task Force, develop diagnostic and prescriptive indicators, and they publish annual reports that apply them to assess state compliance with international standards (Bewley-Taylor 2012; Nance 2015). The US government also operates as self-appointed global sheriff by monitoring the anti-crime policies of foreign countries in an array of areas, including human trafficking, digital piracy, tax evasion, and money laundering. It threatens to impose economic and political sanctions on aid-recipient countries that fail to meet standards of compliance that it unilaterally determines (Chuang 2006; McLeod 2010). The chapters in this book examine the conditions under which these instruments succeed in reducing the scope of ambiguity regarding the interpretation of international criminal justice norms and thus advancing normative settlement at the international level.

One of the key thrusts of TLO theory is that assessing the settlement of norms at the international level is insufficient because it does not come close to guaranteeing their successful implementation and application by national and local authorities. Even when there is a strong consensus about the appropriate interpretation of a norm among actors operating at the international or regional levels, normative understandings can remain highly contested among domestic legal actors who wield power at the implementation stage (Christensen 2018; Meierhenrich and Ko 2009). TLO theory highlights the challenges of domestic implementation of transnational criminal justice norms, underscoring the processes through which domestic actors translate norms into local vernaculars and the conditions under which these processes lead to concordant settling of the meaning of norms *within* a domestic legal system. In this respect, our project also contributes to the emerging research field of comparative international law, which analyzes the domestic and international factors shaping how legal actors understand, interpret, apply, and approach the seemingly universal norms of international law (Roberts, Stephan, Verdier, and Versteeg 2018).

Even when framing practices successfully change laws and regulations at the international and national levels, they still have varying impacts on day-to-day practice and legal consciousness (Boyle 2000; Nelken 2010), giving rise to "localized globalisms" (de Sousa Santos 2002). Nonetheless, shared ideas can shape the values and identities of actors in different sectors of national legal systems, spurring greater convergence in these actors' construal of social problems and influencing their behavior. For example, there is evidence that the framing of migration as a security threat that must be addressed through stricter measures of criminalization, detention, and deportation has become increasingly embedded in the practices of police officers, prosecutors, and judges in the United States and Europe at both the national and subnational levels (Stumpf 2006, 2013; Barker, Chapter 5).

In various issue areas, however, normative settlement and concordance erode over time, whether as a result of endogenous pressures or due to contests among TLOs. TLO theory helps explain how the unsettling of norms and the construction of new normative equilibriums is driven by four structural attributes that shape transnational recursive processes: *the indeterminacy of legal norms* (which often results from the strategic preference of transnational lawmakers to use vague language to achieve a negotiated outcome), *contradictions in the law* (which often emanate from the divergent interests and ideological commitments of actors within a transnational lawmaking ecology), *diagnostic struggles* over how social problems should be understood and addressed, and *mismatches* between actors who formulate transnational norms and those who wield power in implementing them (Halliday 2009; Halliday and Carruthers 2007). As Neil Boister (2012: 130) points out, UN crime suppression treaties do not stipulate the quantum or method of punishment. Because they are designed to facilitate consensus across a broad spectrum of states that differ in their penal standards and constitutional structures, the conventions usually employ open-ended language that implies an obligation to punish effectively but does not specify the type or amount of punishment to be inflicted. Typically, crime suppression treaties require states to apply severe penalties proportionate to the gravity of the offense, but they steer clear of establishing uniform standards of penalization across countries. The efforts of international organizations to reduce these ambiguities by promulgating policy prescriptions for the effective implementation of treaty norms often continue to leave national governments with considerable leeway to mold domestic policies to accommodate powerful interests that might oppose the TLO's regulatory goals. In her study of the implementation of transnational anti-corruption norms in Australia, for example, Radha Ivory (Chapter 3) shows how states may choose among a variety of crime control models, which, in turn, may permit business actors to influence the legal rules governing their activities. Depending on their preferences, corporations may support or impede the concordance of legal norms across a TLO's transnational, national, and local levels – for example, if they find that they benefit from harmonization or from deviation in light of the transnational norms in question.

The prescriptions issued by transnational lawmakers fall prey to pitfalls also encountered by national initiatives to control the exercise of law enforcement agents' discretion (Aharonson 2013; Gelsthorpe and Padfield 2003). As Leigh Payne (2015: 446) writes in the context of the anti-impunity TLO, "although the duty to prosecute gross violations of human rights seems to be a clear mandate in international law, its application soon reveals its ambiguity. The law does not stipulate how many trials, what types of perpetrators or crimes, or how much justice in terms of convictions, sentencing, jails, subsequent pardons, or reversals on appeals constitute that duty." Because of the mismatch between the actors shaping global norms of criminal justice at the international level and those implementing those norms in national and local settings, it is difficult to secure the norms' concordant settlement. Ultimately, criminal justice systems involve large, fragmented bureaucracies, including an array of policing and prosecutorial units that have distinct organizational priorities (Loftus 2010; Reiner 2010; Stuntz 2001) and operate under the long shadow of entrenched professional traditions (Lacey 2014; Lacey and Zedner 2012; Langer 2004, 2014). The failure of a TLO to regulate domestic law enforcement officers' exercise of discretion can, in turn, catalyze legitimacy challenges that jeopardize the TLO's institutionalization and survival. Yet recursive cycles of lawmaking and implementation at different levels of a TLO can also spur new normative settlement and consequent development in the legal order's regulatory performance (Halliday and Shaffer 2015: 55).

A separate dimension affecting the institutionalization of a TLO is the degree of its alignment with the issue it is to address (Halliday and Shaffer 2015: 46–51). The concept of *issue alignment* concerns the relation of a TLO to a targeted problem. A TLO may correspond closely to an issue, cover only a subset of the issue, extend well beyond the issue of concern, or compete with another or multiple TLOs, applying different frames to address the issue. Some TLOs may dominate the policy agenda for an issue area; others operate within a crowded regulatory environment in which they compete with TLOs that offer alternative frames regarding the issue and apply distinct governance tools to address it. The chapters in this book identify and explain the relationships that evolve between criminal justice TLOs and other governance mechanisms operating in an issue area, and the impact of different configurations of issue alignments on a criminal justice TLO's regulatory performance. Some chapters illustrate the capacity of a criminal justice TLO to branch out and cover broader subsets of a targeted problem, displacing other TLOs. For example, the expanding reach of the TLO governing the criminalization of migration facilitated its encroachment into regulatory domains covered by administrative (immigration) law and human rights instruments (Mitsilegas 2015; Stumpf 2006). Vanessa Barker (Chapter 5) stresses that "criminalization has a performative and communicative power that cannot be under-estimated, nor easily undone," which enables it to change public understandings of the nature of a targeted problem. Other chapters shed light on how a weak degree of issue alignment impedes the institutionalization of criminal justice TLOs and lessens their regulatory impact. Joachim Savelsberg (Chapter 7) shows how the mission of bringing criminal prosecutions against perpetrators of grave human rights violations is only partially fulfilled because of an antagonistic alignment between the anti-impunity TLO and the norms guiding the activities of organizations and actors in the fields of diplomacy and humanitarian aid. Concerned that an increase in prosecutions against political and military leaders may have a detrimental effect on diplomatic efforts to stabilize a political situation, as well as on humanitarian aid operations, these actors and organizations resist the institutionalization of the anti-impunity TLO and impede its prospects of becoming the dominant frame for governing responses to atrocities.

Table 1.1 summarizes the book's findings regarding variation across our three broad criminal justice areas in terms of the facilitating circumstances, predominant actors, vehicles for norm settlement, and factors impeding settlement and conducive to a TLO's decline.

1.4   THE CONSEQUENCES OF CRIMINAL JUSTICE TLOS

The production of new legal norms and institutional forms is not an end in itself. Rather, it is a means to shape behavior. The TLOs surveyed in

TABLE 1.1 Variations across types of criminal justice TLOs

	TLOs governing transnational crimes	TLOs governing international crimes, such as war crimes and crimes against humanity	TLOs governing human rights abuses in domestic criminal justice systems
Facilitating circumstances	• Perceived increase in the illicit flow of products, capital, and people across national borders as a result of technological and political changes; • A growing mismatch between national regulation and global markets.	• Escalation of armed conflicts and humanitarian crises; • Development of international human rights institutions after the Cold War.	• Growing concern over the use of repressive policing and penal measures by states; • Shifts in conceptualizations of social problems with the diffusion of liberal values.
Major actors driving the formation of TLOs	• Great powers; • National governments; • International organizations; • Intergovernmental security networks.	• International and regional bodies; • Human rights NGOs; • National governments.	• International and regional bodies (particularly the EU); • Human rights NGOs.
Major vehicles of norm settlement and norm concordance	• International and regional crime suppression treaties; • Prescriptive indicators and legislative guides (issued by the US, EU, UN agencies, among others).	• Rome Statute; • Court decisions and prosecutorial policies of international criminal tribunals.	• International and regional human rights treaties; • Decisions of regional human rights tribunals and UN human rights bodies.

TABLE 1.1 (*cont.*)

	TLOs governing transnational crimes	TLOs governing international crimes, such as war crimes and crimes against humanity	TLOs governing human rights abuses in domestic criminal justice systems
Factors explaining the curtailing and decline of TLOs	• Concerns regarding the effectiveness and legitimacy of a criminal justice TLO; • Decline in the capacity and commitment of powerful global actors to enforce compliance; • Failure to address domestic barriers to effective implementation.	• Legitimacy deficits from unequal enforcement of anti-impunity norms; • Resistance by US and other powerful global actors; • Competition with other transnational legal and political orders (as with fields of humanitarian aid and diplomacy).	• Mounting popular concerns about criminal threats and law and order; • National governments' resistance to effective implementation; • Resistance to implementation by rank-and-file police, prison guards, and prosecutors.

this book seek to motivate criminal justice officials to increase enforcement through arrests, prosecutions, and asset confiscations. They aim to deter would-be offenders and to facilitate victims' access to justice. They attempt to generate social disapproval of particular behaviors, some of which were not previously regarded as wrongful, and to establish norms of accountability for abuses of power by police and prison officials. The studies evaluate the conditions under which transnationally induced legal reforms succeed and fail. They empirically assess the factors that enable and constrain criminal justice TLOs' success in promoting desired regulatory outcomes, as well as the unintended consequences that these TLOs produce.

The success of criminal justice TLOs in achieving their intended regulatory goals depends on a range of structural variables, including the institutional design, governance capacities, and perceived legitimacy of the institutions that formulate and implement their normative prescriptions. It also depends on the practices and attitudes of a range of actors who serve as intermediaries between a TLOs' transnational, national, and local levels, including bureaucratic elites, activists within transnational and local NGOs, criminal lawyers, prosecutors and police, journalists, academics, and other professionals. Intermediaries play a critical role in translating transnational scripts of criminal justice policy into local vernaculars, facilitating their integration into everyday practices (Halliday and Carruthers 2006; Merry 2006b). TLO theory provides a framework for assessing the interactions of structural forces, individual agents, and social practices that shape behavioral outcomes.

In their analysis of the determinants enabling and constraining the impact of the death penalty TLO on national policies, Stefanie Neumeier and Wayne Sandholtz (Chapter 10) show that institutional arrangements that facilitate non-majoritarian policy making enable domestic norm entrepreneurs to promote abolitionist reforms, even under conditions where there is considerable popular support for retention. They find that national institutional arrangements that provide for proportional representation in the parliament and that secure judicial independence from the political branches increase political elites' ability to advance liberal criminal justice initiatives. In these institutional contexts, transnational systems more effectively create political incentives and induce normative socialization of elites. The death penalty TLO, however, is distinct from other criminal justice TLOs in that it promotes policy outcomes implemented by national legislative and judicial institutions, rather than by the wider range of institutional actors – such as police officials, prosecutors, jurors, and lower court judges – that operate in other criminal justice contexts. The domestic institutional context, in short, affects the TLO's influence. As a result, the TLO gained notable achievements in promoting its goal, despite the fact that it only partially succeeded in convincing domestic publics that the issue of capital punishment should be construed as an international human rights problem, rather than as an expression of moral condemnation and demand for security.

Other case studies in this book, in contrast, show that the failure to transform domestic attitudes concerning the moral status of criminalized behaviors and abusive law enforcement measures has a critical impact on a TLO's regulatory performance. Kotiswaran (Chapter 4) notes that, between 2010 and 2012, 41 percent of state parties to the Trafficking Convention reported having fewer than ten convictions for trafficking offenses (see also Kangaspunta 2015). Likewise, Ivory notes that the sequence of legislative reforms widening the scope of criminal responsibility for bribery offences in Australia has not triggered serious efforts to prosecute offenders (Chapter 3). These forms of under-enforcement compromise the deterrent effect of transnationally induced criminal justice reforms. They could also express skepticism of domestic enforcement actors about whether the transnational policy scripts address the concerns and priorities of local communities or, instead, represent the interests of powerful countries and elites. The case of the cannabis prohibition TLO (Aaronson, Chapter 6) and the burgeoning literature on the impact of the global war on drugs in Latin America and the Caribbean (Bowling 2010; Stokes 2005) show how the legitimacy deficits of criminal justice TLOs not only constrain their success in reducing crime rates but also can exacerbate levels of violence and insecurity.

A range of epistemological and methodological problems constrain our ability to empirically measure the regulatory impact of criminal justice TLOs. For TLOs addressing transnational crimes, these limitations arise from the clandestine nature of the activities under scrutiny (Andreas and Greenhill 2010). Even if reliable data on changes in the incidence of transnational crimes could be produced, we would struggle to assess whether these changes were caused by the TLO's instruments or by other explanatory variables, such as economic, demographic, or cultural forces. Efforts to assess the deterrent effect of criminal prosecutions of atrocities have provoked lively scholarly debates that hinge largely on methodological disputes. While some studies argue that criminal prosecutions can deter governments and rebel groups that seek international legitimacy (Jo and Simmons 2016), others question whether the rationalistic assumptions of deterrence theory are valid in the context of the "chaos of massive violence, incendiary propaganda, and upended social order" in which atrocities occur (Drumbl 2005: 590).

The acute methodological difficulties of producing credible quantitative and qualitative data on the effectiveness of criminal justice TLOs have nonetheless proven no barrier to the expansion of their regulatory reach or their steady institutional growth. Against this background, some chapters address why criminal justice TLOs persist even in the face of scant evidence of their positive impact. Halliday, Levi, and Reuter and Sally Merry (Chapters 2 and 12) highlight the role of *institutional inertia*. Once criminal justice TLOs institutionalize distinctive modes of framing social problems and establish bureaucratic structures to which resources are channeled, they can become entrenched, reducing their vulnerability to criticism of their failure to combat criminal activities and human rights abuses. Halliday et al. (Chapter 2) suggest that the persistence of criminal justice TLOs is associated with their ability to reflect plausible folk theories that reassure the public that serious measures are being taken to address security concerns (see also Halliday 2018). As noted by Halliday et al. in Chapter 2, a folk theory's influence "is built not on robust empirical foundations but on parsimony, face validity, a compactness of rhetorical expression, sufficient ambiguity to accommodate potentially conflicting understandings of what it purports to explain, an affinity with extant beliefs about such things as crime ... and a failure or resistance to examining too closely the premises and logic of the theory itself."

In communicating these messages, criminal justice TLOs provide national governments with powerful instruments to reinforce their authority and present themselves as guarantors of human security (Bauman 2000). The efforts of international organizations and transnational networks to impel national governments to adopt stricter measures of criminal regulation often converge with domestic pressures to score political points by deploying *tough on crime* rhetorical templates (Garland 2001; Simon 2006). In an era characterized by a trend in many countries from welfare-oriented to punitive-focused strategies of social governance, criminal justice TLOs promote policy reforms that resonate with (and can reinforce) neoliberal thinking about the role of the state and its priorities over social and penal programs (cf. Lacey

2013; Wacquant 2009). As this analysis suggests, the severity of crime problems cannot, in and of itself, explain the proliferation of transnational legal ordering in this area of governance. To gain a deeper understanding of the driving forces and consequences of the transnationalization of criminal justice law and policy, we need to investigate the complex interaction of the regulatory, institutional, and symbolic functions that TLOs perform across different levels of social organization, from the international to the national and the local.

1.5   THE BOOK'S CONTRIBUTION TO TLO THEORY

Our discussion thus far has focused on how TLO theory contributes to our understanding of current patterns of transnational criminal justice policy making. In this section, building on a broader methodological approach that regards empirical research as a critical and fertile tool for theory building (Nourse and Shaffer 2009), we wish to highlight some of the main research avenues that our empirical focus on the criminal justice terrain opens for TLO theory.

First, much scholarship on the operation of law as a tool of social and economic governance examines the mechanisms of coordination and cooperation that spur compliance. The studies in this book are arguably distinct in light of the unique challenges that characterize the transnational ordering of responses to illegal activities. These activities are, by their very nature, intentionally conducted in a clandestine manner. It is thus commonplace to assume that criminal law serves as the primary tool for combatting them. However, such an assumption is premised on a false dichotomy between legal and illegal spheres of human activity. In a wide variety of market environments, legal and illegal activities are closely intertwined, or the line between them is ambiguous. As David Nelken (2007: 761) describes in his analysis of the "Enron stage of capitalism," competitive strategies and business practices that exploit regulatory loopholes and transgress legal restrictions are embedded within major corporations' organizational cultures. Businesses and their employees often aim to circumvent labor laws, environmental regulations, and tax obligations in highly legalized regulatory areas (Beckert and Dewey 2017). Hence, one would be wrong to assume that this book's lessons apply to a marginal and clearly demarcated social space.

With this in mind, we believe this book opens new paths for empirical and theoretical research concerning how the interfaces between legal and illegal activities affect the performance of transnational legal orders in other fields, including in commercial and private law contexts. For example, the book's case studies identify a cluster of distinctive measurement obstacles inhibiting the production of reliable knowledge regarding the effectiveness of TLOs in regulatory contexts characterized by extensive degrees of clandestine activity. In such contexts, the reliance on social indicators is especially prone to producing blind spots regarding the impact of transnational law and policy. Future research is needed to test whether the methods used to monitor compliance in other areas of transnational legal ordering are attentive to systematic patterns of norm evasion within the regulatory field.

Second, the book's case studies raise difficult questions about the relationship between a TLO's effectiveness and its stability. Since actors form transnational legal orders to resolve (or at least mitigate) perceived regulatory problems, it is often assumed that chronic failure to establish a TLO's effectiveness will foment the creation of an alternative. Some of the chapters in this volume present evidence supporting this proposition. For example, Aaronson (Chapter 6) demonstrates how the war on drugs chronically failed to reduce the incidence of cannabis use and thus stimulated policy makers in various countries to introduce liberal policies defying this TLO's prohibitionist creeds. In other chapters, however, the authors show how criminal justice TLOs experience institutional expansion even when they persistently fail to achieve their intended goals. This observation resonates with a powerful thesis developed by sociologists of punishment to explain the persistent growth of the penal system's administrative bureaucracy, despite its acute failure to offer a remedy to modern society's core problems of crime and recidivism (Foucault 1977). Indeed, periods of increased crime rates are much more likely to generate public demands for the introduction of tougher penal measures than to stimulate critical reflection on the utility of longstanding reliance on punitive strategies (Aaronson 2014: chapter 6). This pattern casts an aura of inevitability around the operation of criminal justice systems in light of the political costs of examining progressive solutions to social problems once they are framed as security issues.

In this context, we again should not readily assume that criminal justice TLOs are *sui generis*. The literature in other areas of transnational governance is littered with examples of how a combination of vested interests and institutional lock-ins block solutions to regulatory problems (Hanrieder 2015). Sally Merry's discussion of institutional inertia's impact on the development of criminal justice TLOs offers a fruitful path for linking this book's empirical findings to other fields. We predict that future studies examining this issue will find a considerable degree of isomorphism across fields of transnational legal ordering, especially when discourses of securitization gain increasing salience (Buzan, Wæver, and de Wilde 1998). As demonstrated by the burgeoning literature in security studies, actors adopt such discourses to frame an ever-expanding ambit of issues, from environmental risks to global health concerns and immigration problems (Bigo 2002; Davies 2008; Huysmans 2000; Trombetta 2008). Successful attempts to frame social issues as security threats lead policy makers to devise measures that heavily rely on – and expand the scope of – the state's policing and surveillance capacities (Bigo 2006; Loader 2002). In this political climate, it is extremely difficult to develop non-punitive policy frameworks to address issues after they are successfully framed as security threats. This dynamic, for example, precludes serious consideration of the failures and externalities of the war on crime crusades. This book thus offers theoretical insights relevant to issues beyond the criminal justice context.

Third, criminal justice TLOs provide a fertile testing ground for examining the role of moralizing discourses in shaping patterns of transnational norm diffusion and domestic resistance. Criminal law has a distinctive capacity to produce moral meanings. Criminal codes and doctrines are mechanisms for formalizing ethical conceptions of blameworthiness (Duff 2018: 18). Emile Durkheim's famous description of punishment as a ritualized form of reaffirming society's moral values continues to provide a starting point for sociological thinking about the social dimensions of penal practices (Garland 2013: 23). This book sheds light on how this moralizing function of criminal law operates within transnational political spaces. The diffusion of legal norms governing transnational and international crimes transforms the social meanings assigned to behaviors and heightens public concern about the social problems they represent. As our case studies reveal, however, the moralizing discourses that criminal justice TLOs propagate also pose complex challenges. They reduce complex social questions to simple categories of good and evil. They serve to legitimize punitive policy agendas that can unwittingly exacerbate the underlying economic and social marginalization producing criminality. The paternalistic undercurrents of moralizing discourses also can prompt resistance from domestic politicians and law enforcement officials responsible for enforcing the norms.

Questions regarding the uses and abuses of moralizing discourses should be closely examined by scholars of transnational legal ordering in other fields. Moralizing discourses play an important role in shaping the public understanding of the nature of a wide range of transnational problems – from climate change (Seidal 2016) to corporate accountability (Shamir 2008). This book's insights pose the challenge of how to raise public awareness of the moral dimensions of transnational problems while steering clear of imposing false universalisms that impede appropriate responses to local contexts.

1.6 OVERVIEW OF THE CHAPTERS

The ten case studies in this book cover three categories of criminal justice TLOs: those dealing with the governance of criminal activities that have transboundary impacts (Part II), those promoting the implementation of anti-impunity norms through international criminal law (Part III), and those addressing the protection of international human rights in domestic criminal justice systems (Part IV). The case studies were selected on the basis of their contribution to building and testing theoretical propositions regarding the causes, manifestations, and impact of transnational legal ordering in the criminal justice sphere and beyond. In terms of case selection, some chapters were selected because they represent extreme case studies (Gerring 2007: 101–102) of the most highly institutionalized systems of norms and institutions that order the behavior of criminal justice officials across jurisdictions. The high level of institutionalization characterizing these TLOs (such as for the issues of human trafficking, money laundering, and the death penalty) offers fruitful testing ground for examining theoretical questions about the conditions under which criminal justice norms diffuse across jurisdictions and the consequences within them. As paradigmatic sites of highly institutionalized TLOs, these case studies can help inform the study of patterns of norm-elaboration and norm-diffusion in more nascent areas of transnational legal ordering. Other chapters address what has been characterized in the literature as *deviant (or outlier) case studies* (George and Bennett 2005: 75), which highlight variance on a particular dimension of the theory under consideration. For example, Aaronson's discussion of the rapid transnational diffusion of legislative models that openly defy the established norms of the cannabis prohibition TLO represents an outlier to the isomorphic trends identified in many issue areas. A longer book could have included chapters with additional case studies – such as the transnational legal ordering of environmental crimes, the transnational legal coordination of policing, and transnational mechanisms of tackling police violence – but we do not believe such case studies would have generated theoretical insights that are significantly different from those developed in this book. Overall, the diversity within the ten case studies enables us to examine a wide range of variables, hypotheses, causal mechanisms, and causal paths. In what follows, we briefly summarize the issues examined and findings of each chapter.

The five case studies in Part II address the conceptualization, propagation, institutionalization, and contestation of norms labeling different conduct transnational crimes. In Chapter 2, Terence Halliday, Michael Levi, and Peter Reuter examine the historical forces that shaped the development of *the anti-money-laundering TLO* and assess the TLO's achievements, limits, costs, and harms. The authors use the case study to analyze broader questions about the factors that enable TLOs to expand their mandates and gain greater regulatory influence, even when their success is far from certain. In the 1980s, an amalgam of powerful states, international and national financial organizations, banking and financial institutions, and transnational epistemic communities established a highly institutionalized TLO dedicated to the suppression of money laundering. Originally designed to suppress the drug trade and fight dirty money, the anti-money-laundering TLO was extended after the 9/11 terrorist attacks to combat terrorism financing and, more recently, to slow the spread of nuclear weapons. The authors examine the legal ordering techniques that major actors developed to produce and propagate transnational norms having global reach, notably through the standards, recommendations, and methodologies developed by the Financial Action Task Force (FATF), an initiative of the G7 countries housed at the OECD in Paris.

The authors then discuss the impact of the anti-money-laundering TLO. They show how assessment of its success depends on how one measures its performance. The anti-money-laundering TLO has had notable achievements in terms of impelling countries to pass anti-money-laundering laws and regulations, create new agencies and enforcement tools, and submit themselves to the scrutiny of the FATF's mechanisms of compliance monitoring. However, when moving from questions about formal compliance to assessments of success in meeting the TLO's objectives, the evidence is less clear. Despite the allocation of massive law enforcement resources, governments have been able to collect (or freeze) only a negligible quantity of stolen assets in relation to the estimated scope of the problem. There is little credible evidence to support the claim that the laws and regulations propagated by the anti-money-laundering TLO have attained the regime's primary goals – strengthening the financial stability of national economies, reducing the extent of tax evasion and corruption, and suppressing criminal organizations. In addition to these structural deficiencies, the anti-money-laundering TLO generates considerable economic costs for countries, international regulatory agencies, and financial services institutions and their customers. By increasing penal risks for financial institutions, the TLO also stems the flow of credit to poor countries desperately in need of it, harming the poor. In addition, it creates new means for authoritarian leaders to surveil and bring charges against the political opposition.

These results lead the authors to ask how the anti-money-laundering TLO continues to expand its regulatory reach despite its considerable costs and despite little evidence of success in reducing the problems that motivated its creation. They analyze a number of possible explanations, including the limited degree of public awareness of the costs of this TLO, the limited power of many of those harmed by anti-money-laundering regulations to mount effective resistance, and the fact that it rests on a surface plausibility that reassures the public of the engagement and ability of national governments and international institutions to find solutions to the risks that illicit activities harnessing globalized financial markets pose.

In Chapter 3, Radha Ivory develops a case study of Australian *anti-corruption law* to consider the strengths and limitations of TLO theory compared to the influential theoretical approach on transnational criminal law developed by Neil Boister (2003, 2012) that focuses on transnational law regimes grounded in crime-suppression treaties. She employs the case study to explore socio-legal questions about how states choose which foreign and transnational models to adopt in order to comply with international treaties and authoritative interpretations of them by international organizations. Drawing on primary and secondary materials, Ivory traces the sources of influence shaping reforms of Australia's anti-corruption laws. These reforms, which focus on holding corporations criminally liable for failing to prevent the bribery of foreign officials, are not required by UN or OECD conventions.

Rather, they were gradually adopted by peer governments (notably, the United Kingdom and the United States) as favored implementation models and were included in non-binding OECD recommendations on the implementation of the Convention.

Ivory's empirical findings raise the question of whether the choice of a model for implementing transnational criminal justice norms is shaped by the capacity of international organizations and powerful countries to coerce and socialize states or, instead, whether it is a byproduct of "colonial histories, common law traditions, and ongoing political, economic, and security ties." She provides evidence regarding the limitations of Boister's conceptualization of the mechanisms shaping transnational criminal law, which focuses on the role of multilateral suppression conventions and other formalized legal sources. As Ivory shows, the impact of these instruments must be understood as part of a more diffuse range of transnational influences illuminated by TLO theory and its emphasis on recursive processes that integrate national and local forces and factors. She finds that a recursive process is at work involving international organizations, national legislators, NGOs, and businesses. This process is marked by moments of borrowing from (former) patrons, the United States, and the United Kingdom. However, it is also punctuated by themes of modernization, efficiency, and reputation. She addresses how Australian anti-corruption activities may result not just in changes to national criminal law, but also in the development of "new" – and controversial – techniques of governance.

The next two chapters explore two TLOs that have emerged to address illicit migration flows. In Chapter 4, Prabha Kotiswaran analyzes the causes and consequences of the uneven degree of institutionalization of anti-trafficking norms across international, regional, and national settings. Although the *anti-trafficking TLO* has its roots in early transnational efforts to combat the perceived "white slavery" epidemic of the early twentieth century, the issue of trafficking has gained unprecedented salience since the 1990s. The Palermo Protocol to Prevent, Suppress and Punish Trafficking in Persons, Especially Women and Children, signed in 2000 in Palermo, Italy, and ratified by 173 countries, has precipitated a global wave of anti-trafficking laws. It also has given rise to the development of new tools for monitoring states' implementation efforts.

However, underneath these apparent indices of cross-national policy convergence, Kotiswaran shows that there are a host of barriers to the successful institutionalization of transnational anti-trafficking norms.

The malleability of the concept of trafficking allows states to tailor their implementation strategies according to their security interests and political needs. It gives rise to perennial diagnostic struggles between actors espousing a narrow construal of the concept of trafficking (focusing on exceptionally egregious slavery-like situations) and those calling for the adoption of a broad conceptualization covering prevalent forms of precarious work. These debates triggered changes in the dominant modes of framing trafficking offenses, which moved from an early approach focused almost exclusively on sex work to more recent policies that criminalize a wide variety of exploitative labor practices. The expanding remit of the anti-trafficking TLO, however, can exacerbate the costs associated with reliance on criminal law to address what is fundamentally a problem of socioeconomic exploitation, including the risk of marginalizing labor rights and economic development approaches to human trafficking.

In Chapter 5, Vanessa Barker examines how transnational legal ordering mechanisms within the European Union facilitate and legitimize a paradigm shift where asylum seeking is framed as a criminal threat rather than a human rights issue, giving rise to a *criminalization-of-migration TLO*. In recent decades, new models of criminalizing an ever-wider range of immigration-related behaviors diffused across EU member states, resulting in the imposition of penal sanctions on migrants, regardless of criminal violations. Political campaigns that conflate the migrant with the criminal and advocate the introduction of tougher tools for policing, confinement, and deportation to regulate new immigration patterns gave rise to sweeping legal reforms. Although this paradigm shift is often associated with the rise of nationalist sentiments in various countries, Barker shows how EU regulations, guidelines, directives, and judicial decisions shaped these legal reforms in important ways. She traces the symbolic and regulatory functions that the criminalization-of-migration TLO performs, which undercut fundamental due process norms. Her chapter also illustrates the erosion of both internal and external aspects of sovereignty. Although this TLO is institutionalized as a regional, rather than a global, enterprise, its impacts extend well beyond the EU's geographical boundaries as it expands the reach of European immigration policies into the high seas and third-world countries.

In Chapter 6, Ely Aaronson places the current crisis of the *TLO governing the criminalization of cannabis* within a broad historical context and considers how this TLO serves as a battleground in a struggle between competing conceptions of criminal law's role in addressing social and medical harms. In an era often characterized by a growing convergence of national laws governing criminal activities, national cannabis policies have become increasingly polarized. Some countries continue to criminalize all forms of personal cannabis use, while others have decriminalized or legalized medical and recreational uses, while regulating and taxing cannabis' commercial sale.

Aaronson shows that the current wave of cannabis liberalization reform has historical roots in debates over the legitimacy of drug prohibitions in the late 1960s and early 1970s. Since the 1990s, local and national contestation of the TLO's legitimacy spread transnationally, leading to the diffusion of new models of decriminalization, depenalization, and legalization. These reforms emerged through different mechanisms of legal change, including through governments taking advantage of the indeterminacy of the treaty norms governing drug prohibition, the persistence of diagnostic struggles over the social issues that should be addressed by the international drug control system, and the mismatch between the actors shaping formal prohibition norms at the international level and those implementing and enforcing these norms nationally and locally. Resistance from powerful actors advocating retention in the global drug control system (including the US federal government and the International Narcotics Control Board), however, has constricted the impact of these liberalization trends. Aaronson shows how, despite the diminishment of its regulatory authority, the cannabis prohibition TLO's path-dependent institutionalization has constrained the development of non-punitive strategies for regulating cannabis markets and impeded efforts to initiate progressive and humane policies in this field.

The two chapters in Part III consider the nature of the relationship between domestic and international norm-making practices in the field of international criminal law. In Chapter 7, Joachim Savelsberg discusses the contribution of TLO theory to understanding the formation, institutionalization, and consequences of legal responses to mass violence and atrocities. Focusing on the case of *Darfur and the anti-impunity TLO*, he assesses how recursive interactions among top-down, bottom-up, and horizontal forms of transnational lawmaking developed new norms establishing political and military leaders' individual criminal responsibility for atrocities, giving rise to a new anti-impunity TLO – one that was then applied to the Darfur civil conflict. The Nuremburg and Tokyo trials provided initial grounding for this process that gained momentum in the final decades of the twentieth century when national prosecutions and prosecutions before newly established international criminal tribunals proliferated. A range of transnational advocacy networks (spearheaded by NGOs like Human Rights Watch and Amnesty International), senior officials within national and international law enforcement institutions, and national governments drove these processes. The UN Security Council's decision to refer the Darfur situation to the International Criminal Court, as well as the investigations, arrest warrants, and indictments that followed, were part of the wider institutionalization of the anti-impunity TLO.

Yet, as the study nonetheless reveals, several factors impeded this criminal justice TLO's institutionalization. Hostile states, especially among the great powers, threaten the anti-impunity TLO's institutionalization, as do fields with potentially competing agendas such as diplomacy and humanitarian aid, internal contradictions within the anti-impunity TLO, and lack of enforcement power. Powerful states resisted the institutionalization of enforcement mechanisms that could be applied against their nationals. The United States, for example, used its diplomatic and political leverage to press less powerful states to agree to immunity agreements pursuant to which they agree not to extradite US citizens to the ICC. Conflicts among different professional and political actors within the TLO, as well as broader conflicts with actors and institutions operating in other social fields using different frames to conceptualize and address the targeted problem (such as humanitarian organizations and diplomatic officials), also eroded the TLO's regulatory authority. The effort to establish international frames of criminal justice triggered legitimation crises that are difficult to resolve. Nation-level forces, which filter transnational socialization processes, diminished concordance between the international and nation-state levels.

Nonetheless, Savelsberg stresses that reduced concordance between the international and the national levels across nation states, while impeding institutionalization, may also have provided the system with needed flexibility to circumvent obstacles and enable its survival. Despite the impediments to its successful institutionalization, the antiimpunity TLO has gained notable achievements in terms of its influence over public perceptions of the legal and moral responsibility of those responsible for atrocities. As Savelsberg shows, criminal indictments have a wider impact on public consciousness than other means of cultural representation. Although the power of criminal law to transform public attitudes depends on country-specific social and cultural conditions, TLOs perform important functions in shaping and institutionalizing these frames of cultural representation. They help constitute historical and political narratives that can profoundly influence collective and individual understandings and reckonings with the past.

In chapter 8, Manuel Iturralde critically assesses the forms of democratic deliberation that emerge under the shadow of the anti-impunity TLO. Focusing on the case of the *anti-impunity TLO and the Colombian peace process*, he shows how the actual and potential interventions of transnational actors implementing anti-impunity norms shaped domestic actors' legal arguments and political strategies in peace negotiations. On October 2, 2016, Colombian voters rejected a landmark peace agreement between the government and the FARC, a Marxist guerilla group, to end the oldest armed conflict in the Western hemisphere. One of the central controversies regarding the peace agreement concerned the legitimacy of provisions granting more lenient punishments to ex-combatants who fully confessed their crimes and asked for forgiveness. Opponents of the agreement argued that these provisions violated fundamental international and regional human rights norms enshrined in the Rome Statute of the International Criminal Court and in the American Convention on Human Rights. They supported their claims by referencing authoritative interpretations developed by the Inter-American Court of Human Rights and the ICC Prosecutor Office, as well as by NGOs such as Amnesty International and Human Rights Watch. Their demands for stricter prosecutions of atrocity crimes served a wider political agenda that favored a minimalist vision of peace. Proponents of the peace agreement, in contrast, offered a different interpretation of Colombia's international obligations, arguing that a less punitive settlement would serve other desirable goals. Namely, it would facilitate perpetrators' engagement with legal processes and foster reconciliation, repairing the wounds of the civil war.

Iturralde's chapter illustrates how international legal norms provide rhetorical and practical tools used in domestic legal and political conflicts. He contends that transnational scripts of retributive penal justice reinforce individualistic, neoliberal frames that preserve political, economic, and social structures that themselves constitute a form of violence. This framing, he contends, hinders the development of more participatory forms of public engagement to address domestic social problems. His chapter invites reflection on the broader socioeconomic implications of criminal justice TLOs.

The three chapters in Part IV consider the promise and challenges of TLOs dedicated to improving human rights standards in domestic criminal justice systems. In Chapter 9, Dirk van Zyl Smit traces the historical evolution of efforts to establish *international standards of prison conditions*. He assesses the achievements and limits of contemporary transnational legal ordering projects in this field, which, overall, have shaped and improved prison conditions. Following a long tradition of prison reform harking back to the classical works of John Howard and Alexis de Tocqueville, human rights activists have attempted to establish transnational mechanisms for establishing minimum standards of penal practice. These mechanisms include international and regional instruments like the 2006 European Prison Rules and the United Nations Standard Minimum Rules for the Treatment of Prisoners (2015), as well as a sizable body of judicial rulings issued by national and international tribunals (such as the European Court of Human Rights). These instruments provide tools that empower NGOs to challenge state practices.

Van Zyl Smit analyzes the complex challenges for implementing transnational norms regarding prison conditions, including those stemming from prison officials' discretion during their day-to-day management of carceral institutions. He sheds light on the complex ways in which this human rights TLO interacts with crime-governance tools that promote cross-border cooperation in prosecuting crimes and in enforcing prison sentences. On the one hand, the mutual recognition of common standards facilitates the extradition of sentenced prisoners between states that apply the standards. On the other hand, it provides states that respond to extradition requests with leverage to demand improvements to prison conditions in receiving states as a condition of cooperation. This study shows the dialectical ways in which human rights TLOs and crime-governance TLOs enable and constrain one another.

Chapter 10, by Stefanie Neumeier and Wayne Sandholtz, focuses on the development of transnational instruments leading to the *abolition of the death penalty*. The death penalty is located at the end of the penal spectrum, and its history is replete with appalling abuses of state power. Unsurprisingly, as a result, the abolition of capital punishment has been a priority for generations of penal reformers. Their analysis treats "bottom-up" and "top-down" effects as interconnected, addresses the formation of the anti-death penalty TLO across national and international levels, and emphasizes recursivity processes linking them. Building on an earlier tradition harking back to eighteenth-century thinkers like Cesare Beccaria, a transnational advocacy network aiming to abolish the death penalty under both international and national law began to gain ground after World War II and reached the height of its influence during the waves of democratization that swept the globe from the 1980s to the early 2000s. As Neumeier and Sandholtz observe, the major challenge for the normative settlement of abolitionist principles at the national level is that, in many countries, the death penalty continues to be seen both as consistent with domestic social values and as a necessary means to enforce them.

Mechanisms of inducement and socialization have institutionalized an anti-death penalty TLO, with the result that most countries have abolished the death penalty, even though this TLO remains highly contested in certain regions, such as the Middle East, North Africa, and much of Asia, as well as in the United States. The support of domestic elites has been critical for the TLO's success. Whether the support is motivated by the moral appeal of liberal values or by reputational concerns, domestic elites operating at a step removed from mass public opinion have been more likely to support abolitionist reforms. Neumeier and Sandholtz show how different aspects of the institutional design of national political systems enable and constrain efforts by political and bureaucratic elites to serve as intermediaries between the transnational and local levels of a criminal justice TLO. In the case of the TLO for the abolition of the death penalty, the relative insulation from mass publics of parliamentary institutions based on proportional representation and of independent judiciaries facilitated the TLO's success.

In Chapter 11, Ron Levi and Ioana Sendroiu use their case study of the United Nation's Universal Periodic Review (UPR) process regarding *state responses to gender-based violence* to connect cultural sociology and field theory with TLO theory. The UPR system institutionalizes a complex multi-scalar process integrating vertical, horizontal, and bottom-up processes of monitoring human rights practices in countries around the world. The review process is based on separate reports submitted by national governments and domestic civil society groups, a UN report integrating information from across UN agencies, and a peer review assessment by three foreign governments. Levi and Sendroiu interpret the UPR process as a multi-level ritual in which states communicate their normative positions to various audiences, including peer governments, transnational NGOs, international donors, and domestic constituencies. They shed light on how the UPR system facilitates normative dialogue across levels of political action by institutionalizing information-sharing mechanisms and help-ing domestic civil society actors bring their grievances to the attention of foreign audiences.

Levi and Sendroiu explore sociological questions regarding the per-formative aspects of transnational norm-making. They find that the recommendations made by countries classified as "free" in the Freedom in the World's report (an index developed by Freedom House) are framed in more specific, legal terms than those made by "unfree" countries. They also find that "unfree" countries are more likely to reject the recommendations made by "free" countries and to accept those made by "unfree" countries. These findings raise important ques-tions about the conditions under which the framing of social problems in legal terms, and the identity of the actors shaping these frames, increase or decrease the likelihood of their endorsement by national governments. They also highlight the complex consequences of human rights monitoring mechanisms that provide local actors with important tools to challenge the legitimacy of domestic criminal justice practices while also allowing national actors to address such challenges through ritualistic forms of performance.

In the concluding chapter, Sally Merry reflects on the book's main themes and raises questions and issues for future investigation. Merry stresses how the processual approach adopted by TLO theory improves our understanding of the complex interactions between three structural components of transnational governance: the ideological construction of transnational problems, the crafting of legal norms to address these problems, and the building of institutionalized infrastructures to imple-ment the norms. Her analysis highlights the mutually constitutive relationship between the materialistic and the ideological dimensions of transnational legal orders. The ideological dimensions of a TLO serve to legitimize the construction of infrastructures that facilitate its institutional expansion. Processes of institutional expansion, in turn, facilitate the transnational diffusion of the ideologies and enhance their impact on legal and administrative actors' attitudes and practices. Merry emphasizes the importance of developing research methods that are attentive to the materialistic and ideological underpinnings of the dispositions, values, and beliefs shaping everyday practices that consti-tute transnational legal orders. The case studies in this book, she concludes, provide useful models for studying the interactions between the materialistic and the ideological dimensions of transnational legal ordering across regulatory domains.

REFERENCES

Aaronson, Ely. 2014. *From Slave Abuse to Hate Crime: The Criminalization of Racial Violence in American History*. New York: Cambridge University Press.

Aas, Katja Franko. 2013. *Globalization & Crime* (2nd ed.). London: Sage.

Aas, Katja Franko. 2017. Criminology, Punishment, and the State in a Globalized Society. In *The Oxford Handbook of Criminology*, eds. Alison Liebling, Shadd Maruna, and Lesley McAra, 353–372. Oxford: Oxford University Press.

Aas, Katja Franko, and Mary Bosworth. 2013. *The Borders of Punishment: Migration, Citizenship, and Social Exclusion*. Oxford: Oxford University Press.

Abbott, Kenneth, and Duncan Snidal. 2000. Hard and Soft Law in International Governance. *International Organization* 54: 421–456.

Aharonson, Ely. 2013. Determinate Sentencing and American Exceptionalism: The Underpinnings and Effects of Cross-National Differences in the Regulation of Sentencing Discretion. *Law and Contemporary Problems* 76: 161–187.

Ali, Nathanael Tilahun. 2018. *Regulatory Counter-Terrorism: A Critical Appraisal of Proactive Global Governance*. New York: Routledge.

Alvarez, José. 2005. *International Organizations as Law-Makers*. New York: Oxford University Press.

Andreas, Peter, and Ethan Nadelmann. 2006. *Policing the Globe: Criminalization and Crime Control in International Relations*. New York: Oxford University Press.

Andreas, Peter, and Kelly M. Greenhill. 2010. The Politics of Measuring Illicit Flows and Policy Effectiveness. In *Sex, Drugs, and Body Counts: The Politics of Numbers in Global Crime and Conflict*, eds. Peter Andreas and Kelly M. Greenhill. Ithaca: Cornell University Press.

Baas, Gary Jonathan. 2000. *Stay the Hand of Vengeance: The Politics of War Crimes Tribunals*. Princeton: Princeton University Press.

Barnett, Michael, and Martha Finnemore. 2004. *Rules for the World: International Organizations in Global Politics*. Ithaca: Cornell University Press.

Barnett, Michael, and Raymond Duvall. 2005. Power in International Politics. *International Organization* 59(1): 39–75.

Bartley, Tim. 2007. Institutional Emergence in an Era of Globalization: The Rise of Transnational Private Regulation of Labor and Environmental Conditions. *American Journal of Sociology* 113: 297–351.

Bauman, Zygmunt. 2000. Social Issues of Law and Order. *British Journal of Criminology* 40(2): 225–241.

Beckert, Jens, and Matias Dewey, eds. 2017. *The Architecture of Illegal Markets: Toward an Economic Sociology of Illegality in the Economy*. New York: Oxford University Press.

Benford, Robert, and David Snow. 2000. Framing Processes and Social Movements: An Overview and Assessment. *Annual Review of Sociology* 26: 611–639.

Bewley-Taylor, David. 2012. *International Drug Control: Consensus Fractured.* New York: Cambridge University Press.

Bigo, Didier. 2002. Security and Immigration: Toward a Critique of the Governmentality of Unease. *Alternatives* 27: 63–92.

Bigo, Didier. 2006. Security, Exception, Ban and Surveillance. In *Theorizing Surveillance: The Panopticon and Beyond*, ed. David Lyon, 46–68. New York: Routledge.

Bigo, Didier. 2013. The Transnational Field of Computerised Exchange of Information in Police Matters and Its European Guilds. In *Transnational Power Elites: The New Professionals of Governance, Law and Security*, eds. Niilo Kauppi and Mikael Rask Madsen, 155–182. New York: Routledge.

Block-Lieb, Susan, and Terrence C. Halliday. 2017. *Global Lawmakers: International Organizations in the Crafting of World Markets.* New York: Cambridge University Press.

Boister, Neil. 2002. Human Rights Protection in the Suppression Conventions. *Human Rights Law Review* 2: 199–227.

Boister, Neil. 2003. Transnational Criminal Law? *European Journal of International Law* 14(5): 953–976.

Boister, Neil. 2012. *An Introduction to Transnational Criminal Law.* New York: Oxford University Press.

Boister, Neil. 2018. The "Bad Global Citizen," "Naked," in the "Transnational Penal Space." In *New Perspectives on the Structure of Transnational Criminal Justice*, eds. Mikkel Jarle Christensen and Neil Boister, 12–39. Leiden: Brill.

Bowling, Ben. 2010. *Policing the Caribbean: Transnational Security Cooperation in Practice.* Oxford: Oxford University Press.

Bowling, Ben, and James Sheptycki. 2012. *Global Policing.* London: Sage.

Boyle, Elizabeth Heger. 2000. National Politics as International Process: The Case of Anti-female-genital-cutting Laws. *Law and Society Review* 34(3): 703–737.

Buzan, Barry, Ole Wæver, and Jaap de Wilde. 1998. *Security: A New Framework for Analysis.* London: Lynne Rienner.

Castells, Manuel. 1998. *The Information Age: Economy, Society and Culture. Vol. 3: End of Millennium.* Oxford: Blackwell.

Christensen, Mikkel Jarle. 2018. International Prosecution and National Bureaucracy: The Contest to Define International Practices within the Danish Prosecution Service. *Law and Social Inquiry* 43(1): 152–181.

Christensen, Mikkel Jarle, and Ron Levi. 2017. *International Practices of Criminal Justice: Social and Legal Perspectives.* New York: Routledge.

Chuang, Janie A. 2006. The United States as Global Sheriff: Unilateral Sanctions and Human Trafficking. *Michigan Journal of International Law* 27: 437–494.

Clark, Ann Marie. 2001. *Diplomacy of Conscience: Amnesty International and Changing Human Rights Norms*. Princeton: Princeton University Press.

Costa Storti, Claudia, and Paul De Grauwe. 2012. *Illicit Trade and the Global Economy*. Cambridge: MIT Press.

Cotterrell, Roger. 2015. The Concept of Crime and Transnational Networks of Community. In *Globalisation, Criminal Law and Criminal Justice: Theoretical, Comparative and Transnational Perspectives*, eds. Valsamis Mitsilegas, Peter Alldridge, and Leonidas Cheliotis, 7–24. Oxford: Hart.

Crawford, Adam, ed. 2011. *International and Comparative Criminal Justice and Urban Governance: Convergence and Divergence in Global, National and Local Settings*. New York: Cambridge University Press.

Cuno, James. 2010. *Who Owns Antiquity? Museums and the Battle over Our Ancient Heritage*. Princeton: Princeton University Press.

Davies, Sara. 2008. Securitizing Infectious Disease. *International Affairs* 84(2): 295–313.

De Sousa Santos, Boaventura. 2002. *Toward a New Legal Common Sense: Law, Globalization, and Emancipation*. Cambridge: Cambridge University Press.

Deflem, Mathieu. 2002. *Policing World Society: Historical Foundations of International Police Cooperation*. New York: Oxford University Press.

Dezalay, Yves, and Bryant Garth. 1996. *Dealing in Virtue: International Commercial Arbitration and the Construction of a Transnational Legal Order*. Chicago: University of Chicago Press.

Dodge, William. 2002. Breaking the Public Law Taboo. *Harvard International Law Journal* 43: 161–236

Drumbl, Mark. 2005. Collective Violence and Individual Punishment: Criminality of Mass Atrocity. *Northwestern University Law Review* 99: 539–610.

du-Bois Penain, Antje, Magnus Ulvang, and Petter Asp. 2017. *Criminal Law and the Authority of the State*. Oxford: Hart.

Duff, R. A. 2001. *Punishment, Communication, and Community*. Oxford: Oxford University Press.

Duff, R. A. 2018. *The Realm of Criminal Law*. Oxford: Oxford University Press.

Durkheim, Emil (1973) [1893]. *The Division of Labour in Society*. Glencoe: Free Press.

Easton, Susan. 2011. *Prisoners' Rights: Principles and Practice*. New York: Routledge.

Efrat, Asif. 2012. *Governing Guns, Preventing Plunder: International Cooperation against Illicit Trade*. New York: Oxford University Press.

Feinberg, Joel. 1974. *Doing and Deserving: Essays in the Theory of Responsibility*. Princeton: Princeton University Press.

Felbab-Brown, Vanda. 2017. *The Extinction Market: Wildlife Trafficking and How to Counter It*. New York: Oxford University Press.

Foucault, Michele. 1977. *Discipline and Punishment: The Birth of the Prison.* New York: Pantheon.

Friman, Richard H., ed. 2015. *The Politics of Leverage in International Relations: Name, Shame, and Sanction.* New York: Palgrave Macmillan.

Gammeltoft-Hansen, Thomas, and Jens Vedsted-Hansen, eds. 2017. *Human Rights and the Dark Side of Globalization: Transnational Law Enforcement and Migration Control.* New York: Routledge.

Garland, David. 1990. *Punishment and Modern Society: A Study in Social Theory.* Chicago: University of Chicago Press.

Garland, David. 2001. *The Culture of Control: Crime and Social Order in Contemporary Society.* Oxford: Oxford University Press.

Garland, David. 2013. Punishment and Social Solidarity. In *The Sage Handbook of Punishment and Society*, eds. Jonathan Simon and Richard Sparks, 23–40. London: Sage.

Gelsthorpe, Loraine, and Nicola Padfield, eds. 2003. *Exercising Discretion: Decision-Making in the Criminal Justice System and Beyond.* Cullompton: Willan.

George, Alexander, and Andrew Bennett. 2005. *Case Studies and Theory Development in the Social Science.* Cambridge: MIT Press.

Gerring, John. 2007. *Case Studies Research: Principles and Practices.* New York: Cambridge University Press.

Goffman, Erving. 1974. *Frame Analysis: An Essay on the Organization of Experience.* Cambridge: Harvard University Press.

Grattet, Ryken, Valerie Jenness, and Theodore R. Curry. 1998. The Homogenization and Differentiation of Hate Crime Law in the United States, 1978 to 1995. *American Sociological Review* 63: 286–307.

Haas, Peter. 1992. Introduction: Epistemic Communities and International Policy Coordination. *International Organization* 46(1): 1–35.

Haber, Eldar. 2018. *Criminal Copyright.* New York: Cambridge University Press.

Hagan, John. 2003. *Justice in the Balkans: Prosecuting War Crimes in the Hague Tribunal.* Chicago: University of Chicago Press.

Hagan, John, Ron Levi, and Gabriel Ferrales. 2006. Swaying the Hand of Justice: The Internal and External Dynamics of Regime Change at the International Criminal Tribunal for the Former Yugoslavia. *Law and Social Inquiry* 31: 585–616.

Halliday, Terence C. 2009. Recursivity of Global Lawmaking: A Sociolegal Agenda. *Annual Review of Law and Social Science* 5: 263–290.

Halliday, Terence C. 2018. Plausible Folk Theories: Throwing Veils of Plausibility over Zones of Ignorance in Global Governance. *British Journal of Sociology* 69(4): 936–961.

Halliday, Terence C., and Bruce Carruthers. 2006. Negotiating Globalization: Global Scripts and Intermediation in the Construction of Asian Insolvency Regimes. *Law and Social Inquiry* 31: 521–584.

Halliday, Terence C., and Bruce Carruthers. 2007. The Recursivity of Law: Global Norm Making and National Lawmaking in the Globalization of Corporate Insolvency Regimes. *American Journal of Sociology* 112: 1135–1202.

Halliday, Terence C., and Pavel Osinsky. 2006. Globalization of Law. *Annual Review of Sociology* 32: 447–470.

Halliday, Terrence C., and Gregory Shaffer, eds. 2015. *Transnational Legal Orders*. New York: Cambridge University Press.

Hanrieder, Tine. 2015. *International Organizations in Time: Fragmentation and Reform*. New York: Oxford University Press.

Hillebrecht, Courtney, and Alexandra Huneeus (with Sandra Borda). 2018. The Judicialization of Peace. *Harvard International Law Journal* 59(2): 279–330.

Houwen, Sara. 2013. *Complementarity in the Line of Fire: The Catalysing Effect of the International Criminal Court in Uganda and Sudan*. New York: Cambridge University Press.

Huneeus, Alexandra. 2013. International Criminal Law by Other Means: The Quasi-Criminal Jurisdiction of the Human Rights Courts. *American Journal of International Law* 107(1): 1–44.

Huysmans, Jef. 2000. The European Union and the Securitization of Migration. *Journal of Common Market Studies* 38(5): 751–777.

Ikenberry, G. John. 2011. *Liberal Leviathan: The Origins, Crisis, and Transformation of the American World Order*. Princeton: Princeton University Press.

Jenness, Valerie. 1995. Social Movement Growth, Domain Expansion and Framing Processes: The Gay/Lesbian Movement and Violence against Gays and Lesbians as a Social Problem. *Social Problems* 42(1): 145–170.

Jo, Hyeran, and Beth Simmons. 2016. Can The International Criminal Court Deter Atrocity? *International Organization* 70: 443–475.

Kangaspunta, Kristiina. 2015. Was Trafficking in Persons Really Criminalised? *Anti-Trafficking Review* 4: 80–97.

Keck, Margaret, and Kathryn Sikkink. 1998. *Activists beyond Borders: Advocacy Networks in International Politics*. Ithaca: Cornell University Press.

Kelley, Judith, and Beth Simmons. 2015. Politics by Number: Indicators as Social Pressures in International Relations. *American Journal of Political Science* 59(1): 55–70.

Knepper, Paul. 2010. *The Invention of International Crime: A Global Issue in the Making, 1881–1914*. New York: Palgrave Macmillan.

Koh, Harold Hongju. 1996. Transnational Legal Process. *Nebraska Law Review* 75: 181–207.

Kotiswaran, Prabha, ed. 2017. *Revisiting the Law and Governance of Trafficking, Forced Labor and Modern Slavery*. New York: Cambridge University Press.

Kotiswaran, Prabha, and Nicola Palmer. 2015. Rethinking the "International Law of Crime": Provocations from Transnational Legal Studies. *Transnational Legal Theory* 6(1): 55–88.

Krisch, Nico. 2014. The Decay of Consent: International Law in an Age of Global Public Goods. *American Journal of International Law* 108(1): 1–40.

Lacey, Nicola. 2013. Punishment, (Neo)Liberalism and Social Democracy. In *The Sage Handbook of Punishment and Society*, eds. Jonathan Simon and Richard Sparks, 260–280. London: Sage.

Lacey, Nicola. 2014. Comparative Criminal Justice: An Institutional Approach. *Duke Journal of Comparative and International Law* 24: 501–527.

Lacey, Nicola, and Lucia Zedner. 2012. Legal Constructions of Crime. In *Oxford Handbook of Criminology* (5th ed.), eds. Mike Maguire, Rod Morgan, and Robert Reiner, 159–181. New York: Oxford University Press.

Langer, Maximo. 2004. From Legal Transplants to Legal Translations: The Globalization of Plea Bargaining and the Americanization Thesis in Criminal Procedure. *Harvard International Law Journal* 45(1): 1–64.

Langer, Maximo. 2014. The Long Shadow of the Adversarial and Inquisitorial Categories. In *The Oxford Handbook of Criminal Law*, eds. Markus Dubber and Tatjana Hornle, 887–912. New York: Oxford University Press.

Lessig, Lawrence. 1995. The Regulation of Social Meaning. *The University of Chicago Law Review* 62: 943–1045.

Limoncelli, Stephanie. 2010. *The Politics of Trafficking: The First International Movement to Combat the Sexual Exploitation of Women*. Palo Alto: Stanford University Press.

Lloyd, Paulette, and Beth A. Simmons. 2015. Framing a New Transnational Legal Order: The Case of Human Trafficking. In *Transnational Legal Orders*, eds. Terry C. Halliday and Gregory Shaffer, 400–438. New York: Cambridge University Press.

Loader, Ian. 2002. Policing, Securitization, and Democratization in Europe. *Criminology and Criminal Justice* 2(2): 125–153.

Loftus, Bethan. 2010. Police Occupational Culture: Classic Themes, Altered Times. *Policing and Society* 20(1): 1–22.

Lukes, Steven. 1974. *Power: A Radical View*. London: Macmillan Press.

Machado, Maira. 2012. Similar in their Differences: Transnational Legal Processes Addressing Money Laundering in Brazil and Argentina. *Law and Social Inquiry* 37: 330–366.

McLeod, Allegra. 2010. Exporting US Criminal Justice. *Yale Law and Policy Review* 29(1): 84–164.

Meierhenrich, Jens. 2014. The Practice of International Law: A Theoretical Analysis. *Law and Contemporary Problems* 76: 1–83.

Meierhenrich, Jens, and Keiko Ko. 2009. How Do States Join the International Criminal Court? The Implementation of the Rome Statute in Japan. *Journal of International Criminal Justice* 7(2): 233–256.

Merry, Sally Engle. 2006a. *Human Rights and Gender Violence: Translating International Law into Local Justice*. Chicago: University of Chicago Press.

Merry, Sally Engle. 2006b. Transnational Human Rights and Local Activism: Mapping the Middle. *American Anthropologist* 108(1): 38–51.

Merry, Sally Engle. 2015. Firming Up Soft Law: The Impact of Indicators on Transnational Human Rights Legal Orders. In *Transnational Legal Orders*, eds. Terry C. Halliday and Gregory Shaffer, 374–400. New York: Cambridge University Press

Merry, Sally Engle. 2016. *The Seduction of Quantification: Measuring Human Rights, Gender Violence, and Sex Trafficking.* Chicago: University of Chicago Press.

Merry, Sally Engle, Kevin E. Davis, and Benedict Kingsbury, eds. 2015. *The Quiet Power of Indicators: Measuring Governance, Corruption, and Rule of Law.* New York: Cambridge University Press.

Minow, Martha, C. Cora True-Frost, and Alex Whiting, eds. 2015. *The First Global Prosecutor: Promise and Constraints.* Ann Arbor: University of Michigan Press.

Mitsilegas, Valsamis. 2015. *The Criminalisation of Migration in Europe: Challenges for Human Rights and the Rule of Law.* London: Springer.

Murphy, Cian. 2012. *EU Counter-Terrorism Law: Pre-Emption and the Rule of Law.* Oxford: Hart.

Nadelmann, Ethan. 1990. Global Prohibition Regimes: The Evolution of Norms in International Society. *International Organization* 44(4): 479–526.

Nadelmann, Ethan. 1993. *Cops Across Borders: The Internationalization of U.S. Criminal Law Enforcement.* University Park: Pennsylvania State University Press.

Naim, Moises. 2006. *Illicit: How Smugglers, Traffickers and Copycats Are Hijacking the Global Economy.* New York: Anchor Books.

Nance, Mark T. 2015. Naming and Shaming in Financial Regulation: Explaining Variation in the Financial Action Task Force on Money Laundering. In *The Politics of Leverage in International Relations: Name, Shame, and Sanction*, ed. Richard H. Friman, 123–142. New York: Palgrave Macmillan.

Naylor, R. T. 2004. *Wages of Crime: Black Markets, Illegal Finance, and the Underworld Economy.* Ithaca: Cornell University Press.

Nelken, David. 2007. White-Collar and Corporate Crime. In *The Oxford Handbook of Criminology* (4th ed.), eds. Mike Maguire, Rod Morgan, and Robert Reiner, 733–770. Oxford: Oxford University Press.

Nelken, David. 2010. Human Trafficking and Legal Culture. *Israel Law Review* 43: 479–513.

Nelken, David, ed. 2011. *Comparative Criminal Justice and Globalization.* Burlington: Ashgate.

Nelken, David. 2015. The Changing Role of Social Indicators: From Explanation to Governance. In *Globalisation, Criminal Law and Criminal Justice: Theoretical, Comparative and Transnational Perspectives*, eds. Valsamis Mitsilegas, Peter Alldridge, and Leonidas Cheliotis, 25–44. Oxford: Hart.

Norrie, Alan. 2000. *Punishment, Responsibility, and Justice*. Oxford: Oxford University Press.

Nourse, Victoria, and Gregory Shaffer. 2009. Varieties of New Legal Realism: Can a New World Order Prompt a New Legal Theory? *Cornell Law Review* 95: 61–138.

Packer, Herbert. 1968. *The Limits of the Criminal Sanction*. Palo Alto: Stanford University Press.

Palan, Ronen. 2006. *The Offshore World*. Ithaca: Cornell University Press.

Pauwelyn, Joost, Ramses Wessel, and Jan Wouters, eds. 2012. *Informal International Lawmaking*. New York: Oxford University Press.

Payne, Leigh A. 2015. The Justice Paradox? Transnational Legal Orders and Accountability for Past Human Rights Violations. In *Transnational Legal Orders*, eds. Terry C. Halliday and Gregory Shaffer, 439–474. New York: Cambridge University Press.

Reiner, Robert. 2010. *The Politics of the Police* (4th ed.). Oxford: Oxford University Press.

Roberts, Anthea, Paul Stephan, Pierre-Hugues Verdier, and Mila Versterg, eds. 2018. *Comparative International Law*. New York: Oxford University Press.

Romaniuk, Peter. 2018. Crime and Criminal Justice. In *The Oxford Handbook of the United Nations* (2nd ed.), eds. Thomas G. Weiss and Sam Daws, 515–527. New York: Oxford University Press.

Rudolph, Christopher. 2017. *Power and Principle: The Politics of International Criminal Courts*. Ithaca: Cornell University Press.

Seabrooke, Leonard, and Lasse Folke Henriksen. 2017. *Professional Networks in Transnational Governance*. New York: Cambridge University Press.

Seidel, Christian. 2016. The Costs of Moralizing: How about a "Government House Climate Ethics"? In *Climate Justice in a Non-Ideal World*, eds. Jennifer Clare Heyward and Dominic Roser, 277–295. New York: Oxford University Press.

Shaffer, Gregory, ed. 2013. *Transnational Legal Ordering and State Change*. New York: Cambridge University Press.

Shaffer, Gregory. 2016. Theorizing Transnational Legal Orders. *Annual Review of Law and Social Science* 12: 231–253.

Shaffer, Gregory, Tom Ginsburg, and Terrence Halliday, eds. 2019. *Constitution-Making and Transnational Legal Order*. New York: Cambridge University Press.

Shaffer, Gregory, and Terrence Halliday. 2020. With, Within, and Beyond the State: The Promise and Limits of Transnational Legal Ordering. In *The Oxford Handbook of Transnational Law*, ed. Peer Zumbansen. New York: Oxford University Press.

Shaffer, Gregory, Nathaniel Nesbitt, and Spencer Weber Waller. 2015. Criminalizing Cartels: A Global Trend? In *Research Handbook on*

Comparative Competition Law, eds. John Duns, Arlen Duke, and Brendan Sweeney, 301–344. Cheltenham: Edgar Elgar.

Shaffer, Gregory, and Mark A. Pollack. 2010. Hard vs. Soft Law: Alternatives, Complements and Antagonists in International Governance. *Minnesota Law Review* 94: 706–799.

Shamir, Hila. 2012. A Labor Paradigm for Human Trafficking. *UCLA Law Review* 60: 76–136.

Shamir, Ronen. 2008. The Age of Responsibilization: On Market-Embedded Morality. *Economy and Society* 37(1): 1–19.

Sharman, J. C. 2011. *The Money Laundry: Regulating Criminal Finance in the Global Economy*. Ithaca: Cornell University Press.

Sikkink, Kathryn. 2011. *The Justice Cascade: How Human Rights Prosecutions Are Changing World Politics*. New York: W. W. Norton.

Simmons, Beth. 2009. *Mobilizing for Human Rights: International Law in Domestic Politics*. New York: Cambridge University Press.

Simmons, Beth, Frank Dobbin, and Geoffrey Garrett. 2006. The International Diffusion of Liberalism. *International Organization* 60: 781–810.

Simon, Jonathan. 2006. *Governing through Crime: How the War on Crime Transformed American Democracy and Created a Culture of Fear*. New York: Oxford University Press.

Slaughter, Anne-Marie. 2004. *A New World Order*. Princeton: Princeton University Press.

Stokes, Doug. 2005. *America's Other War: Terrorizing Colombia*. London: Zed Books.

Stumpf, Juliet. 2006. The Crimmigration Crisis: Immigration, Crime and Sovereign Power. *American University Law Review* 52(2): 367–419.

Stumpf, Juliet. 2013. The Process is the Punishment in Crimmigration Law. In *The Borders of Punishment: Migration, Citizenship, and Social Exclusion*, eds. Katja Franko Aas and Mary Bosworth, 58–75. Oxford: Oxford University Press.

Stuntz, William. 2001. The Pathological Politics of Criminal Law. *Michigan Law Review* 100(3): 505–599.

Trombetta, Maria Julia. 2008. Environmental Security and Climate Change: Analysing the Discourse. *Cambridge Review of International Affairs* 21(4): 585–602.

Tulkens, Francoise. 2011. The Paradoxical Relationship between Criminal Law and Human Rights. *Journal of International Criminal Justice* 9: 577–595.

Valverde, Mariana. 2006. *Law and Order: Images, Meanings, Myths*. New Brunswick: Rutgers University Press.

Van Zyl Smit, Dirk. 2006. Humanising Imprisonment: A European Project? *European Journal on Criminal Policy and Research* 12: 107–120.

Van Zyl Smit, Dirk, and Sonja Snacken. 2009. *Principles of European Prison Law and Policy: Penology and Human Rights*. Oxford: Oxford University Press.

Van Zyl Smit, Dirk, Peter Weatherby, and Simon Creighton. 2014. Whole Life Sentences and the Tide of European Human Rights Jurisprudence: What Is to Be Done? *Human Rights Law Review* 14(1): 59–84.

Wacquant, Loïc. 2009. *Punishing the Poor: The Neoliberal Government of Social Insecurity.* Durham: Duke University Press.

Weber, Max. 1948 [1919]. Politics as a Vocation. In *From Max Weber: Essays in Sociology*, eds. Hans Heinrich Gerth and C. Wright Mills. London: Routledge and Kegan Paul.

Zedner, Lucia. 2003. *Criminal Justice.* Oxford: Oxford University Press.

PART II

TRANSNATIONAL LEGAL ORDERING AND TRANSNATIONAL CRIMES

CHAPTER TWO

WHY DO TRANSNATIONAL LEGAL ORDERS PERSIST?

The Curious Case of Money-Laundering Controls

Terence Halliday, Michael Levi, and Peter Reuter[*]

2.1 INTRODUCTION

Transnational legal orders (TLOs) proliferate. They offer solutions to economic, social, and political problems, ranging from business and financial regulation to climate change, from human rights to constitution making. They come in many forms, rising and falling at different rates, and cooperating or conflicting as they come into contact with each other (Halliday and Shaffer 2015a; Shaffer, Ginsburg, and Halliday 2019).

This chapter enquires into the case of one of the most comprehensive, far-reaching, most deeply penetrating, and most punitive of TLOs. It is so punitive that we suggest there is value in considering whether it points to a species of TLO that differs in kind from those hitherto identified in the literature on financial regulation, business, environmental, human rights, and constitution making.

Since the 1980s an amalgam of clubs of nations, powerful states, international financial institutions, banking and financial institutions, and emergent "issue professionals" have created a worldwide regulatory order to stem tides of money laundering and thereby attempt to forestall the very many harms that anti-money-laundering (AML) entrepreneurs perceive follow from the flow of dirty money inside states and

[*] We are grateful for the cooperation of staff at the International Monetary Fund, the Financial Action Task Force, and other international and domestic regulators and nonprofit organizations integral to the AML/CMT international regulatory order. Opinions expressed are entirely our own. We thank Gregory Shaffer, Ely Aaronson, and the participants in the 2018 conference for their valuable insights.

beyond (Levi and Reuter 2006; Nance 2018). Not only does this order rely on potentially heavy punitive measures against citizens and institutions within states; it also has the capacity, often threatened and occasionally effected, to bring punitive action against states.

This chapter draws on an intensive study of the AML/CFT order[1] at a moment when its governing norms and methodologies of implementation were undergoing revision and expansion (Halliday, Levi, and Reuter 2014), as well as on observation of and participation in AML/CFT activities over three decades. This enables us to bring rich empirical evidence to bear on two theoretical questions.

First, despite its seemingly successful institutionalization, the AML TLO exhibits many deficiencies and imposes extensive costs on the private and public sectors, and harms upon the public. Its benefits are elusive and unmeasured with any serious specificity. Why doesn't it fail? What explains its persistence? Here we seek to contribute to the theory less on the rise of TLOs and more on their persistence and the conditions under which they are likely to fail (Halliday and Shaffer 2015: 500–511).

Second, the pervasiveness and penetration of this particular TLO suggests that it has qualities that distinguish it from other TLOs which have been observed in the domains of business, finance, rights, constitution making, and private legal ordering. The chapter asks if the AML TLO, or indeed criminal TLOs, more generally,[2] are a particular species of a TLO that might be characterized as "disciplinary" TLOs.

We, first, briefly sketch the thirty-year development of the AML TLO and describe how it works; second, we consider its benefits, costs, deficiencies, and harms, both intended and unintended; third, we confront the puzzle of its persistence; and, fourth, we conclude with considerations on its distinctiveness as a disciplinary TLO.

2.2 THE RISE OF THE AML TLO

Although the Council of Europe adopted in 1980 a weak measure for banks to develop some vigilance over who deposited or transferred cash

---

[1] Technically speaking, this regulatory regime or order now embraces anti-money-laundering (AML), combating the financing of terrorism (CFT), and counter-proliferation financing (CPF). We are not arguing that CFT and CPF are unimportant. However, the vast majority of criminal prosecutions and regulatory actions are focused on money laundering. Hereafter we shorten this to the AML TLO.

[2] TLOs of international criminal justice might include legal orders concerned with human trafficking, corporate foreign bribery, prison standards, sexual violence, the death penalty, crimes against humanity, and drugs prohibition.

(as part of its counterterrorism efforts against left-wing groups, primarily in Italy but also Germany), a sharpening focus on money laundering in the 1980s came principally as a response to the drug trade, organized crime, and domestic terrorism. Money laundering is statutorily defined (with some variation between nations) as actions that attempt to conceal the criminal origins of assets, and generally includes self-laundering by primary offenders as well as by third parties, some of whom are lawyers and accountants.

Initially responses by some states came in the form of domestic legislation to detect and deter money laundering, almost entirely focused on the banking industry (Levi 1991). The UK enacted legislation allowing for bank account access (with prior judicial approval) in crime investigations (1984); drug-trafficking offenses (1986); other crimes for gain, excluding tax fraud (1988); and prevention of terrorism (1989), which strengthened law enforcement's capacity to reach dirty money in the banking sector with police powers. It gave bankers civil immunity for reporting their suspicions of account-holder transactions. The UK set up a Serious Fraud Office in 1987, though it never had any clear role in relation to money-laundering prosecutions other than via its later transnational bribery mandate (from the Bribery Act 2010, whose extra-territorial effect also included money-laundering offenses). For the UK, too, detecting dirty money was part of a strategy to suppress the financing of terrorism, then focused on the Provisional IRA and, to a lesser extent, Protestant paramilitaries in Ireland. For domestic political reasons, prior to the latter stages of the Clinton administration and his role in the 1999 peace agreement, the United States did not play an active role in combating the financing of Irish terrorism.

Following a presidential commission on organized crime that reported in 1986, the United States enacted its Money Laundering Control Act (1986), which criminalized money laundering with sentences of up to ten years for individuals who knowingly laundered dirty money. *Money laundering* refers to efforts to use the financial system to make the fruits of specific crimes ("predicate crimes") appear to be legitimate. In all these cases, government responses to money laundering were seen more broadly as a way of suppressing domestic crimes for gain (particularly drug dealing and to a lesser extent financial crimes) and threats from national and international organized crime groups.

International legal responses to the financial proceeds of crime and laundering of dirty money[3] gathered momentum in the later 1980s and early 1990s. The 1988 UN Vienna Convention for the first time named money laundering as an offense in international law in an effort to deprive illicit drug dealers of their ill-gotten financial gains. For the financial sector, the 1988 Basle Committee on Banking Principles issued principles to increase vigilance over customers who might be engaged in criminal activity. The Council of Europe followed with a 1990 convention on laundering, search, seizure, and confiscation of the proceeds of crime – a law mirrored by the 1991 European Community Directive on Money Laundering (Levi 2006).

The painstaking, time-consuming, and exhausting effort to produce the multilateral Vienna Convention convinced the United States and the G7 that treaties were not the appropriate legal method to handle the fast-moving, sophisticated, and shadowy world of dirty money (Nance 2018). The United States had no interest in lodging new surveillance and enforcement capacities in the UN, which was not regarded as appropriate for efficient conduct of business. Instead the United States proposed a task force, subsequently accepted by the G7, that would take one year to review and report on domestic AML laws across the world. Formed in 1989 to focus narrowly on money generated from the illicit drug trade, the Financial Action Task Force on Money Laundering (hereafter FATF) began as a network with eleven members and no standing in international law.

Contrast this tentative moment of origin with the global enterprise described in the 2014 report to the IMF on *Global Surveillance of Dirty Money*:

> 10. **The FATF has accomplished a remarkable feat of global standard-setting since its founding in 1989.** From a world in which there were no global standards on anti-money laundering and few national standards, FATF has forged a single global standard for AML, then CFT, and now financing of proliferation of weapons of mass destruction. The Standard comprises a set of Recommendations which were first issued by the FATF in 1990 and revised in 1996, 2001 (where eight provisions were added on terrorism), 2003, 2004 (where a 9th recommendation was added on terrorism) and 2012. To guide assessments of countries, the

---

[3] Note these are not identical. Although proportions are not empirically established, there is considerable evidence that except for more elite offenders, most proceeds from criminal activities are spent immediately on lifestyles and relatively less is laundered for future consumption.

FATF created an assessment Methodology in 2013 for all AML/CFT assessor bodies, namely the FATF, the eight FATF-Style Regional Bodies (FSRBs), the Fund and the World Bank.

11. **Since its founding, the FATF has forged a global network of states and non-state bodies.** It has created an amalgam of thirty-seven member jurisdictions and two regional organizations, nine regional bodies, and 22 observer bodies, including the International Monetary Fund and World Bank. The FATF-led standard setting and assessment program has produced substantial convergence on core elements of a universal AML/CFT regime which in turn has facilitated international communication and cooperation in the efforts to prevent money laundering and terrorism, to freeze and recover proceeds of crime, and ease financial investigation and prosecution of offenders. This is a significant political achievement. (Halliday, Levi, and Reuter 2014: 10)

2.3 HOW DOES IT WORK?

The AML regime utilizes assessments of country compliance with the FATF standards as a mechanism of surveillance and control. They are conducted in two ways: by teams from other nations and international organizations (IOs), including the FATF, IMF, and World Bank; and by peers from other countries who appraise one of their regional neighbors. In both instances, the result is a Mutual Evaluation Report (MER).

For the IO evaluations that occurred in the Third Round of evaluations between 2004 and 2012, certainly those involving the IMF's dedicated Financial Integrity Group, the process generally proceeded through the following steps. The IO would conduct a "desk analysis" of a country's financial and legal system to provide background. The IO would then send an extensive questionnaire to national authorities asking about aspects of their financial and legal systems that relate to the FATF Standards. After reviewing the responses in the questionnaire, the IO would send a team of about four to six specialists for a two- to three-week on-site visit with state and non-state stakeholders. Based on the accumulated documentary and interview materials, the IO would prepare a draft report, including recommendations and provisional ratings on a checklist of key factors. In draft form these were shared with state officials, invariably leading to several rounds of informal comments and responses as the assessors and country officials moved toward a final, agreed-upon text.

The final text would then be reviewed by the FATF Secretariat as a quality control and consistency check. If the country being assessed was a member of FATF, the report would come to one of the periodic FATF plenaries, where all FATF members and IOs convened in a general assembly, for confirmation (or rejection) of recommendations and ratings. There might be some amendments made to the report at the plenary, sometimes after very vigorous discussion. After FATF approval, the report would be made public. Sometimes countries with compliance problems would go through several rounds of reform and assessments until the FATF considered the country was sufficiently compliant and could exit the reporting process (CLG Final Report 2014: 27).

Since the implementation of a new 2013 methodology, there have been some small changes in this process,[4] reflecting modest rethinking about issues that were working better or less well, along with the integration of FATF and FSRB processes. For mutual evaluations conducted by regional FATFs, there were some variations in the process, but these have now been harmonized, at least formally.

2.4 COMPLIANCE LEVERS AND MECHANISMS

The AML TLO is built upon an architecture of positive inducements and negative sanctions. There are four principal inducements, although they are not explicitly stated. Countries that perform well in the assessments are publicly affirmed. There is no direct evidence that such affirmations provide tangible benefits to their economies, although they are welcome politically. Countries that face challenges or criticism may be eligible for technical assistance by the IMF or other bodies in order to strengthen their institutions and governance capabilities. Countries may believe that AML regulatory measures strengthen their capacity to control domestic and imported crime more generally, and help strengthen Financial Intelligence Units in their bid to obtain inter-agency support for creating a more compliant AML system. And, as an unanticipated by-product of enhanced executive powers in AML regimes, authoritarian leaders obtain new tools to monitor and perhaps more efficiently suppress opposition, for example

---

[4] In February 2013 (R.37, R.40); October 2015 (Note to R.8); June 2016 (R.8); October 2016 (R.5 and definition of "funds or other assets"); June 2017 (R.7 and glossary definitions); November 2017 (R.18, R.21); February 2018 (R.2) (www.fatf-gafi.org/publications/fatfrecom mendations/documents/fatf-recommendations.html#UPDATES).

via corruption and/or money-laundering charges, most easily via a compliant police and judiciary.

The inducements are complemented by three sets of negative sanctions. Diffuse diplomatic and social pressure, significantly through shaming for low ratings, comes from the influence of both "peer" states and powerful states to comply. Financial pressures can follow from low ratings; money center banks may charge more for providing correspondent banking services because their own regulators require enhanced due diligence for transactions involving that country, or they may even "de-risk" large sectors of the low-rated economy by refusing to process their dollar or other transactions.

Much more serious in its consequences is blacklisting by the International Cooperation Review Group (ICRG). According to IMF and country officials, even the threat of blacklisting through ICRG was a "very good driving engine" to get countries to push for reforms. No country, except for the occasional microstate such as Nauru, along with Iran and North Korea, has stayed on the list for long. But its effects on access to affordable international finance produce tangible impacts ranging from a reduction or withdrawal of correspondent banking privileges for a given country to increased difficulty and higher costs in raising capital on international financial markets.[5] The combined risks of these two alone can galvanize governments to react vigorously, initially in efforts to upgrade the ratings they receive from assessors and subsequently in legal and institutional reforms. Even in a country such as Germany, which was at no real risk of being put on the ICRG list, our research found how seriously its senior officials reacted to the draft IMF report's criticisms, even to the extent of bringing a delegation to Washington to confer with IMF officials.[6] The "folk memory" of poor ratings can stimulate them to do better in the next review, many years later and, for those placed on the ICRG gray list, stimulates remediation in follow-up meetings that are reported back to the FATF or FSRB.

The combination of inducements and sanctions has led to a remarkable degree of formal compliance in the adoption of laws and regulations, the creation and enhancement of state institutions, and at

---

[5] It is currently difficult to estimate with hard data how long these impacts persist.
[6] The sanctions regimes are often concatenated with AML but have their own processes. Among the large literature on this subject, see *Targeted Sanctions: The Impacts and Effectiveness of United Nations Action 2016*, by Thomas J. Biersteker, Sue E. Eckert, and Marcos Tourinho (Cambridge University Press). Sanctions on both countries and individuals have increased in popularity in the current decade as a tool of political and economic pressure, but this is outside our remit in this chapter.

least a measure of conformity by domestic economic and civil society actors. However, one effort to assess the performance of rich countries (OECD members) at the end of the third round of evaluations (OECD 2013) showed that many countries were seriously deficient in their compliance. For example, not one out of twenty-nine members fully complied with Recommendation 24 concerning Regulation of Designated Non-Financial Businesses and Professions; only three of the countries were Largely Compliant and thirteen were judged as Non-Compliant. Not all the Recommendations carry the same weight in the eyes of the member countries.

When we apply conceptual criteria to empirical evidence, it is evident that the AML/CFT governance regime constitutes a well-institutionalized TLO (Halliday and Shaffer 2015b). First, its architects have created a certain kind of normative *order* that seeks to solve a "problem" in predictable ways through laws and regulations, and their regulatory accompaniments such as financial supervision. Second, it is *transnational* insofar as its norms are produced ultimately by social organizations that transcend the state. Third, it is *legal* not so much because its norms are expressed in recognizably legal forms, but insofar as those norms are directed to legal institutions and legal regulation within the state. Fourth, it can be said to be institutionalized on three interrelated criteria: (a) there is an alignment, even if partial and con-tested, between underlying issue areas (e.g., illicit drug trade, organized crime, transnational crime, financial instability, security) and the order created to govern them; (b) the norms are well settled in the governing transnational recommendations and their adoption in national laws, regulations, and institutions, and somewhat settled in local norms that infuse the mentalities of police or bankers or professionals; and (c) there is recognizable concordance in the norms at global, regional, national, and local levels of adoption and internalization.

2.5 SUCCESS?

If one measure of success is the formalization of norms, the institutio-nalization of a global regulatory apparatus, and the construction of domestic monitoring and enforcement agencies, then the AML regime has been highly successful. Almost all states, and tiny jurisdictions ranging from the Vatican and the Cayman Islands to Nauru and Turks and Caicos Islands, are now either members of the FATF itself or one of the FATF-style regional bodies. Put another way, if we evaluate outcomes of this TLO by the GAO criteria of *formal compliance* and *program implementation*,[7] then the outcomes can be counted as substantially achieved. States submit themselves to the MER scrutiny and have already put in place much of the legal and institutional structure that FATF requires – all this without FATF being either a treaty body or a UN agency.

If, however, we apply the stricter standards of program effectiveness and outcome effectiveness,[8] then the verdict is very different. Our research concluded that the FATF efforts have almost entirely been focused on formal compliance, and "very little emphasis, if any, was given to program effectiveness and outcome effectiveness" (Halliday, Levi, and Reuter 2014: 5). In spite of the claims made in the revised FATF methodology 2013 that they were shifting toward real-world effectiveness evaluations, the fourth round MERs show little evidence of serious measurement of effectiveness. For example, the AML goals were specified in a way that made operationalization impossible, mixing outcomes with hortatory statements.

Many of the grander claims made for the efficacy of the regime are not sustained by empirical evidence and are belied by media headlines the world over.[9] Major international banks in prominent financial centers, such as London, Frankfurt, and New York, continue to astound with the scale of money laundering over extended periods that involve

---

[7] *Formal compliance* refers to legal authorizations for a country to comply with FATF standards by placing substantive and procedural laws on the books, issuing regulations, and passing enabling law that authorizes the setting up or reform of agencies.

    Program implementation refers to practices that put into effect the authorizations of formal compliance. There are two aspects of program implementation: (a) the setting up, funding, and staffing of agencies, creating educational and reporting obligations for state and non-state bodies, designing reporting protocols and procedures, among others; and (b) the operation of these agencies and programs in the public and private sectors through activities such as obtaining and analyzing STRs (suspicious transaction reports) and/or SARs (suspicious activity reports), investigating and prosecuting crimes, freezing and confiscating proceeds of crime/ terrorist finance, sanctioning criminals, exchanging information between countries on money laundering and terrorist financing and predicate crimes, as well as instituting actions by the private sector (Halliday, Levi, and Reuter 2014: 13–14).

[8] *Program effectiveness* refers to the extent of actual attainment of the goals and objectives of a particular AML/CFT regime as indicated by activities and behaviors that display a *net* effect of formal compliance and program implementation. That is, these are effects of formal and program compliance whose impact would not have occurred without the AML/CFT interventions.

    Outcome effectiveness refers to a country's attainment of ultimate AML/CFT objectives *whether or not* those objectives were met through the FATF AML/CFT tools and regime.

[9] Cf. "The Ghost Companies Connected to Suspected Money Laundering Corruption, and Paul Manafort," *Buzzfeed*, August 23, 2018. www.buzzfeed.com/janebradley/shell-companies-money-laundering-uk-paul-manafort.

tens of billions of dollars. The most recent of these – Denmark-based Danske Bank's alleged laundering of Russian-origin funds via its small Estonian branch – shows that even apparently small countries scoring well in the Transparency International corruption indices can be the conduits for vast sums of illicit monies. Levi's (Levi 1997) conclusion in 1997 remains largely true today: "there is little evidence that stripping offenders of their profits has had much impact on levels or organisation of crime."

It is doubtful that any AML monitoring would have picked up the $500,000 or less that entered the United States to fund the 9/11 terrorist attacks, and certainly not the 1998 attacks on US embassies in East Africa or major European terrorist attacks this century (Levi 2010).[10] And the report on Global Surveillance of Dirty Money concluded that "no credible scientific evidence has yet been presented that there is a direct relationship between installation of effective AML/CFT regimes and the IMF mandate to produce domestic and international financial stability" (2014: 5). Despite considerable investment from international donors and a growing number of cooperation initiatives, the World Bank/UNODC Stolen Asset Recovery (StAR) Initiative has managed to collect – or even to freeze – only a negligible quantity of stolen assets compared with the estimated size of the problem.[11] The most recent consolidated review in 2014 found that there had been an increase in assets frozen (though – we would add – not confiscated) to US$1.398 billion in 2010–2012, up from US$1.225 billion in the period of 2006–2009. A total of US$423.5 million was returned for the entire period of 2006–2012, with an increasing percentage of the assets going to developing countries in the more recent period (compared to earlier data showing most returns from OECD countries went to developed countries).[12]

Just as striking as the lack of evidence for effectiveness is the lack of sustained interest in that aspect of the system. Neither the individual nations driving the system (such as the United States, UK, and France)

---

[10] It should be noted that one-off attacks may be low cost, but maintaining terrorist organizations that sustain them over a long period can be costly.

[11] https://star.worldbank.org/sites/star/files/networks-15.pdf. The World Bank budget to StAR in 2017 was US$650,000; UNODC's budget to StAR in 2017 was US$489,466; and Disbursements from the Multi-Donor Trust Fund in 2017 were US$1,015,5000: https://star .worldbank.org/sites/star/files/star-annual-08.pdf, p. 30. The StAR annual report presents a cogent narrative but little evidence of short-term recovery effectiveness.

[12] https://star.worldbank.org/sites/star/files/few_and_far_the_hard_facts_on_stolen_asset_recov ery.pdf.

nor the International Financial Institutions have undertaken any substantial evaluation effort or put resources into developing a methodology for this very difficult evaluation task. Yet the IMF, World Bank, and major nation treasury departments have substantial research units that contribute to many aspects of agency missions on other issues. There is a curious lack of concern about AML. Much of the final section of this chapter is devoted to understanding why this state of affairs persists.

2.6   COSTS, DEFICIENCIES, AND HARMS

Not only is there limited evidence that the return on investment in the AML regime has been effective in pursuing its many putative goals; there is growing attention to what had previously been manifestly ignored by the states, IOs, and entrepreneurs that drive the AML order. It has very considerable deficiencies, and it cannot be taken for granted that it produces only public goods, and no public or private "bads." There is growing argument and evidence of internal fragilities that might render this invasive and pervasive regulatory order vulnerable.

First, its objectives are eclectic, unclear, and potentially in conflict. In their report to the IMF, Halliday, Levi, Reuter (2014) judge that it remains "very difficult to articulate clear objectives" for this "regime," as they call it. The array of objectives has been astonishing in its expansiveness. A good AML regime, promised an IMF Guidance Note,[13] might be to prevent or act as a palliative for "threats to financial stability and macroeconomic performance," "loss of access to global financial markets and destabilizing inflows and outflows," undermining "the rule of law," a "corrosive, corrupting effect on society," "tax evasion" and "budget deficit shortfalls," "bank fraud," "Ponzi schemes," as well as suppressing crime and denying criminals the fruits of their illegality or terrorists the fruits of their violence. It is true that while the FATF did not articulate clear objectives in its 2003 standards and methodology, it did make an attempt to produce a three-level more systematic hierarchy of objectives in its 2013 Methodology. Even here the objectives are diverse and reach to suppressing underlying predicate crimes, lessening money laundering and financing of terrorism risks, detecting proceeds of crime, keeping proceeds of crime out of the

---

[13] International Monetary Fund, "Anti-Money Laundering and Combating the Financing of Terrorism Inclusion in Surveillance and Financial Stability Assessments – Guidance Note," December 14, 2012, pp. 5–6.

financial system, depriving criminals and terrorists of illicit funds, and preventing terrorist acts, "thereby strengthening financial sector integrity and contributing to safety and security."[14]

Some of these concepts are not clearly defined. Relations among objectives are unspecified (2014: 13–19), and there is no "logic-model" or coherent causal theory that indicates what levers of public policy might be pulled that plausibly will reduce crime, money laundering, or terrorism. While this multiplicity of goals and definitional weaknesses are not uncommon in the global governance of crime, it is especially problematic when certain objectives conflict with others. For instance, if sanctions were to apply to a country that was not considered adequately compliant with global norms, then that in turn might destabilize a country's financial system, precisely one of the goals that the AML TLO supposedly is designed to prevent. Indeed the best interpretation of the few national crises that are usually identified as caused by money laundering (namely, Latvia and Estonia in 2018/19, Nauru in 2000, and the Dominican Republic and Serbian bank crises in 1993) is that they are crises triggered by concerns that major financial fraud and country takeovers by criminal kleptocrats would lead to international AML sanctions as well as to a run on the bank(s). Except in EU member states or other wealthy nations, depositors are unlikely to be compensated by the government or by an industry collective body.

Second, even if objectives were clear, the quality of data on which the TLO rests is weak or even nonexistent in critical respects. Measures of various objectives are neither agreed upon nor readily available in scientific circles (2013 Technical Report; Levi, Reuter, and Halliday 2018). For instance, it is exceedingly difficult to measure the scale of the underlying problem of predicate crime that yields dirty money – that is, the proceeds of crime (Reuter 2013; Reuter and Truman 2004), at least in most parts of the world. Thus there is no adequate denominator that allows measurement of how much dirty money is in the illicit market for money laundering, even if we accept that funds simply deposited in financial institutions by predicate offenders are all self-laundered funds. Measurement of the efficacy of punishment – arrests, sentences, asset confiscation – or of the destabilizing effects of cross-border flows of dirty money lag far behind the "measurement" of how many laws are enacted or rules are adopted. While this problem is not confined to the AML TLO, and may be true of criminal law at all

---

[14] Methodology 2013, p. 15, para. 43.

sophisticated levels, it nevertheless remains the case that the AML TLO rests on flimsy and often purely rhetorical foundations (Levi, Reuter, and Halliday 2018).

These deficiencies are paralleled in practice by defects in the assessments of how AML regimes are working in nation-states. Our close review of IMF Detailed Assessment Reports, if typical of FATF reports more generally, indicates that data collection and data analysis remained well behind the state of the art in the applied social sciences that specialize in behavioral observation and institutional analysis. Deficiencies included no systematic methodology for collecting data on country fundamentals (each evaluation produces its own opportunistic set of descriptors); no sampling design for collecting information from non-state stakeholders (a degree of bias from primary reliance on government officials within the evaluated state to choose informants and sources on private sector compliance); no methodology for systematic analysis of media reports, including investigative journalist reports on crime and money laundering; no systematic methodology for qualitative analysis; and no systematic methods for gathering and appraising scientific and academic research on ML/FT, crime, or regulation in a given country. Though "mystery shopping," by which an investigator simulates a money-laundering transaction to see if financial institutions respond appropriately, has been shown to provide useful information (van der does de Willebois 2011), it has never been used in any MER. See van Duyne, Harvey, and Gelemerova (2019), for a strident methodological critique of the application of and evidential basis for AML.

Third, seldom does appraisal of the AML disciplinary order count the costs.[15] These are of at least three kinds. One set of costs are economic. There are substantial costs to states, especially for poor countries, of erecting an AML regime. In addition to diverting domestic lawmaking toward this externally induced policy agenda, there are tangible costs in personnel, infrastructure, and expertise involved in the creation of Financial Intelligence Units, the hiring and training of civil servants

---

[15] In a range of regional studies, Lexis-Nexis (2017a, b; 2018a, b) estimates that annual anti-money-laundering compliance costs US financial services firms US$25.3 billion; European firms US$83.5 billion; and in six Asian markets, US$1.5 billion. We are not in a position to review the validity of these estimates, and skeptics might note that both they and other consulting firms have an interest in high estimates to get clients to focus on their offerings on how to reduce them. A serious effort was made by the Clearing House (2017), which noted that large financial firms will spend at least US$8 billion on AML compliance around the world, not much less than the US$9.5 billion budget of the FBI.

and regulators in commerce and revenue ministries, the training of police to handle financial crimes, and the recruitment and training of judges to comprehend what are often complex financial dealings. The proportion of AML government administrative costs to the total budget of a developing country will be substantial and entail policy costs for other goals that governments may consider more pressing. In Mauritius, a country of 1.3 million, there were a total of twenty-five positions in its FIU in 2012. For a middle-income country with such a small population, that is a significant component of its financial regulatory resources, especially for largely non-prudential regulation. Even in an advanced economy, Amicelle and Iafolla report that Canada has some eleven federal departments and law-enforcement agencies dedicated to law enforcement and intelligence on money laundering, with a combined budget of C$70 million (Amicelle and Iafolla 2018). FinTrac, Canada's financial intelligence unit, had a staff of 350.

There are enormous costs to businesses as well, such as banks, which have been co-opted by the state to monitor customers on the state's behalf. While these costs are usually closely held, the director of a major international bank's compliance division recently guesstimated[16] that it cost his bank approximately $2 billion annually to implement AML standards through its compliance division. There are also transaction costs to bank customers in time-consuming demands for more and more information when originating a home mortgage or loans for expensive items such as new cars, boats, or private planes. Transferring money internationally through a bank has become slower and more expensive. Risk aversion by financial institutions, which seek to protect themselves from undue scrutiny or sanctions by financial regulators, can lead to denial of financial services to customers by "de-risking practices" in which "banks [decide] to discontinue business relationships with customers who are deemed too risky" (Artingstall et al. 2016; Board 2018; Erbenova et al. 2016). This may be not because of individualized judgments but because of categorical judgments based on their membership of a suspect class, often but not exclusively because they come from or are associated with an occupation or a country deemed to be high risk, and/or because it is more expensive to monitor them properly than the profits they bring to the bank or other institution. Further potential adverse impacts can occur through false positives when individuals are mistakenly cut off from sources of credit or certain kinds of

---

[16] Private communication with the authors.

business activity because over-cautious bankers or faulty algorithms flag them as high risk (Amicelle and Iafolla 2018: 857–858). There is, in most countries, no recourse against such decisions, which banks can cloud in secrecy or in vague references to their "risk appetite."

Entire industries have grown around consulting and advising businesses and governments on AML/CFT compliance, an area stimulated by large fines and threats of prosecution to major international banks. HSBC's $1.9 billion fine in 2012 for violations both of AML and of the sanctions regimes against various nations was large enough to catch the attention of bank boards, though substantial violations have postdated that and other fines. Even as this chapter was being written, the largest bank in Denmark was reporting (under severe media pressure) that it had probably laundered tens of billions of Euros through its Estonian branch, though the problem had been drawn to the attention of the bank board many years earlier by one of its managers. The CEO of Danske Bank – who had presided over the enormous expansion of business – was required to resign in 2018, followed by its chairman.

There are also transaction costs for global regulatory institutions and the expense involved in national evaluations, both to the surveillance institutions and the nation-state. The IMF earlier reported that each of its national assessments cost the Fund more than $300,000. A MER might cost a state $1 million, a minimal amount for an advanced economy, but not inconsequential for a poor state. Over the near thirty years of an AML TLOs existence, cumulative costs may be very high indeed – costs disproportionately (per GDP) borne by states with limited resources.

Furthermore, it is impossible to establish that economic benefits outweigh the economic costs since benefits are at present impossible to calculate.[17] We reported that as of 2014 there was

> no significant effort by any of the standard-setting or assessor bodies to undertake a cost-benefit analysis despite positive but incomplete moves in some jurisdictions.... . National officials and private stake-holders state that discussion or information on benefits and costs of an AML/

---

[17] Fifteen years ago, Peter Reuter and Edward M. Truman (2004) produced a rough estimate of the cost of implementation of AML for the US economy (partitioned among government, corporations, and the general public). There does not seem to be any more recent or more refined estimate, despite the substantial growth of coverage of legislation and regulatory institutions nationally and internationally. The cost studies referred to earlier do not calculate the costs to government or to the general public. In no cases are benefits calculated, though some countries specify asset recoveries from proceeds of crime, some of which are reasonably attributable to AML.

CFT regime are limited or non-existent. Little consideration has been given, they say, to the costs of implementing an AML/CFT regime, and little evidence has been adduced to demonstrate that the costs produce commensurate benefits in their own or indeed in any other jurisdiction. (Halliday, Levi, and Reuter 2014: 47–48)

Indeed, apart from the ability to occasionally convict senior members of criminal enterprises and to trace some proceeds of some crimes more easily, it is hard to measure any specific benefits from the AML regime.

Economic harms to poor countries can adversely affect the most vulnerable populations. Within countries, the AML transnational order has pressed countries to draw informal markets into the formal economy where they can be better monitored. This may have adverse economic effects on the poorest populations, who rely on cheap informal methods for moving money, for example from city workers to rural parents. Between countries an even more severe economic cost may be incurred when money-laundering and counterterrorism measures reduce remittances that overseas workers can send back to their country of origin. The volume of remittances can be high. For instance, it is reported that "every year, Somali migrants around the world send approximately $1.3 billion to friends and families at home, dwarfing humanitarian aid to Somalia. . . . A recent report by the UN Food and Agricultural Organisation shows that up to 40 percent of families receive some form of remittance, and that the money is integral to their survival." The Report continues, "banks in the West are closing down the accounts of money transfer operators, thereby threatening to cut the lifeline to hundreds of thousands of Somali families."[18]

In the United Kingdom, the United States, and Australia, around 2012, banks came to perceive the transfer of funds to countries such as Somalia and Pakistan as exposing them to high risk of violation of counterterrorism finance (CTF) regulations. Many of the transfers occurred through money service businesses (MSBs) that knew little about their customers in the receiving countries; some of the money might be going to terrorist organizations such as Al Shabab. Rather than attempt to decide which MSBs could be trusted – an expensive undertaking – the banks terminated accounts for all MSBs transmitting money to Somalia. "Banks frequently characterize the entire remittance sector as high risk" (Financial Stability Board 2018).

[18] Report, p. 51, para. 119.

When formal means of transmitting moneys are suppressed, and when banking institutions clamp down on remittances as a way of "de-risking," the poorest populations in the world may be forced to use unregulated and unmonitored enterprises for their only lifeline to well-being. Hawalas became more important for Somali remittances: "[D]e-risking measures make it difficult to receive transactions through the formal banking system in a timely fashion. They also block money transfer operators as a viable channel for financial access and the transfer of remittances from the Somali diaspore" (El Taraboulsi-McCarthy 2018: iii). In 2017 the World Bank commented for MSBs generally that "[t]he country authorities are worried about the shift to the informal market."[19] Economic harms in practice can result from discriminatory behaviors by financial institutions when individuals are not excluded on manifest criteria such as race or gender but "on the basis of a certain criterion of risk," which happens to be highly correlated with certain racial or gender attributes (Amicelle and Iafolla 2018: 859).

There are also harms to other institutions that have been seldom confronted, at least until recently. Arguably political harms may be caused by supplying new monitoring and surveillance tools to authoritarian leaders. Charges of corruption, tax evasion, fraud, and money laundering can provide convenient ways for authoritarians to marginalize their rivals, and AML weapons enhance their armory for bringing such charges.[20] Harms to civil society can occur through increased registration and reporting demands on civil society organizations, not to mention the administrative burdens on small charities that already struggle to survive.[21] Reporting itself is not only a possible administrative and financial burden, but it enables authoritarian states to penetrate more deeply into voluntary associations and thereby subject them to surveillance and even control.

Not least, there are massive contradictions within the AML TLO that erode its legitimacy (Levi 2006). There is apparent inequity: those countries most heavily sanctioned are poor and weak. Despite the enormous problems of non-compliance in rich countries, such as the United States and United Kingdom, those countries (though not some of their major banks) are rarely sanctioned, yet they are prime drivers of

[19] http://pubdocs.worldbank.org/en/227971497448351308/WB-work-on-derisking-2017.pdf.
[20] China and Russia, for instance, use data on theft of state or private assets as part of criminal and corruption charges, but the specific contribution AML makes to these charges is unknown and, given the secrecy surrounding them in an authoritarian regime, unknowable at present.
[21] See www.theguardian.com/money/2017/may/08/banks-charity-accounts-shut-without-notice-money-laundering; www.fca.org.uk/your-fca/documents/research/drivers-impacts-of-derisking.

the international order. A recent news story on British shell companies offered the unsubstantiated figure of an estimated £90 billion "that is laundered through the country each year."[22] Certainly there is a great deal of evidence that stolen money from Russia and other nations with high levels of corruption are laundered through real estate in London, New York, and other international cities in wealthy countries (Sharman 2011; Sharman 2017). A 2016 Global Witness investigation of prominent New York law firms found a great willingness to provide services for very suspect financial prospects.[23]

And then there is the allegation that the AML TLO is merely another arrow in the quiver of US foreign policy: Iran and North Korea are blacklisted. There is an undercurrent of geopolitical cherry-picking: China and India are not sanctioned, whereas numbers of less powerful countries are. There is the resistance by business, which bears the heavy burden of co-optation by the state and, in most countries, of professions, particularly the legal profession, which consider reporting and surveillance demands on them to be inconsistent with their hallowed values of privacy and client confidentiality. Though the United States is the leading AML hawk, driving much of the FATF decision-making, it has been unable to meet FATF standards with respect to AML regulation of the legal profession and shows no sign of being willing to do so.

Indeed, most of the critiques of the system registered by Levi and Reuter (2006) over a decade ago remain salient. The AML regime is "elaborate and intrusive." It has demonstrated lack of success in suppressing predicate crime, "rooting out major criminals or recovering a large percentage of crime proceeds" (Levi and Reuter 2006: 365).

2.7 CONFRONTING THE PUZZLE OF PERSISTENCE

At once we are confronted with a two-sided question for TLO theory. From one side, how is it possible for a TLO with so many ambiguities and contradictions, costs and harms, brittleness and fragility, and with so little evidence of reducing the problems that motivated its creation, to continue to reproduce its seemingly well institutionalized order? Why is it so resilient? From the other side, under what conditions will

---

[22] "The Ghost Companies Connected to Suspected Money Laundering Corruption, and Paul Manafort," *Buzzfeed*, August 23, 2018. www.buzzfeed.com/janebradley/shell-companies-money-laundering-uk-paul-manafort.

[23] See www.globalwitness.org/shadyinc/.

a TLO fail – even a TLO as highly developed as the AML TLO (Halliday and Shaffer 2015a)? At present the empirical evidence indicates there is no immediate sign this TLO will fracture or collapse. How is this to be explained?

In the first place, it does work to some degree. It is likely that some generic benefits of the regime identified by Levi and Reuter more than a decade ago still remain largely true (Levi and Reuter 2006). The AML regime makes it more difficult and expensive for offenders to carry out crime and enjoy its benefits. Its mechanisms generate more evidence about the occurrence of crime and link particular individuals to that crime, at least if those links are pursued (which requires both resources and a financial mind-set among law enforcement agencies). Convictions and news stories from time to time have the social appeal that criminals are not getting to enjoy the fruits of their criminality. The most prominent cases involving financial crimes in the United States in recent years, such as Enron, Bernie Madoff, and Paul Manafort, have involved convictions for money laundering, even though fraud and/or corruption may have been the principal offences. Moneys confiscated contribute to the state treasury; indeed, there are occasional complaints that the New York state bank supervisor, who issues licenses for operation on Wall Street, funds the office's operations by putting pressure on for settlements from banks who might be charged with money laundering. And it is possible the measures put in place to enforce money-laundering laws may increase the efficiency of law enforcement (not necessarily by reducing predicate crime).

Second, even if the AML regime imposes harms, it may be the case that those harmed are disproportionately weak as political actors and thus in no position to mount effective resistance to the regime. The senders or recipients of remittances, those injured financially by false positives, small civil-society NGOs, the small-time money launderers occasionally convicted all confront problems of collective action. Even if those hurdles were surmounted, their probable impact on domestic politics would be slight and their ability to influence the transnational legal order would be minimal. Others, such as international NGOs or religious institutions, might speak on their behalf, as has been the case with some positive effect with remittances, but even there, significant difficulties remain. On the other hand, FATF and the system as a whole certainly saw de-risking as a serious challenge to the legitimacy of the AML regime. Roger Wilkins, the Australian who served as FATF president at the height of the de-risking crisis, made some strong statements to this effect.[24] It appears that the AML regime did respond in a constructive fashion, though concerted action against de-risking requires cooperation between regulators, prosecutors, and civil courts in many countries, and this is extraordinarily difficult to achieve.

There are occasional vocal and potentially powerful sources of resistance; see, for example, the 2017 report by prestigious US banking organization The Clearing House (2017). The most notable resistance has come from the legal professions in the United States and elsewhere, but their impact has been at the margins since their principal focus has been on the effort to bring them into the set of AML regulated professions rather than against AML as such. Indeed, for advocacy groups in the world of economic development, the moral high ground is on the side of the enforcers.

Third, even if there are certain financial harms and costs, these are hidden from a public that has only the vaguest sense of what additional costs this imposes on their everyday banking. While they may observe that getting home loans has become more onerous, the borrowers will have little awareness of how much these burdens can be attributed to the AML regime. Banks may also treat the monitoring obligations upon them partly as a barrier to entry to new competition – in particular, the costs of AML decline with scale, so that large banks will be advantaged compared to small new entrants. They will be indifferent to costs so long as all banks bear the same costs. One might even infer from the massive cheating of the previous decade that some banks may have liked the regime because deviating from it gave them a competitive advantage – that being willing to evade the regime enabled them to expand business at the expense of more AML compliant competitors.

Fourth, the AML TLO may be resilient because it rests on a surface plausibility. Cocaine is dangerous, and most people accept that it should be tightly controlled – that may not justify criminalization but it gives prohibition credibility. The notion that banks should keep out dirty money has a similar face plausibility. In fact, the promoters of the AML TLO have had considerable success in building a plausible folk theory to underwrite their enterprise (Halliday 2018). A plausible folk theory is built not on robust empirical foundations but on parsimony, face validity, a compactness of rhetorical expression, sufficient ambiguity to accommodate potentially conflicting understandings of what it

---

[24] See, for example, www.fatf-gafi.org/publications/fatfgeneral/documents/roger-wilkins-speech-fatf-plenary-jun-2014.html.

purports to explain, an affinity with extant beliefs about such things as crime and dirty money, and a failure or resistance to examining too closely the premises and logic of the theory itself. The most succinct version of the folk theory underlying the AML order can be expressed as (1) billions of dollars of dirty money are generated by crime; (2) those funds cause harms by destabilizing markets, governments, or even the international financial system; and (3) the regulatory order constructed by the FATF will mitigate or eliminate both (1) and (2). Part of the appeal of a plausible folk theory to an international organization lies precisely in the fact that they induce optimism that solutions abound for challenging problems, their promise offers an umbrella under which actors with diverse interests can find common ground, and it relieves IOs or states from the very difficult and resource-intensive tasks of subjecting the practices of crime and money laundering to rigorous empirical research.

Fifth, the AML regime covers not just money laundering but also CTF. There is good reason to be skeptical that the system has contributed much to the control of terrorism incidents. As already noted, terrorism is not very expensive. The British government's independent monitor of counterterrorism has presented data to suggest that it is rare for the government to have financial information about detected terrorists. Yet there is an understandable reluctance to criticize anything that is plausibly a component of effective anti-terrorism policy.

Relatedly, the AML TLO satisfies certain symbolic and social needs of publics and governance institutions. While the AML TLO may not rest on empirical foundations, it does offer a compelling narrative. Its real work is not to change behavior or stop rule breakers but to "unite good consciences, to show purity in the face of danger, to do cultural work." It creates a persuasive account of a world in which there are dark, nefarious activities that must be stopped. It joins fear of the unknown and of the criminal with the opportunity for states and supra-state institutions to be styled as rescuers. It offers comfort that good is fighting evil. It assures publics that the fear of the unknown is being addressed – that leaders are acting to assuage fears and control the dark side of globalization.[25]

Not least, the AML TLO is sustained by geopolitics. The AML regime, originally aimed at drug trafficking, has been extended to the

---

[25] We are indebted to Sally Merry and David Nelken for these insights.

international sanctions regime, which has been a central element of US foreign policy for twenty years. Some of the largest fines (e.g., Paribas's $9 billion in 2014 and $80 million against ABN Amro in 2005) have been for violations of the US Treasury financial sanctions regime aimed at Iran, Libya, North Korea, and Russia. The AML TLO has been important for the United States in forcing strategic opponents such as Iran and North Korea to enter into unpalatable bargains. Put in another idiom, this TLO is sustained, critical theories would say, because they are tools of US imperialism or hegemony.[26]

These explanations of TLO resilience lead us back to the hypotheses generated in earlier studies of resistance to TLOs and the conditions under which they might falter or fail (Halliday and Shaffer 2015a: 500ff). The AML TLO might be expected to confirm the hypothesis that resistance to TLOs will increase in inverse proportion to the legitimacy of its institutions or norms (Halliday and Shaffer 2015a: 500, 508). The master norms of the AML order are crafted principally by a few powerful states and international organizations. In theory, poorer and weaker states and non-state actors participate in the development of both AML Standards and its Methodology. In practice, their involvement is more pro forma. Yet this seems not to have detracted from the legitimacy of the AML TLO. In so many of the poorer nations, the leadership is seen as kleptocratic, with a deep interest in weakening money-laundering controls; this presents these governments as seemingly weak opponents to FATF, with its visibly moral position. Each time a kleptocrat falls (e.g., Mubarak in Egypt or Suharto in Indonesia) and it is revealed that they have laundered large amounts overseas, the position of developing countries for rolling back the FATF TLO is weakened. Such events typically result in NGO support for toughening the regime in the Global North.

More pointed is the hypothesis that poorer and weaker nation-states and other actors are more likely to resist a TLO when norms are "perceived to be instruments of imposition, coercion, surveillance, or control by stronger actors on weaker states" (Halliday and Shaffer 2015a: 500). Since we have seen that AML norms emerged primarily from a few states at the center of the world economic and financial systems, and have been sustained by international governance bodies (e.g., IMF, World Bank) where those states wield disproportionate

---

[26] We are indebted to Mariana Valverde for underlining this point.

influence, resistance would seem probable from states in the periphery. While this is not overt in the last revision of either the Standards or Methodology, it is more probable that resistance takes the form of symbolic compliance where states adopt laws and create institutions but cannot or will not implement them in practice. Normative concordance, in other words, is accompanied by a discordance between the expression of those norms and changes in behavior.

The hypothesis has been advanced that TLOs have a greater probability of failing the more that internal contradictions intensify (Halliday and Shaffer 2015a: 508). If, for instance, retributive sanctions by AML governors are brought against a state or financial institution, then it may actually produce the very condition of financial instability the regime was erected to forestall. Yet there appears to be little evidence this has occurred or occurred sufficiently often enough to fracture the TLO. Another contradiction might follow from the very expansiveness and penetration of the TLO itself, thereby engendering a backlash from constituencies that are harmed. Here again, apart from occasional critiques from academics and some professional insiders, such a backlash has not eventuated.

It has further been hypothesized that a change in the embedding contexts that facilitated emergence of the TLO might subsequently render a TLO irrelevant or sclerotic. Institutional rigidities might reduce adaptive flexibility (Halliday and Shaffer 2015a: 524). Yet the AML TLO has shown itself to be remarkably adaptive. From its beginning in the war on drugs, it managed to pivot swiftly to encompass the war against terrorism and pivot again to embrace the financing of nuclear proliferation and assist the fight against tax evasion and wildlife crime along the way. This might of course produce its own contradictions – a sheer overload of not always consistent goals. But it may also signify the agility of a soft law institutional foundation built on high-level principles (Block-Lieb 2019) and the minimal bureaucratic infrastructure that might inhibit change.

Moreover, while some TLOs have diminished or fallen when confronted with a more potent rival (Genschel and Rixen 2015), no rival TLO can be observed on the horizon of AML/CFT/FNP. It is true that there is much passive resistance in the implementation of norms in practice. And there is a good deal of decoupling between states' compliance with global norms that intentionally (or not) do not make it into national or local practice. There is gamesmanship of various kinds, as peers in the mutual evaluation of other states may favor (or appear to favor) each other, or hold back from criticizing more powerful countries, in implicit reciprocities of disciplinary restraint.

Finally, there is the view that the AML TLO has proven itself valuable to monitoring groups in international civil society that seek to constrain corruption and kleptocracy.[27] Some of the tax and AML-evasive activities revealed in WikiLeaks, the Panama and Paradise Papers, and other outlets enable investigative journalists and NGOs to follow trails of money and asset purchases across borders and thereby to hold accountable political leaders and others who siphon off state moneys and seek to transmit them to safe havens for private consumption elsewhere in the world.[28] That accountability effect may also be deployed in domestic politics when, for instance, a special prosecutor seeks evidence of malfeasance in financing of political campaigns by candidates for office or elected politicians. It has been said that local liberal elites in Iran appeal to FATF standards in their own domestic struggles to hold national leaders accountable.[29]

In sum, on the one side, viewed from the vantage point of its champions, the AML TLO persists because (1) it works in small respects; (2) it has surface plausibility insofar as it is underwritten by a plausible folk theory; (3) it offers a culturally satisfying, protective narrative of hope; (4) its minimalist bureaucracy and soft law properties have given it significant adaptive capacity; (5) it offers geopolitical benefits to the most powerful states, especially the United States; and (6) it demonstrates to the world and to regions that international governance institutions are effectively confronting the dark forces of globalization.

On the other side, viewed from the stance of its critics and opponents, it has survived assaults on its mission and practices because (1) most domestic actors harmed or hurt by it either do not realize the costs they bear (e.g., to privacy) or those costs are born most directly by institutions such as banks which can bear them; (2) even if costs were widely recognized, collective action by such diverse economic and civil society actors presents an immense barrier; (3) even if collective action

---

[27] Oral conference discussion, UCI, September 21–22, 2018.

[28] This is not to minimize the challenges posed by the fact that reports to Financial Intelligence Units are classified and that the identities of reporting bodies are protected from external disclosure, including disclosure in court. NGO efforts may be eased if beneficial ownership registers help expose or deter deviants, but this is a deeply contested issue.

[29] "The Ghost Companies Connected to Suspected Money Laundering Corruption, and Paul Manafort," *Buzzfeed*, August 23, 2018. www.buzzfeed.com/janebradley/shell-companies-money-laundering-uk-paul-manafort.

barriers were surmounted, those who are adversely harmed are weak actors; (4) attacks on its legitimacy and practices come from weak or discredited actors; (5) weak states disproportionally harmed by it don't have the ability to mobilize collectively against it, but they can mitigate its local unwanted effects through symbolic compliance; (6) its internal contradictions haven't yet swelled to disruptive levels; (7) the institution has no looming rivals at the global level; and (8) it is immunized from much criticism because a TLO invoking protections from terrorism is rhetorically unassailable.

Indeed, more generically, we may hypothesize that when a TLO is deeply embedded within and supported by other normative institutions, and when its rules become an integral guide to the practices of hundreds or thousands of organizations beyond the state, within the state and across markets, the legal order becomes highly resilient when confronted by attacks or changed contexts. Moreover, if its technical features prove applicable to new problems, then it can move sideways to take on tasks that further widen its appeal to even broader constituencies. Insofar as the AML TLO has accomplished these feats of a legal order, it should be presumed the greater probability is that it will persist rather than fail, despite its costs and harms.

2.8   A DISCIPLINARY TLO?

Nevertheless, while the preceding factors go some distance toward an explanation of resilience, they may serve as elements in a more comprehensive theory. Ultimately, might it be the case that its persistence results not from demonstrable results in achieving its ostensible goals[30] but from its disciplinary character? How does it serve as a disciplinary institution whose interests are advanced by those facilities?

Much currency in contemporary sociology on the topic of discipline derives from the writings of Foucault. The recent revisionist work by Mariana Valverde (Valverde 2016) on Foucault and criminology, law, justice, and penology asserts that conventional English understandings of the French verb *surveiller*, frequently translated as "discipline," are too constrictive. Rather than a negatively inflected tone directed toward predominantly top-down control, in her view, "discipline" better connotes an amalgam of "keeping an eye on things" – watching

---

[30] Or as Peter Andreas cleverly puts it, "a policy failure that is a political success."

over activities, monitoring, and supervising.[31] Extrapolating from Foucault's work on modern prisons, "whole populations would come to be controlled, monitored and supervised. The panopticon is the paradigmatic exemplar, even the extreme. Silently, every inmate of the prison is constantly observed." In society this gaze proceeds thru "hierarchical observation" where "techniques for supervising or monitoring groups of people . . . allow and foster surveillance by authorities" and where "the few are employed to watch the many." Great power is exercised "in a silent, impersonal, and almost automatic manner."[32]

In AML regimes, much of the surveillance is silent and unobserved. Backroom bank employees scan transactions for a whiff of suspicion, or computers run algorithms to identify patterns of abnormal or illegal transactions. Officers in financial systems create lists of both domestic and foreign politically exposed persons (PEPs) who will be subject to heightened scrutiny. Recent research on Canada, for instance, indicates that any citizen can be watching a neighbor for out-of-the-ordinary financial activity or lifestyle and submit a report to a government agency, unbeknownst to the hapless neighbors (Amicelle and Iafolla 2018). Keeping an eye out, thereby, simultaneously occurs from below and above. In AML regimes, much of the monitoring is routinized and observable, though not intrusive, whether at the mundane level of bank deposits or the use of cash for payments or in annual reporting of NGOs and the activities of charities.

The tools that enable such monitoring and eyes on behavior at the bank or in leisure activities offer varieties of value for quite different actors. For state officials, they may offer intelligence for law enforcement of a broad spectrum of crimes, especially grand corruption. Tax authorities obtain an added tool to lessen tax evasion. The security apparatus adds a window into potential threats of violence against the state. For states who dominate this transnational order, they gain another weapon in the armory against "terrorism" or nuisance-some players in regional politics or a bloodless alternative to military action.

For authoritarian regimes, the imperative for control of their populations may be well served by comprehensive and largely unobserved means of tracking who opponents are, what they own, and what they do. Empirical research on use of AML tools for political purpose is in

---

[31] See Valverde (2016), pp. 1–2, fn. 1.
[32] See Valverde (2016), pp. 55, 47, 61.

its infancy. Yet, for authoritarians currently in power, the most dangerous of opponents, whether the leader of an opposition party, a prior ruler, the media, or a civil society irritant, the payoff of keeping an eye on opponents' affairs through the legitimate means of financial surveillance at once may keep current rulers abreast of the threat of insurgency and at most gives them weapons to quash and silence voices perceived to threaten them.[33] For bankers, even if costly to implement, the actuality of monitoring and the threat of AML enforcement may contribute to an even playing field so that competitors do not get undue advantage through devices designed to attract dirty money.

Foucault spoke of the punitive city where "tiny theaters of punishment" were staged in parks and at intersections so passersby could observe the little dramas and heed their moral lessons. The AML regime scales up to the regional and global: a (moderately) punitive global order where monitoring and punishing and shaming take place on a global stage, whether in the form of international media exposes with or without prosecutions; the high drama of the unfolding Danske Bank[34] scandal, with criminal charges and investigations in several European countries and potentially in the United States; or blacklisting threats for punitive actions taken by the entire international financial system.

It is reasonable to ask whether the TLO actually disciplines those it is intended to discipline and/or claims to discipline. The fact that money laundering and underlying predicate crimes continue is not sufficient in itself to belie the impact of disciplinary measures. While discipline might not achieve all or any of its intended effects, it might well impel financial institutions or criminal organizations to develop new techniques of bypassing the rules, at least when local or institutional profitability provides sufficient incentives. The disciplinary apparatus shapes unforeseen ways of crime displacement, where the place, time, or method of offending is changed to avoid detection. Thus there may be a disciplinary effect, even if the crime reduction effect is minimal or difficult to observe.[35]

---

[33] Of course, authoritarian rulers have armories of weapons to wield against opponents, and financial surveillance may be only one of these. To make this point is not to be construed as an argument that authoritarian states could or do exert influence in FATF for this specific purpose. However, they may well concur with stronger measures that have collateral political benefits.

[34] www.ft.com/content/519ad6ae-bcd8-11e8-94b2-17176fbf93f5; www.theguardian.com/world/2018/oct/04/danske-bank-faces-us-investigation-into-money-laundering.

[35] We are indebted to the editors of this volume for this insight.

In sum, is it possible that the persistence of this disciplinary TLO can be attributed to the symbolic and tangible appeal of "discipline" itself? That is, a disciplinary TLO has multi-faceted appeal that gives it viability despite the manifest inadequacies or limitations we have noted. Like much lawmaking on crime, the AML TLO gestures toward serious consideration of problems that trouble publics and rulers without necessarily doing much about these problems in practice. This disciplinary TLO gives powerful states, especially the United States, legitimate cover to leverage surveillance and control in pursuit of domestic policy priorities. And because it is exceedingly difficult to be publicly in favor of dirty money, the illicit drug trade, financing of terrorism, and nuclear proliferation by "rogue states," those institutions that would prefer to escape the TLO cannot legitimately do so and will not thereby defect. Hence this TLO, even if erected on weak foundations to control problems for which it is ill-suited, may nonetheless persist because its collateral benefits give it enduring resilience.

2.9 SINGULAR?

The disciplinary properties of the AML TLO offer a capstone explanation for its resilience. Are those properties distinctive to an AML institution or are they indicative of a class of TLOs that share some of its properties? In comparison to many other partially or wholly institutionalized TLOs previously studied in the scholarly literature, the AML TLO does appear to be distinctive. We can explore this putative distinctiveness more systematically by asking, what makes a TLO disciplinary?

First, there is a pervasive assumption that there are identifiable recalcitrant actors in society who must be monitored to reduce the harms they may cause society. On its face, a disciplinary order offers an attractive way of doing so. This is not an assumption underlying most commercial, finance, and trade TLOs. Nor is it an assumption about actors in a climate change TLO or a value chain TLO, although one might get to recalcitrance in types of deviance for both. This assumption might be a secondary concern for a multilateral trade or carriage of goods by sea regime, since deviance of some sort may factor in either TLO, but these don't seem quite in the same category as the AML order.

Second, we have seen that the AML TLO has erected a pervasive surveillance apparatus into many corners of society. Is this merely a difference in degree, or is it a difference in kind? Perhaps it is true that banking and taxation TLOs come close to this level of surveillance. And perhaps it is the case that the burgeoning reliance of states and international organizations on indicators begin to approach or aspire to such pervasive monitoring (Davis et al. 2012). Human rights TLOs monitor broad swaths of social behavior, yet they tend to more focused on one or another right and leave entire arenas in a society (e.g., its financial institutions or its leisure activities) outside their gaze.

Third, the pervasive AML surveillance apparatus is yoked to punitive criminal and regulatory institutions and practices. This TLO is anchored in public law and the institutions of the state erected to control crime – the police, courts, and prisons – though it has significant regulatory dimensions as well, inflecting the supervisory practices of financial and professional regulators. The qualifier "punitive" is deliberately chosen because despite considerable attention to regulating the suspicious activity reporting regime, the model of crime control underlying the AML TLO is principally retributive and confiscatory, relying on punishment to deter both the criminals who generate financial proceeds of crime and the enablers who allow them to enjoy or use those proceeds for malign purposes.

Fourth, the AML TLO has constructed an elaborate repertoire of discipline. Socialization into disciplinary norms occurs for government officials through their participation in FATF global and regional bodies, for workers in the financial sector through their training, and for professionals in collegial education such as ACAMS (Association of Certified Anti-Money Laundering Specialists) membership. Reports by the FATF and ROSCs (IMF Reports on the Observance of Standards and Codes) from the global financial institutions calibrate degrees of deviance by ratings that concentrate the minds of state officials and incur the evaluative judgments of supra-state monitors. It is a short step from rating to naming and shaming, and then to tangible threats of gray- or blacklisting. How extensively can this repertoire of discipline be found in commercial, financial, environmental, or private contracting or human rights TLOs?

Fifth, we have seen that the AML TLO has multiplied its subjects of discipline to include states; financial institutions (e.g., a bank); non-state collective actors such as charities; organized crime families; individuals in their many guises of PEPs, lawyers, or accountants; or everyday participants in their myriads of transactions in an integrated global financial system. Again, the geographical and legal scope of this disciplinary TLO appears unusually extensive, so much so that it appears different in kind rather than in degree from other TLOs identified in scholarship to date.

The question of singularity therefore points to a wider question: are criminal justice TLOs[36] in general distinctive as a class? There are reasons to suggest they are. TLOs directed to control of crime involve (1) a particular moral sanction (i.e., that of being labeled a "criminal"); (2) the threat or deployment of coercion by the state; and (3) the use of disciplinary powers beyond those deployed in governmentality more generally. Moreover, a criminal justice TLO targets a subset of behavior (i.e., that which is illegal), in contrast to TLOs which target legal behavior that may be deviant in its forms of action but is controlled by civil or regulatory measures.[37]

Placing the AML TLO within a set of TLOs that is as expansive as law itself, public and private, domestic and international, thereby compels us to confront the possibility that the AML TLO is singular or, more probably, is one instance of a class of TLOs not hitherto explored or well understood. Those singular properties may in fact be shared substantially by other TLOs directed at crime. The site of criminal justice thereby encourages a more differentiated understanding of TLOs in twenty-first-century settings, and concomitantly TLO theory reveals aspects of international criminal justice that amplify understandings of crime control, markets, and politics in the contemporary global order.

2.10   SCENARIOS OF TLO COLLAPSE

We conclude with a brief consideration of circumstances under which the AML TLO might collapse. There is little prospect that it becomes irrelevant. It is hard to imagine what would lead to much diminution in transnational money laundering, unless the TLO itself becomes effective, which would lead to its continuation rather than disappearance. Nor, to take contrary extreme, is its failure likely to lead to its collapse. It survives despite almost annual occurrences of attention-riveting incidents showing that major institutions ignore the fundamentals, as illustrated by Danske Bank and ABN Amro as recently as 2018.

The true threat may come from the country most responsible for the formation of the TLO – namely the United States. The threat could

---

[36] See the other chapters in this volume.
[37] We appreciate these insights of the volume's editors on the distinctiveness of criminal TLOs.

come in one of two contrasting forms. In one, the United States, as part of its general withdrawal from international agreements (witness its notification of ending participation in the International Postal Union), drops out of FATF, which then loses its most powerful tool, namely eliminating access to dollar transactions. It is perhaps not unfair to speculate that the Trump administration is not enthusiastic about efforts to control money laundering. The contrasting threat comes from excessive US aggression. Already there is discomfort about the ways in which, as discussed previously, FATF's Recommendations further US foreign policy goals. Further extensions of FATF's jurisdiction in that direction might lead some other important countries to defect from FATF and to the collapse of the TLO, and/or to the undermining of whatever legitimacy its regulations and evaluations has in the international community.

Neither scenario is likely in the near future. Neither scenario, however, seems wholly fanciful.

REFERENCES

Amicelle, Anthony, and Vanessa Iafolla. 2018. "Suspicion-in-the-Making: Surveillance and Denunciation in Financial Policing." *British Journal of Criminology* 58: 845–863.

Artingstall, David, Nick Dove, John Howell, and Michael Levi. 2016. *Drivers and Impacts of Derisking*. London: Financial Conduct Authority. www.fca.org.uk/your-fca/documents/research/drivers-impacts-of-derisking.

Block-Lieb, Susan. 2019. "Soft and Hard Strategies: The Role of Business in the Crafting of International Commercial Law." *Michigan Journal of International Law* 40: 433–477.

The Clearing House. 2017. *A New Paradigm: Redesigning the U.S. AML/CFT Framework to Protect National Security and Aid Law Enforcement*. www.theclearinghouse.org/~/media/TCH/Documents/TCH%20WEEKLY/2017/20170216_TCH_Report_AML_CFT_Framework_Redesign.pdf.

Davis, Kevin E., Angelina Fisher, Benedict Kingsbury, and Sally Engle Merry, eds. 2012. *Indicators as a Technology of Global Governance*. New York: Oxford University Press.

Erbenova, Michaela, Yan Liu, Nadim Kyriakos-Saad, Aledjandro Lopez Mejia, Jose Giancarlo Gasha, Emmanuel Mathias, Mohamed Norat, Francisco Fernando, and Yasmin Almeida. 2016. *The Withdrawal of Correspondent Banking Relationships: A Case for Policy Action*. Washington, DC: International Monetary Fund.

Financial Stability Board. 2018. *Stocktake of Remittance Service Providers' Access to Banking Services*. Basel: Financial Stability Board.

Genschel, Philipp, and Thomas Rixen. 2015. Settling and Unsettling the Transnational Legal Order of International Taxation. Pp. 154–186 in *Transnational Legal Orders*, edited by Terence C. Halliday and Gregory Shaffer. New York: Cambridge University Press.

Halliday, Terence C. 2018. "Plausible Folk Theories: Throwing Veils of Plausibility over Zones of Ignorance in Global Governance." *British Journal of Sociology* 69(4): 936–961.

Halliday, Terence C., Michael Levi, and Peter Reuter. 2014. *Global Surveillance of Dirty Money: Assessing Assessments of Regimes to Control Money Laundering and Combat the Financing of Terrorism*. Chicago: Center on Law and Globalization, American Bar Foundation, and University of Illinois College of Law. www.americanbarfoundation.org/uploads/cms/documents/report_global_surveillance_of_dirty_money_1.30.2014.pdf.

Halliday, Terence C., and Gregory Shaffer. 2015a. "Researching Transnational Legal Orders." Pp. 473–528 in *Transnational Legal Orders*, edited by Terence C. Halliday and Gregory Shaffer. New York: Cambridge University Press.

Halliday, Terence C., and Gregory Shaffer. 2015b. "Transnational Legal Orders." Pp. 1–72 in *Transnational Legal Orders*, edited by Terence C. Halliday and Gregory Shaffer. New York: Cambridge University Press.

Levi, Michael. 1991. "Pecunia non olet: Cleansing the Money Launderers from the Temple." *Crime, Law and Social Change* 16: 217–302.

Levi, Michael. 1997. "Evaluating 'The New Policing': Attacking the Money Trail of Organised Crime." *Australia New Zealand Journal of Criminology* 30: 1–25.

Levi, Michael. 2006. "Pecunia non olet? The Control of Money-Laundering Revisited." Pp. 161–182 in *The Organised Crime Community*, edited by F. Bovenkerk and Michael Levi. New York: Springer.

Levi, Michael. 2010. "Combating the Financing of Terrorism: A History and Assessment of the Control of 'Threat Finance.'" *British Journal of Criminology* 50(4): 650–669.

Levi, Michael, and Peter Reuter. 2006. "Money Laundering." *Crime and Justice* 34: 289–375.

Levi, Michael, Peter Reuter, and Terence Halliday. 2018. "Can the AML System Be Evaluated without Better Data?" *Crime, Law and Social Change* 69: 307–328.

Lexis-Nexis. 2017a. *Future Financial Crime Risks 2017*.

Lexis-Nexis. 2017b. *True Cost of AML Compliance – Europe*.

Lexis-Nexis.2018a. *The True Cost of Anti-Money Laundering Compliance: A LexisNexis Risk Solutions Report Study on Financial institutions across Six Markets in Asia*. www.lexisnexis.com/risk/intl/en/resources/research/true-cost-of-aml-compliance-apac-survey-report.pdf.

Lexis-Nexis. 2018b. *The True Cost of Anti-Money Laundering Compliance in the United States*.

Nance, Mark T. 2018. "The Regime That FATF Built: An Introduction to the Financial Action Task Force." *Crime, Law and Social Change* 69(2): 109–129.

Organization for Economic Co-operation and Development. 2013. *Measuring OECD Responses to Illicit Financial Flows from Developing Countries*. Paris: OECD.

Reuter, Peter. 2013. "Are Estimates of Money Laundering Volume Either Feasible or Useful?" Pp. 224–231 in *Research Handbook on Money Laundering*, edited by Brigitte Unger. Cheltenham: Edward Elgar.

Reuter, Peter, and Edwin M. Truman. 2004. *Chasing Dirty Money: The Fight against Money Laundering*. Washington, DC: Institute for International Economics.

Shaffer, Gregory, Tom Ginsburg, and Terence C. Halliday, eds. 2019. *Constitution-Making and Transnational Legal Orders*. New York: Cambridge University Press.

Sharman, Jason C. 2011. *The Money Laundry: Regulating Criminal Finance in the Global Economy*. Ithaca and London: Cornell University Press.

Sharman, Jason C. 2017. *The Despot's Guide to Wealth Management: On the International Campaign against Grand Corruption*. Ithaca: Cornell University Press.

Valverde, Mariana. 2016. *Michel Foucault*. New York: Routledge.

Van Duyne, Petrus, Jackie H. Harvey, and Liliya Y. Gelemerova. 2019. *The Critical Handbook of Money Laundering: Policy, Analysis and Myths*. London: Palgrave Macmillan.

Van der Does de Willebois, E., E. M. Halter, R. A. Harrison, J. W. Park, and J. C. Sharman. 2011. *The Puppet Masters: How the Corrupt Use Legal Structures to Hide Stolen Assets and What to Do about It*. Washington, DC: The World Bank.

CHAPTER THREE

TRANSNATIONAL CRIMINAL LAW OR THE TRANSNATIONAL LEGAL ORDERING OF CORRUPTION?

Theorizing Australian Corporate Foreign Bribery Reforms

Radha Ivory[*]

3.1 INTRODUCTION

The bribery of foreign public officials is an inherently transnational offense. But are the rules against foreign bribery best viewed as "transnational criminal law"? For international lawyers, concepts of transnational criminal law are an obvious place to start categorizing supra-state anti-corruption controls (Ivory 2018). As most elaborately theorized by legal academic Neil Boister, "TCL" is "the indirect suppression by international law through domestic penal law of criminal activities that have actual or potential transboundary effects" or "transborder moral impacts" (Boister 2003: 955; Boister 2014: 13; Boister 2015: 13; Boister 2018: 17). TCL is a legal system, field, order, or space comprising state-to-state and state-to-person obligations with transnational crime as their focus. The bribery of foreign public officials can be seen as an example of TCL, so conceived, due to the multiple nationalities of its protagonists and its underlying matrix of international and domestic legal standards. In addition, the international norm against foreign bribery is a relatively recent prohibition that would appear to have

[*] The research was conducted in August/September 2018 and updated in December 2018 and in August 2019 for major developments. My thanks to Gregory Shaffer, Ely Aaronson, Terrence Halliday, Felix Lüth, Ross Grantham, Liz Campbell, and Julia Howell, as well as all the participants in the UCI Workshop on the Transnational Legal Ordering of Criminal Justice, for their very useful comments on an earlier draft of this chapter. An earlier version of this study was published in the *UCI Journal of International, Comparative, and Transnational Law* (2019, vol. 4, 101–126).

resulted from the type of international moral politics that Boister would stress.

However, as I argue elsewhere (Ivory 2018), there are important discrepancies between Boister's conception of transnational criminal law and international anti-corruption standards and practice. Supra-state rules against corruption are not only cross-border or penal in the ways elaborated by transnational criminal lawyers; international standards and domestic obligations are but one modality for global anti-corruption control. More overtly sociological approaches to transnational law are a better fit for the development and patterning of these anti-corruption laws. More regulatory or preventive concepts of crime control may better capture the nature of, and problems with, their measures. Thus I proposed Terrence Halliday and Gregory Shaffer's transnational legal ordering (TLO) theory as a more effective tool for explaining and critiquing anti-corruption law as it emerges between international institutions, jurisdictions, and non-state organizations.

Extending that analysis, this chapter tests the utility of Boister's conception, and of Halliday and Shaffer's alternative approach, by examining a case of corporate foreign bribery reform from Australia. A federation of former British colonies in the Asia-Pacific, Australia belongs to several international economic crime initiatives, not least the United Nations Convention against Corruption (UN Convention) and the Convention on Combating Bribery of Foreign Public Officials in International Business Transactions of the Organisation for Economic Co-operation and Development (OECD Convention).[1] Australia's federal government has implemented these anti-corruption treaties inter alia with an offense against the bribery of foreign public officials and statutory corporate criminal liability principles in the Schedule to the Criminal Code Act 1995 (Cth; i.e., Code). These provisions have been pronounced internationally compliant with duties to hold legal persons liable for foreign bribery under the OECD and UN Conventions. But they have also been questioned for their relative lack of accompanying prosecutions. In December 2017, shortly before International Anti-corruption Day, the Commonwealth government proposed a Crimes Legislation Amendment (Combatting Corporate Crime) Bill 2017 (CCC Bill). That Bill would have repealed

---

[1] Organisation for Economic Co-operation and Development Convention on Combating Bribery of Foreign Public Officials in International Business Transactions, December 17, 1997, (1998) 37 ILM 1; United Nations Convention against Corruption, October 31, 2003, (2005) 2349 UNTS 41.

and replaced the generic foreign bribery offense and created a new corporate crime of failing to prevent foreign bribery, along with a system for negotiating corporate settlements in listed federal criminal matters. The Bill lapsed with the prorogation of Parliament for the May 2019 general election (Parliamentary Library 2019: 240). However, its proposals have been identified as issues for the new government, and the OECD's anti-corruption watchdog has flagged the failing to prevent offense, in particular, as an item to monitor (OECD-WGB 2017b: 59, para. 7 (h)). Meantime, the Australian Law Reform Commission (ALRC) has been asked to review the broader issue of corporate criminal responsibility in federal law (ALRC 2019; Porter 2019).[2]

In this chapter, I analyze domestic and international documents surrounding the proposed Australian corporate bribery offense so as to compare the TCL and TLO approaches for their explanatory power. I argue that there is a repetition of the global problems with TCL theory in the Australian case and a clear example of the potential for a TLO analysis. First, the Australian case materials indicate a more hetero-geneous set of inspirations for the corporate failing to prevent offense than Boister's account suggests. A mixture of drivers – international, multinational, and domestic – are evident behind the proposed offense of corporate omission. This mixture of factors better fits Halliday and Shaffer's conceptualization, which emphasizes the recursivity of trans-national lawmaking processes. Second, the proposed Australian failing to prevent offense can be seen, not only as an instance of criminal law, but also as an example of law reform that deploys a "new" and con-troversial approach to governance. Transnational legal ordering theory is better able than TCL theory to illuminate these "non-criminal" features for evaluation and categorization, and to consider the impact of those features on the eventual settlement of – or resistance to – the reforms. In sum, although the future of the measures in the CCC Bill was still uncertain as of August 2019, the Australian case already shows the importance of viewing transnational law reform as a social process in the setting of particular jurisdictions, issue areas, and points in time.

The argument takes four steps toward its core conclusions. Section 3.2 summarizes the rival accounts of transnational law in the work of

---

[2] In May 2019, the author participated in a public call for comments on the "scope of the inquiry and any issues relevant to the terms of reference" (ALRC 2019) and, as of August 2019, is organizing a seminar on the regulation of corporate ethics, with the ALRC and the University of Queensland's Schools of Law and Business.

Boister and of Halliday and Shaffer, respectively. Section 3.3 then provides background to the case study from Australia and my approach to the materials on the Australian case. Section 3.4 sets out my two findings from the analysis, examining the "transnational legality" and "transnational criminality" of Australia's potential corporate foreign bribery offense, in turn. I conclude in Section 3.5 but, to be clear, not with an estimation of the exact reasons for or against the proposed offense or a judgement as to whether it would be "good" or "bad" for anti-corruption work or Australia. Instead, I summarize some key influences on, and characterizations of, the corporate crime so as to identify the strengths and limitations of the TCL and TLO conceptions of transnational criminal justice.

3.2 TWO THEORIES OF TRANSNATIONAL LAW IN CRIMINAL JUSTICE

So, what is "transnational criminal law" and what is the "transnational legal ordering" alternative? In Boister's oft-cited account (Ivory 2018), transnational criminal law is a composite theory of international and domestic criminal law, which draws on positivist and constitutionalist traditions of jurisprudence, as well as on empirical accounts of norm emergence, especially from international relations. According to Boister, some laws are transnational because of their multiple sources and their cross-border crime focus. Hence, TCL consists of multilateral suppression conventions (or other supra-state arrangements) that commit countries to standardizing their domestic laws on particular crime problems and to cooperating with each other in ways that enable the enforcement of those laws (Boister 2003: 962; Boister 2018: 21–23). These "horizontal" rules are implemented through "vertical" obligations imposed by states on people (Boister 2003: 972; Boister 2014: 14, 18; Boister 2015: 14, 19; Boister 2018: 18). Such a collection of norms forms a legal system linked by analytical relationships and/or a legal order or field constituted by its subject matter (i.e., transnational crime; Boister 2003: 956–957; Boister 2014: 12–13, 21–22; Boister 2015: 25–26; Boister 2018: chapter 1, 2).

That transnational criminal subject matter is both normatively and analytically significant. Boister does not dispute that some crimes or harms cross borders or that legal change is recursive. As he writes, "the traffic" between international and domestic legal systems may go both ways (Boister 2018: 20). However, citing Nadelmann's theory of "prohibition regimes" in international relations, he argues that transnational criminal law tends to reflect the preferences of powerful Western countries, especially the United States and the United Kingdom (Boister 2015: 26–28; Boister 2018: 20–21, citing Nadelmann 1990). The resulting legal instruments are therefore likely to suffer from legitimacy deficits, as well as to authorize disproportionate interferences with individual civil rights (Boister 2002). Boister calls for "general" or "ordering" principles that would correct TCL's negative effects on state sovereignty and the administration of individual justice (Boister 2015: 28–30; Boister 2018: 422–427; see also Gless 2015).

By contrast, "transnational legal ordering" theory is a sociolegal methodology that can be used to examine the "changing nature of the relationship between domestic and international forms of criminal justice policy making" in particular places and spaces (Aronson and Shaffer, Chapter 1, this volume). Like Boister, Halliday, Shaffer, and colleagues foreground the social construction of transnational issues and recognize the influence of international politics in these processes (Halliday and Shaffer 2015a: 7, 21). However, TLO scholars are less concerned with whether a rule pertains to a (perceived) cross-border situation or whether that (perceived) phenomenon is ultimately regulated by an international instrument or regime. Rather, taking off from a new legal realist conception of law (Nourse and Shaffer 2009; Halliday and Shaffer 2015a: 17; Shaffer 2015), they see transnational law as embodying norms that are transported across national frontiers via cross-border social structures, and which are possibly changed in the process.

A transnational legal order is "a collection of formalized legal norms and associated organizations and actors that authoritatively order the understanding and practice of law across national jurisdictions" (Halliday and Shaffer 2015b: 475). A TLO may be recorded in an array of instruments on the "soft" to "hard" law spectrum (Halliday and Shaffer 2015a: 16); it may concern an array of socially constructed problems, from the purely domestic to the typically cross-border (Halliday and Shaffer 2015a: 7; Shaffer 2013a: 8); and it may change states in their "legal" and "non-legal" dimensions (Shaffer 2013a: 11–12; Shaffer 2013b: 24–33). The extent to which change occurs is likewise a function of a range of factors. Some relate to the character ("legitimacy, clarity, and coherence") of the rules or processes, and others reflect the relative power of the receiving state, as well as its domestic circumstances, exposure to intermediaries, and the occurrence of "historic events" (Shaffer 2013b: 33–46). Either way, the change-making process is not one-way or one-shot, but recursive. The concept of recursivity "posits that changes and transformations of states will be a function of three processes operating concurrently and cyclically – a politics within international and transnational lawmaking, a politics within domestic lawmaking, and a politics between them" (Shaffer 2013a: 14). In contrast to Boister, Halliday, and Shaffer give recursivity a central place in their analysis. This focus on recursivity allows for the identification and analysis of the splintering, decline, or failure of transnational efforts at criminal law reform in particular domestic settings (Aronson and Shaffer, Chapter 1, this volume; Halliday and Shaffer 2015a: 46; Halliday and Shaffer 2015b).

3.3 COMPARING THE THEORIES IN A CASE OF FOREIGN BRIBERY REFORM

How do these theories of transnational law compare to each other at the global level of anti-corruption controls, and how were they compared in this chapter through the prism of the Australian case? Before discussing my findings on the heuristic value of the two approaches, I briefly describe the CCC Bill in its wider context along with my approach to the case analysis.

3.3.1 Approach to the Comparison

As stated in the Introduction, this chapter proceeds from a parallel work in which I argued that anti-corruption departs, in important respects, from transnational criminal law conceptions (Ivory 2018). Within the broader literature on international and transnational criminal law, Boister's conceptualization of TCL has contributed significantly to exposing under-theorized and under-researched areas of state coordination (Currie 2015: 1166–1167; O'Keefe 2015: para. 7.204; van Sliedregt 2016: 2). Nonetheless, his framework for TCL is an uneasy fit with the diversity of supra-state anti-corruption standards and practices. These norms and activities have both global and local qualities that escape the transnational criminal lawyers' conceptions of space and their allied concerns about regime legitimacy. Further, the treaties could be considered both criminal and regulatory (newly governmental), insofar as they require states to adopt administrative and civil measures of social control. These non-criminal strategies are praised as pragmatic and participatory, though they pose their own normative and practical challenges. Finally, suppression conventions are not the only, or necessarily the most important, source of supra-state proscriptions of corrupt behavior. "Anti-corruptionism" is equally undergirded by international instruments that are nonbinding or internally binding and/or diagnostic in nature.

To address these deficiencies, I argued, it is necessary to situate extant conceptions of TCL within a larger set of doctrinal and socio-legal inquiries into new forms of global governance. My approach would mandate studies that deploy "a combination of sociological, historical, and ecological methods to explore the effect of a transnational legal order on corruption within particular countries or organisations, and vice versa" (Ivory 2018: 438).

3.3.2 Selecting Australia

To begin that undertaking for this chapter, I conducted a desk-based study of a proposed federal anti-corruption reform in my home jurisdiction, Australia. This research formed part of a larger project of inquiry into foreign bribery laws in the UK and Australia. The choice of Australia as the case study stemmed from both my existing knowledge of the Australian situation and from Australia's suitability for comparing TCL and TLO approaches.

Australia, it is said, has an ambivalent, if not anxious, relationship with international law (Charlesworth et al. 2003). Under its constitution, Australia is broadly a dualist state, its commonwealth executive concluding agreements at the international level and its legislature transposing those obligations in the domestic realm via legislation (Appleby et al. 2014: 347). The capacity of the executive to thereby alter the federal balance of power or compromise Australian freedom of action (sovereignty) has been a matter of controversy as relates to criminal justice. Notoriously, Australian governments campaigned for the creation of the International Criminal Court (ICC) in the 1990s before declaring Australia's jurisdictional primacy when ratifying the Rome Statute in the 2000s (Charlesworth et al. 2006: 71–80).

In turn, the ICC debate is said to reflect Australia's occasional roles as "good international citizen" or "middle power" (Tyler et al. 2017). With these labels, Australia is ascribed some scope to act through multilateral institutions and as a norm entrepreneur despite its dependence on great power allies (Ralph 2017: 52; Tyler et al. 2017: 9–11, 18–22). Hence, Australia's reticence with respect to the ICC is partly attributed to its deference to the United States, which ultimately refused to join the Court (Charlesworth et al. 2006: 80). Conversely, in the area of anti-corruption, Australia has adopted and promoted key international treaties favored by the United States, but has been criticized for insufficiently implementing those agreements (Gilbert and Sharman 2016: 82–86).

Viewed against this backdrop, the CCC Bill had much to offer as vehicle for comparison. The Bill has the hallmarks of a relatively orderly response to international pressure (a la Boister's theory) and yet its history exhibits the more recursive pattern of influence predicted by transnational legal process scholars, Halliday and Shaffer.

3.3.3   Background to the CCC Bill

As put to Parliament by Malcolm Turnbull's conservative coalition government in December 2017, the CCC Bill proposed significant changes to the Australian rules on corporate liability for foreign bribery (see generally Barker and Biddington 2018). Since the late 1990s, Division 70 Commonwealth Criminal Code has prohibited the intentional provision and so forth of illegitimate benefits to "foreign public officials" within and outside Australia's territory. Under Part 2.5 Code, a "body corporate" may be attributed with the physical elements of such an offense that is committed by a corporate "employee, agent, or officer" (s. 12.2). The mental elements are ascribed to a corporation who "authorised or permitted" the behavior (s. 12.3(1)), as determined inter alia by analyzing the conduct of its board or "high managerial agent[s]" or assessing the quality of its "corporate culture" (s. 12.3(2)).

Though noted internationally for these detailed and "holistic" provisions (Wells 2001: 102; Wells 2019: 260), Part 2.5 still requires the prosecutor to prove all the physical and mental elements of an offense, like foreign bribery, beyond reasonable doubt (see Code, ss. 13.1–13.2). Proposed s. 70.5A CCC Bill would have departed from this position by rendering certain bodies corporate strictly liable for failing to prevent their associates from bribing a foreign public official; to avoid liability a defendant firm would have had to establish that it had in place procedures adequate to prevent the associate's corruption (CCC Bill, Sch. 1, cl. 8, s. 70.5A(5); see further Gardiner 2018: 42–44). A minister would have been required to publish a guidance for corporations on possible preventive measures (CCC Bill, Sch. 1, cl. 8, s. 70.5B), and corporations may have had the option of negotiating with prosecutors for a deferred prosecution agreement (DPA; CCC Bill, Sch. 2), at least in relation to the primary offense of foreign bribery in s. 70.2 Code.

At the time of writing, it was not clear whether and, if so, when the measures in the CCC Bill would be passed into law. Later in December 2017, the Australian Federal Police (AFP) and Commonwealth Director of Public Prosecutions (CDPP) released a "guideline" on corporate self-reporting of foreign bribery (AFP and CDPP 2017). In June 2018, the Attorney General opened consultations on a Code of Practice, which would have complemented the DPA scheme in the CCC Bill (Porter 2018b). However, by late 2018, the conservative parties had changed their prime minister, and the CCC Bill was awaiting debate in Parliament. With the May 2019 general election, the Bill lapsed (Parliamentary Library 2019: 240), and as of the time of this writing, a matter of months into the reinstated Morrison government, it has yet to be proposed again. In contrast, roughly contemporaneous bills on protections for private-sector "whistleblowers" and corporate reporting with respect to "modern slavery" have been enacted.[3] That said, the broader issue of legal person liability is on the table, with the Attorney General tasking the ALRC to review Australia's corporate criminal responsibility regime (ALRC 2019; Porter 2019). Among other things, the law reform body is to consider "the availability of other mechanisms for attributing corporate criminal responsibility and their relative effectiveness," as well as the possibility of "introducing or strengthening other statutory regimes for corporate criminal liability" (Porter 2019). The ALRC is due to release an initial discussion paper in mid-November 2019 (ARLC 2019). In December 2019 the OECD will discuss its Phase 4 Follow-Up report on Australia.

3.3.4 Method of Analysis

To compare TCL and TLO theories in the Australian case, I undertook a content analysis of documents justifying and describing the corporate foreign bribery measures in the CCC Bill. My selection of materials was motivated by two questions: (1) "What were the international, transnational, and domestic influences on this proposal for reform?" and (2) "Is the failing to prevent offense an example of criminal, preventive, or 'new governance' approaches to behavior control?"

From the domestic sources, I selected three categories of documents to review: (1) the Bill itself, (2) statements on the Bill and its exposure

---

[3] *Modern Slavery Act 2018* (Cth); *Treasury Laws Amendment (Enhancing Whistleblower Protections) Act 2019* (Cth).

draft from the Attorney General's Department (AGD), and (3) Senate committee reports on the Bill and the broader topic of foreign bribery. As my review progressed, I also focused on materials that discussed the failing to prevent offense rather than the DPA scheme.

I then cross-checked my reading of AGD documents against domestic and international sources. As to the domestic sources, I searched the past three years of annual reports of the AFP, CDPP, and the Australian Securities and Investments Commission (ASIC; the corporate regulator) for discussion of anti-foreign-bribery work with possible bearing on the reforms. For the international materials, I considered OECD and UN monitoring body reports on Australia, the United Kingdom, and the United States. As relevant, I drew on United Kingdom and United States corporate foreign bribery laws and associated guidelines on compliance and sentencing.

Analysis of the selected texts yielded data relevant to the research questions in clusters of themes. Using and refining related key words, I searched the PDF documents manually, extracting relevant passages, and organizing the extracts. Through this process, important texts were identified for a second round of data extraction, in which the steps were repeated and larger passages taken out and coded.

3.4 TCL AND TLO THEORY IN THE AUSTRALIAN CASE

The content analysis yielded two main answers to the question "How do TCL and TLO theory perform when applied to a specific case of anti-corruption reform?" The findings of the analysis are grouped around the concepts of "transnational law" (Section 3.4.1) and "criminal law" (Section 3.4.2) in what follows.

3.4.1 "Transnational Law" and the Proposed Australian Reforms
The first finding concerns the extent to which the proposed Australian corporate foreign bribery offense conforms to TCL or TLO pictures of "transnational law." In the parallel study just described, I found that supra-state anti-corruption laws depart, in subtle but significant ways, from Boister's concept of norms that cross borders (Ivory 2018: 423–427). In the Australian case, the corporate failing to prevent offense would "transcend national frontiers" (Jessup 1956: 2), insofar as the putative bribe-taker would be a "foreign public official" (to Australia) and the Commonwealth's geographical jurisdiction would be extended beyond Australian territory (CCC Bill, Sch. 1, cl. 8,

s. 70.5A(1)(b), (7)).[4] The proposed offense would also appear to have implemented Australia's duties to criminalize foreign bribery, hold legal persons responsible, and punish entities for wrongs under the OECD and UN Conventions (AGD 2017: 9; McGrath 2017: 9908; Senate 2017: para. 7). The OECD treaty is cited in the literature, moreover, as the prima facie output of a global prohibition regime due to its close association with the United States and its Foreign Corrupt Practices Act 1977 (FCPA; Andreas and Nadelmann 2008: 55–56; see also Abbott and Snidal 2002).[5] The Turnbull government recalled the international consensus on the immorality of corruption when it described foreign bribery as injurious due to its effect on communities, business, and markets (McGrath 2017: 9906; see also AGD 2017: 1; Senate 2017: para. 6). All that said, with the failing to prevent offense, Australia would appear to have been responding to soft instruments as well as to changes in other "Anglo" countries and additional agentic and structural drivers.

3.4.1.1 International Standards
For a start, neither the OECD Convention nor the UN Convention expressly requires Australia to criminalize corporate failures to prevent foreign bribery. The treaties are silent on the rules for attributing guilt to legal persons other than to say that state parties shall take measures "in accordance" or "consistent with [their] legal principles" (OECD Convention: Art. 2; UN Convention: Art. 26(1)). Commentary suggests that the treaties were designed to accommodate the traditional reluctance of some states to recognize the criminal responsibility of legal persons (Pieth 2014: 223, 225). Instead, the idea that corporations should be liable for foreign bribery through managerial omission is mentioned in a non-binding 2009 OECD Recommendation on the implementation of Art. 2 OECD Convention. According to Annex I of the 2009 Recommendation, member states should ensure that their legal systems allow corporations to be held responsible for the crimes of a range of associated actors, including senior leaders who fail to prevent bribery at "lower level[s]" (OECD 2009: Annex I, para. B(b), third intent). Previously, the European Commission had utilized a similar concept to harmonize

---

[4] The definition of foreign public official under s. 70.1 Code includes persons formally or functionally associated with foreign states, foreign governments, and public international organizations, as well as intermediaries of those persons.
[5] Pub. L. No. 95–213 (1977), 15 U.S.C. §§ 78dd-1.

member state rules on corporate liability for certain forms of economic malfeasance affecting the European Union.[6] More recently, G20 leaders borrowed and broadened the language in the OECD's Annex I in their 2017 High-Level Principles on the Liability of Legal Persons for Corruption.[7]

Numerous international and non-governmental organizations (NGOs) then tell companies themselves what they should do to ensure compliance with anti-bribery duties. For example, the AGD (2018b: 12) intended to be informed inter alia by "ISO 37001" (International Organization for Standardization 2016) as well as a joint OECD, United Nations Office on Drugs and Crime (UNODC), and World Bank handbook on compliance, which purports to digest six other "internationally recognised business instruments on anti-bribery" (2013: 15).[8] That handbook places compliance measures in the context of an international legal framework on corruption and is "complemented by" multilateral lender debarment processes for corrupt consultants or contractors (2013: 9). According to Low (2014: 618), the World Bank's Sanctions Board has deployed a concept of corporate liability that is strict but moderated by an assessment of organizational efforts at prevention and detection of misconduct.

Given this diversity, it cannot be assumed that the OECD or UN Conventions are the actual or analytical "match" for the proposed Australian rule. It could also be that Australia responded to a wider understanding – even an emerging general legal principle or custom – on the optimal interpretation of international corporate criminal liability obligations.

---

[6] Second Protocol, drawn up on the basis of Article K.3 of the treaty on European Union, to the Convention on the protection of the European Communities' financial interests, June 19, 1997, (1997) O.J. (C 221), July 19, 1997, 12, Art. 3(2) (requiring states to ensure the liability of legal persons where lack of supervision or control by senior persons made possible fraud, active corruption, or money laundering as defined). See also Criminal Law Convention on Corruption, January 27, 1999, (1999) 2216 UTS, 225, Art. 18(1); Directive (EU) 2017/1371 of the European Parliament and of the Council of 5 July 2017 on the fight against fraud to the Union's financial interests by means of criminal law, July 5, 2017, (2017) O.J. (L 198), July 28, 2017, 29, Art. 6(1)–(2).

[7] G20, Leaders' Declaration: Shaping an Interconnected World, Annex: G20 High-Level Principles on the Liability of Legal Persons for Corruption, July 8, 2017, available at: www.g20g ermany.de/Webs/G20/EN/G20/Summit_documents/summit_documents_node.html, Principle 4. For example, whereas the OECD would have states take a flexible approach to the status of the triggering person, the G20 would have them make the relevant status flexible or disregard status entirely.

[8] For a discussion of "stakeholder" views on the relative benefits of these and other standards, see Senate 2018a: para. 4.76 et seq.

3.4.1.2 International Statements

Further, neither the international anti-corruption watchdogs nor the federal government presented the failing to prevent offense as necessary for Australian compliance with treaty law. Both the UN Implementation Review Mechanism and the OECD Working Group on Bribery in International Business Transactions (OECD-WGB) depicted Australia as having adequately transposed the conventions' articles on the criminalization of bribery and corporate liability. The difficulties lay with Australia's enforcement of its existing legislation.

Initially, in its Phase 1 review, the OECD-WGB endorsed Australia's legal framework for prohibiting foreign bribery and attributing guilt to corporations (1999: 23). In Phase 2, the Working Group praised "section 12 [as] ambitious and progressive," if untested (OECD-WGB 2006: paras. 2, 148–153). Only from Phase 3 did the examiners express "serious concer[n]" with Australia's low rate of enforcement (OECD-WGB 2012: paras. 7, 42–43; see also OECD-WGB 2015: para. 2). The Phase 4 report, which was released less than two weeks after the CCC Bill, stops short of describing the proposed provisions as necessary, though it "welcome[d]" the failing to prevent offense as an attempt to remove "barriers" to prosecution and "recommend[ed] ... follow-up on ... enact[ment]" (OECD-WGB 2017b: paras. 153–154). The UN reviewers did not have the opportunity to report on the proposed Australian offense, but they endorsed a related UK model in a review of that state's implementation of arts. 12 and 26 UN Convention on corporate liability and corruption prevention in the private sector (UNCAC-COSP 2013: paras. 32, 48; UNCAC-COSP 2019: 9; cf. UNCAC-COSP 2012: 3).

Australian government documents echoed this narrative by asserting that Australia had already executed its international obligations (AGD 2017: 1; Senate 2017: para. 7; see also Senate 2018b: para. 1.3) and that the s. 70.5A offense would have "[gone] beyond the requirements of the [OECD] Convention" (AGD 2018a: 7). On the governmental account, all changes in the Bill would have enhanced the Commonwealth's capacity to enforce international and domestic norms against foreign bribery, particularly with respect to companies in corporate groups and transnational supply chains (AGD 2018a: 7; AGD 2018b: 2–3; Senate 2017: paras. 7–8; see also AGD 2017: 8–9; Senate 2018: paras. 2.85–2.86).

3.4.1.3 Anglo-American Precedents

In addition, when selecting the failing to prevent offense, Australia would appear to have followed an Anglo-American precedent that was not so much required but recommended and perhaps extended through international instruments and processes. Already in the early 2000s, the OECD-WGB had described the general US federal corporate criminal attribution rules as "reinforc[ing] the effectiveness of the FCPA [and] also ... encourag[ing] corporations to implement measures of deterrence throughout their organisations" (2002: para. 15). The FCPA's bribery offense may be committed by legal persons (Kohli 2018: 1280–1282), who are strictly vicariously liable, at common law, for an employee acting "within the scope and nature of his employment and ... at least in part, to benefit the corporation" (Weiner et al. 2018: 964–965). There is no defense that the corporation prohibited misconduct with internal policies and procedures (Weiner et al. 2018: 966, 968). Nevertheless, US courts may reduce financial penalties for firms with "effective compliance and ethics program[s]" (US Sentencing Commission 2018: §§ 8B2.1, 8C2.5(f)). Prosecutors should consider "the adequacy and effectiveness of the corporation's compliance program at the time of the offense, as well as at the time of a charging decision," when determining how to "trea[t] ... a corporate target" (US Department of Justice 2018: § 9–28.300). Corporations are afforded "insights" into the "hallmarks of effective compliance practice" via a non-binding prosecutorial guidance document (US Department of Justice and US Securities and Exchange Commission 2012: 57–65).

Back at the OECD, by the start of the 2010s, the Working Group had endorsed a similar UK offense, defense, and guidance model (OECD-WGB 2010b: paras. 79–80, 83; OECD-WGB 2011: para. 2), after having been highly critical of prior British laws (OECD-WGB 2005: paras. 195–206; OECD-WGB 2008: paras. 65–92). The Bribery Act 2010 (UK) came into force at the very end of the Blair Labor government and made it a crime for "commercial organisation[s]" to fail to prevent bribery by an "associated person," defined in s. 8(3) to include an "employee, agent or subsidiary." Corporate liability under s. 7(1) is no-fault (strict). However, the organization has a defense if it can show that it had implemented procedures adequate to prevent bribery under s. 7(2). Adequate procedures are discussed further in a non-binding guidance issued by the Ministry of Justice under s. 9 (Ministry of Justice 2011). The Crime and Courts Act 2013 (UK; Sch. 17) later established a system of DPAs, which may be concluded with corporations that were, or commit to becoming, compliant, among other things (Serious Fraud Office 2014: paras. 2.8.1(iii), 2.8.2(iii), 7.10(iii)). Therefore, the UK would seem to have created a corporate anti-foreign-bribery framework that is broadly similar to the US model, albeit via a strict organizational offense, adequate procedures defense, and negotiated settlement scheme.[9]

Returning to Australia, both the OECD-WGB (2017: para. 153) and the government acknowledged that proposed s. 70.5A was to be "similar to" the offense in s. 7 Bribery Act 2010 (UK; AGD 2017: 8; AGD 2018a: 7; AGD 2018b: 3; McGrath 2017: 9907), if not "modeled on" that provision (AGD 2018a: 4). The AGD cited both the UK Ministry of Justice's "guidance" (2011) and a US Department of Justice compliance questionnaire (2017, now 2019) among the standards it would consider when devising the Australian compliance principles under s. 70.5B CCC Bill (2018b: 12). Its proposed DPA regime was "consistent with" and a "hybrid of" US and UK practice (AGD 2018a: 3, 12; AGD 2018b: 26, 35; see also Senate 2017: 9907).

3.4.1.4 Australian and Multinational Drivers

Looking finally from text to subtext, the CCC Bill showed signs of influence from other less public international actors and factors than predominate in the TCL model. First, the Bill appears to be a means for government to maintain Australia's status and meet evolving demands for performance of its sovereign functions. Thus the AGD described its review of the Code as "appropriate" given that "[i]t has been 18 years since the foreign bribery offence was introduced" and there was a need "to ensure [that] the law reflects community expectations and does not present unnecessary barriers to effective prosecution" (AGD 2017: 3). Discussing the final version of the Bill, the executive described foreign bribery as a danger to Australia's "reputation" and "international standing," among other things (McGrath 2017: 9906; Senate 2017: para. 6; see also AGD 2017: 1, 9). The documents did not mention any particular source of threat to Australia's relative position; however, it is noteworthy that the country's performance on the Transparency International Corruption Perceptions Index had suffered in previous years (Transparency International Australia 2018; Wyld 2019: 16). An

---

[9] While the transnational origins of the UK scheme is beyond this chapter's scope, it is at least interesting to note that British examiners had participated in the Phase 2 and 3 OECD-WGB reviews of the US: OECD-WGB 2002: para. 2; OECD-WGB 2010: para. 6.

earlier governmental press release mentioned that NGO's rankings in connection with Australia's pride in its "position and reputation ... as one of the least corrupt countries in the world" (Keenan 2014).

Second, the surrounding documents indicate that the AGD detected support for the failing to prevent offense among multinational businesses within Australia's jurisdiction. When discussing the s. 70.5B guidance, the AGD noted that benchmarking against the UK governmental compliance guidelines "[was] in line with the preference Australian industry expressed during the 2017 consultation process and [would] ensure minimal impact on Australian corporations that have already framed their anti-bribery policies on international guidelines" (AGD 2018b: 12). In other statements, the Department indicated that standardized compliance requirements would confer efficiency gains (rather than impose compliance burdens) on Australian firms, which "operat[e] overseas" (AGD 2017: 9; AGD 2018a: 9; see also Senate 2018b: para. 2.89). Multinational businesses, in other words, would need to make a lesser investment of resources to gain equal or greater confidence that their internal systems and procedures meet the Australian standards. The Senate Economics References Committee, somewhat by contrast, recorded private sector concern about the strict liability offense in proposed s. 70.5A CCC Bill. However, the Committee ultimately formed the view that the burden of proof was justified by the compliance defense and an alignment with longstanding UK practice (Senate 2018a: para. 4.98).

Third, the materials reflect ideas about crime and corporations that predate or parallel the OECD Convention and anti-corruptionism. Hence, the CCC Bill is said to address "serious corporate crime," a category described by reference to the complexity, opacity, and sophistication of its offenses and offenders, as well as the cross-border qualities of its investigations (AGD 2017: 1, 3–4, 8; AGD 2018b: 3, 8; McGrath 2017: 9906; Senate 2017: paras. 2, 8; see also Senate 2018b: paras. 2.85–2.88). The nomenclature of "seriousness," as used in the UK, is connected to broader trends toward preventive approaches to justice (Ogg 2015), which are discussed below. Further, there is a history in Australian federal criminal law of corporate liability norms being addressed to the perceived difficulties of attributing mental states to "modern" business organizations. Already in the early 1990s, less hierarchical corporate structures and greater use of delegation were judged to inhibit the identification of individuals who were sufficiently senior to enable the imputation of guilt to corporations. Moreover, it was recognized that particular organizational ("corporate") cultures could tacitly authorize a wrong (Criminal Law Officers Committee of the Standing Committee of the Attorneys-General 1992: 105, 113). Part 2.5 Code was addressed to these concerns. That said, for extreme and "difficult to detect" dangers, it was always the intention of the Code's drafters that the burden of proof could be reversed and liability thereby extended (Senate 1994: 2379, 2381).

3.4.1.5   Theorizing Transnational Law Reforms

To summarize, there are interesting questions to be asked about the cross-border qualities of the "failing to prevent" offense that was proposed for Australian foreign bribery law. However, these questions are not only about the alignment of domestic and international standards in the abstract, or the formation of the global rules through a prohibition regime. Of equal concern are the actual processes by which international organizations, foreign states, and other factors and actors contributed to the choice of reform – and whether, when, and in what final form that choice will be enacted.

Clearly, the AGD responded to OECD critique when it proposed this overhaul of Division 70 Code. However, the Working Group's criticism concerned Australia's relative lack of anti-bribery investigations and prosecutions – not the duty to criminalize corporate foreign bribery, with which it had pronounced Australia compliant. When choosing the failure to prevent offense, moreover, the Department borrowed a British model, with its OECD influences and echoes of US law. It appears to have preferred an Anglo-American hybrid, but one with some basis in international standards as these have changed over time. Probing further, proposed s.70.5A CCC Bill resonated with older governmental understandings of the nature of both "serious" and "modern" corporate crime, as well as the (perceived) expectations of multinational companies and notions of national reputation.

These conclusions are not incompatible with the transnational criminal approach of Boister, but they are better illuminated by Halliday and Shaffer's theory of transnational legal ordering. An initial advantage is that this avowedly sociolegal and process-oriented conception of transnational law avoids the need for analytical matching between domestic and international rules. Such matching is complicated by the diversity of sources on corruption and corporate foreign bribery, in particular. From the TLO view, the issues are as follows: To what extent were the OECD and UN Conventions the inspiration for the proposed Australian rules? To what extent did specific international peer review procedures prompt Australian action, compared to more diffuse international norms about the state of the art in domestic corporate foreign bribery legislation?

Next, the core TLO hypothesis – that transnational lawmaking is recursive – has more heuristic power in revealing and unpacking the messy motivations for reform, which are apparent in the Australian case. A recursivity approach would problematize the internal processes of decision-making within the OECD and UN, US and UK, as well as capture factors native to Australia and the interactions between these "levels" of lawmaking institutions. It could raise questions, for instance, about how the UK came to adopt the failing to prevent model; how the OECD or US influenced the British (or vice versa); and whether Australia contributed to OECD, US, or UK preferences with its earlier "corporate culture" rules.[10] Other issues that would come to the fore when adopting the TLO approach would be the medium of influence between the UK, US, and Australia: Was the OECD the "active ingredient" or an epiphenomenon of colonial histories, common law traditions, and ongoing political, economic, and security ties? Already there are reports of anti-corruption networks among law enforcement officials of "like-minded countries."[11] Also, insofar as the proposed reform followed an Anglo-American precedent and/or responded to a commercial appetite for reform driven by other jurisdictions, to what extent are (perceived or anticipated) changes within the United States and the United Kingdom relevant to the measures' future "success," "failure," or form?[12]

[10] In its Phase 2 report on Australia, the OECD-WGB (2006: para. 148) described s. 12 Code as "a commendable development, and well-suited to prosecutions for foreign bribery" and as "ambitious and progressive, with many elements that are not contained in the criminal legal systems of most other countries, in particular liability based on a corporate culture."

[11] The annual reports of the AFP (2017: 61) and CDPP (2018: 53) mention involvement in an International Foreign Bribery Taskforce with the UK, US, and Canada. The AFP (2017: 59, 61) also records its involvement as a founding member of the International Anti-corruption Coordination Centre, which is based in the UK National Crime Authority (NCA) and has participants from those states plus New Zealand and Singapore (NCA n.d.). See further Barker 2019: 10–11; Wyld 2019: 18.

[12] As to the United Kingdom, the OECD-WGB (2019: 4) has recently noted "relatively low" absolute numbers of foreign bribery cases, "[d]espite an increased level of [British] enforcement of foreign bribery laws." The UK government has also responded equivocally to a Select Committee's suggestions that it consider extending the corporate failing to prevent model to economic crimes generally (Ministry of Justice 2019: paras. 55–56; cf. House of Lords 2019: paras. 227–232). The government did however express its "gratitude" for the Committee's endorsement of the Bribery Act 2010 and the DPA regime (Ministry of Justice 2019: para. 6). Concerns with the impact of Brexit on UK enforcement efforts were noted in both the international and domestic reports (House of Lords 2019: paras. 154–166; OECD-WGB

Further, TLO theory provides greater scope for considering the role of non-state actors in transnational criminal justice. On the one hand, the Australian materials hinted at the role of NGO indictors in shaping perceptions of states as more or less corrupt (Davis, Kingsbury and Merry 2015). On the other, the materials signaled the importance of perceived "big" business preferences for local laws that reflect emerging de-nationalized standards. This is not to point to an international commercial conspiracy in Australia. Nor is it to downplay the role of the state and, within states, the interests of law-enforcers or more obviously "moral" norm entrepreneurs in pushing for harmonized or extended laws.[13] The claim, rather, is that researchers need to consider the ways in which business actors contribute to a choice of crime control and transpose international crime-fighting obligations (Shaffer 2009). Here, too, a recursive lens may be apt. One set of questions could concern notions of "adequate procedures" or "effective compliance." Which national or international conceptions have Australian business actors internalized? Where did those conceptions originate, and to what extent are such private transpositions affecting public and/or non-state understandings of "best practice"? Do they align with, or do they depart from, each other?

Finally, TLO theory is better suited to placing internationally salient law reforms in their local historical contexts. In the Australian case, a TLO lens would prompt an examination of Australia's past failures to enforce its foreign bribery laws, as well as any future failure of the legislature to enact the corporate failing to prevent offense. TLO theory affords this additional explanatory power because it prompts questions about whether norms have been institutionalized within states and how those rules impact upon human behavior. TCL theory does conceive of transnational law as the product of an international process of regime formation that affects people through domestic law. However, Boister's

2017a: paras. 11, 106, 198). As to the US, President Trump's public criticism of the FCPA, among other things, was said to have prompted some commentators to predict changes in US foreign bribery legislation and practices (for examples, see Koehler 2018: 153, 186–187). However, to date, assessments of developments under his administration have been mixed. Garrett (2020: 111,117) has calculated a "decline in corporate penalties and enforcement," though "more stab[ility]" in FCPA penalties and some consistencies with Obama-era trends. Vuona (2019: 1025–1032) and Husisian (2017) note a mixture of structural and agentic factors both for and against the continuation of past FCPA enforcement practices, as does Koehler (2018), albeit favoring a continuity hypothesis in less equivocal terms.

[13] The Senate Economics References Committee (Senate 2018a: paras. 4.69, 4.75) also cites an Australian church group as being in support of the failing to prevent offense and adequate procedures defense.

account does not lend itself to a focus on the ways that states implement international rules, or the strength and weakness of those rules in aligning social practice. What accounts for the apparent cooling in appetite for corporate foreign bribery law reform Down Under? Do we understand the current ambivalence to reflect domestic considerations, international political calculations, and/or the persuasiveness of international rules and institutions? In light of such questions, my first finding is that TCL theory is comparatively less able to expose and account for variations in how states and non-state actors respond to international standards.

3.4.2 "Criminal Law" and the Proposed Australian Reforms

My second finding concerns the challenge of applying the concept of "transnational criminal law" with respect to the proposed Australian corporate foreign bribery controls. Is the failing to prevent offense an example of a criminal approach to behavior control and, if not, why should this matter?

In recent work, Boister acknowledges that the suppression conventions also recommend or require non-criminal forms of intervention: civil and administrative, "preventive and regulatory" (Boister 2018: 29). Yet his attention remains on the criminal law – implicitly conceived of as a relatively discrete group of prohibitions, procedures, and punishments with particular risks of stigmatization and coercion (see, e.g., Boister 2018: 422–427). This focus would appear to be justified insofar as all but one of the anti-corruption treaties require states to criminalize certain behaviors.[14] The crime control treaties also authorize incursions into the private sphere and encourage states to reduce protections for persons subject to international judicial cooperation (Ivory 2014: chapter 4). Be this as it may, notionally non-criminal measures for corruption control may also be a source of tension or conflict with individual civil liberties (Ivory 2014; Boucht 2017). The non-criminal features of the anti-corruption treaties may indicate an alternative (and problematic) approach to behavior control (Ivory 2018: 427–432). The Australian case materials indicate that there are "new" or "non-criminal" qualities to the failure to prevent offense that are central to its categorization, historicization, and appraisal.

---

[14] See, e.g., OECD Convention, supra note 1, Arts. 1, 7; UN Convention, supra note 1, Arts. 15–25. The exception is the Civil Law Convention on Corruption, November 4, 1999, (2005) 2246 UNTS 3.

3.4.2.1 An Example of "New Governance"?

From one angle, the proposed Australian corporate foreign bribery reforms take a stance on criminalization that is characteristic of "new governance" approaches to business regulation. The term "new" ("regulatory" or "experimental") governance describes a broad range of public sector "tools" deployed to motivate private sector self-regulation and cooperation in community problem-solving (de Búrca and Scott 2006: 2–3; Lobel 2004; Lobel 2012). Criminal sanctions are not disregarded in this conceptual framework and mode of intervention, but they are placed toward the tip of a regulatory pyramid. There, they serve to deal with more egregious violations and to motivate compliance with less coercive enforcement activities (Ayes and Braithwaite 1992: 35–39; Freiberg 2017: 423).

Read with the surrounding documents, the CCC Bill recalled this collaborative and staged approach to governmental intervention. The AGD did reject a suggestion that the failing to prevent offense was a "regulatory breach" that should attract lesser penalties (AGD 2018a: 8). Proposed s. 70.5A was to be made punishable with a fine equal to that in s. 70.2 Code (CCC Bill, Sch. 1, cl. 8, s. 70.5A(6)) so as to "ensure … deterre[nce]" of willful blindness in companies (AGD 2018a: 8; AGD 2018b: 3). However, by its terms, s. 70.5A would have excused corporations that "had in place adequate procedures designed to prevent" foreign bribery. The government was to have told corporations the steps they could take, using "principles-based" guidance rather than a "prescriptive checklist" that established a presumption of (non-) compliance (AGD 2018b: 10, 13–14; Porter 2018a: 10; Senate 2018c: para. 5). The Senate Legal and Constitutional Affairs Legislation Committee, which examined the Bill in 2018, recommended that "corporate stakeholders" be permitted to comment on an exposure draft of the "adequate procedures" guidance (Senate: 2018b, para. 2.93). The very opportunities for self-governance justified the no-fault offense, the reversal of the burden of proof, and the broad concept of associates (AGD 2017: 8; AGD 2018b: 16; Senate 2017: paras. 30, 95; Senate 2018a: xiii; Senate 2018b: para. 2.86).

3.4.2.2 The Prospects and Pitfalls of New Governance

Considered as an example of new governance approaches, the CCC Bill could have entailed regulatory risks and returns other than just those emphasized by Boister. For its advocates, new governance is an innovative response to socio-economic complexities, "a third-way vision between unregulated markets and top-down government controls" (Lobel 2012: 65). The AGD thus acknowledged that lengthy court battles are an economic cost for defendant companies, while indictments may themselves pose a possibly fatal threat of corporate stigma (AGD 2016: 9–10; Senate 2017: para. 11). The CCC Bill offered an alternative to that top-down enforcement model insofar as proposed s. 70.5A would have motivated corporate harm prevention, and the DPA provisions would have allowed the deferment of corporate prosecutions in exchange inter alia for compliance reforms (CCC Bill, Sch. 2; see also Bronitt 2018: 50; Campbell 2019). On an appreciative assessment, this "carrot and stick" approach would have maximized opportunities for ethical expression within for-profit organizations, while minimizing the threat to communities from corrupt enterprises and overzealous prosecutors. The CCC Bill could thus be seen to have responded to the complexity of cross-border corporate regulation in ways that would have utilized private resources and expertise, while minimizing the costs and risks of enforcement.

Equally, the scheme could have been liable to elite manipulation of various sorts, such as emerges from a recent Australian corporate governance inquiry, and is evident in the international academic literature. Within Australia, there has been high-level disapproval of conciliatory corporate regulatory practices in both the interim and final reports of the Royal Commission into Misconduct in the Banking, Superannuation, and Financial Services Industry (Hayne Royal Commission; Hayne 2018: xix; Hayne 2019: 3–4). Prepared by a retired High Court judge on the basis of televised witness testimony and major institutional disclosures, the reports do blame financial services entities themselves for misconduct and poor behavior in their organizations (Hayne 2018: 268; Hayne 2019: 4). However, the Commissioner also concluded that Australian corporate and prudential regulators had enabled improper industry practices by being too reticent to prosecute contested allegations of wrongdoing (Hayne 2018: 269–270; Hayne 2019: 424–428, 451–453). ASIC, in particular, was criticized for prioritizing the commercial interest in reaching an agreement over the public interest in penalty proceedings (Hayne 2018: 277; Hayne 2019: 424–425).

Within the academy, scholars have also problematized approaches that seek to motivate corporations to prevent unethical or criminal behavior. Legal sociologist Lauren Edelman illustrates some of the functional problems with her studies of American anti-discrimination law. Through a process of "legal endogeneity," she argues, corporations have used ambiguous legal provisions to shape judicial understandings of compliance in their favor (Edelman 2016: 12–16). She sees "new governance" approaches as generative of such symbolic structures (Edelman 2016: 223, 236) and quite possibly also US corporate criminal liability rules (2016: 226–229).

Applying her insights to the Australian case, it could be argued that the defense of "adequate procedures" was overtly broad as it appeared in the proposed s. 70.5A CCC Bill. The breadth (ambiguity) of that concept was not likely to have been moderated by a "guidance" that was also general ("principles-based") and developed with input from the corporate sector, a skeptic could say. Moreover, if international practice was to have been a guide, the concepts in ss. 70.2 and 70.5A would have been interpreted, not by courts as a rule but by prosecutors in negotiating with corporate defendants for various non-trial resolutions (Abikoff et al. 2014: para. 12.2; Garrett 2014; OECD 2019: 13–14). To the extent that such settlements result from executive discretion (Bronitt 2018: 49; Pieth and Ivory: 2011) and a process of bargaining, one could have hypothesized greater potential for prosecutorial accommodation of corporate preferences. The evaluative question would have then become: "To what extent would the risk of legal endogeneity have been off-set by prosecutorial codes of practice and review procedures in Australia?"

Deploying Foucault and risk theories that adopt a Foucauldian approach, others have configured global economic crime controls as an example of private security governance, (global) governmentality, and/or preventive justice (Catá Backer 2008: 119–120; Ivory forthcoming; Liss and Sharman 2015; see further Ivory 2018). Taking this view of the CCC Bill, the corporate duty of care could have been seen to shift some of the federal government's power for policing onto private organizations. These organizations would have then become more motivated instruments for monitoring (surveilling) "dangerous" populations of employees, contractors, and intermediaries, and encouraging, among them, greater self-control. In this way, the CCC Bill could have been said to reflect a neoliberal rationality, in that it sought to utilize profit driven-actors and market processes to achieve a public ethical good. Foreign bribery was not to have been eradicated but limited to situations where it could not have been forestalled through adequate risk mitigation measures.

Though these latter approaches are not explicitly normative, they may be used to inquire into the logic of trends in regulation, as well as effects of those trends on established legal principles and practices (Ashworth and Zedner 2014; Garland 2001; Mazerolle and Ransley 2006). In terms of regulatory consequences, it could have been asked whether the strict nature of the failing to prevent offense was justified in liberal theories of coercion by its harm reduction objectives (Bronitt and Brereton 2017: para. 5.4 citing Ashworth and Zedner 2008). Alternatively or in addition, it could have been probed how transnational compliance obligations affect the distribution of risk for wrongdoing between small and large businesses in exporting states, like Australia. Moreover, a critical lens would have led us to consider whether and, if so, to what extent privatized corporate surveillance duties actually enhance economic freedoms (World Bank 2016) and sovereignty in Australia's globally southern trading partners (see further Ivory 2018).

3.4.2.3 Theorizing Non-criminal Law Reforms

How would TLO theory, in contrast to TCL theory, accommodate these alternative characterizations and critiques of the Australian failing to prevent offense such as was proposed? In light of the above, I argue that a TLO approach is better suited to illuminating the qualities and consequences of the failure to prevent offense in the CCC Bill, as it stood and as it could be enacted.

The advantage of TLO theory here is its analytical openness. Belonging to the "contextualist" branch of the New Legal Realist tradition, TLO theory departs from the "Jamesian/Deweyan" position that "theory must come from the world" (Nourse and Shaffer 2009: 82, 84). Hence, scholars deploying the TLO approach do not privilege criminal law as the most important means by which societies approach "transnational crimes" (Kotiswaran, Chapter 4, this volume; Kotiswaran and Palmer 2015). Further, unlike transnational criminal lawyers, TLO theorists do not provide a framework for evaluating transnational legal orders as such (Halliday and Shaffer 2015a: 27). Instead, they emphasize the perceived legitimacy of a law as a variable in compliance, as well as the way that "ideological contradictions" within a TLO can spark recursive processes, which affect the settlement of legal meanings and practices (Halliday and Shaffer 2015a: 39–40; Halliday and Shaffer 2015b: 507–508; Shaffer 2013b: 34).

Neutrality vis-à-vis legal taxonomies and fundamental rights enables a reform, like the CCC Bill, to be both described and appraised from a wider range of perspectives. British failing to prevent offenses are queried for their due process implications for corporations and individuals (Ashworth 2017: 627; Ashworth 2018; cf. Campbell 2018: 61–63). Defendants' rights are an important constraint on the enforcement of foreign bribery law in Australia, as a recent High Court case has shown.[15] However, as emerges from the above, the CCC Bill embedded a range of pragmatic and normative challenges, which TCL's focus on the criminal law and its procedures may have concealed. TLO theory may perform better insofar as it is used to illuminate how measures affect and are perceived by relevant groups, from corporate compliance officers and sales personnel to the legal and allied professionals who act as external investigators or advisors. That information could aid reflections on the reasons for the eventual adoption or rejection of the measures in the CCC Bill and, if they are adopted, could help determine the CCC Act's "regulatory performance," to use Lord's language (2014: chapter 8).

In addition, TLO and TCL approaches could be combined to probe the operation – for good or for ill – of anti-foreign bribery compliance systems. Such studies could start, for instance, with questions about how companies subject to s. 70.5A (or an equivalent provision) respond to their duties to prevent, both on paper and through their internal and external counsel and compliance functions. They could then continue to probe how firms discharge their quasi-law enforcement powers (e.g., in trainings and internal investigations) and how those exercises of power are perceived by employees, agents, and contractors in Australia, along with a range of countries that host Australian investments. These findings could illuminate new opportunities for individual ethical expression or possibilities for domination, when viewed through a liberal-criminal law or a knowledge-power lens.

3.5 CONCLUSION

What do the findings in the Australian case say about the relative strengths of TCL or TLO theories? Does Boister's "TCL" theory deliver

---

[15] *Tony Strickland (a pseudonym)* v. *Commonwealth Director of Public Prosecutions; Donald Galloway (a pseudonym)* v. *Commonwealth Director of Public Prosecutions; Edmund Hodges (a pseudonym)* v. *Commonwealth Director of Public Prosecutions; Rick Tucker (a pseudonym)* v. *Commonwealth Director of Public Prosecutions* [2018] HCA 53.

on its promise to match explanatory, descriptive, and normative accounts of transnational crime controls? To the extent that there are difficulties, how does Halliday and Shaffer's "TLO" approach correct the problems with the TCL analysis?

In this chapter, I explored these questions via a preliminary study of a proposed corporate foreign bribery reform in Australia. Through a structured reading of Australian government documents and associated international materials, I found that the transnational criminal account struggled to capture the complex history and ambiguous form of the proposed Australian failing to prevent offense. On the one hand, a corporate crime of omission was not required by the UN or OECD Conventions, nor was it recommended in the reports of those conventions' monitoring bodies. Rather, the CCC Bill corresponded to "soft" OECD standards and other non-binding or non-public international standards on corruption. In particular, the 2017 Australian proposal would seem to have borrowed from the Bribery Act 2010 (UK), and thus to have incorporated the outcomes of earlier battles between the OECD and the British government, as well as US regulatory preferences. On the other hand, the CCC Bill had some of the hallmarks of a new governmental approach to corruption control, with its defense for adequate procedures and its provisions for negotiated corporate settlements (DPAs). In combination, these measures seem designed to enhance the Commonwealth's capacity to prosecute corporate foreign bribery and to engage the corporate sector as partners in law enforcement. Transnational criminal law theory, as framed by Boister, would tend to deemphasize the non-criminal features of the recent Australian proposal and its potential normative and practical implications.

This analysis then opened up the way for applying TLO theory in the Australian case. Halliday and Shaffer's approach would be useful initially for illuminating the range of actors and factors that seemed to motivate the proposed Australian reforms and may affect their progression into law. TLO theory not only points to the role of powerful states and non-state moral entrepreneurs in diffusing social norms through international networks and organizations; in addition, it calls for an examination of how agents and structures interact at multiple levels of governance, and with respect to each other, in the context of particular governmental decisions. Hence, in the Australian case, TLO theory draws attention to the processes by which the OECD and United Nations, United States, and United

Kingdom contributed to the CCC Bill, in addition to the role of Australian officials, companies, and policy traditions in shaping the drafters' preferred corporate criminal liability concepts. TLO theory then takes an agnostic stance on the most relevant features of domestic criminal justice reforms and the possibilities of appraising those measures in any absolute sense. In the case of Australia, this agnosticism permits both the new governance and traditional criminal features of the CCC Bill to come to the fore. A TLO approach would allow the CCC Bill to be considered for its possibilities, as well as its pitfalls, and from the perspective of a range of affected parties. In this way, the avowedly sociolegal orientation of TLO theory exposes the challenge of evaluating rules without assuming particular notions of legitimacy or "good" crime governance. It also places questions about rightfulness in the context of questions about a law's prospects for success or failure, as is important in the case of Australia's nascent corporate foreign bribery reforms.

REFERENCES

Abbott, Kenneth, and Duncan Snidal. 2002. "Values and Interests: International Legalization in the Fight against Corruption." *Journal of Legal Studies* 31: S141–177.

Abikoff, Kevin T., Edward J. M. Little, John F. Wood, and Michael H. Huneke. 2014. The International Perspective: Lessons from US Authorities' Enforcement of the Foreign Corrupt Practices Act. Pp. 439–483 in *Lissack and Horlick on Bribery*, edited by Richard Lissack and Fiona Horlick, 2nd ed. London: LexisNexis.

AFP. 2017. Amended Annual Report 2016–2017. www.afp.gov.au/about-us/publications-and-reports/annual-reports.

AFP and CDPP. 2017. Self-Reporting of Foreign Bribery and Related Offending by Corporations. December 8, 2017. www.cdpp.gov.au/sites/g/files/net2061/f/20170812AFP-CDPP-Best-Practice-Guideline-on-self-reporting-of-foreign-bribery.pdf.

AGD. 2016. Improving Enforcement Options for Serious Corporate Crime: Consideration of a Deferred Prosecution Agreements Scheme in Australia: Public Consultation Paper. March 2016. www.ag.gov.au/Consultations/Pages/Deferred-prosecution-agreements-public-consultation.aspx.

AGD. 2017. Proposed Amendments to the Foreign Bribery Offence in the Criminal Code Act 1995: Public Consultation Paper. April 2017. www.ag.gov.au/Consultations/Pages/Proposed-amendments-to-the-foreign-bribery-offence-in-the-criminal-code-act-1995.aspx.

AGD. 2018a. Submission to the Legal and Constitutional Affairs Legislation Committee, Crimes Legislation Amendment (Combatting Corporate Crime) Bill 2017, Sub. No. 7. www.aph.gov.au/Parliamentary_Business/C ommittees/Senate/Legal_and_Constitutional_Affairs/CombattingCrime/ Submissions.

AGD. 2018b. Response Senate Legal and Constitutional Affairs Legislation Committee, Crimes Legislation Amendment (Combatting Corporate Crime) Bill 2017: Questions on Notice, March 7, 2018. www.aph.gov.au/ Parliamentary_Business/Committees/Senate/Legal_and_Constitutional_A ffairs/CombattingCrime/Additional_Documents.

ALRC. 2019. Review into Australia's Corporate Criminal Responsibility Regime. April 10, 2019. www.alrc.gov.au/inquiries/review-australia%E2% 80%99s-corporate-criminal-responsibility-regime.

Andreas, Peter, and Ethan Nadelmann. 2008. *Policing the Globe: Criminalization and Crime Control in International Relations.* Oxford: Oxford University Press.

Appleby, Gabrielle, Alexander Reilly, and Laura Grenfell. 2014. *Australian Public Law,* 2nd ed. Melbourne: Oxford University Press.

Ashworth, Andrew. 2017. "Positive Duties, Regulation and the Criminal Sanction." *Law Quarterly Review* 133: 606–630.

Ashworth, Andrew. 2018. "A New Generation of Omissions Offences?" *The Criminal Law Review* 5: 354–364.

Ashworth, Andrew, and Lucia Zedner. 2008. "Defending the Criminal Law: Reflections on the Changing Character of Crime, Procedure, and Sanctions." *Criminal Law and Philosophy* 2: 21–51.

Ashworth, Andrew, and Lucia Zedner. 2014. *Preventive Justice.* Oxford: Oxford University Press.

Ayes, Ian, and John Braithwaite. 1992. *Responsive Regulation: Transcending the Deregulation Debate.* New York: Oxford University Press.

Barker, Cat. 2019. Australia's Implementation of the OECD Anti-Bribery Convention. August 28, 2019. *Parliamentary Library Research Paper.* https:// parlinfo.aph.gov.au/parlInfo/search/display/display.w3p;query=Id%3A%22li brary%2Fprspub%2F6300407%22.

Barker, Cat, and Monica Biddington. 2017–2018. Crimes Legislation Amendment (Combatting Corporate Crime) Bill 2017, *Parliamentary Library Bills Digests* 105.

Boister, Neil. 2002. "Human Rights Protections in the Suppression Conventions." *Human Rights Law Review* 2: 199–227.

Boister, Neil. 2003. "Transnational Criminal Law?" *European Journal of International Law* 14: 953–976.

Boister, Neil. 2014. The Concept and Nature of Transnational Criminal Law. Pp. 11–26 in *Routledge Handbook of Transnational Criminal Law,* edited by Neil Boister and Robert Currie. Abingdon: Routledge.

Boister, Neil. 2015. "Further Reflections on the Concept of Transnational Criminal Law." *Transnational Legal Theory* 6: 9–30.

Boister, Neil. 2018. *An Introduction to Transnational Criminal Law*, 2nd ed. Oxford: Oxford University Press.

Boucht, Johan. 2017. *The Limits of Asset Confiscation: On the Legitimacy of Extended Appropriation of Criminal Proceeds*. Oxford: Hart.

Bronitt, Simon. 2018. Deferred Prosecution Agreements: Negotiating Punishment Before Conviction? Pp. 45–59 in *The Evolving Role of the Public Prosecutor: Challenges and Innovations*, edited by Victoria Colvin and Philip C. Stenning. New York: Routledge.

Bronitt, Simon and Zoe Brereton. Submission to the Attorney General's Department, Proposed Amendments to the Foreign Bribery Offence in the Criminal Code Act 1995 (Cth) Public Consultation Paper. May 10, 2017. www.ag.gov.au/Consultations/Documents/Proposed-amendments-to-the-foreign-bribery-offence-criminal-code-act-1995/Foreign-bribery-submission-Bronitt-Brereton.pdf.

Campbell, Liz. 2018. "Corporate Liability and the Criminalisation of Failure." *Law and Financial Markets Review* 12: 57–70.

Campbell, Liz, 2019. "Trying Corporations: Why Not Prosecute?" *Current Issues in Criminal Justice* 31: 269–291.

Catá Backer, Larry. 2008. "Global Panopticism: States, Corporations, and the Governance Effects of Monitoring Regimes." *Indiana Journal of Global Legal Studies* 15: 101–148.

CDPP. 2018. Annual Report 2017–2018. www.cdpp.gov.au/publications.

Charlesworth, Hilary, Madelaine Chiam, Devika Hovell, and George Williams. 2003. "Deep Anxieties: Australia and the International Legal Order." *Sydney Law Review* 25: 423–465.

Charlesworth, Hilary, Madelaine Chiam, Devika Hovell, and George Williams. 2006. *No Country Is an Island: Australia and International Law*. Sydney: UNSW Press.

Conley Tyler, Melissa, Emily Crawford, and Shirley V. Scott. 2017. Australia's International Personality: Historical, Legal, and Policy Perspectives. Pp. 1–22 in *International Law in Australia*, 3rd ed., edited by Emily Crawford and Donald R. Rothwell. Pyrmont: Thompson Reuters.

Criminal Law Officers Committee of the Standing Committee of the Attorneys-General. 1992. Model Criminal Code: General Principles of Criminal Responsibility (Final Report).

Currie, Robert. 2015. "Neil Boister, An Introduction to Transnational Criminal Law." *Journal of International Criminal Justice* 13: 1166–1169.

Davis, Kevin, Benedict Kingsbury, and Sally Engle Merry. 2015. The Local-Global Life of Indicators: Law, Power, and Resistance. Pp. 1–24 in *The Quiet Power of Indicators: Measuring Governance, Corruption,* and *Rule of Law*, edited by Sally Engle Merry, Kevin E. Davis, and Benedict Kingsbury. Cambridge: Cambridge University Press.

de Búrca, Gráinne, and Joanne Scott. 2006. Introduction: New Governance, Law and Constitutionalism. Pp. 1–12 in *Law and New Governance in the EU and the US*, edited by Gráinne de Búrca and Joanne Scott. Oxford: Hart.

Edelman, Lauren. 2016. *Working Law: Courts, Corporations, and Symbolic Civil Rights*. Chicago: University of Chicago Press.

Freiberg, Arie. 2017. *Regulation in Australia*. Annandale: Federation Press.

Gardiner, Jock. 2018. "Arendt and Corporate Culture: Instilling Thoughtfulness into the Commonwealth Criminal Code." *Australian Journal of Corporate Law* 33: 25–54.

Garland, David. 2001. *The Culture of Control: Crime and Social Order in Contemporary Society*. Oxford: Oxford University Press.

Garrett, Brandon. 2014. *Too Big to Jail: How Prosecutors Compromise with Corporations*. Cambridge: Harvard University Press.

Garrett, Brandon. 2020. "Declining Corporate Prosecutions." *American Criminal Law Review*. https://papers.ssrn.com/abstract=3360456.

Gilbert, Jo-Anne, and Jason Sharman. 2016. "Turning a Blind Eye to Bribery: Explaining Failures to Comply with the International Anti-corruption Regime." *Political Studies* 64: 74–89.

Gless, Sabine. 2015. "Bird's-Eye View and Worm's Eye View: Towards a Defendant-Based Approach in Transnational Criminal Law." *Transnational Legal Theory* 6: 117–140.

Halliday, Terrence C., and Gregory Shaffer. 2015a. Transnational Legal Orders. Pp. 3–72 in *Transnational Legal Orders*, edited by Terrence C. Halliday and Gregory Shaffer. Cambridge: Cambridge University Press.

Halliday, Terrence C., and Gregory Shaffer. 2015b. Researching Transnational Legal Orders. Pp. 475–528 in *Transnational Legal Orders*, edited by Terrence C. Halliday and Gregory Shaffer. Cambridge: Cambridge University Press.

Hayne, The Hon. Kenneth M.A.C. 2018. Q.C. Interim Report: Royal Commission into Misconduct in the Banking, Superannuation and Financial Services Industry, vol. 1. September 21, 2018. https://financialser vices.royalcommission.gov.au/Documents/interim-report/interim-report-volume-1.pdf.

Hayne, The Hon. Kenneth M.A.C. 2019. Q.C. Final Report: Royal Commission into Misconduct in the Banking, Superannuation and Financial Services Industry, vol. 1. February 1, 2019. https://financialservi ces.royalcommission.gov.au/Pages/reports.aspx#final.

House of Lords, Select Committee on the Bribery Act 2010. 2019. Report of Session 2017–2019, The Bribery Act 2010: Post-Legislative Scrutiny. March 14, 2019. www.parliament.uk/bribery-act-2010.

Husisian, Gregory. 2017. "The Future of the Foreign Corrupt Practices Act under the Trump Administration." *International Trade Law and Regulation* 23: 97–108.

International Organization for Standardization (ISO). 2016. *ISO 37001: Anti-Bribery Management Systems – Requirements with Guidance for Use.* www .iso.org/standard/65034.html.

Ivory, Radha. 2014. *Corruption, Asset Recovery and the Protection of Property in Public International Law: The Human Rights of Bad Guys.* Cambridge: Cambridge University Press.

Ivory, Radha. 2018. "Beyond Transnational Criminal Law: Anti-corruption as Global New Governance." *London Review of International Law* 6: 413–422.

Ivory, Radha. Forthcoming. From Content to the Construction of Risk: Due Diligence Debates in International Anti-corruption and Money Laundering Law. In *Due Diligence in International Law*, edited by Anne Peters, Heike Krieger, and Leonhard Kreuzer (manuscript accepted by Oxford University Press and on file with author).

Jessup, Phillip. 1956. *Transnational Law: Storrs Lectures on Jurisprudence*, vol. 2. New Haven: Yale University Press.

Keenan, The Hon. Michael, MP, Minister for Justice. 2014. Media Release: AFP-Hosted Anti-fraud and Anti-corruption Centre. July 31, 2014. http://pandora .nla.gov.au/pan/143276/20141001-1307/www.ministerjustice.gov.au/Mediarel eases/Pages/2014/ThirdQuarter/31July2014-AFPHostedFraudAndAntiCorrup tionCentre.html.

Koehler, Mike. 2018. "Foreign Corrupt Practices Act: Continuity in a Transition Year." *South Carolina Law Review* 70: 143–208.

Kohli, Rahul. 2018. "Foreign Corrupt Practices Act." *American Criminal Law Review* 55: 1269–1331.

Kotiswaran, Prabha, and Nicola Palmer. 2015. "Rethinking the 'International Law of Crime': Provocations from Transnational Legal Studies." *Transnational Legal Theory* 6: 55–88.

Liss, Carolin, and Jason Sharman. 2015. "Global Corporate Crime-Fighters: Private Transnational Responses to Piracy and Money Laundering." *Review of International Political Economy* 22: 693–718.

Lobel, Orly. 2004. "The Renew Deal: The Fall of Regulation and the Rise of Governance in Contemporary Legal Thought." *Minnesota Law Review* 89: 342–470.

Lobel, Orly. 2012. New Governance as Regulatory Governance. Pp. 65–82 in *The Oxford Handbook of Governance*, edited by David Levi-Faur. Oxford: Oxford University Press.

Lord, Nicholas. 2014. *Regulating Corporate Bribery in International Business: Anti-corruption in the UK and Germany.* London: Routledge.

Low, Lucinda. 2014. Preventing and Defending Against Vicarious and Successor Liability under National and International Transnational

Bribery Regimes. Pp. 611–683 in *The OECD Convention on Bribery: A Commentary*, 2nd ed., edited by Mark Pieth, Lucinda Low, and Nicola Bonucci. Cambridge: Cambridge University Press.

Mazerolle, Lorraine, and Janet Ransley. 2006. *Third Party Policing*. Cambridge: Cambridge University Press.

McGrath, Senator the Hon. James. 2017. Second Reading Speech: Crimes Legislation Amendment (Combatting Corporate Crime) Bill 2017. Commonwealth Parliamentary Debates. Senate Official Hansard, December 6, 2017. 15: 9906–9908.

Ministry of Justice. 2011. The Bribery Act 2010: Guidance about Procedures Which Relevant Commercial Organisations Can Put into Place to Prevent Persons Associated with them from Bribing. March 2011. www.gov.uk/government/publications/bribery-act-2010-guidance.

Ministry of Justice. 2019. Government Response to the House of Lords Select Committee on the Bribery Act 2010, May 2019. www.gov.uk/government/publications.

Nadelmann, Ethan A. 1990. "Global Prohibition Regimes: The Evolution of Norms in International Society." *International Organization* 44: 479–526.

National Crime Agency. Undated. International Anti-corruption Coordination Centre. www.nationalcrimeagency.gov.uk/about-us/what-we-do/national-economic-crime-centre/international-anti-corruption-coordination-centre.

Nourse, Victoria, and Gregory Shaffer. 2009. "Varieties of New Legal Realism: Can a New World Order Prompt a New Legal Theory?" *Cornell Law Review* 95: 61–137.

O'Keefe, Roger. 2015. *International Criminal Law*. Oxford: Oxford University Press.

OECD. 2009. Recommendation of the Council for Further Combating Bribery of Foreign Public Officials in International Business Transactions, C(2009)159/REV1/FINAL (November 26, 2009) as amended by C(2010)19 (February 18, 2010).

OECD. 2019. Resolving Foreign Bribery Cases with Non-trial Resolutions Settlements and Non-trial Agreements by Parties to the Anti-Bribery Convention. www.oecd.org/corruption/Resolving-Foreign-Bribery-Cases-with-Non-Trial-Resolutions.htm.

OECD, UNODC, and World Bank Group. 2013. *Anti-corruption Ethics and Compliance Handbook for Business*. www.oecd.org/corruption/anti-corruption-ethics-and-compliance-handbook-for-business.htm.

OECD-WGB. 1999. Australia: Review of the Implementation of the Convention and 1997 Recommendation. www.oecd.org/corruption/countryreportsontheimplementationoftheoecdanti-briberyconvention.htm.

OECD-WGB. 2002. United States: Phase 2 Report on the Application of the Convention on Combating Bribery of Foreign Public Officials in

International Business Transactions and the 1997 Recommendation on Combating Bribery in International Business Transactions. October 2002. www.oecd.org/corruption/countryreportsontheimplementationoftheoec danti-briberyconvention.htm.

OECD-WGB. 2005. United Kingdom: Phase 2 Report on the Application of the Convention on Combating Bribery of Foreign Public Officials in International Business Transactions and the 1997 Recommendation on Combating Bribery in International Business Transactions. March 17, 2005. www.oecd.org/corruption/countryreportsontheimplementationofth eoecdanti-briberyconvention.htm.

OECD-WGB. 2006. Australia: Phase 2 Report on the Application of the Convention on Combating Bribery of Foreign Public Officials in International Business Transactions and the 1997 Recommendation on Combating Bribery in International Business Transactions. January 4, 2006. www.oecd.org/corruption/countryreportsontheimplementationofth eoecdanti-briberyconvention.htm.

OECD-WGB. 2008. United Kingdom: Phase 2bis Report on the Application of the Convention on Combating Bribery of Foreign Public Officials in International Business Transactions and the 1997 Recommendation on Combating Bribery in International Business Transactions. October 16, 2008. www.oecd.org/corruption/countryreportsontheimplementationofth eoecdanti-briberyconvention.htm.

OECD-WGB. 2009. Australia: Phase 2 Follow-Up Report on the Implementation of the Phase 2 Recommendations, Application of the Convention on Combating Bribery of Foreign Public Officials in International Business Transactions and the 1997 Recommendation on Combating Bribery in International Business Transactions. August 29, 2009. www.oecd.org/corruption/countryreportsontheimplementationoftheoecdanti-briberyconvention.htm.

OECD-WGB. 2010a. Phase 3 Report on Implementing the OECD Anti-Bribery Convention in the United States. October 2010. www.oecd.org/co rruption/countryreportsontheimplementationoftheoecdanti-briberyconven tion.htm.

OECD-WGB. 2010b. United Kingdom: Phase 1ter Report on the Application of the Convention on Combating Bribery of Foreign Public Officials in International Business Transactions and 2009 Recommendation on Combating Bribery in International Business Transactions. December 16, 2010. www.oecd.org/corruption/countryreportsontheimplementationofth eoecdanti-briberyconvention.htm.

OECD-WGB. 2011. United Kingdom: Phase 2bis Follow-Up Report on the Implementation of the Phase 2bis Recommendations. May 23, 2011. www .oecd.org/corruption/countryreportsontheimplementationoftheoecdanti-br iberyconvention.htm.

OECD-WGB. 2012. Phase 3 Report on Implementing the OECD Anti-Bribery Convention in Australia. October 12, 2012. www.oecd.org/cor ruption/countryreportsontheimplementationoftheoecdanti-briberycon vention.htm.

OECD-WGB. 2015. Australia: Phase 3 Follow-Up to the Phase 3 Report and Recommendations. April 3, 2015. www.oecd.org/corruption/countryreport sontheimplementationoftheoecdanti-briberyconvention.htm.

OECD-WGB. 2017a. Phase 4 Report: United Kingdom. March 16, 2017. www .oecd.org/corruption/countryreportsontheimplementationoftheoecdanti-bri beryconvention.htm.

OECD-WGB. 2017b. Phase 4 Report: Australia. December 15, 2017. www .oecd.org/corruption/countryreportsontheimplementationoftheoecdanti-br iberyconvention.htm.

OECD-WGB. 2019. Implementing the OECD Anti-Bribery Convention: Phase 4 Two-Year Follow-Up Report: United Kingdom. March 2019. www .oecd.org/corruption/countryreportsontheimplementationoftheoecdanti-br iberyconvention.htm.

Ogg, James Thomas. 2015. *Preventive Justice and the Power of Policy Transfer.* Basingstoke: Palgrave Macmillan.

Parliamentary Library (Parliament of Australia, Department of Parliamentary Services). 2019. *Briefing Book: Key Issues for the 46th Parliament.* Commonwealth of Australia. www.aph.gov.au/About_Parliament/Parliam entary_Departments/Parliamentary_Library/pubs/BriefingBook46p.

Pieth, Mark. 2014. Article 2: The Responsibility of Legal Persons. Pp. 212–251 in *The OECD Convention on Bribery: A Commentary,* 2nd ed., edited by Mark Pieth, Lucinda Low, and Nicola Bonucci. Cambridge: Cambridge University Press.

Pieth, Mark, and Radha Ivory. 2011. Emergence and Convergence: Corporate Criminal Liability Principles in Overview. Pp. 3–60 in *Corporate Criminal Liability: Emergence, Convergence, and Risk,* edited by Mark Pieth and Radha Ivory. Dordrecht: Springer.

Porter, The Hon. Christian, MP, Attorney General. 2018a. Letter to Senator Helen Polley, Chair, Senate Scrutiny of Bills Committee, No. MS18-000369. March 6, 2018. www.aph.gov.au/Parliamentary_Business/Commit tees/Senate/Scrutiny_of_Bills/Scrutiny_Digest/2018.

Porter, The Hon. Christian, MP, Attorney General. 2018b. Media Release: Consultation on New Measures to Combat Corporate Crime. June 8, 2018. www.attorneygeneral.gov.au/Media/Pages/Consultation-on-new-measure-t o-combat-corporate-crime-8-june-2018.aspx.

Porter, The Hon. Christian, MP, Attorney General. 2019. Media Release: Review into Australia's Corporate Criminal Responsibility Regime. April 10, 2019. www.attorneygeneral.gov.au/Media/Pages/Review-into-Australia%E2% 80%99s-corporate-criminal-responsibility-regime-10-april-19.aspx.

Ralph, Jason. 2017. "The Responsibility to Protect and the Rise of China: Lessons from Australia's Role as a 'Pragmatic' Norm Entrepreneur." *International Relations of the Asia-Pacific* 17: 35–65.

Senate. 1994. Explanatory Memorandum, Criminal Code Bill 1994 (Cth).

Senate. 2017. Explanatory Memorandum, Crimes Legislation Amendment (Combatting Corporate Crime) Bill 2017 (Cth).

Senate. 2018a. Economic References Committee, Foreign Bribery (Report), March 2018. www.aph.gov.au/Parliamentary_Business/Committees/Senate/Economics/Foreignbribery45th/Report.

Senate. 2018b. Senate Legal and Constitutional Affairs Legislation Committee, Crimes Legislation Amendment (Combatting Corporate Crime) Bill 2017 (Report), April 2018. www.aph.gov.au/Parliamentary_Business/Committees/Senate/Legal_and_Constitutional_Affairs/CombattingCrime.

Senate. 2018c. Addendum to the Explanatory Memorandum, Crimes Legislation Amendment (Combatting Corporate Crime) Bill 2017 (Cth).

Serious Fraud Office. 2014. Deferred Prosecution Agreements Code of Practice: Crime and Courts Act 2013, February 14, 2014. www.sfo.gov.uk/?wpdmdl=1447.

Shaffer, Gregory. 2009. "How Business Shapes Law: A Socio-Legal Framework." *Connecticut Law Review* 42: 147–183.

Shaffer, Gregory. 2013a. Transnational Legal Ordering and State Change. Pp. 1–22 in *Transnational Legal Ordering and State Change*, edited by Gregory Shaffer. Cambridge: Cambridge University Press.

Shaffer, Gregory. 2013b. Dimensions and Determinants of State Change. Pp. 23–49 in *Transnational Legal Ordering and State Change*, edited by Gregory Shaffer. Cambridge: Cambridge University Press.

Shaffer, Gregory. 2015. "The New Legal Realist Approach to International Law." *Leiden Journal of International Law* 28: 189–210.

Transparency International Australia. 2018. Media Release: Corruption Perceptions Index (CPI) 2017 Shows Australia Falls again in Corruption Perceptions Index Scores. http://transparency.org.au/corruption-perceptions-index-cpi-2017-shows-australia-falls-corruption-perceptions-index-scores.

UNCAC-COSP. 2012. Implementation Review Group, Review of Implementation of the United Nations Convention against Corruption, Executive Summary: Australia. UN Doc. No. CAC/COSP/IRG/I/2/1. www.unodc.org/unodc/treaties/CAC/country-profile.

UNCAC-COSP. 2013. Implementation Review Group, Country Review Report of the United Kingdom. www.unodc.org/unodc/treaties/CAC/country-profile.

UNCAC-COSP. 2019. Implementation Review Group, Review of Implementation of the United Nations Convention against Corruption, Executive Summary: United Kingdom of Great Britain and Northern

Ireland. UN Doc. No. CAC/COSP/IRG/II/2/1/Add.4. www.unodc.org/un
odc/treaties/CAC/country-profile.

US Department of Justice. 2018. Justice Manual. November 2018. www
.justice.gov/jm/jm-9-28000-principles-federal-prosecution-business
-organizations.

US Department of Justice. 2019. *Evaluation of Corporate Compliance Programs.*
www.justice.gov/criminal-fraud/page/file/937501/download.

US Department of Justice and US Securities and Exchange Commission.
2012. A Resource Guide to the U.S. Foreign Corrupt Practices Act.
November 14, 2012. www.justice.gov/sites/default/files/criminal-fraud/lega
cy/2015/01/16/guide.pdf.

US Sentencing Commission. 2018. Guidelines Manual, §3E1.1. November 1,
2018. www.ussc.gov/sites/default/files/pdf/guidelines-manual/2018/GLMFu
ll.pdf.

van Sliedregt, Elies. 2016. "International Criminal Law: Over-Studied and
Underachieving?" *Leiden Journal of International Law* 29: 1–12.

Vuona, Bridget. 2019. "Foreign Corrupt Practices Act." *American Criminal
Law Review* 56: 979–1032.

Weiner, Blake, Kimberly Austin, John Lapin, and Mary McCullough. 2018.
"Corporate Criminal Liability." *American Criminal Law Review* 55: 961–999.

Wells, Celia. 2001. *Corporations and Criminal Responsibility*, 2nd ed. Oxford:
Oxford University Press.

Wells, Celia. 2019. Economic Crime in the UK: Corporate and Individual
Liability. Pp. 253–276 in *White Collar Crime: A Comparative Perspective*,
edited by Katalin Ligeti and Stanislaw Tosza. Oxford: Hart.

World Bank. 2016. De-risking in the Financial Sector. October 6, 2016. www
.worldbank.org/en/topic/financialsector/brief/de-risking-in-the-financial
-sector.

World Bank Group. 2013. Anti-corruption Ethics and Compliance Handbook
for Business. www.oecd.org/corruption/anti-corruption-ethics-and-
compliance-handbook-for-business.htm.

Wyld, Robert. 2019. Australia. Pp. 11–59 in *From Baksheesh to Bribery:
Understanding the Global Fight against Corruption and Graft*, edited by
T. Markus Funk and Andrew S. Boutros. Oxford: Oxford University Press.

CHAPTER FOUR

TRANSNATIONAL CRIMINAL LAW IN A GLOBALIZED WORLD

The Case of Trafficking

Prabha Kotiswaran

4.1 INTRODUCTION

Not a day goes by without a sensationalist report on the travails of modern slaves, be it the saga of Indian teenagers trafficked into sex work as depicted in the Hollywood movie *Love Sonia* (2018); or workers trafficked into the UK's nail bar and car wash shops (Lawrence 2018); or the 2018 Global Slavery Index released by the Walk Free Foundation, founded by mining magnate Andrew Forrest, which estimates that there are 40.3 million modern slaves around the world (Walk Free Foundation 2018: 21). Antislavery groups remind us that modern slavery afflicts almost everything that we consume on a day-to-day basis. This includes basic commodities like tea, sugar (Richardson 2016), coffee (Anti-Slavery International 2016), prawns (Hodal, Kelly, and Lawrence 2014), chicken, eggs, onions, mushrooms (LeBaron 2016: 33), "slave chocolate" from Cote D'Ivoire, and cotton from Uzbekistan (Anti-Slavery International 2016). Exploitation is also rife in wartime captivity in Nigeria, bonded labor in Pakistan, fishing boats in Thailand (Quirk 2016: 18), households employing overseas migrant domestic workers (Sloan 2015), Qatari construction sites with Nepali workers, the brick kiln industry in India, Brazilian garment factories employing Bolivian workers (Lerche 2016: 76), in Unilever's supply chain in Vietnam, and in Kenyan flower and green bean cultivation (Wilshaw 2016: 78).

Drafters of the 2000 UN Protocol to Prevent, Suppress and Punish Trafficking in Persons, Especially Women and Children (Trafficking

Protocol; UN 2000a), which supplements the UN Convention against Transnational Organised Crime 2000 (UN Convention; UN 2000b), could have hardly imagined that the Protocol would one day cover labor exploitation in global commodity chains. This chapter explains how this came to be. Despite being one of the most ratified UN instruments (UNODC 2016: 48), the transnational legal order (TLO) generated by the Trafficking Protocol is poorly institutionalized. This chapter elaborates on the reasons for this by mapping the various phases of its development, the discursive and ideological issues that are at its core, the factors for its institutionalization relating to concordance and issue alignment, and the varied regulatory fields that it has implicated. Paradoxically, however, the criminal justice approach to trafficking remains hegemonic. This hegemony however cannot be simply attributed to the unidirectional influence and dissemination of transnational (and Western) ideas about how to address the problem. Rather, using the example of the India, I show how national legal contexts are crucial to when and how the logic of criminalization is pursued. The recursive nature of the trafficking TLO is therefore significant and helps explain the normative basis for the authority of transnational law.

4.2   TRAFFICKING: GLOBALIZATION'S PROBLEM CHILD

When drafters of the Trafficking Protocol sat down to draft it in the late 1990s, they envisaged trafficking as an offense involving the cross-border movement of persons against their will for exploitative purposes. Although international law had historically targeted the "traffic" in women and children across borders, particularly for prostitution, in the 1990s, this traditional concern converged with several developed states' interests in stemming illegal international labor migration to create a criminal law regime against "trafficking." Consequently, under the Trafficking Protocol and the Protocol on Migrant Smuggling (UN 2000c), which supplemented the UN Convention, participating states promised to criminally sanction anyone assisting another to migrate illegally (migrant smuggling) as well as recruiting, harboring, or transporting a person through means of coercion, force, and deception for purposes of exploitation (trafficking). Under the Trafficking Protocol, the trafficked person cannot be criminally punished in the receiving country for being trafficked and may be able to obtain a visa to stay there, but is most likely to be repatriated. Negotiated within two years "at lightning speed on the UN clock" (Lloyd and Simmons 2015: 423), the Trafficking Protocol was adopted in 2000, came into force in 2003, and has been exceptionally well ratified – by 175 countries to date.

Although presented and often discussed as a problem of massive proportions requiring urgent attention, the prevalence of trafficking is notoriously difficult to verify (UNODC 2016: 47). Estimates vary wildly from 1.3 million people (Danailova-Trainor and Laczko 2010: 57) to 45.8 million as estimated by the Walk Free Foundation (Kelly 2016). Indeed, Savona and Stefanizzi observe that available information on trafficking is "fragmentary, heterogeneous, difficult to acquire, uncorrelated and often out-dated" (Savona and Stefanizzi 2007). Underlying these highly varied estimates of the problem of trafficking, however, is the acknowledgment, even by the United Nations Office on Drugs and Crime (UNODC), the only UN entity focusing on the criminal justice aspects of trafficking, that the data on the extent of the problem is woefully inadequate (UNODC 2014a: 16). The UNODC attributes this inadequacy to the lack of international standardization of definitions along the lines of the Trafficking Protocol, the failure of even countries with similar legal systems to count the same things, and countries' failures to include domestic crimes amounting to trafficking in their data.

This wide variance can also be attributed to the fact that trafficking as an issue has been over-determined by many competing discursive frames and ideologies promoted by the epistemic communities that have developed around them for the past two decades. These discursive frames include sex work, migration, smuggling, human rights, security, crime control, criminal justice, forced labor, slavery, border control, and increasingly, extreme exploitation – especially forced labor and modern slavery (Lee 2007: 2; Choi-Fitzpatrick 2016: 6). As I will demonstrate, these discursive frames are mirrored in the paradigmatic approaches to addressing the problem of trafficking and the choice of law used to counter it, highlighting the significance of the frame (Clifford 2015) through which the problem is sought to be understood.

4.3   A TRANSNATIONAL LAW APPROACH TO TRAFFICKING

In adopting a transnational legal approach, this chapter "places processes of local, national, international, and transnational public and private lawmaking and practice in dynamic tension within a single analytic frame" (Halliday and Shaffer 2015: 3). Transnational law is recursive so that "the production and implementation of transnational legal norms among international, transnational, national, and local lawmakers and law practitioners dynamically and recursively affect each other" (Halliday and Shaffer 2015: 38). Further, a "transnational legal order" or TLO is a "collection of formalized legal norms and associated organizations and actors that authoritatively order the understanding and practice of law across national jurisdictions" (Halliday and Shaffer 2015: 11).[1] The legal form includes both norms enacted by the state through formal law, but also those developed by networks, that are directed toward enactment or recognition and enforcement within nation-states (Halliday and Shaffer 2015: 12). Thus a TLO encompasses both hard law as well as soft law norms such as codes of conduct and diagnostic and prescriptive indicators.

TLOs are dynamic and in flux such that they "can rise or fall in rapid bursts or in long drawn-out, incremental cycles. They may entail trial and error or big bang-like events" (Halliday and Shaffer 2015: 32). Further, TLOs may become institutionalized over time with a convergence of legal norms and practices so as to guide actors over what norms apply to given situations (Halliday and Shaffer 2015: 42). This can reflect con-cordance (or alternatively discordance) at varied levels – the transna-tional, national and local. Institutionalization is also reflected in the alignment of a given TLO with the issue at hand. One could thus imagine competing TLOs, which may regulate the very same issue to varying extents in which case, it becomes possible to delineate these interactions in terms of (1) correspondence, (2) partition (especially where the legal scope and geographical scope do not converge), (3) misalignment/non-alignment, and finally (4) antagonistic competition between them (Halliday and Shaffer 2015).

Like transnational legal studies, the field of transnational criminal law is relatively new. In fact, Neil Boister coined the term "transna-tional criminal law" in 2001 to study a distinct area of international criminal law relating to "the indirect suppression by international law through domestic penal law of criminal activities that have actual or potential trans-border effects" (Boister 2003: 955). The core compo-nent of transnational criminal law is often a crime suppression treaty,

---

[1] The term "order" connotes some regularity of behavioral orientation, communication, and action, while a "legal" order "involves international or transnational legal organizations or networks, [which] directly or indirectly engage multiple national and local legal institutions, and assumes a recognizable legal form" (Halliday and Shaffer 2015: 11).

whether agreed bilaterally, regionally, or through a large UN-backed multilateral convention directed at suppressing conduct that is subsequently criminalized through domestic law. This is the "horizontal" component of transnational criminal law and "[t]he vertical component in transnational criminal law involves domestic criminalization of the specified conduct of individuals and the enactment of allied procedures and provisions for cooperation in regard to those individuals by the states parties to the particular suppression convention" (Boister 2015: 19). Transnational criminal law is therefore conformal in nature, which explains its patterns of settlement and institutionalization. This chapter brings into conversation insights from transnational legal studies and transnational criminal law through this study of the trafficking TLO.[2]

4.4 ASSESSING THE TRAFFICKING TLO

Human trafficking is one of the most hotly debated areas of transnational criminal law. As mentioned earlier, few international legal instruments have been ratified as widely as the Trafficking Protocol. According to the UNODC, since the Protocol's entry into force, the number of countries criminalizing trafficking in persons on the basis of the Protocol definition saw a near fivefold increase, from 33 in the year 2003 to 158 in August 2016 (out of the 179 countries considered; UNODC 2016: 48). Certainly, the number of states that criminalized sex and labor trafficking in domestic laws increased from 10 percent in 2000 to about 73 percent in 2013 (Lloyd and Simmons 2015: 436) to 90 percent in 2014 (UNODC 2014a). Some scholars observe that anti-trafficking law has percolated to the local level and that its reach is deep and extensive (Lloyd and Simmons 2015: 414, 416). In addition, trafficking encompasses various forms of exploitation, including practices similar to slavery and forced labor, thereby implicating other international treaties (e.g., on forced labor and slavery), non-treaties, and soft law codes of conduct (Lloyd and Simmons 2015: 414) at the international and national levels. There are also varied forms of norm-setting on trafficking, including, indicators, labor codes, corporate social responsibility initiatives, "ethical audits," rankings, and naming and shaming techniques, such as the publication of a "dirty list" of

---

[2] See the special issue (Vol. 6, Iss. 1) of *Transnational Legal Theory on Transnational Criminal Law* (2015).

companies using forced labor. Viewed through the legal pluralist, multi-scalar lens of transnational legal studies, the stunning legal architecture spawned by the Trafficking Protocol constitutes a TLO.[3]

Despite the existence of the trafficking TLO for the past twenty years, the low rates of conviction for trafficking-related offenses indicate its poor institutionalization. Chapter 1 of the 2016 UNODC Global Report on Trafficking is revealing in this respect. While one subheading speaks to the extensive incorporation of the Protocol into national law and is labeled "The United Nations Trafficking in Persons Protocol: A Universal Legal Standard," the second (which speaks to its enforcement) is labeled "Investigations, Prosecutions and Convictions for Trafficking in Persons: Stagnation at a Low Level." Despite the spectacular figures of modern slaves already mentioned, only 44,758 trafficked persons around the world have been identified (Chuang 2017; Plant 2017), resulting in 5,776 convictions (Chuang 2014: 642). According to the UNODC, 6,800 persons were convicted for trafficking between 2012 and 2014 (UNODC 2016: 34). Conviction rates have remained "stubbornly low" since 2003 (Chuang 2014: 642); 41 percent of countries have not had any convictions or have recorded less than ten convictions between 2010 and 2012 (Kangaspunta 2015: 86). This held true for the period between 2012 and 2014 (UNODC 2016: 51). Although the rate of conviction is positively related to the length of time that an anti-trafficking law has been on the books, the UNODC notes that "the criminal justice system response, however, appears to be stagnating at a low level. For most countries, the number of processed cases is limited, regardless of stage (investigation, prosecution or conviction)" (UNODC 2016: 50–52). Not surprisingly, anti-trafficking offenses have proved ineffective in comparison to other serious offenses such as homicide or rape for which conviction rates are higher (Kangaspunta 2015: 88).

Arguably there is a gap between the "law in the books" and "law in action," as is typical when it comes to the enforcement of criminal laws. The police force is a large bureaucracy with limited resources and its own priorities, so that while criminalizing a certain act like trafficking has great symbolic value, the police may not prioritize the enforcement of the anti-trafficking law. Even if they did prioritize anti-trafficking laws, there is wide variance in charging and prosecutorial practices. Especially given that trafficking touches on various other practices that

---

[3] See the later discussion on a trafficking mega-TLO.

are outlawed in many parts of the world, such as slavery and forced labor, prosecutors may not limit themselves to offenses framed in terms of trafficking as defined in the Trafficking Protocol, although only prosecutions for such offenses may be counted for purposes of trafficking statistics. Further, although the Trafficking Protocol visualizes trafficking as involving organized crime, in many parts of the world, traffickers may in fact be small-time offenders who are mobile.

Further, the poor enforcement of the Trafficking TLO can be attributed to the indeterminacy of the concept of trafficking, the malleability of its definition in Article 3 of the Trafficking Protocol, the lack of alignment and concordance within the TLO, deep ideological differences on how to address trafficking, and the varied frames through which to understand the problem of trafficking. These factors have resulted in the poor settlement of legal norms on trafficking even at the international level. It is no different at the national and local levels. Concordance across the international, national, and local levels is more symbolic than substantive as the exact scope of the offense of trafficking continues to be in doubt. Alternate modes of governance like indicators moreover replicate the conceptual indeterminacy and operational inconsistencies of state anti-trafficking laws.

4.5 INDETERMINACY AND CONCEPTUAL MALLEABILITY OF THE TRAFFICKING TLO

Article 3 of the Trafficking Protocol defines trafficking as follows:

> Art. 3. (a): "Trafficking in persons" shall mean the recruitment, transportation, transfer, harbouring or receipt of persons, by means of the threat or use of force or other forms of coercion, of abduction, of fraud, of deception, of the abuse of power or of a position of vulnerability or of the giving or receiving of payments or benefits to achieve the consent of a person having control over another person, for the purpose of exploitation. Exploitation shall include, at a minimum, the exploitation of the prostitution of others or other forms of sexual exploitation, forced labor or services, slavery or practices similar to slavery, servitude or the removal of organs; (b): The consent of a victim of trafficking in persons to the intended exploitation set forth in subparagraph (a) of this article shall be irrelevant where any of the means set forth in subparagraph (a) have been used.

> (UN 2000a: 61)

We can disaggregate the definition as the mode of action required for trafficking (recruitment, transportation, transfer, etc.), the means by which it is obtained (threat or use of force or other forms of coercion, etc.), and the purpose for which it is obtained (namely exploitation). In the case of people aged eighteen and over, all three elements must be proved for a case of trafficking (Gallagher 2001: 987; Dottridge 2007: 4). The Trafficking Protocol offers an expansive understanding of both the means of trafficking as well as the purpose for which one is trafficked, namely, exploitation. The concepts of coercion and exploitation are central to the Trafficking Protocol. Yet the Trafficking Protocol does not define these and related terms and their meaning is far from definitive, even when available in international law.

Each of the two central legal concepts in the law of trafficking – namely, the means and purpose – both span a continuum of possibilities. The means of coercion can range from legally recognizable and fairly narrowly construed notions of coercion, deception, fraud, and abduction to the capacious, outlier concept of the abuse of a position of vulnerability. Similarly, while Article 3 points to specific labor conditions that constitute exploitation and are recognized and understood under international law, this list of labor conditions is not exhaustive and could well include a range of working conditions that are best described as precarious, exploitative, normatively reprehensible, and "contradictory to human dignity" (Skrivankova 2010: 16), as described in court rulings in some European countries.

A narrow construction of the offense of trafficking might entail coercive means of entry, including violence, deception, or fraud resulting in a slavery-like situation (e.g., young woman recruited for a nanny job but duped into forced sex work). In contrast, a broader construction of the offense of trafficking may penalize the recruitment of a victim by abuse of a position of vulnerability resulting in precarious work with less than minimum-wage pay (e.g., undocumented migrant workers working in a Dutch restaurant for less than the Dutch minimum wage; UNODC 2012b: 38–39). This malleability of the definition of trafficking means that states can tailor the offense according to their needs and political, ethical, and normative preferences (Allain 2014).[4] Moreover, although the offense of trafficking (at least in adults) requires both the means and exploitative purpose to be proved, states often dispense with

---

[4] Allain speaks of the wide-ranging interpretation of exploitation in domestic laws that cover begging, illegal adoption, servile or forced marriage, pornography, sex tourism, surrogacy, and removal of cells, blood, organs, body parts, or tissues (Allain 2014: 125, 126).

the one or the other (UNODC 2012b: 5, 48–55), and their domestic legal mediations of the coercion-exploitation balance vary quite dramatically. Interestingly, even soft law norms such as the ILO's Operational Indicators of Trafficking in Human Beings (ILO 2009b) variously interpret Article 3 (Kotiswaran 2014: 371–372). This is further complicated when the means of entry and/or the sector in which trafficked labor is carried out is legal. Where either is legal, enforcement personnel presume the lack of coercion, exploitation, and, ultimately, trafficking.

Based on this analysis, it appears that states prosecute trafficking offenses involving extreme forms of coercion and exploitation while ignoring categories of trafficking involving intermediate levels of coercion and exploitation. Thus some states have focused unduly on targeting sex work through anti-trafficking law. Given its highly stigmatized nature, sex work ticks the boxes of both coercion and exploitation per se, the reasoning being that who but a coerced person would want to do sex work, and how can sex work be anything other than exploitative? Moreover, sex work itself is likely to be illegal in many countries, making travel for sex work difficult, with countries specifically inquiring if the migrant has ever been prosecuted for sex work. But apart from sex work, which forms of labor exploitation warrant the label of trafficking is often unclear. According to the ILO, discussions among jurists and lawmakers on the definitional aspects of trafficking continue without clear resolution (ILO 2013: 17). A survey of the laws relating to trafficking in twelve jurisdictions found a widespread lack of clarity on the definition of trafficking (UNODC 2012b: 5). The UNODC further admits that this lack of clarity over the parameters of trafficking hinders detection of trafficked victims and overall enforcement efforts (UNODC 2012a: 89).

4.6 LACK OF ALIGNMENT WITHIN THE TRAFFICKING TLO

Another factor for the weak institutionalization of the trafficking TLO is its lack of alignment with TLOs in related areas such as sex work, slavery, and forced labor. Recall that exploitation in the Article 3 definition of trafficking is an umbrella term for these varied forms of exploitation. Starting in the 1900s, international law developed regarding several forms of exploitation, such as the exploitation of the prostitution of others, slavery, practices similar to slavery, servitude, and forced labor, which resulted in divisions of labor among UN agencies (Dottridge 2017). Thus there exists a long *duree* of preexisting TLOs on slavery and forced labor, which, while coexisting prior to the passage of the Trafficking Protocol, are now brought together in definitional terms under Article 3 without a corresponding align-ment among TLOs, leading to misalignment if not outright competi-tion between these various TLOs. This is exacerbated by the fact that the trafficking TLO itself has undergone dynamic transformation over the past twenty years.

At least three phases of anti-trafficking law since the negotiation of the Trafficking Protocol can be discerned:

1. a phase between 2000 and 2009, which was the heyday of sex work exceptionalism;
2. a phase between 2009 and 2014, when closer attention to labor trafficking rendered visible the competing frames of "modern slav-ery" and "forced labor"; and
3. from 2014, when legal interventions framed explicitly in terms of slavery and forced labor began to be enacted at the national and international levels.

4.6.1 Trafficking and Sex Work Exceptionalism: 2000–2009

Lloyd and Simmons offer a compelling explanation for the emergence of the trafficking TLO and how trafficking was initially introduced as part of the UN's postwar concern with human rights, but then formed part of the post–Cold War international anti-transnational crime efforts of the late 1990s (Lloyd and Simmons 2015: 434). In other words, consensus around the trafficking TLO depended crucially on the prominence of the transnational crime frame (Lloyd and Simmons 2015: 433).

Trafficking had, however, long been associated with prostitution, and hence it was little surprise that the preexisting sex work TLO (emerging from the 1950 UN Convention for the Suppression of the Traffic in Persons and of the Exploitation of the Prostitution of Others; UN 1950) cast a long shadow over the trafficking TLO. Associated actors, both governmental and nongovernmental, dis-agreed fundamentally and along ideological lines on the normative status of sex work and therefore the remit of the crime of traffick-ing. Anglo-American feminists occupied a range of positions on prostitution, from neo-abolitionism to pro-sex-worker agency, and played a crucial role in the negotiation of the Trafficking Protocol (Chuang 2010). Neo-abolitionists' influence on the Trafficking Protocol negotiations compromised the definitional clarity of trafficking, resulting in vague terms such as the "abuse of power or of a position of vulnerability" (UNODC 2012b: 22). The Protocol also clarified that consent of the victim to exploitation is immaterial where any of the means listed in Article 3 are used. These provisions were meant to cover even "voluntary" sex workers who had consented to sex work where their vulnerability had been abused. Thus, in the initial years of the Trafficking Protocol, trafficking was invariably conflated with sex trafficking and sex work (Dottridge 2007: 4; Chuang 2010: 1655). I term this development *sex work exceptionalism*, by which I mean (a) the characterization by abolitionist groups (who model themselves after eighteenth century abolitionists of slavery, like William Wilberforce) of the sale of sex for money as an egregious violation of human dignity and an exceptionally harmful activity, and (b) the overwhelming association of trafficking with trafficking for sex work and with sex work itself.

The Bush administration in the United States in particular interpreted the anti-trafficking regime as primarily concerned with forced migration for sex work. The then US government, keen to abolish the sex industry, named and shamed countries through the annual Trafficking in Persons (TIP) Report issued under the Trafficking Victims Protection Act 2000. This had ripple effects across the world when countries felt compelled to specifically target prostitution in their anti-trafficking laws as a way of moving up the TIP Report rankings (Chuang 2014: 610). Western states thus used anti-trafficking policy for curbing sex work and for border control, while emerging economies like Brazil, China, and India narrowly construed trafficking as trafficking for sex work to deflect attention away from their vast domestic problem of labor trafficking. A robust sex panic (Weitzer 2006) thus accompanied the first phase of the development of the trafficking TLO. This has been extensively documented by feminists, both in relation to its historical antecedent, the anti-white-slavery campaigns at the turn of the twentieth century (Doezema 2000), and its contemporary use to allay fears about globalization through a yearning for a familiar race and gender order (Andrijasevic 2007: 27), wherein women's migration was sought to be discouraged (Parreñas 2006: 178).

4.6.2 Expanding Trafficking to Include Labor Exploitation: 2009–2014

By 2007, the consensus among scholars and activists alike was that the conceptualization and implementation of the Trafficking Protocol was over-inclusive in targeting coerced and voluntary sex workers and that it was under-inclusive in addressing the labor exploitation of millions of workers. Beginning in 2005, the ILO through its report *A Global Alliance against Forced Labor* (ILO 2005) argued for an expansive understanding of trafficking to include both sexual and labor exploitation. Registering the heightened (and unexpected) visibility of the issue of trafficking, the ILO initiated internal dialogue and reoriented institutional priorities by setting up the Special Program Against Forced Labor. It adopted key strategies of measurement and quantification through periodic reports (estimating that there were 12.3 million forced laborers in 2005 and 20.9 million in 2012), and it leveraged existing political capital within its tripartite configuration. By 2009, with the change in regime in the United States under the Obama administration, the US State Department in its annual TIP Reports began to focus on labor trafficking in place of its previous sole preoccupation with sex trafficking and sex work. Janie Chuang claims that this focus on forced labor and slavery was also a result of attempts at bureaucratic capture by the Trafficking in Persons Office over other departments within the US government, such as the State Department's Bureau of Democracy, Human Rights and Labor (DRL), and the Labor Department's International Labor Affairs Bureau (ILAB), which were concerned with human rights, labor exploitation, and migration reform. The goal was thus to maintain the hegemony of the criminal justice approach to addressing trafficking (Chuang 2014: 611, 620). A combination of the waning of an exclusive emphasis on sex work, the increased visibility of the ILO's interventions on forced labor, and the US State Department's expanding remit to encompass forced labor and slavery heralded a new phase in thinking about the scope of anti-trafficking law.

Critics of the anti-trafficking framework put forward what they called the "labor paradigm of trafficking" (Pope 2010; Shamir 2012). Moreover, where trade unions and other workers' groups had consciously stayed away from the issue of trafficking, they soon came to form networks with conventional anti-trafficking nongovernmental organizations (NGOs; Chuang 2014: 622). The entry of forced labor into activists' vocabularies put on the table the possibility of regulatory plurality through the deployment of labor law mechanisms to address trafficking in addition to the criminal law (see also Skrivankova 2010). Where anti-trafficking laws earlier defined trafficking purely in terms of sex trafficking, they now defined it more broadly to cover labor trafficking as well (UNODC 2016).

4.6.3 Trafficking, Forced Labor, and Modern Slavery as Competing Umbrella Terms: 2014–Present

From around 2012, trafficking became increasingly reframed in terms of both slavery and forced labor. Chuang calls this conflation of trafficking with forced labor and modern slavery, "exploitation creep" (Chuang 2014). A new term coined by sociologist Kevin Bales – namely, "modern slavery" (which has no definition under international law) – was added to the mix. The definition of modern slavery has varied over time (Bales 1999, 2007). The Walk Free Foundation was influenced by Bales and released the Global Slavery Index in 2013 and subsequently in 2014, 2016, and 2018, ranking countries in terms of their "modern slavery" problem. The 2013 Global Slavery Index defined modern slavery to include "slavery, slavery-like practices (such as debt bondage, forced marriage, and sale or exploitation of children), human trafficking and forced labor" (Walk Free Foundation 2013: 2). In 2014 the definition was "Modern slavery involves one person possessing or controlling another person in such a way as to significantly deprive that person of their individual liberty, with the intention of exploiting that person through their use, management, profit, transfer or disposal" (Walk Free Foundation 2014: 10).

By 2016, the Global Slavery Index defined modern slavery to refer to "situations of exploitation that a person cannot refuse or leave because of threats, violence, coercion, abuse of power or deception, with treatment akin to a farm animal" (Walk Free Foundation 2016: 12). The 2017 Global Estimates of Modern Slavery produced by the Walk Free Foundation and the ILO defines modern slavery as an umbrella term to cover forced labor (as defined by the ILO's 1930 Convention) and forced marriage (as situations where a person is forced to marry without consent; ILO et al. 2017: 3). The Global Slavery Index 2018 defines modern slavery as "an umbrella term that focuses attention on the commonalities across concepts such as human trafficking, forced labor, debt bondage, forced or servile marriage, and the sale and exploitation of children." The commonalities refer "to situations of exploitation that a person cannot refuse or leave because of threats, violence, coercion, deception, abuse of power, or deception" (Walk Free Foundation 2018: 7). Each global slavery index has been accompanied by an estimate as to the number of modern slaves in the world: 29.8 million in 2013, 35.8 million in 2014, and 45.8 million in 2016. The 2018 Index refers to numbers produced by the Global Estimates of Modern Slavery (GEMS) – namely of 25 million forced laborers and 15 million men and women in forced marriage.

This expansion of the remit of trafficking found purchase with governments. The UNODC notes that while the term "modern slavery" has an important advocacy impact and has been adopted in some national legislation to cover provisions related to trafficking in persons, the lack of an agreed definition or legal standard at the international level results in inconsistent usage (UNODC 2016: 16). The UK has, for instance, passed the Modern Slavery Act 2015. The law is essentially a criminal law, but includes a supply chain transparency clause that calls on corporations above a certain economic turnover to report on the existence of forced labor in their supply chains. Although the California Transparency in Supply Chains Act existed prior to the passage of the Modern Slavery Act, 2015, several countries and provincial governments, including the Australian state of New South Wales, Australia (with recently passed federal legislation), France, and the Netherlands, have followed suit, often with more stringent requirements for corporate accountability and vigilance that go beyond disclosure statements.

In relation to forced labor, the ILO's efforts culminated in the negotiation in 2014 of a significant Protocol and Recommendation, revising and in effect updating one of the most highly ratified ILO Conventions, Convention No. 29 Against Forced Labor (1930) ("Forced Labor Convention"; ILO 1930). The 2014 Protocol and Recommendation constituted a long overdue attempt to update the Forced Labor Convention, as the 1930 Convention and its 1957 counterpart (ILO 1930, 1957) were drafted and revised in the context of state-imposed forced labor, whereas 90 percent of the forced labor in the world today is exacted by private-sector employers. The 2014 Protocol was also a normative response to the highly carceral approach of the Trafficking Protocol, which prioritized prosecution over its broader mandate to prevent trafficking and protect the rights of those trafficked. Indeed, Andrees and Aikman (2017) highlight the 2014 Protocol's human rights approach and its provisions on victim assistance and compensation, irrespective of immigration status, a non-penalization clause, "a labor-based, integrated approach to combating forced labor" that recognizes the crucial role of the labor administration, employers, and businesses against forced labor as well as national-level policy-making mechanisms that include all relevant stakeholders. The requirement for both ratifying and non-ratifying countries to report under the 2014 Protocol offers a more robust implementation system. The Protocol entered into force in November 2016 and has been ratified by forty-five countries. Thus, notwithstanding the misalignment and competition within the trafficking TLO, it has spurred the development of the forced labor TLO, thereby generating an overlapping zone of governance for those trafficked and in forced labor to benefit from human rights protections.

The definitional relationship between trafficking and forced labor has, however, not been resolved. It is still unclear whether trafficking is a subset of forced labor or if forced labor is a subset of trafficking (ILO 2013a: 16; ILO 2013b: 12–13). Early ILO reports, particularly in 2005, distinguished between trafficked forced labor and non-trafficked forced labor (ILO 2005: 14) based on the assessment that trafficking involved the cross-border movement of persons. However, as the requirement for movement became less certain, a 2009 ILO Report steered clear of its earlier distinction between trafficked and non-trafficked forced labor (ILO 2009a). By 2013, when representatives of employers, workers, and states came together to negotiate the 2014 Protocol, they remained undecided, with one camp insisting that trafficking encompassed all forced labor and another camp claiming that trafficking was merely one form through which forced labor was exacted (ILO 2013a: 57; ILO 2013b: 51). Yet the executive summary to a 2014 report on the profits of forced labor claimed that "all exploitative purposes of trafficking are covered by the ILO's Forced Labour definition with the exception of trafficking for the purpose of the removal of organs" (ILO 2014: 4). It is not surprising then that the ILO has claimed that the forced labor TLO encompasses the trafficking TLO with the UNODC claiming the reverse. Although the UNODC praised the ILO on concluding the 2014 Protocol and the ILO defers to the UNODC's mandate on trafficking and is keen for coherent anti-trafficking policies and strategies rather than on widening the trenches between them, only a veneer of institutional cooperation exists between the UN agencies. As the ILO perseveres to remain relevant and ensure its survival, it has recently joined hands with the Walk Free Foundation to produce the Global Estimates of Modern Slavery (GEMS; ILO et al. 2017).

Without dwelling on definitional conundrums, GEMS defines "modern slavery" as an umbrella term to encompass forced labor, trafficking, slavery, and practices similar to slavery.

Although the shifting of frames through which trafficking is understood at the international level (e.g., from "trafficking" to "forced labor" to "modern slavery") may appear to be a response to preexisting frames, this is not always the case. The shifting of frames seems to be related more to institutional politics than purely a normative response to the deficiencies of any particular frame. Thus in the case of the United States, Chuang documents how the growing conflation of trafficking with forced labor and modern slavery on the part of the US Department of State had to do with expanding its bureaucratic remit. Similarly, the focus on forced labor on the part of the ILO and its recent capitulation to the modern slavery discourse through its joint enumerative exercise in producing the Global Estimates of Modern Slavery has to do with the need for the ILO to source funds and maintain institutional relevance as much as its need to temper the rhetorical flourishes of modern slavery discourse.

The settlement of the definition of trafficking at the international level is thus tenuous. The resultant misalignment and competition between related TLOs on sex work, forced labor, slavery, and now "modern slavery" have been replayed at the domestic and local levels in various national contexts, along with the attendant diagnostic struggles, ideological and institutional contradictions, and mismatch between actors. There is neither high concordance nor discordance between laws at the international, national, and local levels. We instead find what Shaffer and Halliday call "symbolic compliance." Experts, however, disagree on the extent of this intermediation. Jean Allain claims that no effective definition of trafficking exists, as the adoption of general principles and definitions are not mandated by the Trafficking Protocol, leaving states in the absence of any direction on core concepts of Article 3 to make legislative choices in creating the offense of trafficking (Allain 2014: 122). Moreover, "trafficking" can have little resonance in domestic contexts with rich histories of activism against forms of extreme exploitation. In Brazil, for instance, trafficking is understood as an imported concept, and the country's own successful anti-slave labor movement is "loath to change their brand" (Grupo Davida 2015: 161).

Anne Gallagher meanwhile argues that the core aspects of Article 3 have made their way into numerous domestic laws. However, both she and Chuang, who participated in the negotiation of the Trafficking Protocol)[5] are critical of the steady doctrinal expansion of the concept of trafficking in international and US law, or "exploitation creep" (Chuang 2014). They attribute these expansionist doctrinal developments to definitional ambiguities in Article 3, which, brokered through a series of compromises at the negotiating table, literally gave states a "blank check" (Chuang 2017) to operationalize the definition of trafficking in domestic law. They argue that clarity, certainty, and coherence in the definition of trafficking are crucial, given its criminal law implications for the rights of the defendant and in order to end impunity and seek justice for the victims of trafficking. However, invoking the criminal law to address the full spectrum of labor exploitation detracts attention away from its extreme forms, including slavery, practices similar to slavery, and forced labor. Gallagher and Chuang therefore call for a realignment of the trafficking TLO around what they view as properly constituting the underlying offense of trafficking – namely, "instances in which individuals are moved into and/or maintained in a situation of egregious exploitation through means that were themselves highly abusive" (Gallagher 2017: 15), involving abusive, clandestine migration. In other words, they argue to retain the conceptual and legal distinctness of trafficking as "an extremely serious crime carrying severe penalties" and call for a return to the originally intended scope of the trafficking TLO, suggesting in the process, a clear partition of the trafficking TLO from associated TLOs relating to slavery and forced labor and consequently, a sensible division of labor between criminal law and labor laws in countering exploitation.

Whether we are persuaded by Allain that no effective definition of trafficking exists or by Gallagher and Chuang that a discrete definition of trafficking exists and should be followed, given this weak institutionalization of the trafficking TLO, one might consider whether this is in fact one trafficking TLO or a trafficking mega-TLO. Shaffer and Halliday use the term "mega-TLO" to refer to the Financial Stability Forum, which in 1999 brought together "fragmented supervisory structures" within the global financial systems relating to banking, securities, and accounting (Halliday and Shaffer 2015: 495). However, the Financial Stability Forum in fact acted as a "coordinating and

---

[5] Anne Gallagher also authored the three Issue Papers commissioned by the UN Office on Drugs and Crime dealing with various aspects of Article 3 of the Trafficking Protocol , namely, consent, exploitation, and abuse of a position of vulnerability (UNODC 2012b, 2014b, 2015).

integrative structure" in relation to sub-transnational financial legal orders, unlike the trafficking TLO, which currently performs no such function. If anything, as I have shown, the various TLOs, some established (e.g., forced labor, sex work, slavery) and others incipient (e.g., modern slavery), align with different subsets of the issue of trafficking giving rise to tensions and resulting in the uncertain institutionalization of the trafficking TLO (Halliday and Shaffer 2015: 521). As Halliday and Shaffer predict, when an issue-area is vast in legal and geographical scope with "extraordinarily variegated actors with enormous economic stakes," this may give rise to multiple-micro TLOs with little prospect of an integrative mega-TLO (Halliday and Shaffer 2015: 523–524).

4.7 IDEOLOGICAL DIFFERENCES IN THE DEVELOPMENT OF ANTI-TRAFFICKING LAW

Apart from conceptual elasticity and the lack of alignment, the trafficking TLO has been from the very start, affected by deep ideological disagreements, especially over sex work. These differences have persisted despite an expansive understanding of the concept of trafficking beyond sex work to include extreme forms of exploitation. These are reflected in the three main approaches to trafficking that shape the very construction of the problem and the appropriate legal response to it. These approaches are the criminal justice approach that views trafficking as a problem of organized crime against which to direct the criminal law; the human rights approach that is keen to ensure the human rights of survivors of trafficking; and the labor approach to trafficking, which views trafficking as a problem of migration to which a coordinated immigration and labor law response is needed.

The criminal law paradigm views trafficking as an exceptional aberration to otherwise normal circuits of commerce and exchange in a globalized world, thus warranting the use of the heavy, corrective hand of the criminal law. This criminal law response to trafficking is said to have arisen from a particular alignment of geopolitical interests of developed countries in the wake of globalization. As Lloyd and Simmons explain, a "broad coalition of states had much to gain by choosing a prosecutorial model over one that makes human rights or victim protection its top priority" (Lloyd and Simmons 2015: 400). Thus the high rate of diffusion of the Trafficking Protocol transnationally could be attributed to the popularity of the "transnational organised crime frame" among states over the "human rights" frame preferred by non-state actors (Lloyd and Simmons: 429). In this, the trafficking TLO is like other regimes of transnational criminal law (e.g., drug trafficking laws), which are emblematic of vast power differentials between countries in the Global North and those in the Global South (Mitchell 1998; Raustiala 1999: 102; Shapiro 2010; Jenner 2011; Lloyd 2011; O'Connor and Rumann 2011; Avelar 2012) and lack political legitimacy at the points of enactment and enforcement (Boister 2003: 957–958).

The human rights approach to trafficking seeks to mitigate the harshness of the criminal law regime by bolstering the human rights of victims of trafficking. As Gallagher notes, the UN Trafficking Principles and Guidelines issued by the UN High Commissioner for Human Rights in 2002 "provided a way forward that has supported the evolution of a cohesive 'international law of human trafficking' which weaves together human rights and transnational criminal law" (Gallagher 2015: 21). Similarly, in 2005, the Council of Europe adopted its own Convention on Action against Trafficking in Human Beings (Allain 2014), which produced a human rights paradigm whereby the criminal law thrust of anti-trafficking law was retained but was softened vis-à-vis the victims of trafficking who were often prosecuted for committing crimes when trafficked.

The labor approach rejects the criminal justice view of trafficking. It understands coercion and exploitation as spanning a continuum of social scenarios so that the difference between the exploitation of workers and trafficking is a matter of degree not of kind (Shamir 2012: 110). Advocates of the labor approach view trafficking funda- mentally as a problem of labor migration and call for addressing struc- tural systems of subordination and exploitation in labor sectors across the world by preventing the criminalization and deportation of workers who report exploitation and eliminating binding arrangements (where a migrant worker must only work for the employer sponsoring his or her visa), reducing recruitment fees, guaranteeing the right to unionize, and extending labor and employment laws to vulnerable workers (Shamir 2012: 76). They point to "general processes that create low pay, long hours, arbitrary employment conditions, as well as silence the voices of labour and labour organisations," ignoring in the process employment relations in export and domestic industries, along with the general absence of labor inspectors and the non-implementation of labor laws (Lerche 2016: 75; Rittich 2017). Corporate anti-trafficking interventions meanwhile focus on exceptional and violent forms of labor trafficking such as sex trafficking and trafficking in the Global South, particularly in informal markets, while perpetuating precarious working arrangements in the formal economy back home. These interventions in Bernstein's words recast "temporary labor, bonded labor, and brokered labor, all key features of capitalist production under conditions of neoliberal globalisation – as progressive, good, and free" (Bernstein 2017), thus providing what Thomas calls a legitimation effect (Halley et al. 2006).

At the very minimum, then, the criminal justice and human rights approaches view trafficking through an individualist, liberal frame. The criminal justice approach is driven by "a powerful mythology of isolated 'bad apples' (i.e., traffickers)," who inflict extreme violence on vulnerable victims for purposes of exploitation. The heavy hand of the state is warranted in order to free the victim of trafficking and punish the trafficker. The labor approach instead assumes a structural view of the problem by attributing it to "root causes" and the structures of patriarchy, capitalism, and racism that legitimize a range of exploitative working conditions. Thus, addressing only the criminal acts of individual traffickers entrenches a "politics of exception" (Quirk and Bunting 2016: 67), and depoliticizes extreme exploitation (O'Connell Davidson 2010) that arises from "the smooth functioning of global capitalism and official policies, rather than amoral individuals and corrupt institutions" (Quirk and O'Connell Davidson 2016: 16). These fundamental ideological differences in conceptualizing and responding to trafficking have further undermined the settlement of legal norms within the trafficking TLO.

4.8   A DEVELOPMENT APPROACH TO TRAFFICKING?

Twenty years after its negotiation, the trafficking TLO has entered a new phase with the adoption by the UN in 2015 of the Sustainable Development Goals (SDGs). SDG 8 seeks to promote sustained, inclusive, and sustainable economic growth; full and productive employment; and decent work for all. Target 8.7 in particular calls on states to "take immediate and effective measures to eradicate forced labour, end modern slavery and human trafficking and secure the prohibition and elimination of the worst forms of child labour, including recruitment and use of child soldiers, and by 2025 end child labour in all its forms."

The global "development goal" to end trafficking is new. However, the developing world has long been the playground of humanitarian interventions in the guise of anti-trafficking initiatives. The indicator culture that has developed around trafficking in the form of the annual Trafficking in Persons Report and the Global Slavery Index (McGrath and Watson 2018) has long encoded states' responses to trafficking in terms of their stage of development. Developing countries thus often perform the worst and developed countries the best, even if the 2018 Global Slavery Index recently acknowledged that developed countries have more modern slaves than previously thought (Walk Free Foundation 2018). The entry of trafficking into the SDG agenda is, however, also an occasion to bring back into focus the structural approach to extreme labor exploitation adopted by certain developing countries.

In this chapter, I briefly consider the experience of India, a country with a long-standing problem of extreme exploitation and the most "modern slaves" (18 million according to the 2016 Global Slavery Index), where a large percentage of trafficking is internal, and which has dealt with the problem in ways that are at variance with the criminal justice model of the Trafficking Protocol. I ask whether this could be labeled "a development approach to trafficking," why it has been eclipsed by the globally hegemonic criminal justice approach, and whether this can be attributed to the influence of the trafficking TLO.

Long before Western governments began to address extreme labor exploitation, including in the context of migration, in the 1970s, India developed labor laws on bonded labor, contract labor, and inter-state migrant labor – all forms of exploitation amounting to "trafficking" (Kotiswaran 2014). These laws pioneered innovative strategies by prioritizing welfare over rescue and rehabilitation, proposing community-based rehabilitation rather than institutionalized rehabilitation, imposing liability on intermediaries with a backstop to the principal employer to ensure decent work conditions and by sparingly using criminal law, which resulted in a more prominent role for the executive than the police. And although there are several similarities between a labor approach and development approach to trafficking, in the latter, the state is not simply an arbiter of relations between labor and capital. The postcolonial state assumes a strong developmental role and is responsible for the welfare of its citizens. Often the developmental state is also the employer extracting forced labor from workers on vast projects such as the building of dams or stadia as the Indian cases on contract and bonded labor of the 1980s bear out. Further, in the 1980s, an activist judiciary conceptualized forced labor broadly (much like the American legal realists) to encompass economic coercion rather than as an exceptional occurrence in the world of work requiring police action. Similarly, judges interpreted exploitation as involving any pay less than the minimum wage (not unlike some EU countries today). This model, directed toward structural reform would on paper, has been a powerful counter to the criminal justice model that has been diffused by the Trafficking Protocol.

Unfortunately, however, these innovative labor laws were chronically under-enforced. The general criminal law (Indian Penal Code, 1860) and India's anti-sex-work criminal law (the Immoral Traffic Prevention Act, 1986 or ITPA) meanwhile criminalized various forms of trafficking and developed on parallel tracks rather than in conversation with the labor law innovations noted previously. Contestations over the normative status of sex work meanwhile continued during the 1980s and 1990s. In the 2000s, when trafficking became a high-profile international issue, India, like many other countries, conflated trafficking with trafficking for sex work and with sex work itself.

Two camps became central to the trafficking debates: sex worker groups on the one hand and neo-abolitionist groups on the other. The latter included radical feminist groups and culturally nationalist and socially conservative NGOs, which sought to protect the "dignity" of Indian women and children. Neo-abolitionist NGOs were heavily invested in raids, rescue, and rehabilitation, and they subscribed to a crime-control paradigm of trafficking. As efforts to amend the ITPA did not materialize, these groups took to public interest litigation (PIL) as a route to achieving institutional reform. As repeat players in such litigation, they collaborated with the police in raids and rescue operations, compensating for the executive's lack of resources. Consequently, a small number of neo-abolitionist groups infiltrated the bureaucracy so that they were appointed to every single expert committee constituted by the courts or the relevant ministry (typically the Ministry for Women and Child Development [MWCD]) to address trafficking. In 2013 when the Indian Parliament passed sweeping rape law reforms, these neo-abolitionist groups lobbied the government for an offense criminalizing trafficking (defined by and large in consonance with Article 3 of the Trafficking Protocol). As if this was not enough, a PIL filed in 2004 by a neo-abolitionist group came up for decision in

2015, and the Supreme Court dismissed the petition on the assurance of the MWCD that it would introduce a comprehensive anti-trafficking legislation. This led to the formulation of the Trafficking of Persons (Prevention, Protection and Rehabilitation) Bill, 2018 (2018 Bill).

The MWCD introduced the 2018 Bill in Parliament in July 2018; it was passed by the lower house but lapsed before introduction before the upper house in 2019. The Bill is a draconian legislation that entrenches a classic raid-rescue-rehabilitation model, alongside a robust criminal law system with stringent penalties, reversals of burden of proof, provisions for forfeiting traffickers' assets, and an extensive surveillance machinery that is meant to prevent trafficking. It proposes the offense of aggravated trafficking for bonded labor, forced labor, bearing a baby through assisted reproductive technologies, marriage, and begging, thus detailing various forms of exploitation not specifically listed in the Trafficking Protocol. Offenses are cognizable and non-bailable. The Bill's focus on recue and rehabilitation is perplexing, as existing homes have historically been ineffective at best (causing women to escape and return to sex work) and have facilitated sexual abuse and even suicide at worst (Deccan Chronicle 2018; *Economic and Political Weekly* 2016; Govindan 2013; Ahmed and Seshu 2012; Magar 2012). Importantly, the Bill does not repeal the ITPA or labor laws on bonded labor, making the relationship between them unclear. The Bill unthinkingly applies techniques developed in the context of sex work, such as raids, rescues, and rehabilitation, to all forms of extreme exploitation and exemplifies neo-abolitionist thinking. Although the Bill now covers sectors of labor exploitation beyond sex work, the letter and spirit of labor law jurisprudence is entirely missing from the Bill.

What accounts for the dissonance between a labor/development approach to trafficking that India pioneered in the 1970s and 1980s and the hegemonic criminal law approach of the trafficking TLO that the 2018 Bill uncritically follows today? One reason is simply the triumph of neo-liberal capitalist ideologies around the world, and the concomitant weakening of trade unions and the radical dismantling of labor laws. Another is the influence of the trafficking TLO as it has proliferated worldwide over the past twenty years. The initial impetus to introduce anti-trafficking laws came from India's international law obligations under the Trafficking Protocol. The TIP reports were also instrumental in triggering law reform. Thus India came close to criminalizing the customers of sex work (and adopting the Swedish model) in 2005, although this failed due to international pressure from public health actors who feared its negative consequences on HIV prevention efforts. As international opinion shifted to construe trafficking broadly to go beyond sex trafficking, so did that of the Government of India. Thus, by 2013, despite attempts to conflate trafficking and sex work, Indian sex workers groups' opposition was robust enough to defeat such a move, resulting in a trafficking offense under Section 370 of the IPC, which reflected a generic Article 3 formulation of trafficking.

Just as in the West, in India too, one found the "strange bedfellows" phenomenon whereby radical feminist groups became aligned with evangelical Christian organizations like the International Justice Mission in pushing for anti-trafficking legislation. Moreover, state and civil society actors routinely interacted (with each other and their respective counterparts internationally) in spheres of transnational modernity (Merry 2016), often deriving legitimation from each other. Thus, in response to a statement from the UN Special Rapporteurs on Trafficking and on Contemporary Forms of Slavery criticizing the 2018 Bill, the Minister for Women and Child Development Smt Maneka Gandhi claimed how she and the founder of a neo-abolitionist group, Kailas Satyarthi shared the draft 2018 Bill at a child labor conference in Argentina in 2017 to considerable praise from other governments. Moreover, to the extent that the trafficking TLO privileges a criminal justice response to trafficking, which increases the executive (surveillance and police) powers of the state, governments are likely to embrace it (Halliday and Shaffer 2015: 519). Thus international developments on trafficking have certainly influenced the development of Indian anti-trafficking law.

However, the soft power exercised by the international community has not always been well received by the Indian government. The government of India long resented the TIP ranking system and refused to fill out questionnaires circulated by the US government (Ramachandran 2010). More recently, India vigorously protested the Global Estimates of Modern Slavery (GEMS) released by the Walk Free Foundation, the International Labour Organization, and the International Organization for Migration (Debroy 2017), and lodged a complaint on its faulty methodologies with the ILO. Similarly, it is rumored that the 2018 Global Slavery Index had no negative comments on India (unlike in 2016, when the headlines screamed about India having the largest number of "modern slaves" in the world) because the Indian government had of late denied visas to researchers from the Walk Free Foundation.

I argue further that the influence of the trafficking TLO is not ultimately determinative. For instance, the introduction of the offense of trafficking (Section 370) in 2013 was triggered by a domestic political opportunity, namely the Delhi rape case and the occasion it afforded neo-abolitionist groups to lobby for a trafficking offense. Before then, trafficking was not a priority issue for the Indian women's movement or the government, which was looking to amend the ITPA to meet its international law obligations under the Trafficking Protocol. Similarly, once Section 370 was passed, there was no need per se to enact a separate statute building it out. And although the London-based Freedom Fund suggested that the 2016 version of the Trafficking Bill (a precursor to the 2018 Bill) was drafted to respond to the 2016 Global Slavery Index, which was damning of India (Grono 2016), in reality, the 2018 Bill resulted from the domestic legal innovation of PIL. A neo-abolitionist NGO launched PIL on trafficking in 2004, little expecting the promise of an anti-trafficking statute a decade later. The political opportunity structures are thus resolutely local. Unlike in the West, trafficking has also failed to capture the popular imagination of the Indian public where, despite its ramifications for millions of desperately poor Indian laborers, trafficking cannot even begin to compete with several other issues jostling for national attention.

The cultural content of the domestic iteration of neo-abolitionism also varies from its Western version. In a social history of the predecessor statute of the ITPA, namely the Suppression of Immoral Traffic Act, 1956 (SITA), legal historian Rohit De elaborates on how women leaders of the Indian nationalist movement, elevated to key positions in the newly independent state, worked tirelessly both from within the government (as architects of a massive social welfare bureaucracy) and from outside (through NGOs) to pass India's anti-sex work law (De 2018). They did not wish to criminalize the sex worker herself, who in their view was a victim of economic circumstance and whose freedom to practice an occupation of choice was protected by the Constitution.[6] Feminists instead prioritized rehabilitation to be operationalized by female police officers and state-run homes staffed by female social workers, over penalization. This form of welfare governmentality forms the basis of the ITPA and continues to be mobilized by socially

---

[6] Constitution of India Art. 19(1)(g), http://lawmin.nic.in/olwing/coi/coi-english/coi-4March2016.pdf.

conservative neo-abolitionist groups who oppose sex work (voluntary sex work included) on the grounds that it offends human dignity. Some of these groups are closely aligned with the ruling Bharatiya Janata Party (BJP) at the federal level, which has increasingly resorted to carceral techniques to address social problems with the aid of surveillance mechanisms. This has in fact fractured relationships between Bachpan Bacho Andolan, a neo-abolitionist group, and Apne Aap, a radical feminist organization, where the former supported the 2018 Bill and the latter protested its passage. There is thus a long tradition of nationalist humanitarianism that helps explain the overwhelming support for the 2018 Bill.

4.9 CONCLUSION

The jury is still out on the value of the trafficking TLO. Some experts like Gallagher argue that it "has done more than any other single legal development of recent times to place the issue of human exploitation firmly on the international political agenda" (Gallagher 2015: 16). Plant similarly claims that the Trafficking Protocol has challenged various international organizations working on different forms of abject labor in Article 3 by introducing the expansive and indeed, elastic concept of exploitation (Plant 2017).

Yet prosecutions for trafficking are disproportionately low in comparison to the resources expended on the issue. Rather, the trafficking TLO is actively misused to disproportionately target sex workers, migrants, migrant brides, and sexual minorities in countries as diverse as Romania, Bulgaria, Mexico, Sweden, Brazil, Singapore, and Myanmar (de Castilho 2015: 179; Grupo Davida 2015: 162; Hackney 2015: 101; Jahnsen and Skilbrei 2015: 158; Wijers 2015: 71). In Southeast Asia, the TLO has contributed to "miscarriages of justice on a significant scale" as countries seek to appease their donors and those in charge of drafting the annual TIP reports (Gallagher 2016: 10). Even as the ILO collaborates with Walk Free to settle the trafficking TLO, GEMS has muddied the waters by focusing on forced marriage, an issue neither amenable to a clear definition nor around which international consensus can be built. Moreover, under the trafficking TLO, victims of trafficking continue to be prosecuted for engaging in illegal activities. Even the benefits of the expanded trafficking TLO are questionable because only the most "egregious" forms of labor trafficking are addressed, leaving the exploitation of migrant workers to be addressed by labor and employment laws (Baer 2015: 171). The informal economy is villainized as a site for trafficking when the formal sector is increasingly predicated upon precarious labor (e.g., Verite 2014). The trafficking TLO has triggered changes in the forced labor TLO. It has also contributed to the passage of supply chain transparency laws. However, the Commonwealth version of supply chain transparency provisions is, for the most part, weak (e.g., Modern Slavery Act 2015) when compared to corporate vigilance laws passed by civil law countries like France.

The incorporation of target 8.7 within the broader SDG agenda on creating decent work meanwhile has mixed implications for the future development of the trafficking TLO. While we may hope for a renewed consideration of systemic approaches to trafficking (including from developing countries, which could close the loop of transnational law making), Western countries that were central to the adoption of the Trafficking Protocol may continue to use SDG 8.7 to name and shame developing countries for their "modern slavery" problem.

Ultimately, the trafficking TLO is only one of many issues to have emerged in the aftermath of two decades of globalization that confounds the regulatory efforts of states. Issues that plague the trafficking TLO – namely, the lack of normative coherence on the question of precisely what trafficking is, the range of regulatory frameworks (whether criminal, labor, immigration, international) that can be brought to bear on it, the ineffectiveness of cross-border criminal law, the rise of indicators as a technique of governance, and the multitude of actors involved in creating legal and social norms through formal state law and "soft law" at the international, regional, domestic, and local levels around trafficking – are hardly unique. Interestingly, the TLO's resilience despite its weak institutionalization, democracy deficit, and high negative externalities can be attributed to what Halliday labels as "plausible folk theory" in the context of the anti-money laundering TLO. He explains that

> a plausible folk theory is built not on robust empirical foundations but on parsimony, face validity, a compactness of rhetorical expression, sufficient ambiguity to accommodate potentially conflicting understandings of what it purports to explain, an affinity with extant beliefs about such things as crime and dirty money, and a failure or resistance to examining too closely the premises and logic of the theory itself.

The rhetorical reach of the trafficking TLO shows no sign of abating, and as it seeps into our popular consciousness, it is this folk theory that continues to justify the use of criminal law to address what is fundamentally a problem of socioeconomic exploitation.

REFERENCES

Allain, J. 2014. "No Effective Trafficking Definition Exists: Domestic Implementation of the Palermo Protocol." *Albany Government Law Review* 7: 111–142.

Andrees, B., and A. Aikman 2017. Raising the Bar: The Adoption of New ILO Standards against Forced Labour. Pp. 359–394 in *Revisiting the Law and Governance of Trafficking, Forced Labour and Modern Slavery*, edited by P. Kotiswaran. Cambridge: Cambridge University Press.

Andrijasevic, R. 2007. "Beautiful Dead Bodies: Gender, Migration and Representation in Anti-Trafficking Campaigns." *Feminist Review* 86: 24–44.

Anti-Slavery International. 2016. International Cotton Campaign against Slavery. https://www.antislavery.org/take-action/campaigns/end-uzbek-cotton-crimes/ (accessed March 17, 2017).

Avelar, F. 2012. "Alternative Drug Policies in the Americas." *Law and Business Review of the Americas* 18: 403–410.

Baer, K. 2015. "The Trafficking Protocol and the Anti-Trafficking Framework: Insufficient to Address Exploitation." *Anti-Trafficking Review* 4: 167–172.

Bales, K. 1999. *Disposable People: New Slavery in the Global Economy*. Berkeley and Los Angeles: University of California Press.

Bales, K. 2007. *Ending Slavery: How We Free Today's Slaves*. Berkeley and Los Angeles: University of California Press.

Bernstein, E. 2017. "Brokered Subjects and Sexual Investability." Pp. 329–358 in *Revisiting the Law and Governance of Trafficking, Forced Labour and Modern Slavery*, edited by P. Kotiswaran. Cambridge: Cambridge University Press.

Boister, N. 2003. "Transnational Criminal Law?" *European Journal of International Law* 14: 953–976.

Boister, N. 2015. "Further Reflections on the Concept of Transnational Criminal Law." *Transnational Legal Theory* 6(1): 9–30.

Choi-Fitzpatrick, A. 2016. "The Good, Bad, the Ugly: Human Rights Violators in Comparative Perspective." *Journal of Human Trafficking* 2(1): 1–14.

Chuang, J. A. 2010. "Rescuing Trafficking from Ideological Capture: Prostitution Reform and Anti-Trafficking Law and Policy." *University of Pennsylvania Law Review* 158: 1655–1728.

Chuang, J. A. 2014. "Exploitation Creep and the Unmaking of Human Trafficking Law." *American Journal of International Law* 108(4): 609–649.

Chuang, J. A. 2017. Contemporary Debt Bondage, "Self-Exploitation," and the Limits of the Trafficking Definition. Pp. 112–133 in *Revisiting* the Law and Governance of Trafficking, Forced Labour and Modern Slavery, edited by P. Kotiswaran. Cambridge: Cambridge University Press.

Clifford, B. 2015. "Re-framing Exploitation Creep to Fight Human Trafficking: A Response to Janie Chuang." AJIL Unbound. June 11, 2015. https://www.ca mbridge.org/core/journals/american-journal-of-international-law/article/refram ing-exploitation-creep-to-fight-human-trafficking-a-response-to-janie-chuang/ 6953C5CFD765CD49954A1FD24279E222 (accessed March 17, 2017).

Danailova-Trainor, G., and F. Laczko. 2010. "Trafficking in Persons and Development: Towards Greater Policy Coherence." International Migration 48 (4): 38–83.

De, Rohit. 2018. People's Constitution: The Everyday Life of Law in the Indian Republic. Princeton University Press.

de Castilho, E. W. V. 2015. "Human Trafficking in Brazil: Between Crime-Based and Human Rights-Based Governance." Anti-Trafficking Review 4: 174–185.

Debroy, B. 2017. "International Labour Organisation's Omissions." Indian Express. November 30, 2017. https://indianexpress.com/article/opinion/columns/inter national-labour-organisation-modern-slavery-forced-marriage-4960954/.

Deccan Chronicle. 2018. "Hyderabad: Rescued Uzbek Woman Ends Life in Shelter Home." April 15, 2018. www.deccanchronicle.com/nation/crime/ 150418/hyderabad-rescued-uzbek-woman-ends-life-in-shelter-home.html.

Doezema, J. 2000. "Loose Women or Lost Women? The Re-emergence of the Myth of White Slavery in Contemporary Discourses of Trafficking of Women." Gender Issues 18(1): 23–50.

Dottridge, M. 2007. Introduction. Pp. 1–27 in Global Alliance against Traffic in Women, Collateral Damage: The Impact of Anti-Trafficking Measures on Human Rights Around the World, edited by M. Dottridge, www.gaatw.org/ Collateral%20Damage_Final/singlefile_CollateralDamagefinal.pdf (accessed March 17, 2017).

Dottridge, M. 2017. Trafficked and Exploited: The Urgent Need for Coherence in International Law. Pp. 59–82 in Revisiting the Law and Governance of Trafficking, Forced Labour and Modern Slavery, edited by P. Kotiswaran. Cambridge: Cambridge University Press.

Economic and Political Weekly. 2016. Review of Women's Studies 51: 44–45.

Gallagher, A. T. 2001. "Human Rights and the New U.N. Protocols on Trafficking and Migrant Smuggling: A Preliminary Analysis." Human Rights Quarterly 23: 975–1004.

Gallagher, A. T. 2015. "Two Cheers for the Trafficking Protocol." Anti-Trafficking Review 4: 14–32.

Gallagher, A. T. 2016. "Editorial: The Problems and Prospects of Trafficking Prosecutions: Ending Impunity and Securing Justice." Anti-Trafficking Review 6: 1–11.

Gallagher, A. T. 2017. The International Legal Definition of "Trafficking in Persons": Scope and Application. Pp. 83–111 in Revisiting the Law and

Governance of Trafficking, Forced Labour and Modern Slavery, edited by P. Kotiswaran. Cambridge: Cambridge University Press.

Govindan, P. 2013. "Rethinking Emancipation: The Rhetorics of Slavery and Politics of Freedom in Anti-Trafficking Work in India." *Interventions: International Journal of Postcolonial Studies* 15(4): 511–529.

Grono, N. 2016. "Measuring Slavery Encourages Governments to Do Better." *Thomson Reuters Foundation News*. July 16, 2016. http://news.trust.org/item/20160716164413-tig2w (accessed March 17, 2017).

Davida, Grupo. 2015. "Trafficking as a Floating Signifier: The View from Brazil." *Anti-Trafficking Review* 4: 161–166.

Hackney, L. K. 2015. "Re-evaluating Palermo: The Case of Burmese Women as Chinese Brides." *Anti-Trafficking Review* 4: 98–119.

Halley, J., P. Kotiswaran, H. Shamir, and C. Thomas. 2006. "From the International to the Local in Feminist Legal Responses to Rape, Prostitution/Sex Work, and Sex Trafficking: Four Studies in Contemporary Governance Feminism." *Harvard Journal of Law and Gender* 29: 335–423.

Halliday, T. C., and G. Shaffer. 2015. *Transnational Legal Orders*. New York: Cambridge University Press.

Hodal, K., C. Kelly, and F. Lawrence. 2014. "Revealed: Asian Slave Labour Producing Prawns for Supermarkets in US, UK." *The Guardian*. June 10, 2014. https://www.theguardian.com/global-development/2014/jun/10/supermarket-prawns-thailand-produced-slave-labour (accessed March 17, 2017).

International Labour Office, Walk Free Foundation and International Organization for Migration. 2017. Global Estimates of Modern Slavery: Forced Labour and Forced Marriage. Geneva: ILO.

International Labour Organization. 1930. Convention Concerning Forced or Compulsory Labour (No. 29), Geneva, 28 June 1930, in force 1 May 1932, 39 UNTS 55.

International Labour Organization. 1957. Convention Concerning the Abolition of Forced Labour (No 105), Geneva, 25 June 1947, in force 17 January 1959, 520 UNTS 291.

International Labour Organization. 2005. A Global Alliance against Forced Labour. International Labour Conference 93rd Session 2005, Report I(B). Geneva: ILO.

International Labour Organization. 2009a. The Cost of Coercion: Global Report under the Follow-Up to the ILO Declaration on Fundamental Principles and Rights at Work. International Labour Conference 98th Session 2009, Report I(B). Geneva: ILO.

International Labour Organization. 2009b. Operational Indicators of Trafficking in Human Beings: Results from a Delphi Survey Implemented by the ILO and the European Commission. Geneva: ILO.

International Labour Organization. 2009c. Fighting Forced Labour, The Example of Brazil. Special Action Programme to Combat Forced Labour. Geneva: ILO.

International Labour Organization. 2013a. Report for Discussion at the Tripartite Meeting of Experts Concerning the Possible Adoption of an ILO Instrument to Supplement the Forced Labour Convention, 1930 (No. 29). Geneva: ILO.

International Labour Organization. 2013b. Report and Conclusions of the Tripartite Meeting of Experts on Forced Labour and Trafficking for Labour Exploitation. Geneva: ILO.

International Labour Organization. 2014. Profits and Poverty: The Economics of Forced Labour. Geneva: ILO.

Jahnsen, S. O., and M. L. Skilbrei. 2015. "From Palermo to the Streets of Oslo: Pros and Cons of the Trafficking Framework." *Anti-Trafficking Review* 4: 156–160.

Jenner, M. S. 2011. "International Drug Trafficking: A Global Problem with a Domestic Solution." *Indiana Journal of Global Legal Studies* 18(2): 901–927.

Kangaspunta, K. 2015. "Was Trafficking in Persons Really Criminalised?" *Anti-Trafficking Review* 4: 80–97.

Kelly, A. 2016. "46 Million People Living as Slaves, Latest Global Index Reveals." *The Guardian.* June 1, 2016. https://www.theguardian.com/global-development/2016/jun/01/46-million-people-living-as-slaves-latest-global-index-reveals-russell-crowe (accessed March 17, 2017).

Kotiswaran, P. 2014. "Beyond Sexual Humanitarianism: A Postcolonial Approach to Anti-Trafficking Law." *UC Irvine Law Review* 4: 353.

Lawrence, F. 2018. "How Did We Let Modern Slavery Become Part of Our Everyday Lives?" *The Guardian.* April 2, 2018. https://www.theguardian.com/commentisfree/2018/apr/02/modern-slavery-daily-life-exploitation-goods-services.

LeBaron, G. 2016. It's Time to Get Serious about Forced Labour in Supply Chains. Pp. 8–13 in *E-Book on Forced Labour in the Global Economy, Beyond Trafficking and Slavery Series,* edited by G. LeBaron and N. Howard. www.opendemocacy.net (accessed March 17, 2017).

Lee, M., ed. 2007. *Human Trafficking.* New York, Routledge.

Lerche J. 2016. ILO Campaigns: Missing the Wood for the Trees? Pp. 74–77 in *E-Book on Forced Labour in the Global Economy, Beyond Trafficking and Slavery Series,* edited by G. LeBaron and N. Howard. www.opendemocacy.net/beyondslavery (accessed March 17, 2017).

Lloyd, M. B. 2011. "Conflict, Intervention, and Drug Trafficking: Unintended Consequences of United States Policy in Colombia." *Oklahoma City University Law Review* 36(2): 293–349.

Magar, V. 2012. "Rescue and Rehabilitation: A Critical Analysis of Sex Workers' Antitrafficking Response in India." *Signs* 37(3): 619–644.

McGrath, S., and S. Watson. 2018. "Anti-Slavery as Development: A Global Politics of Rescue." *Geoforum* 93: 22–31.

Merry, S. E. 2016. *Human Rights and Gender Violence: Translating International Law Into Local Justice*. Chicago: University of Chicago Press.

Mitchell, A. 1998. "The United States Extraterritorial War on Drugs." *Southern Cross University Law Review* 2: 36–75.

Modern Slavery Act. 2015, C30.

O'Connell Davidson, J. 2010. "New Slavery, Old Binaries: Human Trafficking and the Borders of 'Freedom.'" *Global Networks* 10: 244–261.

O'Connor, M. P., and Rumann, C. M. 2011. "Market Solutions to Global Narcotics Trafficking and Addiction." *Phoenix Law Review* 5: 123–149.

Parrenas, R. S. 2006. "Trafficked? Filipino Hostesses in Tokyo's Nightlife Industry." *Yale Journal of Law and Feminism* 18: 145–180.

Plant, R. 2017. Combating Trafficking for Labour Exploitation in the Global Economy: The Need for a Differentiated Approach. Pp. 422–442 in *Revisiting the Law and Governance of Trafficking, Forced Labour and Modern Slavery*, edited by P. Kotiswaran. Cambridge: Cambridge University Press.

Pope, J. G. 2010. "A Free Labor Approach to Human Trafficking." *University of Pennsylvania Law Review* 158: 1849–1976.

Quirk, J. 2016. The Rhetoric and Reality of "Ending Slavery in Our Lifetime." Pp. 20–25 in *E-Book on Popular and Political Representations, Beyond Trafficking and Slavery Series*, edited by J. Quirk and J. O'Connell Davidson. www.opendemocracy.net (accessed March 17, 2017).

Quirk, J., and A. Bunting. 2016. The Politics of Exception: The Bipartisan Appeal of Human Trafficking. Pp. 64–68 in *E-Book on Popular and Political Representations, Beyond Slavery and Trafficking Series*, edited by J. Quirk and J. O'Connell Davidson. www.opendemocracy.net (accessed March 17, 2017).

Quirk, J., and J. O'Connell Davidson. 2016. Introduction. Pp. 10–19 in *E-Book on Popular and Political Representations, Beyond Trafficking and Slavery Series*, edited by J. Quirk and J. O'Connell Davidson. www.opendemocracy.org (accessed March 17, 2017).

Ramachandran. 2010. The Politics of the US State Department's TIP Report in India: Ethnographic Vignettes and Theoretical Possibilities.

Raustiala, K. 1999. "Law, Liberalization and International Narcotics Trafficking." *N.Y.U Journal of International Law and Politics* 32: 89–145.

Richardson, B. 2016. Still Slaving Over Sugar. Pp. 43–47 in *E-Book on Forced Labor in the Global Economy, Beyond Trafficking and Slavery Series*, edited by G. LeBaron and N. Howard. www.opendemocracy.net (accessed March 17, 2017).

Rittich, K. 2017. Representing, Counting, Valuing: Managing Definitional Uncertainty in the Law of Trafficking. Pp. 238–272 in *Revisiting the Law and Governance of Trafficking, Forced Labour and Modern Slavery*, edited by P. Kotiswaran. Cambridge: Cambridge University Press.

Savona, E. U., and Stefanizzi, S. 2007. Introduction. Pp. 1–4 in *Measuring Human Trafficking: Complexities and Pitfalls*, edited by in E. U. Savona and S. Stefanizzi. Verlag and New York: Springer.

Seshu, M. and Ahmed, A. 2012. "'We Have the Right Not to Be Rescued . . .': When Anti-trafficking Programmes Undermine the Health and Well-Being of Sex Workers." *Anti-Trafficking Review* 1: 149–165.

Shamir, H. 2012. "A Labor Paradigm for Human Trafficking." *UCLA Law Review* 60: 76–137.

Shapiro, J. B. 2010. "What Are They Smoking?! Mexico's Decriminalization of Small-Scale Drug Possession in the Wake of a Law Enforcement Failure." *Inter-American Law Review* 42(1): 115–144.

Simmons, B. A., and P. Lloyd. 2015. Framing and Transnational Legal Organization: The Case of Human Trafficking. Pp. 400–438 in *Transnational Legal Orders*, edited by T. C. Halliday and G. Shaffer. New York: Cambridge University Press.

Skrivankova, K. 2010. Between Decent Work and Forced Labour: Examining the Continuum of Exploitation. Joseph Rowntree Foundation Programme Paper: Forced Labour. York: JRF.

Sloan, A. 2015. "UK Tied Visa System Turning Domestic Workers into Modern Day Slaves." *The Guardian*. March 17, 2015. https://www.theguardian.com/world/2015/mar/17/uk-tied-visa-system-turning-domestic-workers-into-modern-day-slaves (accessed March 17, 2017).

United Nations. 1950. Convention for the Suppression of the Traffic in Persons and of the Exploitation of the Prostitution of Others, New York, 21 March 1950, in force 25 July 1951, 96 UNTS 271.

United Nations. 2000a. Protocol to Prevent, Suppress and Punish Trafficking in Persons, Especially Women and Children, Supplementing the United Nations Convention Against Transnational Organized Crime, New York, 15 November 2000, in force 25 December 2003, 2237 UNTS 319.

United Nations. 2000b. Convention against Transnational Organized Crime, New York, 15 November 2000, in force 29 September 2003, 2225 UNTS 209.

United Nations. 2000c. Protocol against the Smuggling of Migrants by Land, Sea and Air, Supplementing the United Nations Convention against Transnational Organised Crime, New York, 15 November 2000, in force 28 January 2004, 2241 UNTS 507.

UN Office on Drugs and Crime. 2012a. Global Report on Trafficking in Persons. https://www.unodc.org/documents/data-and-analysis/glotip/Trafficking_in_Persons_2012_web.pdf (accessed March 17, 2017).

UN Office on Drugs and Crime. 2012b. Abuse of a Position of Vulnerability and Other "Means" within the Definition of Trafficking in Persons. Issue Paper. https://www.unodc.org/documents/human-trafficking/2012/UNOD

C_2012_Issue_Paper_-_Abuse_of_a_Position_of_Vulnerability.pdf (accessed March 17, 2017).

UN Office on Drugs and Crime. 2014a. Global Report on Trafficking in Persons. New York: United Nations.

UN Office on Drugs and Crime. 2014b. The Role of Consent in the Trafficking in Persons Protocol. Issue Paper. www.unodc.org/documents/human-trafficking/2014/UNODC_2014_Issue_Paper_Consent.pdf.

UN Office on Drugs and Crime. 2015. The Concept of Exploitation in the Trafficking in Persons Protocol. Issue Paper. https://ec.europa.eu/anti-trafficking/sites/antitrafficking/files/unodc_ip_exploitation_2015.pdf.

UN Office on Drugs and Crime. 2016. Global Report on Trafficking in Persons. New York: United Nations. www.unodc.org/documents/data-and-analysis/glotip/2016_Global_Report_on_Trafficking_in_Persons.pdf.

Verite. 2014. Forced Labor in the Production of Electronic Goods in Malaysia: A Comprehensive Study of Scope and Characteristics. https://www.verite.org/wp-content/uploads/2016/11/VeriteForcedLaborMalaysianElectronics2014.pdf (accessed March 17, 2017).

Victims of Trafficking and Violence Protection Act. 2000. Pub. L. No. 106–386, § 106, 114 Stat. 1464, 1474 (2000) (codified at 22 U.S.C. § 7104 (2012)).

Walk Free Foundation. 2013. *Global Slavery Index*. Australia: Walk Free Foundation.

Walk Free Foundation. 2014. *Global Slavery Index*. Australia: Walk Free Foundation.

Walk Free Foundation. 2016. *Global Slavery Index*. Australia: Walk Free Foundation.

Walk Free Foundation. 2018. *Global Slavery Index*. Australia: Walk Free Foundation.

Weitzer, R. 2006.Moral Crusade against Prostitution. *Society* 43(3): 33–38.

Wijers, M. 2015. "Purity, Victimhood and Agency: Fifteen Years of the UN Trafficking Protocol." *Anti-Trafficking Review* 4: 56–79.

Wilshaw, R. 2016. What Would Loosen the Roots of Labour Exploitation in Supply Chains? Pp. 78–83 in *E-Book on Forced Labour in the Global Economy, Beyond Trafficking and Slavery Series*, edited by G. LeBaron and N. Howard. www.opendemocracy.net (accessed March 17, 2017).

Womark, D. (producer), and T. Noorani (director). 2018. *Love Sonia* [Motion picture]. India: Zee Studios.

CHAPTER FIVE

THE CRIMINALIZATION OF MIGRATION

A Regional Transnational Legal Order or the Rise of a Meta-TLO?

Vanessa Barker

5.1 STRUCTURAL REALIGNMENT: THE CRIMINALIZATION OF MIGRATION CHALLENGES HUMAN RIGHTS NORMS

On August 21, 2018, an Italian Coast Guard ship, the *Diciotti*, rescued 177 people off the coast of Lampedusa. The people on board had fled Eritrea, Syria, Egypt, and Bangladesh, and were seeking asylum in Europe. After Malta refused their entry, they had been left at sea until the *Diciotti* picked them up. When the Coast Guard ship docked in Catania, Sicily, the migrants were not allowed to disembark as the Italian Interior Minister, Matteo Salvini, refused their entry. Criticized by the UN's refugee agency in Italy, Carlotta Sami explained that the people on board were victims of human trafficking and torture and "They urgently need assistance and the right to claim asylum. A fundamental right, not a crime" (Sami quoted by CNN, August 21, 2018). When pressed to take responsibility, the European Commission said, "It's a matter for national authorities" (press briefing cited by CNN, August 21, 2018). When EU member state Sweden was contacted to take in the migrants, Prime Minister Stefan Löfven said no – it was time for other European countries to do their part, as Sweden had done enough already. In just the course of a week, EU member states effectively immobilized a group of asylum seekers, blocking their entry and denying their right to make a claim. As European law scholars Francesca Cancellaro and Stefano Zirulia (2018) explain, European authorities had essentially denied the personal liberty of more than a hundred people, detaining them on board, without a detention order. In Italy they were cast as illegal, in Sweden as drains on the state. In this case, migrants were immobilized and confined on board, their loss of liberty justified on the basis of their status rather than on a criminal offense.

How did we get here? How is this series of events possible? One easy answer is the rise of anti-immigrant sentiment and the growing effects of far-right movements across Europe and North America. The *Diciotti* incident reflects the backlash against immigration and governmental resistance to admit additional asylum seekers or other unwanted migrants to appease a restless populous. While these factors are certainly at work in Italy, Sweden, and in the United States, this incident is much more complicated than the far-right or populist accounts allow. I argue instead that the *Diciotti* and the people on board were caught in a paradigm shift. They were caught in a historic movement away from humanism and human rights norms and toward resurgent nationalism and its darker undercurrents. These undercurrents are backed by the violence of the state that tend to be glossed over by the perceived legitimacy of criminal justice measures. The Global North – that is, affluent democratic societies – are in the middle of a major transformation of governance and transnational legal orders are at the center of it. Anti-immigrant and populist politics are at the surface of these deeper structural and legal realignments. Legal orders, as Terence Halliday and Gregory Shaffer (2015) explain, provide the underlying rules, norms, and expectations that shape, if not govern, complex social relations. Today, these rules are fast changing, and in particular, the postwar norm about the value of human life is being overtaken by expanding criminalization processes. As we shall see below, only some lives matter in law as an emerging transnational criminal legal order contributes to the hierarchy of human worth.

From the *Diciotti* incident, we can see the tension between competing legal norms and values with an outcome tipped toward criminal justice. First, there is the fact that the Italian Coast Guard, operating under European Union directives, International Maritime law, and its own naval traditions, rescued the migrants at sea and brought them to shore. They were not left to drown, and that is significant. The duty of care, the obligation to rescue those in distress at sea as governed by international maritime law (United Nations Human Rights Council [UNHRC], n.d.), also applies to commercial vessels and has been mobilized by civilians and civil society organization. MSF (Médecins Sans Frontières), for example, has conducted numerous search and rescue operations in cooperation with the Italian Coast Guard and with permission from the Libyan authorities (Medecins sans Frontiers, n.d.). At sea, we can see the strength of transnational legal norms at work, preventing further loss of life and upholding the value of human life. Second, on a similar track, we see the United Nations refugee agency bolstering these norms and values by advocating for the *Diciotti* migrants and their right to make landfall. Yet, third, once in port, national authorities refused their entry and did so without formal sanctions from the international community, despite the blatant disregard for the life and liberty for those on board. The migrants were deprived of liberty, detained, and confined, as if they had committed a crime. Even as mobility, free movement, and rights to seek asylum are supported by international legal frameworks, the right to make landfall, to claim asylum, to settle in a particular place remains the prerogative of domestic, national governments, which increasingly rely on criminalization to legitimize these exclusions. It is the criminalization not of acts but of people that portends significant shifts in the transnational legal order.

5.2 TRANSNATIONAL LEGAL ORDER: A NEW LENS TO EXAMINE THE CRIMINALIZATION OF MIGRATION

This chapter examines the criminalization of migration through the lens of transnational legal orders (TLOs). By doing so, it seeks to explain dramatic episodes such as the *Diciotti* incident but also provide socio-legal analysis for far-reaching practices such as immigration detention, removal, and refusal of entry, all of which depend on the development of a formalizing legal order and specific regulation, such as the EU Returns Directive, that transcends national boundaries (see Halliday and Shaffer 2015: 4).

Here I use a broad conceptualization of the criminalization of migration that includes three components:

1. substantive criminal law, which makes certain immigration acts or statuses criminal offenses subject to criminal sanctions (Mitsilegas 2015: 2; Stumpf 2006);
2. the use of criminal justice tools, personnel, and institutions to regulate migration, including the imposition of penal sanctions

and penal harm, such as detention regardless of criminal violations (Aas 2015; Barker 2017; Bosworth 2014); and

3. the discursive framing of migration as a crime and public order problem rather than as an expression of rights or economic imperatives (Barker 2017; Franko 2020; van der Woude et al. 2014).

These elements are applicable to most cases across the Global North, such as the United States of America, Australia, and Europe. To keep this chapter empirically coherent, I focus on the development of a regional TLO in the European Union. Despite the regional focus, this European TLO is likely to have global impacts as political and legal decisions in Brussels or Strasbourg impact mobility from Turkey, Ghana, Libya, and elsewhere around the world. The case selection of the European Union is motivated based on the EU's historical role as an innovator in transnational governance, its role as an important immigration region, and its Member States' historically restrictive use of criminal justice to respond to social problems (van Zyl Smit and Snacken 2009). The restrained use of criminal law and penal sanctioning makes the EU a critical case to examine how and why it has come to rely on these measures in response to migration as it goes against expectations and established norms (for more on case studies, see Flyvbjerg 2011). For these reasons, the European Union makes for an empirically rich and theoretically significant site to examine transnational legal ordering, particularly in relation to the criminalization of migration.

The criminalization of migration entails a series of developments that together have blocked the free movement of people into Europe at a rate that outpaces mass incarceration in the United States (Eurostat 2018; Global Detention Project 2018). In just two years, from 2015 to 2017, for instance, the European Union ordered more than 1.5 million non-EU citizens to leave the European Union (Eurostat 2018). The transnational legal order framework offers analytical leverage into this particular issue as it pulls criminal justice measures out of their ordinary frame, the national context, and opens them up for analysis in a transnational or cross-border frame. By doing so, we can better appreciate the scale and character of this transformation. For example, as the foremost expert on the topic Valsamis Mitsilegas (2015) explains, as the European Union has sought to prevent unwanted migration, it has moved the criminalization process outside national territories and into transnational spaces on the high seas, in third countries, and recently at "reception centers" located well outside the borders of the EU in Northern Africa. If we were to focus only on domestic criminal law or immigration law, we would miss this major site of legal exclusion.

In another example, the European Union has long been criminalizing human trafficking, that is the nonconsensual trade of human beings across borders for the purpose of forced labor or sexual exploitation, with the intention to target criminal networks and slow down, if not prevent unwanted migration into the EU (Mitsilegas 2015). In terms of human smuggling, which is defined as voluntary illegal movement across borders, the Facilitators Package (Directive 2002/90/EC) made it a crime for anyone to help, aid, or facilitate "unauthorized entry, transit, or residence" in the European Union, and subjected this activity to criminal sanctions (European Parliament 2018). Recently, this criminalization process has radiated outward toward civil society actors and nongovernmental organizations (NGOs) engaged in search and rescue in the Mediterranean, unlikely groups now subject to sanction for aiding migrants reach EU territories. A TLO lens illuminates new kinds of activity and new kinds of actors that are subject to sanctions who might not otherwise be visible.

From this perspective, we can not only see but perhaps better explain how nationalized criminal justice measures are being repurposed to suit new kinds of interests (Aaronson and Shaffer, Chapter 1). Domestic and national police forces, for example, are routinely called upon to conduct border control, to protect the domestic population against existential threats and material harm, from unwanted people to transnational crime. Benjamin Bowling and James Sheptycki (2012) identified the rise of transnational policing to respond to cross border crimes such as terrorism, human trafficking, and the drug trade, a trend that has become more sophisticated and integrated with the European Surveillance System (EUROSUR), a type of big data technology, replete with shared norms and practices. Likewise, Prabha Kotiswaran (this volume) shows how sex trafficking became identified and framed as a transnational crime problem, and one that required new forms of cooperation and new forms of legal regulation, a movement that led to the international agreement against human trafficking, the United Nations 2000 Palermo Protocol. The transnational legal order lens can effectively expose how "certain social issues are framed as 'global problems' addressed through transnational legal regulation" (Aaronson and Shaffer, Chapter 1). In a breakthrough for criminology, Katja

Franko, formerly Aas (2013), called attention to how globalization was reshaping our understanding of crime and crime control, as both elements became increasingly unmoored from the national context and subsequently require more sophisticated analytical tools to understand their transnational dimensions.

As particular issues such as crime, trafficking, and migration are framed as transnational issues that require transnational legal regulation, we can also track shifts in enforcement that we might not otherwise notice, as they fall outside traditional criminal justice. Just as local police are now drawn into border control and transnational crime control, national security forces are pulled into domestic politics. Most notably, the US military has been deployed at the US-Mexico border with five thousand active troops awaiting the entry of asylum seekers from Central America. Portrayed as an unruly and illegal "migrant caravan" of violent criminals by the Trump administration, the military was mobilized to guard against this perceived national and criminal threat (for more on the military and migration, see Loyd and Mountz 2018).

We see similar, if unfamiliar, developments in Europe. The European Union recently expanded the budget, personnel, authority, and tasks of the European Border and Coast Guard Agency, established only recently in 2016, after the 2015 refugee crisis. For the upcoming 2021–2027 term, the European Border and Coast Guard Agency has an operating budget of 11.3 billion Euros, expanded executive powers, its own equipment, and a standing core of 10,000 active personnel (European Commission, State of the Union 2018). The European Union traditionally rejected a pan European military force in favor of Member State collaboration. Migration has changed that calculus. It ushered in a new form, the European Coast Guard, for new purposes: to manage the EU's external border through force and removal (European Commission, State of the Union, 2018). In addition, the European Union has partnered with NATO, the North Atlantic Treaty Organization, to patrol territorial and international waters with the expressed purpose to reduce to irregular migration into Europe (NATO, 2016). The specific legal regulations and practices are discussed in more detail below.

The criminalization, securitization, and increased militarization of migration – expanding since 2001 – has been formalized, legitimized, and by now quite possibly entrenched in practice and in law. Without investigating transnational legal ordering, we may miss the scale of this transformation; it is immense. We may miss its particular forms of enforcement through policing, punishment, and the military. Moreover, we may miss the emergence of a "meta-TLO" for migration – that is, a legal order that supersedes the norms, practices, and institutions of other legal orders, as Jothie Rajah (2015) succinctly captured the dominance of the rule of law over all other legal orders. We may miss the consequences of the criminalization of migration, which impact not only individuals but entire societies (Barker 2018). As Halliday and Shaffer (2015a) rightly note, most studies of globalization neglect the law and as a consequence miss the underlying structure of global relations. By paying attention to the changing legal structure, we can map out the changing structure and meaning of social relations. What we are seeing is a fundamental shift toward repression over humanism. Over time, this shift may lead to the closure of democratic societies and their subsequent unraveling.

5.3   TLO CONCEPTS: FRAMING, LEGAL REGULATION, AND NORM SETTLEMENT

This chapter applies key concepts from the TLO framework to analyze the criminalization of migration. As Halliday and Shaffer (2015a, b) outline in their defining volume *Transnational Legal Orders*, TLOs are institutionalized legal orders that cross national borders. To study TLOs, the authors propose a series of terms, hypotheses, and trajectories to help identify TLOs and the processes by which they become formalized, settled, or contested (Halliday and Shaffer 2015a; 2015b). As the range of TLO possibilities is quite expansive, I focus on a specific set of terms that best inform the processes and practices of the criminalization of migration. I illustrate diagnosis or framing, norm settlement vis-à-vis legal regulation and enforcement. In the final section, I take up competing TLOs, namely human rights and the refugee convention, and the possibility of a meta-TLO that regulates mobility.

5.3.1   The Role of Framing: Crime and Solidarity

One of the central tenets of the TLO framework is the recognition that legal problems are socially constructed, are embedded in power imbalances, and entail communicative struggles about social meaning. Here the framing of an issue or diagnosis of a problem is essential to understanding the proposed solutions or remedies – or why an issue becomes subject to transnational legal regulation. Or for understanding why a migrant in this case could be detained without having committed a crime. How is that possible? It is possible because migration, particularly the movement of poorer people of color from the Global South, has been framed as a crime problem requiring increased security, deterrence, public order policing, confinement, penal sanctions, and other means of crime control.

The crime frame works well in European Union context, as it accomplishes two structural tasks:

1. it resonates with national interests, national sovereignty, and national identity (Barker 2017), making the TLO more likely to be accepted and adopted (Halliday and Shaffer 2015a: 39); and
2. it provides an effective resource to reaffirm social solidarity on both the national Member State level and at the transnational European Union level as the crime framework communicates membership and belonging in sometimes diverging polities (Barker 2017; Duff 2001; European Commission 2018).

The criminalization of migration depends upon discursive moves that conflate the migrant with the criminal – the crimmigrant other as Katja Franko explains. The criminal migrant, or crimmigrant other, is perceived as a social threat whose very presence will pollute the moral purity of the social body. Under the Trump administration in the United States, for example, migrants from Mexico and Central America have been characterized a priori as criminal – carrying risk, rape, and danger across the border. This conflation is part of a broad uneasiness or fear of outsiders and perceived others who are scapegoated or blamed for a whole host of social anxieties. World-renowned Norwegian criminologist the late Nils Christie introduced the term "suitable enemies" to captures this process. In the UK, we can see how the Brexit vote turned on anti-immigrant sentiment, as migrants became stand-ins for unease about globalization and austerity and triggers for a romanticized past. Similarly, in Sweden, fear of the criminal migrant fueled anti-immigrant sentiment and altered the electoral map and make-up of the Parliament and government as migrants were perceived to be different, if not, dangerous to social cohesion and the sustainability of the welfare state (Barker 2018). By overlaying a discursive crime frame onto migration, public authorities cast doubt on the moral worthiness of migrants, cast doubt on their capacity to integrate, and offer suitable sanctions for their perceived wrongdoing.

In this framework, migration is portrayed as a crime problem requir-ing crime control responses, including the loss of liberty. The United States, for example, currently confines more than 300,000 migrants in immigration detention centers – prison-like facilities that many scho-lars call "immigrant imprisonment," as it entails many of the same penal harms (Bosworth 2014; Canning 2017) if not punitive purpose of the prison (Fleury-Steiner and Longazel 2016).

In the European Union, the crime frame for migration has been present at least since the late 1990s when the Tampere European Council (1999) pushed for a common asylum system that went hand in hand with the "fight against illegal immigration" (European Parliament, Directive 2008/115/EC). In 2005 the Hague Programme, "Strengthening Freedom, Security and Justice in the European Union," continued this thread by linking migration with public order and secur-ity concerns, backing more efficient removal procedures. While EU policy statements tend to support the idea of reforming asylum policies, what gets passed consistently is stronger enforcement measures against unwanted migration. For example, as Valsamis Mitsilegas (2015: 3) notes, the "first major global effort to legislate immigration control" was based on security and crime control concerns. The Trafficking and Smuggling Protocols, for instance, foregrounded the perceived crimin-ality and duplicity of those involved rather than the rights of migrants. The ensuing Directives increased criminal penalties for trafficking to at least five years imprisonment. Irregular migrants, according to the European Commissioner, are at the "mercy of criminal networks who put profit before human life" and should be stopped (Juncker in a European Agenda on Migration 2014–2015, European Commission 2015a). These criminal networks "which exploit vulnerable migrants must be targeted" (Juncker, A European Agenda on Migration 2014–2015, European Commission 2015a: 3). Moreover, European Union Security and Defense operations would be tasked with operations to "systematically identify, capture and destroy vessels used by smug-glers" (A European Agenda on Migration 2014–2015, European Commission 2015a). All tools are available for this endeavor, including increased enforcement cooperation, intelligence gathering and sharing, surveillance, credit card and internet monitoring, and interventions.

The crime frame and its enforcement measures are used for both nonconsensual trafficking and voluntary illegal entry through smug-gling. This expansive crime control approach contrasts with ethno-graphic research on smuggling. As Gabriella Sanchez (2016) has shown, the social dynamics between those who assist others to cross the US border without legal authorization and those that are crossing are complex – they are as likely to involve a duty of care, norms of reciprocity, and economic survival as much as risk.

The crime control framework has much appeal as it communicates authority and reaffirms solidarity, key findings from the history of punishment (Garland 2001). For the European Union, managing migration through crime control provides a "powerful demonstration of the EU's determination to act" (European Commission 2015a). In the contemporary context, the border spectacle has provided the EU much needed occasions to reaffirm its political authority and capacity to govern as political elites have faced severe strains with their handling of the 2015 refugee crisis, the 2010 financial crisis, and earlier rejection of the EU Constitution. As the European Commission explains, the EU needs to "restore confidence in our ability to bring together European and national efforts to address migration" (Juncker, September 12, 2018). In his State of the Union Address, Jean-Claude Juncker explained, "We cannot continue to squabble to find ad-hoc solutions each time a new ship arrives. Temporary solidarity is not good enough. We need lasting solidarity – today and forever more" (Junker, State of the Union Address, September 12, 2018).

To resolve the solidarity crisis, the European Union would go on to shore up its borders through criminalization and securitization. It would provide internal security for those on the inside at the expense of those on the outside. We should note that this crisis of solidarity was not perceived by elites as a crisis of solidarity with migrants but rather as a crisis of solidarity within the EU. Consequently, the figure of the criminal migrant becomes the body through which solidarity is achieved. The expansion of the European Border and Coast Guard Agency would provide the balm to ease the crisis. As proclaimed by the European Commission Vice President Frans Timmermans, the European Border and Coast Guard and a "reinforced EU Asylum Agency" will "ensure EU solidarity is effectively delivered on the ground – whenever and wherever needed" (Timmermans, State of the Union Press Release, September 12, 2018). Likewise, the EU Commissioner for Migration, Home Affairs and Citizenship Dimitris Avramopoulos stated:

> Today we offer more Europe where more Europe is needed by maximiz-ing EU support on border and migration management. ... We are

putting in place stronger rules on return to ensure a more harmonized and effective return system across the EU. Finally, we call on Member States to deliver credibly and ambitiously on legal pathways, both for humanitarian and economic purposes.

(Avramopoulos, State of the Union Press Release,
September 12, 2018)

Here the EU will offer a more secure Europe while Member States retain responsibility for more humane migration policies. At this historical juncture, EU solidarity is based on externally oriented repression rather than on more liberating norms and values.

5.3.2 Cross-Border Legal Regulation: The Returns Directive, Detention, and Removal

The TLO framework posits that transnational legal orders necessarily cross national borders, engage multiple legal systems, and take on recognizable legal forms (Halliday and Shaffer 2015a: 8–10). The criminalization of migration in the European Union illustrates these critical attributes in several ways. The European Union generates legal regulations, guidelines, laws, and directives that take on a recognizable form that are upheld by supranational courts such as the European Court of Human Rights. The EU generates rules that cross multiple legal systems. For example, Member States are obligated to domesticate certain EU regulations within their own legal systems. In the criminalization of migration there are multiple regulations that fit the criteria, with the Trafficking and Smuggling Protocols as some of the more familiar and potent examples.

Another such example, the Returns Directive is perhaps one of the most significant pieces of the legal framework that underpins the criminalization of migration TLO in Europe. This section highlights key features of the Returns Directive, which to some legal scholars pose serious challenges to the principle of proportionality and the protection of human dignity in European law (Cancellaro and Zirulia 2018; Mitsilegas 2015). To border criminologists, the Returns Directive most clearly upholds the use of detention, the loss of liberty, for immigration violations, legitimizing the use of penal harms and penal sanctions for noncriminal offences, a sign of penal excess, if not state violence (Canning 2017). For TLO scholars, we can understand the Returns Directive as providing some of the substance of criminalization, the form of transnational legal regulation, and to some degree norm settlement as it is the most harmonized aspect of EU migration policy (see Mitsilegas 2015: 94).

The Returns Directive (Directive 2008/115/EC) provides the legal framework for the use of detention (that is, the deprivation of liberty for migrants, including unaccompanied minors), sets the stage for migrants' removal from the European Union, and establishes guidelines for their return to third countries. It is aimed at the efficient removal of those without legal authorization to remain in the EU or Member State.

Recognized as both part of a "humane return policy" and a coercive measure in the directive itself (Article 8), the EU created a set of safeguards and common rules to limit its use and applicability (Directive 2008/115/EC). For example, the use of detention is limited to the removal process and is "subject to the principle of proportionality" (Directive 2008/115/EC). As such, detention can be used only when "less coercive measures" are not possible (Directive 2008/115/EC: Paragraph 16). Despite these safety valves within the system, in practice, the use of detention has exceeded these limits and is now subject to a set of reforms that would expand its use, increase the maximum allowable time in detention, and increase the categories of persons eligible for detention, including those who are considered uncooperative or "pose a threat to public order or national security" (Manieri, 2018).

In the European Union, the Returns Directive has become the centerpiece of migration control as new practices and new regulations are built up around it. The directive has legitimized limits on free movement, authorized the deprivation of liberty for migrants, forcefully removed people from the territory (sometimes returning them to hostile territories), and initiated bilateral agreements with third countries where EU citizens are discouraged (if not prohibited) from traveling, such as Afghanistan or Libya. It has contributed to norm settlement to the degree to which new forms of migration control mirror its key elements. For example, in 2015, in response to the scale of newly arrived migrants in the European Union, the European Commission proposed the "hotspot" approach to migration control. The EU Commission created four hotspots in Italy, including on the island of Lampedusa, and multiple locations in Greece, including its headquarters in Piraeus – both countries considered the front line of migration management. The European Asylum Support Office in collaboration with Frontex and Europol ran "reception centers" to facilitate the identification, registration, and fingerprinting of incoming migrants

(European Commission Hotspot Approach 2015). According to the European Commission, those identified as needing protection were funneled into the asylum system while those deemed "not in need of protection" were removed and returned. The hotspot approach created sites of removal even before migrants had formally entered the EU. In 2018, hotspots were recently recast as "controlled centers" where migrants cannot leave the premises, and subject to a type of preventative detention. None of these practices show signs of retraction but are on an upward trajectory toward expansion. And all were made because of the entrenched norms and practices of return, where migrants are perceived to be threats to the social order and deemed unworthy and unfree to decide to their own fates.

5.4 NORM SETTLEMENT THROUGH ENFORCEMENT

Norm settlement through enforcement is one of the last attributes of TLOs that this chapter considers. Norm settlement occurs when a new TLO becomes taken for granted, a naturalized way of solving problems, part of the institutionalized rules of the game. The criminalization of migration TLO has become normalized in part because it is consistent with past practices of the European Union and is part and parcel of an effective frame, a crime control frame that does the hard work of shoring up solidarity and national sovereignty when needed. Criminalization has a performative and communicative power that cannot be under-estimated, nor easily undone (as the prison abolition movement can surely attest to in the United States; but see Aaronson (Chapter 6) on cannabis legalization). Although the Returns Directive served to illustrate some degree of norm settlement in this area, I highlight entrenchment through the expansion of enforcement measures, mechanisms, and bilateral agreements.

The establishment of the European Border and Coast Guard Agency in 2016 represents elite consensus that the European Union will do what it takes to prevent and deter unwanted migration. Considered "one of the biggest achievements" of the European Union, the Coast Guard has greatly expanded its authority and power, personnel, equipment, budget allocations, and significance. Defined as a "reliable intervention force," the European Border and Coast Guard will now be able to carry out migrant interdiction – that is, it will be able to "intervene wherever and whenever needed" (European Commission, State of the Union, September 12, 2018) to prevent entry of unwanted migrants.

With new executive powers, the Coast Guard will be able to carry out identification checks, authorize travel documents, and refuse the entry of certain migrants as well as remove them from the EU. Perhaps most importantly, this European Coast Guard will have the authority to conduct its operations well beyond the EU border in non-EU countries (European Commission, State of the Union, September 12, 2018).

Offshoring confirms the success of this TLO and heightens its transnational character as a host of non-EU countries nominally adopt its principles and practices. Of course, on the ground, ethnographic work in these countries would nuance the actual practices and provide a clearer picture of adherence. Yet externalization is a striking development. The European Union has not only extended its own operations into new territories; it has sought out "stronger cooperation" with non-EU partners so that other countries will carry out EU migration control. For example, the EU in partnership with Niger, the IOM and UNHCR created a multipurpose center to provide information, legal protection, and "resettlement opportunities" for African migrants. Similarly, the EU has provided donor aid to several Northern and West African countries such as Nigeria, Mali, Sudan, Ghana, and Senegal, in exchange for slowing down migration into Europe, even if open borders are more effective for their own economic development (Statewatch 2018).

Similarly, the EU-Turkey deal, for example, initiated in the wake of the 2015 refugee crisis, is a bilateral agreement between the European Union and Turkey. The agreement is aimed at halting the flow of migrants from Turkey to the EU in exchange for substantial financial assistance. According to the European Parliament, the EU-Turkey Statement is "aimed at stopping the flow of irregular migration via Turkey to Europe. According to the EU-Turkey Statement, all new irregular migrants and asylum seekers arriving from Turkey to the Greek islands and whose applications for asylum have been declared inadmissible should be returned to Turkey" (European Parliament 2018).

This agreement stipulates a series of actions designed to reduce, if not stop, Syrians from leaving Turkey to seek asylum in Europe. It includes NATO activity on the Aegean Sea to target smugglers, in a now familiar crime control approach to migration. It includes the "return" of Syrians who made it to the Greek Islands to Turkey after March 20, 2016. It enables Turkey to "take any necessary measures to prevent new sea or land routes for irregular migration opening from Turkey to the

EU" (EU-Turkey Statement, European Parliament 2018). It makes some of the financial support conditional on the reduction of migration flows. The agreement states that when the "irregular crossings ... have been substantially reduced, a Voluntary Humanitarian Admission Scheme will be activated" (EU-Turkey Statement, European Parliament 2018). Since 2016, the European Commission has allocated 1.6 billion Euros to the construction and development of the Refugee Facility (European Commission Press Release, March 14, 2018). The facilities support 1.2 million refugees in Turkey, including 500,000 children, who have received cash transfers from the EU as well education and health care (European Commission Press Release, March 14, 2018). While the bulk of the budget is dedicated to humanitarian assistance, the facility is meant to prevent mobility. Here humanitarianism was initiated and maintained at service of migration control (on penal humanitarianism, see Bosworth 2017).

The EU-Turkey deal led to the involvement of NATO, a military alliance, in migration control. NATO, the North Atlantic Treaty Organization, founded after the Second World War, is an alliance of twenty-nine countries, including Turkey. In July 2016, NATO responded to its allies' request to patrol the Aegean Sea. Deploying the Standing Maritime Group 2, made up of seven naval ships from Germany, the United Kingdom, the United States, Greece, and Turkey, NATO is specifically "providing support to broader international efforts to stem the flow of illegal trafficking and migration in the Aegean Sea" (NATO's Deployment in the Aegean Fact Sheet, July 2016). These naval ships conduct "reconnaissance, monitoring and surveillance in the territorial waters of Greece and Turkey, and international waters" (NATO's Deployment in the Aegean Fact Sheet, July 2016). In other words, NATO is conducting military-style operations in international waters to prevent outward migration to Europe and doing so in collaboration with Frontex, the European Union's border agency. The militarization of the EU border is a reality and taking place extra-territorially in international waters and off the coast of Turkey. Here military power is used at the service of migration control, itself framed as a response to the transnational crime of smuggling, solidifying this TLO.

These arrangements as part of a more restrictive transnational legal order have serious consequences for the migrants involved. Nominally, they protect asylum seekers and refugees from the treacherous journey across the Mediterranean Sea, especially by illicit means, and provide a safe haven from civil war. Yet they deprive migrants of self-determination, the right to make their own choices, and subject them instead to containment and the loss of liberty. These infringements on human will are arranged by third parties in exchange for cash and promises to improve conditions in the home countries. These decisions are made not by the people most affected by them, but by elites in European capitals.

5.5 DISCUSSION AND IMPLICATIONS: COMPETING TLOS OR THE EMERGENCE OF A META-TLO?

This chapter has examined the criminalization of migration as a transnational legal order and argued that this particular TLO is expansive, normalized, and entrenched in the European Union. Yet the question remains as to the extent to which it is a dominant TLO in terms of crime control and migration, as there are several competing TLOs that are oriented toward the recognition, protection, and dignity of both migrants and criminal offenders.

In terms of criminal justice, legal scholars and criminologists have identified the growth of transnational norms and legal regulations that are intentionally designed to protect the dignity of persons and uphold human rights. Leading prison scholars Dirk van Zyl Smit and Sonja Snacken (2009), for example, have extensively documented these developments in *The Principles of European Prison Law and Policy: Penology and Human Rights*. Here the authors highlight the centrality of human dignity as a core value in the postwar period that sets limits on the use of confinement in European prisons. European prisons are regularly monitored by an independent committee against torture, known as the CPT or the European Committee for the Prevention of Torture or Inhuman or Degrading Treatment or Punishment, an international body of experts attached to the Council of Europe. Likewise, Peter Scharff Smith points to the international campaign to introduce the Mandela Rules of imprisonment across the globe that have been adopted by the United Nations as minimum standards of treatment for prisoners. In a similar case, Scharff Smith (2008) explains how a group of international experts, including Sharon Shalev, a well-known research and advocate against solitary confinement, worked over three years to develop a joint statement and set of standards to eliminate the use of solitary confinement. This effort culminated in the Istanbul Statement of the Uses and Effects of Solitary Confinement. The institutionalization of transnational efforts to mitigate penal harm have clearly created a set of standards, norms, and monitoring bodies that seek to uphold key tenets. These efforts are significant.

But are they enough? Do they counter the powerful criminalization frame? The question remains whether or not these transnational norms apply across criminal justice domains and, specifically, to migrants and migration. We know from current accounts on European penal regimes, when foreign nationals and noncitizens intermix with imprisonment, this configuration tends to change the character and aims of punishment, away from reintegration and toward expulsion (Aas 2015; Barker 2013; on deportability, see De Genova 2010; also see van Zyl Smit and Snacken 2009). When the tools of criminal justice are used to manage migration, when the deprivation of liberty is rationalized for noncriminal offenders, when interdiction is used to block the free movement of people, especially outside EU territory, the preservation of human dignity seems a secondary concern.

In terms of migration TLOs, there is a series of established human rights norms, the 1951 Refugee Convention, and the UN Declaration of Human Rights that should counter, if not neutralize, criminal justice practices and policies that undermine human rights. Yet these norms and provisions, as many legal scholars have shown, are not necessarily institutionalized or written into domestic law, even in high-functioning democracies. In the face of human hardship, they have been ignored. In the borderlands, they are nearly invisible (Weber and Pickering 2011).

By contrast, the criminalization of migration has been readily adopted across jurisdictions and liberally applied to a wide range of divergent cases. Because this TLO tends to amplify national interests, national sovereignty, and national solidarity, it has also gained a high degree of legitimacy and dominance. The criminalization frame, moreover, tends to colonize other policy domains, making resistance difficult or short-lived. The criminalization of migration TLO structures social relations according to its logic and rationale. Consequently, we may be witnessing the emergence of a meta-TLO that dominates other legal orders, including those that uphold human dignity.

REFERENCES

Aas, Katja Franko. 2013. *Globalization and Crime*, 2nd ed. London: Sage.

Aas, Katja Franko. 2014. "Bordered Penalty: Precarious Membership and Abnormal Justice." *Punishment and Society* 16(5): 520–541.

Aas, Katja Franko, and Mary Bosworth, eds. 2013. *Borders of Punishment: Citizenship, Migration, Citizenship and Social Exclusion*. Oxford: Oxford University Press.

Aas, Katja Franko, and Helene Gundhus. 2015. "Policing Humanitarian Borderlands: Frontex, Human Rights and the Precariousness of Life." *British Journal of Criminology* 55: 1–18.

Barker, Vanessa. 2013. Democracy and Deportation: Why Membership Matters Most. Pp. 237–256. In *Borders of Punishment: Citizenship, Migration, Citizenship and Social Exclusion*. Oxford: Oxford University Press.

Barker, Vanessa. 2017. "Penal Power at the Border: Realigning State and Nation." *Theoretical Criminology* 21(4): 441–457.

Barker, Vanessa. 2018. *Nordic Nationalism and Penal Order: Walling the Welfare State*. Abingdon: Routledge.

Bosworth, Mary. 2008. "Border Control and the Limits of the Sovereign State." *Social Legal Studies* 17(2): 199–215.

Bosworth, Mary. 2014. *Inside Immigration Detention*. Oxford: Oxford University Press.

Bosworth, M. 2017. "Penal Humanitarianism: Sovereign Power in an Era of Mass Migration." *New Criminal Law Review*. 39(20).

Bosworth, Mary, Katja Franko, and Sharon Pickering. 2017. "Punishment, Globalization, and Migration Control: 'Get Them the Hell Out of Here.'" *Punishment and Society* 20(1): 34–53.

Bowling, Benjamin, and James Sheptycki. 2012. *Global Policing*. London: Sage.

Cancellaro, Francesca Stefano Zirulia. 2018. Controlling Migration through De Facto Detention: The Case of the *"Diciotti"* Italian Ship. www.law.ox.ac.uk/research-subject-groups/centre-criminology/centre

border-criminologies/blog/2018/10/controlling (accessed December 31, 2018).

Canning, Victoria. 2017. *Gendered Harm and Structural Violence in the British Asylum System*. Abingdon: Routledge.

Chacón, Jennifer. 2009. "Managing Migration through Crime." *Columbia Law Review Sidebar* 109: 135.

De Genova, Nicholas. 2010. The Deportation Regime: Sovereignty, Space and the Freedom of Movement. Pp. 33–68. In *The Deportation Regime: Sovereignty, Space, and the Freedom of Movement*, eds. Nicholas de Genova and Nathalie Peutz. Durham: Duke University Press.

Duff, Antony. 2001. *Punishment, Communication and Community*. Oxford: Oxford University Press.

EU Lex. 2018. EU Directives. EU Lex, Access to European Law. https://eur-lex .europa.eu/legal-content/EN/TXT/?uri=LEGISSUM%3Al14527 (accessed December 9, 2018).

European Commission. 2015a. "Communication from the Commission to the European Parliament, the Council, the European Economic and Social Committee and the Committee on the Regions: A European Agenda on Migration." *European Commission, Brussels*, 13.5. 2015 COM (2015) 240 final.

European Commission. 2015. Hotspot Approach. https://ec.europa.eu/ home-affairs/sites/homeaffairs/files/what-we-do/policies/european-agen da-migration/background-information/docs/2_hotspots_en.pdf (accessed January 1, 2019.)

European Commission. 2015a. Fact Sheet. Questions and Answers on the European Agenda on Migration. Brussels May 13, 2015. https://europa.eu/rapid/press-release_MEMO-15-4957_en.htm (accessed August 28, 2019).

European Commission. 2018. A Strengthened and Fully Equipped European Border and Coast Guard. September 12, 2018.

European Commission. 2018a. State of the Union 2018: Commission Proposes Last Elements Needed for Compromise on Migration and Border Reform. Strasbourg, September 12. Press Release.

European Commission. 2018b. Proposal for a Directive of the European Parliament and of the Council on Common Standards and Procedures in Member States for Returning Illegally Staying Third-Country Nationals (Recast). European Commission, Salzburg on September 19–20, 2018. Brussels, 12.9.2018 COM (2018) 634 final.

European Commission. 2020. The EU Facility for Refugees in Turkey. https://ec.europa.eu/neighbourhood-enlargement/sites/near/files/frit_fact sheet.pdf.

European Parliamentary Research Service. 2019. Priority 8: Toward a New Policy on Migration. European Parliament.

European Union. 2008. Directive 2008/115/EC of the European Parliament and of the Council, December 16, 2008, on Common Standards and Procedures in Member States for Returning Illegally Staying Third-Country Nationals. *Official Journal of the European Union.*

Eurostat. 2018. Statistics on Enforcement of Immigration Legislation. https://ec .europa.eu/eurostat/statistics-explained/index.php?title=Enforcement_ of_immigration_legislation_statistics.

Fleury-Steiner, Benjamin, and Jamie Longazel. 2016. "The Pains of Immigrant Imprisonment." *Sociology Compass* 10: 989–998.

Flyvbjerg, Bent. 2011. Case Study. In *The Sage Handbook of Qualitative Research*, edited by Norman K. Denzin and Yvonne S. Lincoln. Thousand Oaks, CA: Sage.

Franko, Katja. 2020. *The Crimmigrant Other: Migration and Penal Power*, 1st ed. Abingdon: Routledge.

Garland, David. 2001. *The Culture of Control: Crime and Social Order in Contemporary Society*. Chicago: University of Chicago Press.

Global Detention Project. www.globaldetentionproject.org (accessed December 9, 2018).

Halliday, Terence, and Gregory Shaffer. 2015a. Transnational Legal Orders. Pp. 3–72. In *Transnational Legal Orders*, edited by Terence Halliday and Gregory Shaffer. Cambridge: Cambridge University Press.

Halliday, Terence, and Gregory Shaffer. 2015b. Researching Transnational Legal Orders. Pp. 475–528. In *Transnational Legal Orders*, edited by Terence Halliday and Gregory Shaffer. Cambridge: Cambridge University Press.

Heinsen, Johan. 2018. The Scandinavian Empires in the Seventeenth and Eighteenth Centuries. Pp. 97–122. In *Global History of Convicts and Penal Colonies*, edited by Clare Anderson. London: Bloomsbury.

Leutert, Stephanie, Ellie Ezzel, Savitri Arvey, Gabriella Sanchez, Caitlyn Yates, and Paul Kuhne. 2018. Asylum Processing and Waitlists: At the US-Mexico Border. Migration Policy Center, European University Institute. www.migrationpolicycentre.eu/new-report-asylum-processing-and-waitlists-at-the-us-mexico-border (accessed February 6, 2019).

Loyd, Jenna M., and Alison Mountz. 2018. *Boats, Borders and Bases: Race, the Cold War, and the Rise of Migration Detention in the United States*. Berkeley: University of California Press.

Manieri, Maria Giovanna. 2018. Current Trends, Numbers and Routes in EU Migration: Is Existing Law Creating Irregularity? Committee of Civil Liberties, Justice and Home Affairs, European Parliament. Presentation at

Managing Migration through Criminal Law Tools meeting. December 3–4, University of Milano.

Medecins sans Frontiers. n.d. Mediterranean Search and Rescue. www.msf.org.uk/country/mediterranean-search-and-rescue.

Mitsilegas, Valsamis. 2015. *The Criminalisation of Migration in Europe: Challenges for Human Rights and the Rule of Law.* London: Springer.

NATO. 2016. NATO's Deployment in the Aegean Sea: Fact Sheet. www.nato.int/nato_static_fl2014/assets/pdf/pdf_2016_07/20160627_1607-fact sheet-aegean-sea-eng.pdf (accessed February 6, 2019).

Rajah, Jothie. 2015. "Rule of Law" as Transnational Legal Order. Pp. 340–373 in *Transnational Legal Orders*, edited by Terence Halliday and Gregory Shaffer. Cambridge: Cambridge University Press.

Sanchez, Gabriella. 2016. *Human Smuggling and Border Crossing.* Abingdon: Routledge.

Scharff Smith, Peter. 2008. "Solitary Confinement: An Introduction to the Istanbul Statement on the Uses and Effects of Solitary Confinement." *Torture Volume* 18(1): 56–62.

Statewatch. 2018. Dangerous Link between Migration, Development and Security for the Externalization of Borders in Africa: Case Studies on Sudan, Niger, and Tunisia. www.statewatch.org/news/2018/jul/report-frontiere-2018-english-.pdf?utm_source=ECRE+Newsletters&utm_campaign=b7215dda50-EMAIL_CAMPAIGN_2018_08_06_12_37&utm_medium=email&utm_term=0_3ec9497afd-b7215dda50-422285469.

Stumpf, Juliet. 2006. "The Crimmigration Crisis: Immigration, Crime and Sovereign Power." *American University Law Review* 52(2): 367–419.

United Nations Human Rights Council [UNHRC], n.d. Rescue at Sea. www.unhcr.org/4ef3002c9.pdf (accessed February 6, 2019).

van der Woude, Maartje, Johanna van der Leun, and JA Nijland. 2014. "Crimmigration in the Netherlands." *Law and Social Inquiry* 39: 560–579.

van Zyl Smit, Dirk, and Sonja Snacken 2009. *The Principles of European Prison Law and Policy: Penology and Human Rights.* Oxford: Oxford University Press.

Weber, Leanne, and Sharon Pickering. 2011. *Globalization and Borders: Death at the Global Frontier.* London: Palgrave.

Media Sources on the Diciotti Italian Coast Guard Ship

https://edition.cnn.com/ 2018/08/21/europe/diciotti-italy-coast-guard-ship-migrants-standoff-intl/index.html

www.theguardian.com/world/ 2018/aug/25/matteo-salvini-formally-investiga
   ted-over-migrant-ship-standoff
www.thelocal.se/20180822/sweden-turns-down-migrants-docked-in-italy
www.gppi.net/fileadmin/user_upload/media/pub/ 2017/GPPi_DRC_RMM
   S_2017_Protection_Fallout.pdf

CHAPTER SIX

THE STRANGE CAREER OF THE TRANSNATIONAL LEGAL ORDER OF CANNABIS PROHIBITION

Ely Aaronson

There is a crack in everything – that's how the light gets in Leonard Cohen, "Anthem"

6.1 INTRODUCTION

With its roots in international treaties signed during the League of Nations era, the transnational legal order (TLO) of cannabis prohibition represents one of the most sustained efforts to develop internationally applicable standards for criminalizing human behavior. The vast majority of United Nations member states have ratified the three major international drug conventions, which require criminalizing the production, distribution, and use of cannabis. Over the past decades, this TLO has encompassed an extensive array of legal instruments for monitoring national legislative efforts, disseminating information on the activities of drug trafficking networks, and facilitating cooperation among national police forces. However, despite the extensive institutionalization of this TLO, cannabis remains the most widely used illegal drug in the world. The 2018 World Drug Report estimates that at least 192 million people aged 15–64 had used cannabis in the preceding year (UNODC 2018: 43). With the percentage of adults reporting cannabis use in North American and European countries far exceeding the international average, cannabis use has become "a normal part of the leisure-pleasure landscape" (Parker et al. 1995: 25).

In an era that is often characterized as one of a growing isomorphism of the laws governing criminal activities in different countries (Jakobi 2013), the issue-area of cannabis policy has undergone processes of fragmentation and polarization (Bewley-Taylor 2012; Chatwin 2017). Some countries continue to criminalize all forms of medical and recreational uses of cannabis. Others have sought to "separate the market" for cannabis from that of other drugs by de-penalizing, decriminalizing, or legalizing particular forms of cultivating, selling, and consuming cannabis for medical and recreational purposes (Caulkins et al. 2016; Room et al. 2010). These reforms have gained international momentum despite resistance from key actors in the international drug control system, including the International Narcotic Control Board (INCB) and the US federal government (Bewley-Taylor 2012: chapter 5). Drug policy scholars often portray the trend toward liberalizing cannabis policies as a catalyst for the collapse of broader ideological and institutional tenets of the international narcotic control system (Blickman 2018).

How deep is the current crisis of the cannabis prohibition TLO? What are its causes and consequences? How does it differ from earlier crises? What does this case study reveal about the conditions under which criminal justice TLOs rise and fall? This chapter explores these questions by placing the current crisis of the prohibitionist ideology within a broad historical perspective and examining the complex ways in which the formation of cannabis policies has served as a battleground between competing conceptions of the role of criminal law in addressing social and medical harms. This chapter shows that the capacity of the cannabis prohibition TLO to regulate the practices of legal actors at the international, national, and local levels has been eroded as a result of effective contestations of the *input* and *output* legitimacy of its governance instruments. It investigates the ways in which this legitimation crisis have been triggered by four mechanisms of recursive transnational lawmaking (Halliday 2009): the indeterminacy of drug prohibition norms, the ideological contradictions between competing interpretations of their meaning, the impact of diagnostic struggles over the social issues that the international drug control system should address, and the mismatch between the actors shaping formal prohibition norms at the international level and those implementing these norms in national and local contexts. Our analysis then assesses the limits of current cannabis-liberalization reforms and the ways in which the institutionalization of the cannabis prohibition TLO has created path-dependent trajectories constraining the development of non-punitive strategies for regulating cannabis markets. In this context, I argue that it is too early to sound the death knell for the prohibitionist paradigm of cannabis policy. The dense array of UN treaties, transnational and regional monitoring schemes, national laws, and local enforcement arrangements put in place throughout the institutionalization of the cannabis prohibition TLO impedes efforts to initiate more progressive regulatory innovations in this field.

The chapter is organized as follows. Section 6.2 examines the historical formation of the international legal framework governing cannabis regulations. It also identifies the inherent ambiguities giving rise to interpretive disagreements regarding the scope of application of cannabis prohibition norms. Section 6.3 examines the debates that evolved during the 1960s–1970s regarding the criminological logic of cannabis prohibition policies. It then considers the processes leading to the reversal of the cannabis-liberalization reforms introduced in this era. Section 6.4 discusses the causes and consequences of the legitimation crisis that the cannabis prohibition TLO has experienced since the mid-1990s, as well as the global wave of depenalization, decriminalization, and legalization reforms precipitated by this crisis. Section 6.5 considers the implications of this reform movement on the development of cannabis regulations at the international, national, and local levels.

6.2 CANNABIS PROHIBITIONS IN INTERNATIONAL LAW

Up until the early twentieth century, cannabis was regarded as a legal substance that experienced periodic popularity as a medicine and was not widely used for recreational purposes. Debates about the relationship between cannabis and mental illness began to take place in scientific and medical circles during the nineteenth century, largely as a result of colonial encounters with traditional indigenous practices of using hemp and hashish (Abel 1980; Mills 2005; Shamir and Hacker 2001). However, these early debates did not gain much political salience; nor did they trigger the introduction of laws criminalizing the personal consumption of cannabis. Instead, these debates led national policy makers to include measures regulating the commercial trade of cannabis within wider frameworks governing the production and sale of pharmaceuticals. In the United States, the passage of the Pure Food and Drug Act of 1906 – which sought to regulate the sale of cannabis products as part of a wider framework of consumer protection laws governing adulterated and mislabeled food and drug products – signaled the dominant impact of this regulatory approach by the turn of the century (Musto 1999: 218–219). Over the next decades, however, this approach was swiftly replaced by a prohibitionist vision of cannabis policy. Inspired by the legislative inroads of the temperance movement, and expressing nativist sentiments toward Mexican migrants whose habits of marijuana smoking attracted considerable media attention, moral entrepreneurs in various US states mobilized public support for the introduction of penal restrictions on cannabis use (Bonnie and Whitebread 1974; Gieringer 1999). In 1915, California introduced the nation's first anti-marijuana criminal prohibition. Three decades later, such prohibitions appeared in the statute books of forty-six states and a series of marijuana-related federal offenses were included in the Marijuana Tax Act of 1937 (Andreas 2013: 268). This paradigm shift soon brought repercussions that extended well beyond the US borders.

The transnational legal ordering of cannabis regulations originated during the League of Nations era (Knepper 2011: chapter 5). An earlier international drug convention, signed at The Hague in 1912, focused on regulating opium, morphine, and cocaine, and did not include implementation mechanisms. The establishment of the League of Nations, and the appointment of its Advisory Council on Opium and Other Dangerous Drugs, provided a new institutional platform for creating transnational norms addressing drug issues (Pederson 2007: 1110). Before long, the Council was urged by countries that sought to apply stricter measures of policing cannabis trade (within and across borders) to include cannabis within the list of substances brought under international control (Kozma 2011). Although the United States was not a member of the League, it sent delegates to the Council's conferences and lobbied for the recognition of the "cannabis menace" as one of the priorities of the emerging international narcotic control system (Borougerdi 2018: 127–129). These efforts helped get cannabis included in the list of dangerous drugs covered by the 1925 International Opium Convention. They also stimulated the appointment of a subcommittee on cannabis soon thereafter. However, it is important to note that the 1925 Convention (as well as other policies developed under the auspices of the League of Nations) did not focus on formulating and propagating drug prohibition norms. Although the United States had strongly advocated the introduction of strict criminal prohibitions on the use and distribution of illicit drugs, this position was met with resistance from European colonial powers that had significant financial interests in the production of opium and coca and the manufacturing of their derivatives (McAllister 2002). The contours of the debate over cannabis prohibitions were shaped by this wider context of international conflict. Whereas the United States (collaborating with other countries such as Egypt and South Africa) pushed for the introduction of stricter international controls, Great Britain (which drew considerable revenue from taxing cannabis trade in India) opposed such proposals (Mills 2005: chapter 6). In the absence of an international consensus regarding the need to strengthen the criminal regulation of cannabis use, the pre-UN drug control framework focused on the development of administrative measures to govern cross-border commodity flows and to encourage a more effective domestic regulation of local drug markets (Ballotta 2008: 97).

Following the Second World War, the growing capacity of the United States to shape the rules and institutions of the international drug control system facilitated the move of the prohibitionist approach from the periphery to the center of the policy agenda (Bewley-Taylor 2002: 118–120). To a considerable extent, the institutionalization of the cannabis prohibition TLO provides a paradigmatic example of what has been usefully conceptualized as "globalized localism" – a process by which policy models that originated in the distinctive cultural and institutional contexts of a powerful country come to be perceived as global standards due to their inclusion in treaties, diagnostic indicators, interpretive guidelines, and other instruments of transnational legal diffusion (de-Santos 2002: 179). The introduction of the Single Convention on Narcotic Drugs in 1961 served as an important milestone in this process (Bewley-Taylor and Jelsma 2012; Boister 2001). The Convention frames the issue of drug use as a moral problem, stating in its preamble that "addiction to narcotic drugs constitutes a serious evil for the individual and is fraught with social and economic danger to mankind." In line with this moralizing framework, the Convention requires signatory countries to criminalize a wide range of drug-related activities. For example, Article 36 of the Single Convention reads:

> Subject to its constitutional limitations, each party shall adopt such measures as will ensure that cultivation, production, manufacture, extraction, preparation, possession, offering for sale, distribution, purchase, sale, delivery on any terms whatsoever, brokerage, dispatch, dispatch in transit, transport, importation and exportation of drugs contrary to the provisions of this Convention ... shall be punishable offences when committed intentionally.

The two subsequent UN drug conventions adopted in 1971 and in 1988 sought to extend the application of the prohibitionist approach to new contexts of drug regulation. Responding to the increasing production and use of synthetic drugs as part of the rise of the countercultural movements of the late 1960s, the 1971 Psychotropic Drug Treaty applied these policy principles to synthetic psychoactive drugs, such as opioids and amphetamine-type stimulants. The 1988 Convention against Illicit Traffic in Narcotic Drugs and Psychotropic Substances (the Vienna Convention) further expanded the array of criminal justice enforcement measures that states were required to adopt. However, it is important to note that the mandatory criminalization norms established by the UN drug conventions are defined in a manner that leaves two major sources of textual ambiguity regarding their scope of application. First, the conventions deliberately refrain from providing a definition of what constitutes medical and scientific uses of drugs. Second, they clarify that countries should implement the duty to criminalize drug-related activities in accordance with their domestic constitutional principles. As is often the case, these two provisions are products of efforts to paper over divergent policy preferences. During the negotiations of the Single Convention, several countries objected to banning certain drugs that have traditional and quasi-medical uses among indigenous populations. India, for example, expressed concerns regarding the implied need to criminalize traditional uses of *bhang*, which is made from cannabis leaves with a low tetrahydrocannabinol (TOC) content (Bewley-Taylor 2012: 190). Other countries emphasized the need to retain interpretive flexibility in light of the possibility that future research would reveal new medical benefits. The resulting compromise encouraged countries that would not have otherwise supported the prohibitionist principles set by the treaties to come on board. However, these compromises also sowed the seeds of later controversies regarding the ways in which cannabis prohibition norms should be applied. As the following discussion shows, these controversies set recursive processes of transnational legal change in motion, leading to the settling and unsettling of specific interpretations of the scope and meaning of cannabis prohibition norms.

6.3 INSTITUTIONALIZATION AND ITS DISCONTENTS: THE EARLY CRISIS OF THE CANNABIS PROHIBITION TLO

By an irony of history, the first decade following the introduction of the Single Convention experienced a marked increase in the prevalence of cannabis use in Western countries. When the Single Convention was signed in 1961, cannabis use was widespread in a cluster of countries where the plant was traditionally cultivated, while having little impact on mainstream leisure culture in North America and Europe. By the end of the decade, cannabis acquired unprecedented political salience not only in light of objective increases in the prevalence of its use but also due to its symbolic association with emerging countercultures and the perceived threat they putatively posed to public morality. These dramatic changes intensified the enforcement of cannabis offenses. In turn, these enforcement activities generated heightened public attention to the adverse consequences of prohibitionist drug control policies.

In the late 1960s, there was an historical increase in the rates of arrests, prosecutions, and convictions of cannabis users in various Western countries. The magnitude of this change was most remarkable in the United States. In California, for example, the number of people arrested for marijuana offenses increased from 5,156 in 1960 to 50, 327 in 1968 (Zimring and Hawkins 1992: 73). Arrests for cannabis possession became increasingly common in countries such as the United Kingdom, the Netherlands, Germany, and Canada as well (Ballotta 2008: 101; Mills 2013: chapter 6; Van Solinge 2017: 147). The civil rights implications of these increased levels of drug law enforcement generated vigorous public debate on the rationales of treating cannabis on par with other psychoactive substances that are widely perceived to be more dangerous and harmful (Frydl 2013: 350). Disagreements regarding whether cannabis should be classified under the strictest schedules of the UN drug control treaties were already evident during the Plenipotentiary Conference, which drafted the Single Convention. However, it was only in the wake of the increased enforcement of cannabis prohibitions in the late sixties that such disagreements precipitated potent forms of political and legal resistance. Due to increasing public criticism, national governments in several countries appointed public committees to consider the effectiveness of the existing laws. These committees directed strong criticism toward the criminological and medical underpinnings of the prohibitionist approach and called for the decriminalization of mild forms of cannabis use.

In Great Britain, the Advisory Committee on Drugs Dependence (Wootton Report), published in 1969, concluded:

> The long term consumption of cannabis in *moderate* doses has no harmful effects. . . . There is no evidence that this activity is causing violent

crime, or is producing in otherwise normal people conditions of dependence or psychosis requiring medical treatment. ... [T]here are indications that (cannabis) may become a functional equivalent of alcohol. ...
[P]ossession of a small amount of cannabis should not normally be
regarded as a serious crime to be punished by imprisonment.

(Home Office 1968)

Broadly similar conclusions were reached by other committees oper-
ating in the Netherlands (The Baan Commission 1970 and Hulsman
Commission 1971), Canada (The Commission of Inquiry into the
Nonmedical Use of Drugs, commonly referred to as the Le Dain
Commission 1973), and Australia (Senate Social Committee on
Social Welfare 1977). In the United States, the public debate that
followed President Nixon's famous identification of drug abuse as
"America's public enemy number one" led to the nomination of the
National Commission on Marihuana and Drug Abuse (the Shafer
Commission). To the surprise of many, the Commission's 1972
Report, entitled *Marihuana: A Signal of Misunderstanding*, concurred
with the liberal approach endorsed by other national investigation
committees. While the Commission emphasized that cannabis was
not a harmless substance, it stressed that its dangers had often been
overstated. The Report recommended repealing the criminal prohibitions on the possession of small amounts of marijuana and establishing
alternative measures to address the public health concerns associated
with cannabis use. Such reforms, the Commission stated, are needed to
relieve "the law enforcement community of the responsibility for enforcing a law of questionable utility, and one which they cannot fully
enforce" (National Commission on Marijuana and Drug Abuse 1972:
150). These recommendations were repudiated by the Nixon administration. However, they provided considerable momentum to the effort
of grassroots activists to bring about cannabis liberalization reforms at
the state and local levels. In 1973, Oregon became the first state that
decriminalized the possession of small amounts (28.35 grams) of marijuana. Eleven states followed suit during the next half of the decade
(Dufton 2017: 69–70; DiChiara and Galliher 1994).

The failure of the US national administration to secure the compliance of state governments with the prohibitionist norms it sought to
propagate internationally provided a clear indication of the decline of
the cannabis prohibition TLO. However, instead of precipitating the
rise of new models of liberalizing cannabis policy, this early crisis gave
rise to new cycles of recursive transnational lawmaking leading to the

entrenchment of the prohibitionist approach. In the United States, calls to reintroduce tougher drug laws resonated with the wider conservative offensive against the putative "soft on crime" inclinations of liberal policy makers in the post–civil rights era (Beckett 1999). Opponents of legalization sought to challenge the *public health frame* that gained increasing influence in the wake of the Shafer Commission's Report and to contextualize the issue of cannabis use as yet another symptom of a putative law and order crisis in American cities. The proliferation of grassroots movements lobbying for the stricter regulation of marijuana provided considerable political momentum for the introduction of tougher penalties for trafficking and possession offenses (Dufton 2017: chapter 8).

The process by which cannabis prohibition norms again became settled at the national level in the United States provided facilitative conditions for the increasing involvement of the federal government in exporting its drug policies to other countries. This effort became increasingly consequential in an historical moment in which the United States came to perceive itself "not just as a powerful state operating in a world of anarchy" but as "a producer of world order" (Ikenberry 2005: 133). With the end of the Cold War, new discourses of "securitization" emerged as part of the search for a new way of grounding America's internationalist engagement (McLeod 2010: 102–107). Drug policy became increasingly aligned with national security issues pertaining to the activities of insurgent and terrorist groups in Latin American countries and to the risks posed by these groups to the democratic stability and peace in the region (Stokes 2005). This new frame of diagnosing the implications of the illegal drug trade led to the development of new modes of defining the goals of US counternarcotic policies, as well as the strategies through which such goals should be pursued. These new strategies have sought to reduce drug production at the source, combat drug trafficking *en route* to US borders, dismantle international illicit drug networks, reduce drug demand at home and abroad, and incentivize foreign governments to cooperate with US counternarcotic goals.

From the mid-1980s onward, the US government institutionalized an array of multilateral, bilateral, and unilateral measures intended to coerce, induce, and socialize other countries to cooperate with its counternarcotic strategies (McLeod 2010). Its multilateral efforts have largely been based on the extensive funding and support of international and regional organizations that are committed to the

prohibitionist approach. In this context, the United States has consistently pushed for an expansion of the International Narcotic Control
Board's monitoring authority and has served as a staunch defender of its
prohibitionist policies (Bewley-Taylor 2012: 272). The United States
has also made extensive use of bilateral treaties to create an issue-
linkage between states' willingness to adopt zero-tolerance models of
drug policy and their eligibility for foreign aid. Over the next decades,
such bilateral agreements provided a basis for the operation of extensive
cooperation and capacity-building projects in countries as diverse as
Afghanistan, Colombia, Mexico, Nigeria, Peru, Ghana, Thailand, and
many others. Along with these multilateral and bilateral instruments,
the US government has made extensive reliance on unilateral tools to
influence the drug policies of other countries (Arnold 2004: 87–98). In
1986, Congress introduced the Omnibus Drug Enforcement,
Education, and Control Act, which created a certification process for
drug-producing and drug-transit countries. The certification process
requires the president to withdraw financial assistance and support to
multilateral lending institutions from countries that fail to comply with
requisite benchmarks of anti-drug policy. To enable congressional
deliberations over such sanctions, the US Department of State submits
an annual International Narcotic Control Strategy Report (INCSR)
that identifies the major illicit drug-producing and drug-transit countries and evaluates the extent to which their domestic policies comply
with the US counternarcotic agenda. The INCSR explores a wide
range of countries (e.g., seventy countries in the 2018 report). The
certification process applies to countries known as the "majors list"
(which included twenty-two countries in 2018; US Department of
State 2018).

The success of the United States to coerce and induce dozens of
countries to adhere to a prohibitionist stance promoted the convergence of drug laws across jurisdictions and thus increased the degree of
concordance between the transnational and the national levels of this
TLO. However, the global diffusion of tougher cannabis laws throughout the 1980s and 1990s cannot be sufficiently explained by focusing on
the coercive mechanisms employed by the United States alone. Our
analysis must also consider the role played by domestic legal actors
shaping the reception of these prohibition norms in national and
subnational settings (Shaffer 2013: 41). As the contributions to this
book demonstrate, the *crime frame* provides legislatures and criminal
justice bureaucracies with an effective tool of scoring political points

and mobilizing institutional resources (Chapter 1 this volume; see also Simon 2007). In the issue area of drug policy, these gains are largely associated with the capacity of anti-drug crusades to serve as vehicles for constructing "suitable enemies" (Christie 1986) and enlisting support for drastic measures of social control (Alexander 2012; Baum 1997). The international spread of cannabis prohibitions during the final decades of the twentieth century was part and parcel of global currents leading to the adoption of "zero tolerance" punitive policies in various areas of public policy (Garland 2001). In an era during which a broader shift from welfare-oriented to punitive-focused approaches to governing social marginality took place (Wacquant 2009), strengthening state capacities to penalize drug dealers and users proved to be a far more attractive project for politicians than addressing the public health implications of drug use (Friedrichs 2007: chapter 7; Mills 2013: chapter 7).

The institutionalization of the cannabis prohibition TLO was also promoted by international bureaucracies operating in the issue-area of drug control. As the primary international organization responsible for monitoring the implementation of the UN drug conventions, the INCB played an important role in facilitating the concordance between the transnational and national levels of the cannabis prohibition TLO. In particular, the Board used its annual reports as a tool of naming and shaming national governments whose drug policies do not conform to prohibitionist standards (Bewley-Taylor 2012: chapter 5; Friman 2015b). This naming and shaming project has relied on the extensive participation of domestic governmental officials and nongovernmental actors who helped diagnose national trends in drug use, monitor legislative developments and enforcement efforts, and translate the Board's policy prescription into local vernaculars. In turn, this project has served to produce the legitimacy and credibility of prohibitionist policy prescriptions. The INCB has repeatedly supported the "gateway drug thesis," which states that cannabis use increases the user's probability of using harder illicit substances, such as amphetamines, cocaine, or heroin. Based on this thesis (whose scientific validity was and remains controversial; Buxton 2006: 110–111), the 1983 Report criticized those "circles in certain countries" that "apparently assume that to permit unrestricted use of some drug, regarded by them as less harmful, would permit better control of other drugs which they deem more perilous to health" (International Narcotic Control Board 1983: 2). This criticism was leveled at supporters of the *separation of markets* strategy, which came to be endorsed by Dutch policy makers at the time (Van Vilet 1990: 463). In its later reports throughout the 1980s and 1990s, the INCB adopted an increasingly critical stance toward the Dutch attempts to de-penalize cannabis usage. In its 1997 Report, the selling of cannabis in coffee shops was depicted as "an activity that might be described as indirect incitement" (INCB 1997: 6). The predominant focus on the Netherlands reflected the limited degree to which prohibitionist imperatives had faced open contestations during that period.

6.4   THE LEGITIMATION CRISIS AND ITS CONSEQUENCES

The extensive institutionalization of the cannabis prohibition TLO throughout the 1980s and 1990s facilitated the international spread of tougher laws, severer penalties, and more aggressive policing strategies. However, the very success of this effort to promote the global diffusion of prohibitionist policy models highlighted their failure to reduce the prevalence of cannabis use and to eliminate its illicit supply chains. The intensification of enforcement activities also brought into focus the adverse social consequences of implementing the prohibitionist agenda of cannabis regulation. The increasing criticisms of the failures and boomerang effects of the cannabis prohibition TLO prompted both internal and external processes that eroded its legitimacy and compromised its ability to continue guiding the practices of legal actors at the national and local levels.

From the early stages of the institutionalization of the cannabis prohibition TLO, it became vulnerable to criticism of its inherent *input legitimacy* deficiencies. As discussed earlier, the central role played by the United States in shaping the goals and strategies of this TLO has largely depended on the exercise of unilateral measures of coercion and inducement. The degree to which the *certification process* has realized basic standards of transparency, inclusiveness, and accountability is conspicuously limited. The procedures by which the INCB defines and applies its compliance criteria are insulated from ongoing public debates regarding the impact of cannabis prohibition laws on marginalized populations. These legitimacy deficits are conveniently set aside by proponents of the war on drugs, who tend to focus more on the ability of these measures to promote global public goods than on the quality of the processes through which these measures are created. As

Niko Krisch observes, such tendency to prioritize *output legitimacy* considerations is pronounced in various contexts of global governance and often produces pressure to move toward more informal and hier-archical modes of transnational legal ordering (Krisch 2014). However, in the context of cannabis policy, it has become increasingly difficult to use *output legitimacy* justifications given the mounting evidence on the failure of this TLO to achieve its stated goals. Despite the investment of billions of dollars and extensive law enforcement resources, a sizable body of scholarship has documented the growing availability of canna-bis during the 1990s, the widespread prevalence of its usage among adolescents, and the increasingly tolerant attitudes toward cannabis consumption among both users and non-users (Baum 1997; Parker et al. 1998; Reuter 2003).

Drawing analogies to the failure of the "Noble Experiment" of the alcohol prohibition period (Levine and Reinarman 2006), criminolo-gists developed thorough critiques of the underlying assumptions of the cannabis prohibition TLO. The assumption that the availability of cannabis can be meaningfully reduced by the deployment of militarized policing strategies (such as the aerial spraying of crops) has been criticized for overlooking the resilience of cannabis markets and their high levels of adaptability to changes in their regulatory environments (Potter et al. 2011). Studies have shown that rather than eliminating supply chains, such interventions served to disperse, displace, and fragment supply sources and distribution routes (Bowling 2010). In turn, such interventions precipitated a spillover of armed violence to new geographical areas and exposed otherwise uninvolved indigenous populations to new risks and insecurities (Bowling and Sheptycki 2012: 118–120; Klantchnig 2013: 55). The inherent flaws of these policies are often illustrated by referencing the "balloon effect" metaphor, depict-ing the ways in which efforts to suppress the cultivation of cannabis in one geographical area causes a shift of its production elsewhere (Buxton 2006: 107).

The legitimacy of the cannabis prohibition TLO has also been damaged by evidence regarding the immense human rights violations associated with the implementation of the war on drugs. Advocacy networks led by prominent transnational NGOs, such as Amnesty International and Human Rights Watch, have exposed the dispropor-tionate punishments imposed under the banner of the war on drugs in various countries. In the United States, such criticism focused on the contribution of marijuana prohibitions to the nation's internationally unparalleled incarceration rates and its distinctive patterns of racially-skewed law enforcement (Alexander 2012; Provine 2007). A 2013 ACLU report using data extracted from the FBI's Uniform Crime Reporting Program indicates that between 2001 and 2010, there were more than eight million marijuana arrests in the United States, of which 88 percent were for marijuana possession (ACLU 2013). In 2010, there were more than 20,000 people incarcerated for the sole charge of cannabis possession. Outside of the United States, human rights activists focused on the increasing use of capital punishments for drug offenses from the late 1980s onward as part of the broader escalation of enforcement efforts during the war on drugs era (Lines 2017: 87). The exportation and importation of illegal drugs constitute capital offenses in more than 30 countries. In China, Saudi Arabia, and the Philippines, the death penalty is exercised regularly for cannabis trafficking offenses (Sander and Lines 2018).

By the mid-1990s, the criticism leveled at the cannabis prohibition TLO began to stimulate increasing advocacy activity in favor of reform. These activities failed to initiate a paradigm shift at the international level. As Robin Room and Peter Reuter observed in 2012, "the effects of civil society organisations in the drug control system have been much less than in other areas of public health ... people in the official policy community – i.e., on national delegations to the Commission on Narcotic Drugs, or in international bureaucratic positions – have a vested commitment to the existing system and have kept civil society at bay" (Room and Reuter 2012: 85). Indeed, the "outcome document" issued in the wake of the 2016 UN General Assembly Special Session on drugs kept in place the existing framework of cannabis prohibition and did not endorse the calls to reclassify cannabis as a less dangerous drug. However, the criticism of the prohibitionist approach had a considerable transformative impact on the development of drug policies at the national and subnational levels. Before long, the diffusion of liberal cannabis policies across national borders began to jeopardize the normative settlements institutionalized by the cannabis prohibition TLO in previous decades.

The efforts to liberalize cannabis regulations have focused on three distinct models of reform: depenalization, decriminalization, and legalization. Under formal depenalization regimes, the possession of cannabis is still formally prohibited; however, such prohibitions are enforced through intermediate justice measures rather than through conventional penal sanctions such as incarceration. The Netherlands pioneered the experimentation with depenalization strategies in 1976 when it formalized the use of the *expediency principle* to guide the enforcement of drug prohibitions. Based on this principle, Dutch prosecutors are instructed not to bring charges when cannabis use offenses take place within the user's home or within the so-called *coffee shops*, where cannabis can be openly consumed and purchased (Van Solinge 2017). From the 1990s onward, many national and subnational jurisdictions introduced *cautioning* and *diversion schemes* to deal with drug use offenses (Bewley-Taylor 2012: 167–173). Cautioning schemes authorize police officers to avoid arresting suspected drug offenders under certain circumstances. Instead, they require them to issue a written warning of the possible consequences of the illegal behavior. Diversion schemes, which may operate at the pre-trial, pre-sentence, or post-conviction stages of the legal process, are intended to shift offenders from the criminal justice system and its carceral institutions to other channels of intervention, such as treatment or education. When applied before the sentencing stage, such measures may require the offender to participate in certain treatment and education programs as part of the bail conditions. After the sentencing stage, diversion measures may subject a convicted offender to community-based or rehabilitative measures (e.g., community service and therapeutic programs).

The widespread transnational diffusion of depenalization regimes is enabled by the structural mismatch between the actors shaping the formal rules of the international drug control system and those implementing these rules in national and local contexts (Halliday 2009). The diffusion of these regimes was not supported by international organizations or powerful countries. Rather, it has evolved through uncoordinated processes of institutional isomorphism, reflecting converging professional concerns regarding the complexities of implementing criminal prohibitions that are extensively violated by ordinary citizens and that do not reflect widespread social disapprobation of the targeted activity. From the perspectives of ground-level enforcement officials and more senior bureaucratic elites, the implementation of cannabis prohibitions raised pragmatic concerns regarding the limited effectiveness of conventional penal measures and the immense costs that such efforts entailed.

In democratic systems committed to the principle of legality, it seems natural to suppose that schemes of depenalization would translate into de jure changes in the statutory definitions governing processes of criminalization. The international drug conventions place constraints on the ability of national legislatures to introduce such reforms. However, the treaties also contain textual ambiguities that provide leeway for negotiating the ambit of such prohibitions. The rise of the medical cannabis movement provides a powerful illustration of how such processes of normative contestation unfold. The movement began to gain ground in the early 1990s, focusing its efforts on promoting ballot initiatives at the municipal and state levels in the United States (Dufton 2017: chapter 12; Hannah and Mallinson 2018). Within the next two decades, it effectively initiated the enactment of laws decriminalizing the medical use of marijuana in thirty-one states across the United States and inspired entrepreneurs in dozens of other countries to campaign for the adoption of similar models. Countries adopting medical cannabis laws utilize the latitude allowed by the UN drug conventions regarding the definition of the term "medical and scientific purposes." Importantly, they challenge the powerful view (which has long been defended by the US federal government and the INCB) that marijuana has no demonstrated medical use. In this regard, the medical cannabis movement demonstrates the extent to which local practices of grassroots mobilization can trigger effective contestations of the prohibition norms produced by powerful global actors (Halliday and Shaffer 2015: 58).

Building on the successes of the medical marijuana reform movement, advocacy networks in various countries have campaigned for the enactment of more radical models of decriminalizing and legalizing the recreational use of cannabis. The seeds of this development were sown in the 1990s when European countries increased the thresholds of the amounts of cannabis possession exempted from criminal responsibility. Portugal, for example, adopted threshold parameters based on "the quantity required for an average individual consumption during a period of ten days" (Bewley-Taylor 2012: 157). Whereas Portugal adopted this policy as part of a comprehensive redesign of its drug laws based on harm reduction principles (Hughes and Stevens 2010), in other countries, these steps toward legalizing cannabis use were stimulated by court rulings reviewing the constitutionality of cannabis prohibitions. For example, in Argentina, the Supreme Court struck down Article 14 of the country's drug control legislation, which punished the possession of small amounts of cannabis with prison sentences ranging from one month to two years. In the *Arriola* case,[1] the Court stated that

---

[1] Arriola, Sebastian y otros, 9080 (Supreme Court of Argentina, August 25, 2009).

the possession of cannabis is protected by Article 19 of Argentina's constitution, which states that "private actions that in no way offend public order or morality, nor are detrimental to a third party, are reserved for God and are beyond the authority of legislators." Recent developments in Canada and nine US states signify the growing momentum of the trend toward the legalization of recreational uses of cannabis and the development of more complex regulatory models to govern legal cannabis markets (Kamin 2017). In different ways, these jurisdictions grant licenses to professional farmers and pharmacies to produce and sell cannabis commercially and exempt individuals from criminal responsibility for non-commercial uses (Pardo 2014; Room 2013).

The trend toward liberalizing cannabis prohibitions illustrates the recursive nature of transnational processes of legal change. The networks of actors participating in these processes – composed of grassroots activists, legislatures, bureaucratic elites, criminal justice actors, scientists, journalists, and public health officials – created new regulatory models that gradually transformed the application of cannabis prohibition norms in various jurisdictions. These actors invoked the indeterminacy of treaty provisions and highlighted the diverse ways in which the enforcement of criminal prohibitions produces social harms that are severer than those generated by cannabis use. They also utilized the space for norm-making provided by the mismatch between the institutions and actors that formulate global norms and those assigned with the actual implementation of these norms in national and sub-national settings. The success of these campaigns warrants a reflection on the conditions under which (and the extent to which) local and national acts of contesting TLOs can reshape the agenda of global actors invested in preserving the current normative settlements. The following section focuses on this question.

6.5   AFTER THE WAR ON DRUGS?

The rapid and widespread transnational diffusion of new models of decriminalizing, de-penalizing, or legalizing the use of marijuana serves as a product and catalyst of the declining capacity of the cannabis prohibition TLO to shape the policy choices of criminal lawmakers and the routine practices of enforcement officials. However, to what extent do these reforms change the agendas of the global actors that play key roles in shaping the normative and institutional structures of this TLO?

Faced with the global spread of cannabis liberalization reforms, the INCB has positioned itself as the most steadfast defender of the normative expectancies of the cannabis prohibition TLO (Bewley-Taylor 2012: chapter 5). In its annual reports, the Board contested the legitimacy of the legal interpretations underpinning states' engagement with decriminalization, depenalization, and legalization initiatives (Friman 2015b). The Board repeatedly expressed its concern that the introduction of civil sanctions for possession offenses was sending the wrong signal and was underplaying the health risks of marijuana use (INCB 2000: 56). It criticized medical cannabis reforms and questioned the scientific basis on which they are premised (INCB 2013: 66). Most recently, the Board condemned Uruguay and Canada for adopting legalization schemes, stating that such reforms constituted clear breaches of the international conventions (INCB 2018: 74).

The literature examining the roles of naming and shaming mechanisms in international politics observes that most countries are inclined to bring their laws into formal compliance with international standards to avoid being stigmatized as "deviant states" (Hafner-Burton and Tsutsui 2005). The efforts of the INCB to achieve such influence by condemning countries deviating from the prohibitionist expectancies of the international drug conventions failed to generate such adaptive responses (Friman 2015b). Some countries have practically ignored the Board's proposed interpretation of the international obligations set by the conventions. Others have argued that the Board's interpretive approach was too narrow and relied on selective use of the available evidence concerning the medical uses of cannabis. Still others contended that the Board was exceeding its mandate when it adopted a hostile stance toward legitimate policy choices of sovereign states (Bewley-Taylor 2012: 248). To a considerable extent, the limited impact of the Board's naming and shaming strategy reflects its failure to mobilize domestic actors who participate in the construction of national drug policies to serve as "carriers, conduits, and points of entry" (Shaffer 2013: 41) for the circulation of its prohibitionist scripts. This failure is largely the product of the legitimacy deficits suffered by the Board as a result of its relative silence on the human rights abuses inflicted in the name of the war on drugs. Proponents of depenalization, decriminalization and legalization policies have effectively framed these reforms as intended to bring drug policy into fuller conformity with fundamental human rights values as well as with human development concerns (Bone and Seddon 2016). The heavy involvement of the INCB in promoting the global war on drugs damages its ability to reach out to local audiences while criticizing policy initiatives that destabilize the settled meanings of cannabis prohibition norms.

Whereas the INCB has remained unambiguously committed to the task of defending the normative settlements of the cannabis prohibition TLO, the approach taken by the United States has been marked by ambivalence (Kamin 2017). President Barack Obama's administration adopted the ambiguous position of respecting the decisions of US states legalizing the medical and recreational use of marijuana while continuing to condemn steps toward legalization in Latin American and Caribbean countries. Responding to shifts in national public opinion, the administration set out lenient guidelines for the federal prosecution of marijuana users in states that had legalized its medical and recreational uses (Chemerinsky et al. 2015). It thereby allowed legalized drug markets to take root in Colorado and Washington and subsequently in other states. Like other national governments, the US federal government invoked its domestic constitutional principles (particularly the principles governing the distribution of legislative power within the US federal system) to argue that its policies comply with the international standards (Tackeff 2018). However, during the same period, the United States continued to apply its strict punitive approach to evaluating the compliance of other countries with the UN drug conventions. The International Narcotic Control Strategy Report continues to include assessments of the extent to which "drug majors" satisfy crop eradication targets and impose tough penalties on drug offenders. With a majority of Americans supporting the legalization of marijuana and a majority of US states already implementing decriminalization schemes for medical marijuana, lawmakers in the House and Senate are facing increasing pressure to end the federal ban on cannabis. It is too early to predict whether and when such a change will take place or how it will impact the federal government's foreign policy stance on the issue of cannabis legalization. However, as long as the United States adheres to this "do as I say, not as I do" message, its ambivalent posture allows national and local lawmakers to adopt reform measures that effectively unsettle the meaning of cannabis prohibition norms.

Nevertheless, it is important to note that despite its declining regulatory effectiveness, the cannabis prohibition TLO continues to exert considerable influence on the development of drug policies at the international, regional, national, and local levels. In this context, it is notable that countries that have liberalized their cannabis laws emphasize their commitment to remain bound by the confines of the current treaty regimes of the international drug control system. The widespread recognition of the severe failures and counterproductive effects of the cannabis prohibition TLO has not generated viable political efforts to amend the international treaties underpinning its operation. The precedent set by Bolivia – which withdrew from the Single Convention in protest of the classification of coca leaves as an illegal drug and re-acceded to the treaty with reservations on the issue of coca chewing – was not followed by countries supporting the legalization of cannabis. Nor did we see efforts to improve the capacity of this TLO to adapt to changes in scientific knowledge and social attitudes concerning cannabis by introducing into the treaties flexibility mechanisms that would allow pro-legalization countries to promote a new normative settlement (Bewley-Taylor and Fitzmaurice 2018; Helfer 2013). The reluctance to renegotiate the treaty norms governing cannabis policies largely stems from the embedding of the cannabis prohibition TLO within the mega-TLO of the international narcotic control system. By institutionalizing linkages between the international norms applying to cannabis and those governing other narcotic substances, the UN drug conventions deter those countries that oppose the prohibitionist approach from promoting treaty reform initiatives that might destabilize the relatively settled norms prevailing in other contexts of drug policy (e.g., the norms governing the regulation of illicit markets of heroin, cocaine, and synthetic opiates). The fact that these conventions regulate the global trade of both the illicit and licit uses of drugs, including substances on the World Health Organization's list of essential medicines, further escalates the stakes of treaty reform initiatives. In addition, the reputational costs of defecting from UN crime suppression treaties might be higher than those suffered by persistent objectors in other areas of public international law. The branding of countries as pariah states, or "narco-states," as it were, carries a stigma that resonates with the censuring functions performed by criminal labels in domestic contexts (Simpson 2004).

These factors help explain why the current efforts to change the regulatory landscape governing cannabis markets are contained within the narrow space of policy experimentalism created by the textual ambiguity of the current treaties. However, as long as countries that embark on the path toward cannabis-liberalization reform fail to develop a strategy of breaking out of this straitjacket, many of the inherent shortcomings of the prohibitionist approach are likely to resurface (though in a more attenuated form) in the new regulatory landscapes governing the implementation of decriminalization, depenalization, and legalization schemes. The involvement of criminal organizations in illicit drug markets remains significant given the illegality of supply-related activities. The growing formalization of intermediate sanctions has a net-widening effect, which expands the use of control measures against low-risk drug offenders (Shiner 2015). Most fundamentally, the insistence on promoting drug liberalization reforms within the confines of the current system constrains the capacity of individual states and of the international community to imagine more effective and humane alternatives, such as those offered by harm-reduction and development-centered approaches.

6.6 CONCLUSION

Transnational legal orders both enable and constrain the development of new models of legal regulation. The enabling function of TLOs rests not only on the institutionalization of measures of negotiating, codifying, and implementing legal norms with a global reach, but also on their tendency to generate dynamics of resistance and contestation that are conducive to the development of new norms and institutional forms (Halliday and Shaffer 2015: 500–503). This chapter analyzed the ways in which such acts of norm-making have developed the issue of cannabis policy, emphasizing the role played by mechanisms of recursive legal change (including legal indeterminacy, diagnostic struggles, actor mismatch, and ideological contradictions) in shaping the forms and outcomes of reform initiatives. The discussion has also demonstrated that even when transnational legal orders undergo processes of fragmentation and polarization, they continue to constrain the capacity of reform advocates to generate new normative settlements. Mindful of Niels Bohr's advice that "prediction is very hard, particularly about the future," we conclude this chapter by hoping that a better understanding of how transnational legal orders facilitate and hinder recursive legal change can illuminate some of the possible trajectories for the future development of cannabis regulations.

REFERENCES

Abel, Ernest. 1980. *Marihuana: The First Twelve Thousand Years*. New York: Springer.

Alexander, Michele. 2012. *The New Jim Crow: Mass Incarceration in the Age of Colorblindness*. New York: The New Press.

American Civil Liberties Union (ACLU). 2013. *The War on Marijuana in Black and White*. www.aclu.org/sites/default/files/field_document/1114413-mj-report-rfs-rel1.pdf.

Andreas, Peter. 2013. *Smuggler Nation: How Illicit Trade Made America*. New York: Oxford University Press.

Andreas, Peter, and Ethan Nadelmann. 2006. *Policing the Globe: Criminalization and Crime Control in International Relations*. New York: Oxford University Press.

Arnold, Guy. 2004. *The International Drug Trade*. New York: Routledge.

Ballotta, Danilo, Henri Bergeron, and Brendan Hugher. 2008. Cannabis Control in Europe. Pp. 97–118 in *A Cannabis Reader: Global Issues and Local Experiences*, edited by Paul Griffiths. Lisbon: European Monitoring Center for Drugs and Drug Addiction.

Baum, Dan. 1997. *Smoke and Mirrors: The War on Drugs and the Politics of Failure*. Boston: Back Bay Books.

Beckett, Katherine. 1999. *Making Crime Pay: Law and Order in Contemporary American Politics*. New York: Oxford University Press.

Bender, Steven. 2016. "The Colors of Cannabis: Race and Marijuana." *UC Davis Law Review* 50: 689–706.

Bewley-Taylor, David. 2002. *The United States and International Drug Control, 1909–1997*. London: Bloomsbury.

Bewley-Taylor, David. 2012. *International Drug Control: Consensus Fractured*. New York: Cambridge University Press.

Bewley-Taylor, David, and Malgosia Fitzmaurice. 2018. "The Evolution and Modernization of Treaty Regimes: The Contrasting Cases of International Drug Control and Environmental Regulation." *International Community Law Review* 20(5): 403–435.

Bewley-Taylor, David, and Martin Jelsma. 2012. "Regime Change: Re-Visiting the 1961 Single Convention on Narcotic Drugs." *International Journal of Drug Policy* 23: 72–81.

Blickman, Tom. 2018. The Elephant in the Room: Cannabis in the International Drug Control Regime. Pp. 101–131 in *Collapse of the Global Order on Drugs: From UNGASS 2016 to Review 2019*, edited by Axel Klein and Blaine Stothard. Bingley: Emerald Publishing.

Boister, Neil. 2001. *Penal Aspects of the UN Drug Conventions*. Leiden: Brill.

Bone, Melissa, and Toby Seddon. 2016. "Human Rights, Public Health and Medicinal Cannabis Use." *Critical Public Health* 26: 51–61.

Bonnie, Richard, and Charles Whitebread II. 1974. *The Marihuana Conviction: A History of Marihuana Prohibition in the United States.* Charlottesville: University of Virginia Press.

Borougerdi, Bradley. 2018. *Commodifying Cannabis: A Cultural History of a Complex Plant in the Transatlantic World.* Cambridge: Harvard University Press.

Bowling, Ben. 2010. *Policing the Caribbean: Transnational Security Cooperation in Practice.* New York: Oxford University Press.

Bowling, Ben, and James Sheptycki. 2012. *Global Policing.* London: Sage.

Buxton, Julia. 2006. *The Political Economy of Narcotics: Production, Consumption, and Global Markets.* London: Zed.

Carrier, Neil, and Gernot Klantschnig. 2012. *Africa and the War on Drugs.* London: Zed Books.

Caulkins, Jonathan, Beau Kilmer, and Mark Kleiman. 2016. *Marijuana Legalization: What Everyone Needs to Know.* New York: Oxford University Press.

Chatwin, Caroline. 2015. "UNGASS 2016: Insights from Europe on the Development of Global Cannabis Policy and the Need for Reform of the Global Drug Policy Regime." *The International Journal of Drug Policy* 49: 80–85.

Chemerinsky, Erwin, Jolene Forman, Allen Hopper, and Sam Kamin. 2015. "Cooperative Federalism and Marijuana Regulation." *UCLA Law Review* 62: 74–122.

Christie, Nils. 1986. Suitable Enemies. Pp. 34–51 in *Abolitionism: Toward A Non-repressive Approach to Crime,* edited by Herman Bianchi and Rene von Swaaningen. Amsterdam: Free University Press.

Courtwright, David. 2002. *Forces of Habit: Drugs and the Making of the Modern World.* Cambridge: Harvard University Press.

De Santos, Boaventura. 2002. *Toward a New Legal Common Sense: Law, Globalization and Emancipation.* New York: Cambridge University Press.

DiChiara, Albert, and John F. Galiher. 1994. "Dissonance and Contradictions in the Origins of Marihuana Decriminalization." *Law and Society Review* 28 (1): 47–76.

Dufton, Emily. 2017. *Grass Roots: The Rise and Fall and Rise of Marijuana in America.* New York: Basic Books.

Efrat, Asif. 2012. *Governing Guns, Preventing Plunder: International Cooperation against Illicit Trade.* New York: Oxford University Press.

Friedrichs, Jörg. 2007. *Fighting Terrorism and Drugs: Europe and International Police Cooperation.* New York: Routledge.

Friman, Richard, ed. 2015a. *The Politics of Leverage in International Relations: Name, Shame, and Sanction.* Basingstoke: Palgrave Macmillan.

Friman, Richard. 2015b. Behind the Curtain: Naming and Shaming in International Drug Control. Pp. 143–164 in *The Politics of Leverage in*

International Relations: Name, Shame, and Sanction, edited by Richard Friman. Basingstoke: Palgrave Macmillan.

Frydl, Kathleen. 2013. *The Drug War in America, 1940–1973*. New York: Cambridge University Press.

Garland, David. 2001. *The Culture of Control: Crime and Social Order in Contemporary Society*. Chicago: The University of Chicago Press.

Gieringer, Dale. 1999. "The Forgotten Origins of Cannabis Prohibition in California." *Contemporary Drug Problems* 26(2): 237–288.

Hafner-Burton Emily, and Kiyotero Tsutsui. 2005. "Human Rights in a Globalizing World: The Paradox of Empty Promises." *American Journal of Sociology* 110: 1373–1411.

Halliday, Terence C. 2009. "Recursivity of Global Lawmaking: A Sociolegal Agenda." *Annual Review of Law and Social Science* 5: 263–290.

Halliday, Terrence, and Gregory Shaffer, eds. 2015. *Transnational Legal Orders*. New York: Cambridge University Press.

Hannah, A. Lee, and Daniel Mallinson. 2018. "Defiant Innovation: The Adoption of Medical Marijuana Laws in the American States." *Policy Studies Journal* 46(2): 402–423.

Helfer, Laurence. 2013. Flexibility in International Agreements. Pp. 175–196 in *International Perspectives on International Law and International Relations: The State of the Art*, eds. Jeffrey Dunoff and Mark Pollack. New York: Cambridge University Press.

Home Office. 1968. *Cannabis: Report by the Advisory Committee on Drug Dependence*.

International Narcotic Control Board. 1984. *Report of the International Narcotic Control Board for 1983*.

International Narcotic Control Board. 1998. *Report of the International Narcotic Control Board for 1997*.

International Narcotic Control Board. 2000. *Report of the International Narcotic Control Board for 1999*.

International Narcotic Control Board. 2013. *Report of the International Narcotic Control Board for 2012*.

International Narcotic Control Board. 2018. *Report of the International Narcotic Control Board for 2017*.

Ikenberry, John. 2005. "Power and Liberal Order: America's Postwar World Order in Transition." *International Relations of Asia-Pacific* 5: 133–152.

Jakobi, Anja. 2013. *Common Goods and Evils? The Formation of Global Crime Governance*. New York: Oxford University Press.

Jojarth, Christine. 2009. *Crime, War, and Global Trafficking: Designing International Cooperation*. New York: Cambridge University Press.

Kamin, Sam. 2017. Marijuana Regulation in the United States. Pp. 105–119 in *Dual Markets: Comparative Approaches to Regulation*, edited by Ernesto Savona, Mark Kleiman, and Francesco Calderoni. Berlin: Springer.

Klantschnig, Gernot. 2013. *Crime, Drugs and the State in Africa: The Nigerian Connection*. Leiden: Brill.

Knepper, Paul. 2011. *International Crime in the Twentieth Century: The League of Nations Era, 1919–1939*. New York: Palgrave Macmillan.

Knepper, Paul. 2016. Dreams and Nightmares: Drug Trafficking and the History of International Crime. Pp. 208–228 in *The Oxford Handbook of the History of Crime and Criminal Justice*, edited by Paul Knepper and Anja Johansen. New York: Oxford University Press.

Kozma, Liat. 2011. "The League of Nations and the Debate over Cannabis Prohibitions." *History Compass* 9: 61–70.

Krisch, Nico. 2014. "The Decay of Consent: International Law in an Age of Global Public Goods." *American Journal of International Law* 108: 1–40

Levine, Harry, and Craig Reinarman. 2006. Alcohol Prohibition and Drug Prohibition: Lessons from Alcohol Policy for Drug Policy. Pp. 43–76 in *Drugs and Society: U.S. Public Policy*, edited by Jefferson Fish. New York: Rowman & Littlefield.

Line, Richard. 2017. *Drug Control and Human Rights in International Law*. New York: Cambridge University Press.

McAllister, William. 2002. *Drug Diplomacy in the Twenty Century: An International History*. London: Routledge.

McLeod, Allegra. 2010. "Exporting U.S. Criminal Justice." *Yale Law and Policy Review* 29: 83–164.

Mills, James. 2005. *Cannabis Britannica: Empire, Trade, and Prohibition, 1800–1928*. Oxford: Oxford University Press.

Mills, James. 2013. *Cannabis Nation: Control and Consumption in Britain, 1928–2008*. Oxford: Oxford University Press.

Musto, David. 1973. *The American Disease: Origins of Narcotic Control*. New York: Oxford University Press.

National Commission on Marihuana and Drug Abuse. 1972. *Marihuana: A Signal of Misunderstanding*.

Pardo, Bryce. 2014. Cannabis Policy Reforms in the Americas: A Comparative Analysis of Colorado, Washington, and Uruguay. *International Journal of Drug Policy* 25: 727–735.

Parker, Howard, Judith Aldridge, and Fiona Measham. 1998. *Illegal Leisure: The Normalization of Adolescent Recreational Drug Use*. London: Routledge.

Pederson, Susan. 2007. "Back to the League of Nations." *The American Historical Review* 112(4): 1091–1117.

Potter, Gary, Martin Bouchard, and Tom Decorte. 2011. The Globalization of Cannabis Cultivation. Pp. 1–21 in *World Wide Weed: Trends in Cannabis Cultivation and Its Control*, eds. Gary Potter, Martin Bouchard, and Tom Decorte. London: Routledge.

Provine, Doris Marie. 2007. *Unequal under Law: Race in the War on Drugs*. Chicago: University of Chicago Press.

Reuter, Peter. 2003. The Political Economy of Drug Smuggling. Pp. 128–147 in *The Political Economy of the Drug Industry: Latin America and the International System*, edited by Menno Vellinga. Gainesville: Florida University Press.

Room, Robin. 2013. "Legalizing a Market for Cannabis for Pleasure: Colorado, Washington, Uruguay and Beyond." *Addiction* 109: 345–351.

Room, Robin, Benedikt Fischer, Wayne Hall, Simon Lenton, and Peter Reuter. 2010. *Cannabis Policy: Moving beyond Stalemate.* New York: Oxford University Press.

Room, Robin, and Peter Reuter. 2012. "How Well Do International Drug Conventions Protect Public Health?" *Lancet* 379: 84–91.

Sander, Gen, and Rick Lines. 2018. The Death Penalty for Drug Offences: Pulling Back the Curtain to Expose a Flawed Regime. Pp. 49–64 in *Collapse of the Global Order on Drugs: From UNGASS 2016 to Review 2019*, edited by Axel Klein and Blaine Stothard. Bingley: Emerald Publishing.

Santos, Alvaro. 2013. "International Law and Its Discontents: Critical Reflections on the War on Drugs or the Role of Law in Creating Complexity." *American Society of International Law Proceeding* 106: 172–176.

Seddon, Toby. 2016. "Inventing Drugs: A Genealogy of a Regulatory Concept." *Journal of Law and Society* 43(3): 393–415.

Shaffer, Gregory. 2013. The Dimensions and Determinants of State Change. Pp. 23–49 in *Transnational Legal Ordering and State Change*, edited by Gregory Shaffer. New York: Cambridge University Press.

Shaffer, Gregory. 2016. "Theorizing Transnational Legal Orders." *Annual Review of Law and Social Science* 12: 231–253.

Shamir, Ronen, and Daphna Hacker. 2001. "Colonialism's Civilizing Mission: The Case of the Indian Hemp Drug Commission." *Law and Social Inquiry* 26(2): 435–461.

Shiner, Michael. 2015. "Drug Policy Reform and the Reclassification of Cannabis in England and Wales: A Cautionary Tale." *International Journal of Drug Policy* 26: 696–704

Simon, Jonathan. 2007. *Governing through Crime: How the War on Crime Transformed American Democracy and Created a Public of Fear.* New York: Oxford University Press.

Simpson, Gerry. 2004. *Great Powers and Outlaw States: Unequal Sovereigns in the International Legal Order.* Cambridge: Cambridge University Press.

Stokes, Doug. 2005. *America's Other War: Terrorizing Columbia.* London: Zed Books.

Tackeff, Mike. 2018. "Constructing a 'Creative Reading': Will the US State Cannabis Legislation Threaten the Fate of the International Drug Control Treaties?" *Vanderbilt Journal of Transnational Law* 51: 247–295.

United Nations Office of Drugs and Crime (UNODC). 2018. *Analysis of Drug Markets: Opiates, Covaine, Cannabis, Synthetic Drugs.* www.unodc.org/wdr2018/prelaunch/WDR18_Booklet_3_DRUG_MARKETS.pdf.

US Department of State. 2018. *International Narcotic Control Strategy Report.*

Van Solinge, Tim. 2017. The Dutch Model of Cannabis Decriminalization and Tolerated Retail. Pp. 145–169 in *Dual Markets: Comparative Approaches to Regulation*, edited by Ernesto Savona, Mark Kleiman, and Francesco Calderoni. Berlin: Springer.

Van Vilet, Henk. 1990. "Separation of Drug Markets and the Normalization of Drug Problems in the Netherland: An Example for Other Nations?" *Journal of Drugs Issues* 20: 463–471.

Wacquant, Loïc. 2009. *Punishing the Poor: The Neoliberal Government of Social Insecurity.* Durham: Duke University Press.

Wisehart, Daniel. 2018. *Drug Control and International Law.* New York: Routledge.

Zimring, Franklin, and Gordon Hawkins. 1992. *The Search for Rational Drug Control.* New York: Cambridge University Press.

PART III

TRANSNATIONAL LEGAL ORDERING AND INTERNATIONAL CRIMES

CHAPTER SEVEN

THE ANTI-IMPUNITY TRANSNATIONAL LEGAL ORDER FOR HUMAN RIGHTS

Formation, Institutionalization, Consequences, and the Case of Darfur

Joachim J. Savelsberg[*]

7.1 TRANSNATIONAL LEGAL ORDERING AND THE CRIMINALIZATION OF HUMAN RIGHTS VIOLATIONS

The twentieth century is distinct from its predecessors, because humankind sought, for the first time in history, to create institutions suited to prevent and respond to mass violence and atrocities (Minow 1998). In the realm of criminal law, some observe a "justice cascade" (Sikkink 2011), a substantial increase in prosecutions against political and military leaders who order mass killings, and subordinates who execute them (Bergsmo and Lohne 2018; Levi and Hagan 2008; Roht-Arriaza 2005; Vilmer 2015). The International Criminal Court (ICC) in The Hague, the first permanent international criminal court, is but the most prominent example. Created in 2002, based on the 1998 Rome Statute, and with jurisdiction over war crimes, crimes against humanity, the crime of genocide, and the crime of aggression, it follows in the tracks of several ad hoc courts of the 1990s, prominently the International Criminal Tribunal for the former Yugoslavia (ICTY) and its equivalent for Rwanda (ICTR).

This chapter shows great benefits of applying a transnational legal ordering approach to these developments. Doing so sheds fresh light on the formation of a new anti-impunity Transnational Legal Order (TLO), its institutionalization, and its consequences. With Halliday and Shaffer

[*] Research for this paper was supported by a research grant from the National Science Foundation, Program for Law and Social Sciences (SES-0957946). The paper was written during a fellowship at the Stellenbosch Institute for Advanced Study. (South Africa).

(2015a), I refer to a TLO as "a collection of formalized legal norms and associated organizations and actors that authoritatively order the understanding and practice of law across national jurisdictions" (Halliday and Shaffer 2015a: 5). TLOs vary in terms of their geographic and legal scope, alignment with issues and other TLOs, institutionalization and impact. Their boundaries are marked by discursive attributes, underlying ideological frames, and perception of actors whose behaviors are subject to constraint and facilitation by legal norms. The approach replaces methodological nationalism by the recognition of recursivity between the international, national, and local levels of social organization. It pays attention to agency and power, and to the plurality of legal orders, which coexist in a state of tension *and* cooperation.

Socio-legal scholarship and recent research on responses to the mass violence unfolding in the Darfur region of Sudan, beginning in 2003, provide insights into strengths and limits of the new anti-impunity TLO. Based on a comparative eight-country study, involving in depth interviews in four social fields (human rights, diplomacy, humanitarian aid, media) and an analysis of 3,387 media reports, I review judicial steps taken on Darfur, conditions supporting them, and their consequences, interpreting them in terms of the transnational legal ordering approach. The case of Darfur shows the anti-impunity TLO at work, displaying it as a force that delegitimizes mass violence. Yet, it also shows impediments to institutionalization in the form of hostile state actors, fields with potentially competing agendas, internal contradictions, and lack of enforcement power. Nation-level forces filter cultural effects of intervention, resulting in diminished concordance between the global and the national realms and across nation-states.

I proceed in three steps, addressing first the formation of the anti-impunity TLO, second its institutionalization (and impediments), and third its consequences.

7.2 FORMATION OF A CRIMINAL JUSTICE TLO IN THE HUMAN RIGHTS FIELD

Aaronson and Shaffer, in Chapter 1 of this volume, highlight potential forces that contribute to the formation of TLOs in the field of criminal law. They include new risks from globalization that individual nation-states cannot control, the framing of problems as global by interested entrepreneurs, the proliferation of intergovernmental networks, and the transfer of authority from nation-states to international organizations

(IOs). Which of these were at work in the formation of the anti-impunity TLO?

Historically, political and military leaders responsible for mass killings and atrocities were celebrated as heroes (Giesen 2004). In the alternative, those responsible for mass violence were – and still often are – subject to denial and forgetting (Cohen 2001). Yet the twentieth century has brought remarkable change. Martha Minow (1998) suggests that its hallmark was not the horrendous atrocities committed (too many past centuries can compete), but humanity's new inventiveness and efforts toward curbing perpetration against human rights. This is in line with – albeit more broadly conceived than – Kathryn Sikkink's (2011) argument that the late twentieth and early twenty-first centuries are characterized by a "justice cascade," a massive increase in individual criminal accountability for grave human rights violations. Sikkink documents how prosecutions against individual human rights perpetrators in domestic, foreign, and international courts increased almost exponentially in recent decades. She counts by country the number of years, in which prosecutions were conducted. Values, in the single digits during much of the 1980s, rose to about 100 by the mid-1990s, to 300 a decade later, and they approached 450 by 2009 (Sikkink 2011: 21).

Domestic justice systems drive this increase. Yet their role is largely the result of the adoption of international human rights norms by a growing number of countries, attesting to the recursivity of the new transnational legal order. Countries' willingness grew, in recent decades, due to the complementarity principle of the 1998 Rome Statute, the foundation of the ICC. Domestic courts have primary jurisdiction as long as they are able and willing to pursue cases (Rome Statute 1998, Article 17). Operating "in the shadow" of the ICC, nation-states prosecute cases at times specifically to keep them under their own domestic jurisdiction. The adoption of the Rome Statute in 1998 and the establishment of the ICC in 2002, on the heels of a series of ad hoc tribunals (e.g., Yugoslavia, Rwanda, Sierra Leone, Cambodia, East Timor), document the weight at the international level of the justice cascade in its own right. Indeed, international and foreign prosecutions also increased substantially. ICC charges against those responsible for the mass violence in Darfur serve as an example in this chapter.

What were the sources of this remarkable development? Sikkink (2011) provides at least preliminary answers. While not discounting the Nuremberg and Tokyo trials, orchestrated by the victorious powers of World War II, she sets the stage with more challenging cases that did not result from military defeat. Her detailed studies of Greece (1975), Portugal (1976), Spain (1975–1978), and Argentina (1985) show that regional opportunity structures had developed by the 1970s that favored transitional justice proceedings. Examples for such structures are the creation of the European Court of Human Rights in 1959 and the foundation of Amnesty International in 1961, an organization that played a central role in responses to the Darfur crisis.

Initial steps toward human rights prosecutions eventually resulted in a decentralized, interactive system of global accountability that challenged national sovereignty. Sikkink (2011: 96–125) identifies two contributors – "streams" to use her metaphor. The first stream is constituted by international prosecutions, from Nuremberg and Tokyo via the International Criminal Tribunal for the former Yugoslavia (ICTY) and its equivalent for Rwanda (ICTR) and finally on to the ICC with its jurisdiction over cases of aggression, war crimes, crimes against humanity, and genocide. The second stream consists of domestic and foreign prosecutions such as those in Greece, Portugal, and Argentina in the mid-1970s and the Pinochet case of 1998–1999. In addition, a "hard law streambed" provide support, led by various conventions such as the Genocide Convention (1948), Geneva Convention (1949), Apartheid Convention (1980), Torture Convention (1987), the Inter-American Convention on Forced Disappearances (1996), and the Rome Statute (1998).

This spread of human rights initiatives, and their solidification in a system, was not simply the result of contagion. Instead, individuals, associations, trans-governmental networks, an epistemic community of criminal law experts, and NGOs such as Human Rights Watch (HRW) and Amnesty International achieved the progressive institutionalization of individual criminal liability – that is, *criminalization* and *individualization* under international law. This focus on actors builds on earlier work, in which Sikkink, in collaboration with Margaret Keck, examined advocacy in international politics. Their much-cited book drew attention to transnational advocacy networks and the engagement of these networks in information politics that tied them together, leverage politics that shamed evildoers, and accountability politics that "tricked" nations into commitments, which they might have entered into merely for symbolic and legitimate reasons, to then hold them accountable. The 1975 Helsinki Accord is just the most famous example (Keck and Sikkink 1998).

Leaders of the human rights movement, not surprisingly, share a tendency to privilege advocacy as a driving force of criminalization. Aryeh Neier, former Executive Director of HRW and President of the Open Society Institute, confirms that even after the success of early truth commissions, "some in the international human rights movement continued to espouse prosecutions and criminal sanctions against those principally responsible for the most egregious offenses" (Neier 2012: 264). Neier describes the role of the Italian organization No Peace Without Justice (NPWJ), but especially of Emma Bonino, an Italian politician and civil liberties campaign veteran in the establishment of the ICC. "In the period in which the ICC was being established, Bonino was a member of the European Commission ... and she took advantage of her post and her contacts with heads of state to ensure the participation of high-level officials from many countries in NPWJ's conferences. ... The result was that by the time the conference took place in Rome – Bonino's city – many governments were ready to support establishment of the ICC" (Neier 2012: 270). Also on the path to ratification, for which some countries had to go so far as to modify their constitutions, "[l]obbying by a number of nongovernmental organizations – including the Coalition for an International Criminal Court – played an important part" (Neier 2012: 270).

Other analysts emphasize the weight of different types of actors in the establishment and spread of human rights norms. Hagan (2003), for example, in his study of the ICTY, focuses on officials within judicial institutions, specifically successive chief prosecutors, each of whom brought a new form of "capital" to bear. All of them combined innovative strategies with established legal practices: from securing international support (Richard Goldstone) to sealed indictments and surprise arrests (Louise Arbour) to Carla del Ponte's charges against former president Milosevic. Innovative strategies eventually become "doxa," Hagan argues: taken-for-granted legal standards in the emerging international criminal tribunal in The Hague.[1] Yet elsewhere, David Scheffer, former US Ambassador and right hand of US Secretary of State Madeleine Albright, highlights diplomats as crucial contributors in the establishment of international judicial institutions, from the ICTY to the ICC (Scheffer 2012).

---

[1] Once established, the standards diffuse in the international legal system, even if their names shift, as Meierhenrich (2006) has shown regarding the notions of "conspiracy" (US law), "criminal organization" (International Military Tribunal at Nuremberg), and "joint criminal enterprise" (ICTY).

No matter the relative weight of each of these types of actors, their interactions contributed to the passing of the Rome Statute in 1998 and the establishment of the ICC. The ICC entered into force in 2002 when 60 countries had ratified the Statute; the number has since increased to 123.

In short, literature on the rise of criminal law norms against perpetrators of mass violence shows the emergence of a new TLO, challenging impunity in the human rights realm: a collection of formalized legal norms, associated organizations and actors, and an authoritative ordering of legal interpretation and practice across national jurisdictions. It also documents, in line with the TLO approach, that agency and the mobilization of power are necessary preconditions for the definition of mass violence as a problem and for the initiation of global legal responses. Governments, INGOs and IOs played central roles. These patterns support several hypotheses suggested by Halliday and Shaffer (2015b) in an earlier volume on TLOs. This study of the case of Darfur confirms these patterns, but it also leads to consideration of social forces that impede the institutionalization of the anti-impunity TLO.

7.3 RESPONDING TO DARFUR IN THE CONTEXT OF THE NEW ANTI-IMPUNITY TLO

Once a TLO has been established, individual cases still require intervention by a variety of entrepreneurs. The case of Darfur provides an example that sheds further light on the transnational ordering of criminal justice.

A few notes on the situation of Darfur are in order. In the year 2000, disturbing events began to unfold in the Darfur region of Sudan. Activists against Sudan's ruling elite had issued *The Black Book: Imbalance of Power and Wealth in Sudan*. Distributed widely, especially in the surroundings of mosques after Friday prayers, the *Black Book* castigated the domination of Sudan by "only one Region (Northern Region) with just over 5% of Sudan's population" (Seekers of Truth and Justice 2003: 1). A March 22, 2004 translation, signed by "Translater," informs that "[a]s of last year (March 2003), some of the activists involved in the preparation of the Book took arms against the government" (Seekers of Truth and Justice 2003: 1). Indeed, early 2003 saw the formation of the Sudan Liberation Army (SLA) and the Justice and Equality Movement (JEM) – two organizations that led a violent rebellion against the government of Sudan. Their armed actions were surprisingly effective. In April of 2003, rebel groups famously attacked the Sudanese military's el Fasher air base, destroyed numerous planes of the Sudanese air force, and killed almost one hundred soldiers. The government of Sudan and its military, supported by Janjawiid militias, responded with brute force. A first wave of mass killings unfolded between June and September of 2003. Targets did not just include armed rebels but primarily civilian villagers, including elderly men, women, and children. A cease-fire held only for a few months, and in December 2003 President al-Bashir vowed to "annihilate" the Darfur rebels. His vow evoked a second wave of mass killings that lasted from December of 2003 through April of 2004. Massive displacements of the civilian population were the consequence. Tens of thousands of lives were extinguished as a direct result of violence and many more during the Darfuris' flight from the violence and due to problematic conditions in displaced person camps in Sudan and refugee camps in neighboring Chad.

Much of the Western world took note only after the first peak of killings (summer 2003) had subsided and when the second wave (winter 2003–2004) was underway. The first public pronouncement, a "genocide alert," issued by the United States Holocaust Memorial Museum in January of 2004, was followed by op-ed pieces in prominent American media; a speech by UN Secretary-General Kofi Annan on April 7, 2004, the occasion of the tenth anniversary of the Rwandan genocide; United Nations Security Council (UNSC) Resolution 1564, instituting an International Commission of Inquiry on Darfur on September 18, 2004; and the UNSC's referral of the situation of Darfur to the ICC on March 31, 2005. Simultaneously, a massive civil society movement evolved. In the United States, the Save Darfur movement gathered almost two hundred liberal and conservative organizations under its umbrella. The US Congress resolved that the violence in Darfur amounted to genocide. Secretary of State Colin Powell initiated the famous "Atrocities Documentation Survey" of more than one thousand Darfuri refugees in the camps of Eastern Chad. Based on findings from this survey, he determined, at a September 9, 2004, hearing before the Senate Foreign Relations Committee, that genocide was being committed. President George W. Bush followed suit a few weeks later.

Soon after the UNSC referred the situation of Darfur to the ICC on March 31, 2005, the court took action. After almost two years of investigation, on February 27, 2007, the ICC's chief prosecutor Luis

Moreno-Ocampo applied for an arrest warrant against Ahmad Harun, then Sudan's Deputy Minister for the Interior and responsible for the "Darfur Security Desk," and against Ali Kushayb, a Janjawiid leader. Both were charged with crimes against humanity and war crimes. On April 27, 2007, the court issued a warrant of arrest against both actors for war crimes and crimes against humanity. It took another year until the prosecutor also applied for an arrest warrant against Sudanese President Omar al-Bashir, charging crimes against humanity, war crimes, and genocide (July 14, 2008). The judges did not initially follow this application in its entirety, but on March 4, 2009, they issued a warrant against al-Bashir for crimes against humanity and war crimes. With more than a year's delay and five years after the UNSC referral to the ICC, on July 12, 2010, the court followed up with a warrant against the President of Sudan for the crime of genocide.

The ICC thus places itself at the center of the judicial field's engagement with the mass violence in Darfur. Its interventions clearly seek to discredit potential denial of atrocities, or even glorification of those responsible for their perpetration. Consider the following quotation from the initial charging document against President Omar al-Bashir of July 14, 2008. After spelling out several conditions, the first warrant concludes as follows:

> CONSIDERING that, for the above reasons, there are reasonable grounds to believe, that Omar al Bashir is criminally responsible as an indirect perpetrator, or as an indirect co-perpetrator [footnote], under article 25(3)(a) of the Statute, for (i) intentionally directing attacks at a civilian population as such or against individual civilians not taking direct part in hostilities as a war crime . . . ; (ii) pillage as a war crime . . . (iii) murder as a crime against humanity; (iv) extermination as a crime against humanity . . . ; (v) forcible transfer as a crime against humanity . . . ; (vi) torture as a crime against humanity . . . ; rape as a crime against humanity.[2]

The court did not just issue this warrant, but, through its press offices, it sought to communicate it to a broad public.[3] Media from across the globe responded to the indictment and communicated its message to a world audience: the depiction of President al Bashir as a criminal

---

[2] Warrant of Arrest for Omar Hassan Ahmad Al Bashir, ICC-02/05-01/09-104 March 2009, at www.icc-cpi.int/iccdocs/doc/doc639078.pdf.
[3] On ICC efforts to shape public opinion locally, for the case of Northern Uganda, see Golden 2013.

perpetrator (see Savelsberg 2015: chapters 8 and 9; Savelsberg and Nyseth Brehm 2015).

In short, in an act of transnational legal ordering, civil society, INGOs, transnational advocacy networks, national governments, the UN, and the ICC acted to criminalize the violence of Darfur. Darfur thus took its rightful place in the context of the justice cascade and the new anti-impunity TLO.

7.4 CHALLENGERS TO THE INSTITUTIONALIZATION OF THE ANTI-IMPUNITY TLO

The successful formation of the anti-impunity TLO may still leave it vulnerable to forces that impede institutionalization. Its operation may not become matter of course like, for example, that of a domestic criminal justice system.

The introduction to this volume lists mechanisms that may advance institutionalization (Aaronson and Shaffer, Chapter 1): compliance monitoring, naming and shaming, and other mechanisms giving rise to concordance, a convergence of meanings attached to norms between the international and national realms across nation-states. Important as these mechanisms may be, more fundamental forces may determine the fate of the new anti-impunity TLO: powerful nation-states, social fields that pursue different goals, internal contradictions within the TLO, and lack of enforcement powers.

First, most powerful countries, including the People's Republic of China, Russia, and the United States, are not signatories of the Rome Statute. Heavily engaged across the globe, they fear that their citizens may be prosecuted and they jealously guard their sovereignty. Their power position in international relations ensures that they do not face sanctions for such obstruction. In fact, the United States has entered into bilateral immunity agreements with many smaller nation-states, reducing the risk of the extradition of American citizens to the ICC. In addition, smaller countries have threatened to withdraw from the Rome Statute when their leaders feared they might become targets of prosecution.

Second, the anti-impunity TLO lacks enforcement power. For example, in December 2014, Fatou Bensouda, the second chief prosecutor of the ICC, announced the following to the United Nations:

> Given this [UN Security] Council's lack of foresight on what should happen in Darfur, I am left with no choice but to hibernate investigative

activities in Darfur as I shift resources to other urgent cases, especially those in which trial is approaching. It should thus be clear to this Council that unless there is a change of attitude and approach to Darfur in the near future, there shall continue to be little or nothing to report to you for the foreseeable future.

Relatedly, in a February 12, 2015, article, *New York Times* journalist Somini Sengupta, correspondent at the UN, wrote about a growing pile of cases, defiant government authorities, and a Security Council that called for investigations but did little to advance them. Her article was entitled "Is the War Crimes Court still Relevant?" The Darfur case indeed is not the only one where the court's lack of direct access to an enforcement staff comes to a full and, for those in pursuit of criminal justice, painful display.

Third, and relatedly, the anti-impunity TLO coexists with competing fields. The Darfur study illustrates conflicts between the anti-impunity TLO, on the one hand, and the humanitarian aid and diplomacy fields, on the other. The goal of humanitarian aid is to help victims survive. Its actors depend on permits to enter and operate in the country in which mass violence has caused a humanitarian emergency. Support for prosecution of members of the perpetrating government may put their operations at risk. In the words of one MSF (Doctors without Borders) interviewee:

> I then was head of missions ... in Sudan, based in Khartoum, which means more of the overall management of the humanitarian projects – and their representation, negotiation with the [Sudanese] government and other actors. ... You negotiate with representatives of the government in order to secure the delivery of services, to have permission to have international staff in Darfur, and for the particular services as well.

Diplomats, seeking to stabilize a region and to end military confrontation, do not just depend on cooperation by mid-level bureaucrats, but on active participation by high-level government officials. In Sudan in 2011, the pending separation of the South, meant to end a long and destructive civil war, had international negotiators on edge, especially when the ICC began to charge leading Sudanese politicians. Such dependency is reflected in an interview with a political scientist from a foreign ministry affiliated institute:

> If you want to make peace in Darfur through negotiations you have to deal with the Sudanese government and you have to deal with the

people who hold the power in the Sudanese government, and that includes Omar al-Bashir. If you want to achieve justice through the International Criminal Court, well, then you should stigmatise someone who is indicted. You shouldn't talk to Omar al-Bashir, right?

In addition, foreign policy makers have not fully accepted the new TLO. One of my interviewees from the foreign ministry of a large European country, who specialized on issues of the ICC within his ministry's Division of International Law and represented his country in the Assembly of States, expressed his frustration accordingly:

> As to my interlocutors in the [Foreign Ministry] ... there were constantly conflicting perceptions. I do remember quite a number of quarrels I had with my colleagues in the political department. .... And the reason is that we had two different approaches. Their approach was purely political. My approach was both political, but also legal and judicial. And that is extremely difficult to combine at times. Because, if you are only confined to making political assessments, then it is difficult to evaluate the work of a court, to accept a court, to accept any independent legal institution. And that is really something new in the international field where people are trained to assess complex issues by political means only. .... Now there is a new factor, a new player on the ground [ICC], which does not make a political assessment, but which simply applies the law. That is a new phenomenon, and I think for those who have an exclusively political approach that is difficult to accept.

Importantly, the use of different strategies across social fields is not just based on actors' rational calculations. Instead, actors are immersed in their fields' respective missions, through training and practice. They have internalized its goals and its mode of operation. Corresponding with the resulting habitus, there emerge particular knowledge repertoires, a specific mode of thinking and way of seeing the world, including situations of mass violence, and these are likely to differ across fields.

In addition, the Rome Statute opens the window for substantive, political concerns to intrude into the work of the ICC. The UN Security Council, composed of countries that are no strangers to the consideration of geopolitical and economic interests, is authorized to refer cases to the ICC. Intrusion of political rationales into the legal process is further supported by Article 16 of the Rome Statute, a window built into the edifice of the law to keep political considerations in plain view. Article 16 states, "No investigation or prosecution may be commenced or proceeded with under this Statute for a period of 12 months after the Security Council, in a resolution adopted under Chapter VII of the Charter of the United Nations, has requested the Court to that effect; that request may be renewed by the Council under the same conditions." Decision makers on the court will have to be mindful of the UNSC's political reasoning if they hope to maintain control over their cases.

Fourth, the institutionalization of the new anti-impunity TLO is at risk due to the likelihood of internal conflict within the legal realm. Within the ICC, lawyers and technocrats use conflicting reasoning (Meierhenrich 2014), reflecting the tension between a formal and a substantive orientation of law that pervades international law even more than domestic criminal law.[4] On the one side of the divide is law's formal rationality, oriented toward a system of legal criteria alone. These criteria are clearly part of the anti-impunity TLO as reflected in codifications such as the Rome Statute. Having laid the foundation for the pursuit of legal rationales, the Statute has begun to revolutionize a world in which foreign affairs were subject to political reasoning alone.

Yet extra-legal criteria impress themselves on legal decision makers, especially in the human rights realm. Lawyers, always resentful of being reduced to an automaton into which one drops the facts and the fees for them to spew out the decision (Weber 1978), are inclined to consider ethical maxims and practical concerns of a political, economic, and geopolitical nature in their legal decisions. In the anti-impunity TLO, substantive considerations have particular weight, as thousands of lives may be at stake if decision makers disregard conditions on the ground. In the case of Darfur, for example, foreign policy makers, including several interviewees, expressed concern that charges against President al-Bashir might threaten the North-South agreement and the referendum on the independence of South Sudan. It is hard to imagine that these concerns did not affect decision makers at the ICC (Savelsberg 2017).

In short, criminal law is no stranger to internal contradictions and conflicts. Conflicts between formal legal criteria and substantive concerns, while dividing legal and political actors, also create ambivalences and internal tensions within the legal field. The ICC and the case of Darfur are no exceptions. More generally, even once the formation of a TLO has succeeded, its institutionalization is still at

---

[4] This tension, noted by Max Weber (1978), has been subject to more recent work on technocratization (Stryker 1989), substantivation (Savelsberg 1992), responsive law (Nonet and Selznick 1978), and post-liberal law (Unger 1976).

risk. Threats are especially pronounced when powerful nation-states torpedo the TLO, when competing social fields pose challenges to it, when the TLO is marred by internal conflicts, and when enforcement powers are limited. Such conditions clearly impede normative settlement.

7.5 CONSEQUENCES OF THE ANTI-IMPUNITY TLO IN THE HUMAN RIGHTS REALM

Promoters of new TLOs that challenge age-old impunity practices expect an increase in arrests and prosecutions. In Chapter 1 of this volume, Aaronsen and Shaffer state that much. They add that more arrests and prosecutions are likely to generate deterrent effects and social disapproval. In line with such expectations, recent scholarship has not only measured an increase in prosecutions, but also subsequent declines in grave human rights violations, especially where trials were paired with truth commissions (Kim and Sikkink 2010; Neier 2012; Sikkink 2011). Specifically for the ICC, Hyeran Jo and Beth Simmons (2016) find that violence by governments and by rebel groups declines following an increase in prosecutions (also Jo 2015). Others, however, express profound pessimism (e.g., Snyder and Vinjamuri 2003/4; Pensky 2008). As the anti-impunity TLO is historically new and not securely institutionalized, more analyses over longer time periods will be needed for the debate to be settled.

The Darfur project offered a new opportunity to measure consequences of intervention by the anti-impunity TLO, especially with regard to cultural effects yielded by the representational power of international criminal justice. Would the TLO indeed spur social disapproval, as hypothesized by Aaronson and Shaffer (Chapter 1, this volume). ? What is the chance that the framing of mass atrocities by international criminal courts reaches a broad audience across national boundaries and communicates to such audience a perception of mass violence as a form of criminal violence, even against competing narratives? What are the consequences of the new anti-impunity TLO on collective representations and memories of mass atrocities?

7.5.1 Cultural Consequences: Collective Representations and Memories

Classic writings (Mead 1918), supported by a new line of neo-Durkheimian work in cultural sociology, suggest considerable representational power of criminal courts. This literature interprets criminal punishment as a didactic exercise, a "speech act in which society talks to itself about its moral identity" (Smith 2008: 16). The weight of this mechanism for our theme becomes clear if indeed the International Military Tribunal in Nuremberg and the Universal Declaration of Human Rights initiated the extension of the Holocaust and psychological identification with the victims in historical memory, as Jeffrey Alexander (2004) argues. Judicial events like Nuremberg, the Eichmann trial in Jerusalem, and the Frankfurt Auschwitz Trial produced cultural trauma: members of a world audience were affected by an experience to which they themselves had not been exposed. Empirical research shows that criminal trials have the capacity of coloring not just narratives of recent events, but also the collective memory of a more distant past in the minds of subsequent generations (Savelsberg and King 2011). Once generated, delegitimizing memories – in a positive feedback loop – further promote human rights standards. In the words of Daniel Levy and Natan Sznaider (2010: 4), "[t]he global proliferation of human rights norms is driven by the public and frequently ritualistic attention to memories of their persistent violations."

7.5.2 Cultural Consequences of Intervention in the Darfur Situation

The case of Darfur shows how the anti-impunity TLO generated a representation of the violence as a form of criminal violence that news media diffused to a worldwide public. Initial warnings, entailed in a December 2003 confidential memo by Tom Eric Vraalsen, UN special envoy for humanitarian affairs in Darfur, note that "delivery of humanitarian assistance to populations in need is hampered mostly by *systematically denied access* [emphasis in original]."[5] On April 7, 2004, speaking before the UN General Assembly, on the tenth anniversary of the Rwandan genocide, Secretary-General Kofi Annan referred to Darfur, expressing concern "at the scale of reported human rights abuses and at the humanitarian crisis." He quoted the UN Emergency Relief Coordinator's report to the Security Council that "a sequence of deliberate actions has been observed that seem aimed at achieving a specific objective: the forcible and long-term displacement of the targeted

[5] As cited at http://sudanreeves.org/2013/08/05/humanitarian-conditions-in-darfur-a-climate-of-violence-and-extreme-insecurity-2/.

communities, which may also be termed 'ethnic cleansing'" (Annan 2004).

Following Annan's speech, on September 18, 2004, the UN Security Council adopted Resolution 1564, threatening to sanction the Sudanese government should it fail to live up to its obligations on Darfur. It also established an International Commission of Inquiry on Darfur (ICID) to investigate violations of human rights in Darfur and invoked, for the first time in history toward such purpose, the Convention for the Prevention and Punishment of the Crime of Genocide (Genocide Convention). Appointed by Secretary-General Annan in October 2004, the ICID was charged "'to investigate reports of violations of international humanitarian law and human rights law in Darfur by all parties'; 'to determine also whether or not acts of genocide have occurred'; and 'to identify the perpetrators of such violations'; 'with a view to ensuring that those responsible are held accountable'" (ICID 2005: 9). Clearly, the mandate accords with the new anti-impunity TLO.

The selection of Commission members, in terms of their educational backgrounds, careers, and positions, further solidifies the placement of the Darfur issue in transnational criminal law: The ICID consisted of five members whose short bios appear in its report (ICID 2005: 165–166). Commission chair was the late Antonio Cassese from Italy. A renowned law professor, Cassese had published prominently on issues of international human rights law and international criminal law. Previously, he had served as the first president of the ICTY. Mohammed Fayek, from Egypt, is a former minister in his country's government and Secretary-General of the Arab Organization for Human Rights, an NGO. Hina Jilani, from Pakistan, had served as a Special Representative of the UN Secretary-General on Human Rights Defenders and as Secretary-General of the Human Rights Commission of Pakistan. She is a member of the District Court and Supreme Court Bar Association of her country. Dumisa Ntsebeza from South Africa served as a Commissioner on the Truth and Reconciliation Commission of his country. He led the Commission's Investigatory Unit and was head of its witness protection program. Ntsebeza is an Advocate of the High Court of South Africa and a member of the Cape Bar. Finally, Theresa Striggner-Scott from Ghana is a barrister and principal partner with a legal consulting firm in Accra. She served on her country's High Court, as an ambassador to France and Italy, and as a member of the "Goldstone Commission" that had investigated public violence and intimidation in South Africa. In short, the ICID was dominated by members from the Global South with a background in law, especially international human rights law and international criminal law. Three of its five members were from the African continent.

Commissioners and their investigatory team traveled to Sudan and the three Darfur states, holding meetings with the Government of Sudan and with government officials at the State and local levels (on a mixed assessment of Government cooperativeness see ICID 2005: 15–16). They further met with military and police, rebel forces and tribal leaders, displaced persons, victims and witnesses, NGO and UN representatives, and they examined reports issued by governments, inter-governmental organizations, UN bodies and NGOs (ICID 2005: 2–3). Many of these actors, simultaneously driving forces of the anti-impunity TLO, here aid the examination of criminal wrongdoing in a specific case.

The Commission, three months after its constitution, delivered a 176-page report to the UN Secretary-General (January 25, 2005). Following a brief "Historical and Social Background" section (ICID 2005: 17–26), the Commission strictly follows legal logic. It categorizes actors ("1. Government Armed Forces"; "2. Government supported and/or controlled militias – The Janjaweed"; "3. Rebel movement groups" [ICID: 27–39]), spells out the legal rules that are binding on the Government of Sudan and the rebel groups, identifies categories of international crimes, and associates available and legally relevant evidence with those legal concepts (ICID: 40–107).

The ICID speaks to the *actus reus* with regard to "Violations of international human rights law and international humanitarian law": "Firstly, according to United Nations estimates there are 1,65 million internally displaced persons in Darfur, and more than 200,000 refugees from Darfur in neighbouring Chad. Secondly, there has been large-scale destruction of villages throughout the three states of Darfur. The Commission conducted independent investigations to establish additional facts" (ICID: 3). It then links the evidence to the legal categories of the Rome Statute and concludes:

> [T]he Commission found that Government forces and militias conducted indiscriminate attacks, including killing of civilians, torture, enforced disappearances, destruction of villages, rape and other forms

of sexual violence, pillaging and forced displacement, throughout Darfur. These acts were conducted on a widespread and systematic basis, and therefore may amount to crimes against humanity. ... In addition to the large scale attacks, many people have been arrested and detained, and many have been held incommunicado for prolonged periods and tortured.

(ICID: 3)

By identifying the acts of violence as "widespread and systematic," the ICID determines that they amount to crimes against humanity, as defined in the Rome Statute, and thus fall under the jurisdiction of the ICC. The ICID thereby lays the groundwork for its recommendation to the UNSC that the case be referred to that court. It further follows the logic of criminal law by attributing responsibility to individuals in a section on the "Identification of Perpetrators":

Those identified as possibly responsible for the above-mentioned violations consist of individual perpetrators, including officials of the Government of Sudan, members of militia forces, members of rebel groups, and certain foreign army officers acting in their personal capacity. Some Government officials, as well as members of militia forces, have also been named as possibly responsible for joint criminal enterprise to commit international crimes. ... The Commission also has identified a number of senior Government officials and military commanders who may be responsible, under the notion of superior (or command) responsibility, for knowingly failing to prevent or repress the perpetration of crimes. Members of rebel groups are named as suspected of participating in a joint criminal enterprise to commit international crimes.

(ICID: 4–5)

Not only does this segment of the report follow the individualizing logic of criminal law; the Commission also makes use of legal concepts developed and refined in international criminal law, in order to establish criminal responsibility of individuals who act in complex organizational contexts. "Command responsibility" seeks to prevent those from washing their hand of guilt who delegate the dirty work to others, lower in the organizational hierarchy. Working to identify individuals as potential criminal perpetrators who acted in the context of complex organizations, the report applies the notion of "joint criminal enterprise." This term developed out of the concept of "conspiracy" in American criminal law in the context of the fight against organized crime. It mutated into "criminal organization" in the London Charter of 1943, on which the Nuremberg Tribunal was based, and into "joint criminal enterprise" by the ICTY (Meierhenrich 2006). In addition to illustrating the application of concepts from international criminal law, this excursus into legal history illustrates how the global is constituted from below, in this case from US law. Based on the ICID report, the UNSC referred the case of Darfur to the ICC, and the court's first chief prosecutor, Luis Moreno-Ocampo. Ocampo investigated and began his series of prosecutorial decisions against Ahmad Harun, then Sudan's Deputy Minister for the Interior, Ali Kushayb, the Janjawiid leader, and Sudanese President Omar al-Bashir.

While actors and organizations that constitute the anti-impunity TLO thus created a powerful representation of the mass violence in Darfur as a form of criminal violence, actors from the humanitarian aid and diplomacy fields, in line with their distinct agendas, narrated the events differently. Table 7.1 displays ideal typical accounts along a set of analytic dimensions: victims, responsible actors, time dimension, causes of conflict, interpretive frames, and appropriate responses. While ideal types are theoretical constructs, actual knowledge repertoires do approximate them in each of the fields under study.

7.6 EMPIRICAL PATTERNS OF A PREVAILING CRIME FRAME

Given such competition over the depiction of the mass violence in Darfur, which field was most successful in impressing on a global public its representation of Darfur? The intensity of media reporting on Darfur after interventions and the relative frequency of competing frames in reports and commentaries provide some indication.

Figure 7.1 depicts the number of reports over time by years of the conflict and by country. The numbers in this figure reflect the entire population of articles about Darfur that my research team identified in the fourteen newspapers and from which the sample of 3,387 articles was drawn for detailed analysis. The different graph lines distinguish trends by country. Following these lines year by year reveals remarkable patterns.

Note first that the intensity of reporting differs across countries, a result for which I provide a detailed analysis elsewhere (Savelsberg 2015). Second, shifts in the intensity of reporting developed in almost perfect unison. Years with peaks in the number of articles in one

TABLE 7.1 Analytic dimensions of the Darfur conflict and their use by holders of different positions in three social fields

Analytic dimensions	Fields		
	Human rights/ criminal law	Humanitarian aid	Diplomacy
Suffering/ victimization	Graphic accounts, high numbers for killings and rapes, especially among "black African" groups	Graphic accounts, high numbers for displacements, caution on death counts	Caution about numbers, stress of victims on both sides of conflict
Responsible actors	GOS, SAF, Janjawiid, specified individuals	Caution about identifying actors	Vague reference to indirect responsibility, more on rebel side than in other fields
Origins/time Causes	Short-term Ethno-political entrepreneurs	Short-term Complex historical, cross-national processes	Long-term History of colonialism; center-periphery conflicts
Policy Conclusions	Criminal law Toward justice	Humanitarian aid Toward survival	Negotiations Toward peace

country experience the same in the other countries. While the mass killings of 2003 barely evoked any reporting, the years 2004 and 2007, marked by highly visible international interventions, stand out. Some journalist interviewees speak to factors that motivated their first reporting about Darfur in early 2004. In the words of a distinguished Africa correspondent,

> When first messages about a new war in Sudan appeared in 2003, I initially did not take that so seriously. But when the commemorative events unfolded on the tenth anniversary of the Rwandan genocide [April 2004] and Kofi Annan [2004] and others said, "We will no longer tolerate this," then I also decided to take this conflict seriously and I traveled there.
>
> (Interview, translation, JJS)

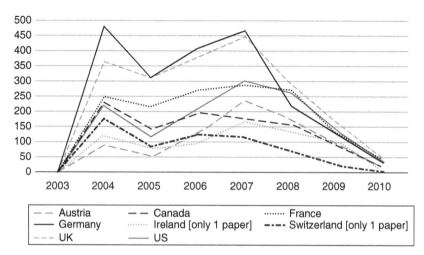

Figure 7.1 Number of articles on Darfur by country by year in 14 newspapers of record.

Figure 7.1 also shows that, despite a relative lull in 2005, media attention remained at a high level for four years. Such unusually sustained attention likely results from several quasi-judicial and judicial interventions. The subsequent drop in 2008 is due to several factors including the obstruction of journalistic work by the government of Sudan, the eviction of aid agencies and the reluctance of those who remained to speak to journalists. Importantly though, interventions kept media attention to Darfur alive for an unusually long time. The question arises how specifically juridical forces acted on the journalistic field. How did they affect the substance of reporting?

Figure 7.2 displays the percentage of articles about Darfur per period that cite the crime frame, in combination with three competing frames. I offer a detailed analysis of the fluctuations of the competing approaches elsewhere (Savelsberg 2015). Suffice it to say here that the crime frame becomes the dominant way of representing the Darfur conflict over time. This is all the more remarkable as the humanitarian emergency and civil war frames started at about the same level as the crime frame before judicial interventions occurred. Multivariate statistical analyses, presented elsewhere, confirm that international criminal justice interventions intensify the depiction of the mass violence in Darfur as a form of criminal violence (Savelsberg and Nyseth Brehm 2015).

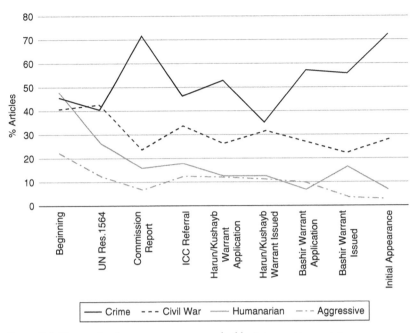

Figure 7.2 Competing frames over stages marked by intervention points

A brief example from *New York Times* reporting provides detail. One day after Ocampo's application for an arrest warrant against President al-Bashir, a long report appeared by staff journalists Marlise Simons (Paris), Lydia Polgreen (Dakar), and Jeffery Gettleman (Nairobi). Their 1,446-word report, reviewing the mass violence of Darfur, reminds the reader of Slobodan Milošević and Charles Taylor, two previous sitting presidents who had been tried before international tribunals. The authors further quote chief prosecutor Ocampo: "Mr. Bashir had 'masterminded and implemented' a plan to destroy three ethnic groups. ... Using government soldiers and Arab militias, the president 'purposefully targeted civilians'" (*New York Times*, July 15, 2008: 1). An editorial of the same day, entitled "Charged with Genocide," opens with this sentence: "The truth can be difficult. That doesn't make it any less true. And so we support the decision by the prosecutor of the International Criminal Court to bring charges of genocide against Sudan's president, Omar Hassan al-Bashir, for his role in masterminding Darfur's horrors" (*New York Times*, July 15, 2008: 18). Also on the same day, an opinion piece by Richard Goldstone, former chief prosecutor of the ICTY and ICTR, strongly supported the arrest warrant against al-Bashir. Both the editorial and Goldstone's piece challenge critics who point at an indictment's problematic consequences for aid delivery and diplomatic efforts. Some twenty additional articles and editorials followed in the *New York Times* in the remainder of the month of July 2008 alone. The editorial messages decidedly stay on course in supporting the prosecution.

In short, an analysis of the comparative representational power of three social fields, all prominently involved in the situation of Darfur, shows that the new anti-impunity TLO prevails over the humanitarian and diplomacy fields. Media play a powerful role in generating such effects. It is conceivable that media, concerned with high ratings, are more attracted by sensational events. International criminal court indictments, especially if propagated by the court's media departments, are thus more promising than are repeated reports about ongoing suffering in refugee camps and behind-the-scenes negotiations of diplomats. Other factors favoring the attractiveness of judicial interventions for news media are the particular ritual power of court proceedings, in line with Durkheimian thought, or – building on Luhmannian ideas – the legitimacy of courts of law resulting from stringent procedural norms. (For a more detailed analysis of media in transitional justice situations, see Savelsberg forthcoming.)

7.7   NATIONAL CONTEXTS AS IMPEDIMENTS TO CONCORDANCE

While the criminalizing narrative generated by the anti-impunity TLO prevailed in the struggle of cultural representation, this effect is not necessarily evenly strong in all countries. Concordance of meaning may vary between the international and national levels and across nation-states. Earlier work on criminal punishment has shown that nation-specific institutional conditions filter global forces (Savelsberg 1994). Specifically for human rights law, McElrath (forthcoming) demonstrates that the adoption into national law of international genocide law is marked by an adaptation to national conditions.

In the case of Darfur, and despite the overall privileging of the crime frame, media from the eight countries differed in their preference for each of the competing narratives. Even those that embraced the criminalizing frame did so to varying degrees. In addition, within the crime

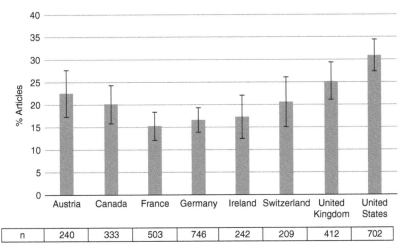

| n | 240 | 333 | 503 | 746 | 242 | 209 | 412 | 702 |

Figure 7.3 Use of the term "genocide" in media reports on Darfur across countries

frame, some countries were more reluctant than were others to apply the category of "genocide" when reporting about Darfur (see Figure 7.3).

US journalists, especially favorably inclined toward the crime frame, also used the genocide label more often than their colleagues from other countries. On the one hand, this may be surprising given their country's reluctance to ratify the Rome Statute, the foundation of the ICC. On the other hand, it is consistent with the broad-based mobilization and genocide rhetoric by the Save Darfur coalition, encompassing some two hundred civil society organizations, liberal and conservative as well as religious and secular. Features of civil society and society-state relations appear to matter here too, enhancing receptivity for the crime frame generated by the anti-impunity TLO in the United States, despite the country's aversion to global institutions.

Ireland offers an interesting contrast. Its journalists were relatively reluctant to use both the crime frame and the genocide label, a reluctance they explained by the strong humanitarian climate in the country. This humanitarian orientation is manifested in a pronounced aid orientation of Irish foreign policy and close coopera-tion between the state and humanitarian aid NGOs, including those affiliated with the Irish Catholic Church. Collective memories of the Irish potato famine and extreme poverty provide cultural support. Multivariate statistical analyses show that a national focus on aid programs is generally associated with less frequent use of the crime and genocide labels, lower victimization counts (with the exception of displacements), and a less frequent identification of the Sudanese state as a criminal organization. The competing humanitarian aid narrative thus prevails in a national context in which organizational and policy practices and cultural sensitivities conflict with the frame suggested by the anti-impunity TLO.

To provide a final example of country-specific patterns, German media reported extensively about Darfur and generously applied the crime frame. Yet, media reports and interviewees quite rarely used the term genocide; respondents explained their reluctance with their caution toward likening mass atrocities such as those in Darfur with the Shoah, not wanting to risk accusations of seeking to relativize the Holocaust. Again, nation-specific cultural sensitivities filter the cultural force projected by the anti-impunity TLO, at least with regard to the term "genocide."

In short, patterns identified in this cross-national analysis of frames demonstrate that the representational power of the anti-impunity TLO is contingent on country-specific structural and cultural conditions. Such conditions thus diminish concordance between the international and national spheres and across nation-states. Some will interpret diminished concordance as a weakness of a new TLO. Yet, we may also recognize in it a flexibility that allows for the acceptance and legitimacy of TLOs across countries with varying types of civil society organization, policy preferences, and cultural sensitivities.

7.8   CONCLUSIONS: TRANSNATIONAL REORDERING OF CRIMES AGAINST HUMAN RIGHTS AND THE CASE OF DARFUR

The build-up of international institutions of criminal justice, culminating in the establishment of the ICC, is a part transnational legal ordering processes. These resulted in a new anti-impunity TLO in the human rights realm. Different from other contexts, as illustrated by the chapters in this volume, criminal law and human rights actors joined forces in the face of grave human rights violations and mass violence, forming a coalition.

Having explored the potential of a transnational legal ordering approach (Aaronson and Shaffer, Chapter 1; Halliday and Shaffer 2015a, b; Shaffer 2016) to advance our understanding of responses to mass violence has taught us two lessons. First, the current case of the anti-impunity TLO yields gains for the TLO approach. Second, the TLO approach provides substantial benefits for an appropriate understanding of the justice cascade in the human rights field. Insights can be gained regarding the formation, institutionalization, and consequences of TLOs.

Regarding *formation*, agency and power, including "soft power," matter. International organizations, INGOs, and selective nation-states are among the driving forces. These forces promote the referral of specific situations, like that of Darfur, to the prosecutor of the ICC. Bottom-up processes create pressures on national governments to join international initiatives. The UN Security Council could not have referred the situation of Darfur to the ICC had the Bush administration vetoed such a step. A veto was prevented by the engagement of human rights NGOs and the Save Darfur coalition, especially due to the substantial engagement of conservative evangelical groups. Under specific circumstances, the agency and mobilization of national and local forces may thus play a central role in the establishment of international criminal justice and in the enforcement of its norms. Simultaneously, the adoption of anti-impunity criminal law is a recursive process: the mere existence of an international legal order promotes the enforcement of human rights norms at the domestic level. In other words, domestic courts operate partially "in the shadow" of the ICC.

Regarding *institutionalization* of the anti-impunity TLO, this chapter points to substantial progress, while it also documents major impediments. The United States and other superpowers challenge international criminal justice, not when they are in control of its deployment (see US support for the ICTY), but when they see their sovereignty threatened as in an ICC case. This trend has been accentuated by recent pronouncements of the US administration under the anti-multilateralism program of the Trump administration. In addition, smaller countries, especially countries under authoritarian leadership, have threatened to withdraw from the Rome Statute when their leaders face prosecution. In the case of Darfur, intervention provoked Sudan's resistance and spurred expressions of solidarity by several African countries against the anti-impunity TNO, resulting in refusal to cooperate with the arrest and extradition of President al-Bashir to the ICC, which led to the hibernation of Darfur prosecutions.

This chapter also shows that the new TLO is not the only field that responds to situations of mass violence. It illustrates the potential for inter-field conflict, in this case with the diplomacy and humanitarian aid fields that aimed at quite different goals than the pursuit of criminal justice. Such conflict is aggravated by intra-field conflicts within a TLO, highlighting the difficulties of reaching and maintaining normative settlements. The lack of enforcement power of the anti-impunity TLO weighed even more in light of its dependence on cooperation by exactly those foreign policy actors and powerful countries that pursue different goals than the pursuit of justice.

Regarding *consequences*, relatively new TLOs require more time for maturation before final judgments can be cast. Yet, statistical analyses provide some indication that the new anti-impunity TLO may result in diminished violence. The causal mechanisms are yet to be explored, but cultural consequences should be taken seriously. The Darfur project showed that the representational power of intervention by the ICC is substantial. The court's framing of the conflict in Darfur mattered for the global spread of representations, despite the availability of alternative frames, including diplomacy and humanitarian aid frames. Dominant representations of Darfur focused on people being killed and forced to flee as a consequence of criminal action. While different orders existed to address the situation, the international criminal law frame became dominant. The role of media in the representational effectiveness of the criminal law TLO appears to be substantial. Note, however, that the receptivity toward the crime frame and the application of the genocide label varied across countries.

Consequences of interventions by the anti-impunity TLO can also be counter-productive, threatening the very system that produced them. A powerful criminal justice frame may generate challenges to the resolution of conflict and to the delivery of humanitarian aid. Criminal law, after all, is bound by legal categories. It focuses on a few individual actors while neglecting structural forces – opposed to a sociological perspective. It dehistoricizes the conflict – in contrast to a historian's perspective. It also operates with a binary logic of guilty versus not guilty – distinct from more fine-grained approaches in social psychology. Such narrowing of perspectives, and the avenues it threatens to block, provokes opposition in the realm of scholarship (Engle 2016; Moyn 2016) and in practice.

Ironically, and this issue warrants further exploration, reduced concordance between the international and the national levels across nation-states, while impeding institutionalization, may simultaneously provide the system with needed flexibility to circumvent obstacles and opposition.

REFERENCES

Alexander, J. C. 2004. "On the Social Construction of Moral Universals: The 'Holocaust' from War Crime to Trauma Drama." Pp. 196–263 in *Cultural Trauma and Collective Identity*, edited by J. C. Alexander et al. Berkeley: University of California Press.

Annan, Kofi. 2004. *Speech before the United Nations General Assembly.* April 7, 2004.

Bergsmo, Morten, Mark Klamberg, Kjersti Lohne and Chris Mahony, eds., 2020. *Power in International Criminal Justice: Towards a Sociology of International Justice.* Oslo: TOAEP.

Bourdieu, Pierre. 1977. "The Force of Law: Toward a Sociology of the Judicial Field." *The Hastings Law Journal* 38: 805–853.

Cohen, Stanley. 2001. *States of Denial.* Oxford: Polity Press.

Engle, Karen. 2016. "A Genealogy of the Criminal Turn in Human Rights." In *Anti-impunity and the Human Rights Agenda*, edited by Karen Engle, Zinaida Miller, and D. M. Davis. Cambridge: Cambridge University Press.

Fourcade, Marion, and Joachim J. Savelsberg. 2006. "Introduction: Global Processes, National Institutions, Local Bricolage: Shaping Law in an Era of Globalization." *Law and Social Inquiry* 31: 513–519.

Giesen, Bernhard. 2004. *Triumph and Trauma.* Boulder: Paradigm.

Golden, Shannon. 2013. *After Atrocity: Community Reconstruction in Northern Uganda.* Doctoral dissertation, University of Minnesota, Minneapolis.

Hagan, John. 2003. *Justice in the Balkans.* Chicago: University of Chicago Press.

Halliday, Terence, and Gregory Shaffer. 2015a. "Transnational Legal Orders." In *Transnational Legal Orders*, edited by Terence Halliday and Gregory Shaffer. Cambridge: Cambridge University Press.

Halliday, Terence, and Gregory Shaffer. 2015b. "Researching Transnational Legal Orders." In *Transnational Legal Orders*, edited by Terence Halliday and Gregory Shaffer. Cambridge: Cambridge University Press.

ICID (International Commission of Inquiry on Darfur). 2005. *Report of the International Commission of Inquiry on Darfur to the Secretary-General of the United Nations.* www.un.org/news/dh/sudan/com_inq_darfur.pdf.

Jo, Hyeran. 2015. *Compliant Rebels: Rebel Groups and International Law in World Politics.* Cambridge: Cambridge University Press.

Jo, Hyeran, and Beth A. Simmons. 2016. "Can the International Criminal Court Deter Atrocity?" *International Organization* 70(3): 443–475.

Keck, Margaret. E., and Kathryn Sikkink. 1998. *Activists beyond Borders: Advocacy Networks in International Politics*. Ithaca: Cornell University Press.

Kim, Hunjoon, and Kathryn Sikkink. 2010. "Explaining the Deterrence Effect of Human Rights Prosecutions for Transitional Countries." *International Studies Quarterly* 54(4): 939–963.

Levi, Ron, and John Hagan, with the collaboration of Sara Dezalay, eds. 2008. *Pacifier et Punir*, special issues of *Actes de la recherche en sciences sociales* 173 and 174.

Levy, Daniel, and Natan Sznaider. 2010. *Human Rights and Memory: Essays on Human Rights*. University Park: Pennsylvania State University Press.

McElrath, Suzy. 2020. *The Global Criminalization of Genocide, 1948–2015*. Doctoral dissertation, University of Minnesota, Minneapolis.

Mead, George Herbert. 1918. "The Psychology of Punitive Justice." *American Journal of Sociology* 23(5): 577–602.

Meierhenrich, Jens. 2006. "Conspiracy in International Law." *Annual Review of Law and Social Science* 2(1): 341–357.

Meierhenrich, Jens. 2014. "The Evolution of the Office of the Prosecutor at the International Criminal Court: Insights from Institutional Theory." In *The First Global Prosecutor*, edited by Martha Minow, Alex Whiting, and Cora True-Frost. Ann Arbor: University of Michigan Press.

Minow, Martha. 1998. *Between Vengeance and Forgiveness: Facing History after Genocide and Mass Violence*. Boston: Beacon Press.

Moyn, Samuel. 2016. "From Aggression to Atrocity: Rethinking the History of International Criminal Law." *Oxford Handbook of International Criminal Law*, https://ssrn.com/abstract=2805952.

Neier, Aryeh. 2012. *The International Human Rights Movement: A History*. Human Rights and Crimes against Humanity, Book 14. Princeton: Princeton University Press.

Nonet, Philippe, and Philip Selznick. 1978. *Law and Society in Transition: Toward Responsive Law*. New York: Octagon Books.

Pensky, M. 2008. "Amnesty on Trial: Impunity, Accountability, and the Norms of International Law." *Ethics and Global Politics* 1(1–2): 1–40.

Roht-Arriaza, N. 2005. *The Pinochet Effect: Transnational Justice in the Age of Human Rights*. Philadelphia: University of Pennsylvania Press.

Rome Statute. 1998. Rome Statute of the International Criminal Court. http://legal.un.org/icc/statute/99_corr/cstatute.htm.

Savelsberg, Joachim J. 1992. "Law That Does Not Fit Society: Sentencing Guidelines as a Neoclassical Reaction to the Dilemmas of Substantivized Law." *American Journal of Sociology* 97(5): 1346–1381.

Savelsberg, Joachim J. 1994. "Knowledge, Domination, and Criminal Punishment." *American Journal of Sociology* 99(4): 911–943.

Savelsberg, Joachim J. 2015. *Representing Mass Violence: Conflicting Responses to Human Rights Violations in Darfur*. Oakland: University of California Press.

Savelsberg, Joachim J. 2017. Max Weber's Formal and Substantive Rationality: Tensions in International Law. Pp. 493–510 in *Recht als Kultur? Beiträge zu Max Webers Soziologie des Rechts*. Frankfurt: Vittorio Klostermann Verlag.

Savelsberg, Joachim J. 2020. "The Representational Power of International Criminal Courts." In *Power in International Criminal Justice: Towards a Sociology of International Justice*, edited by Morten Bergsma and Kjersti Lohne. Oslo: TOAEP.

Savelsberg, Joachim J. forthcoming. "Media and Transitional Justice." In *The Oxford Handbook of Transitional Justice*, edited by Lawrence Douglas, Alexander Hinton, and Jens Meierhenrich. Oxford University Press.

Savelsberg, Joachim J., and Ryan D. King. 2011. *American Memories: Atrocities and the Law*. New York: Russell Sage Foundation.

Savelsberg, Joachim J., and Suzy McElrath. 2018. *"Human Rights and Penal Policy."* Oxford Research Encyclopedia for Criminology and Criminal Justice. Oxford: Oxford University Press.

Savelsberg, Joachim J., and Holly Nyseth Brehm. 2015. "Representing Human Rights Violations in Darfur: Global Justice, National Distinctions." *American Journal of Sociology* 121(2): 564–603.

Scheffer, David. 2012. *All the Missing Souls: A Personal History of the War Crimes Tribunals*. Princeton: Princeton University Press.

Seekers of Truth and Justice. 2003. *The Black Book*. n.p.

Shaffer, Gregory. 2016. "Theorizing Transnational Legal Ordering." *Annual Review of Law and Social Sciences* 12: 231–253.

Sikkink, Kathryn. 2011. *The Justice Cascade: How Human Rights Prosecutions Are Changing World Politics*. New York: W. W. Norton and Company.

Smith, Philip. 2008. *Punishment and Culture*. Chicago: University of Chicago Press.

Snyder, Jack, and Leslie Vinjamuri. 2004. "Trials and Errors: Principle and Pragmatism in Strategies of International Justice." *International Security* 28 (3): 5–44.

Stryker, Robin. 1989. "Limits on Technocratization of Law." *American Sociological Review* 54: 341–358.

Unger, Roberto M. 1976. *Law in Modern Society*. New York: Free Press.

Vilmer, Jean-Baptiste Jeangène. 2015. *La Responsabilité de Protéger*. Paris: Presses Universitaires de France.

Weber, M. 1978. *Economy and Society: An Outline of Interpretive Sociology*. Berkeley: University of California Press.

CHAPTER EIGHT

COLOMBIAN TRANSITIONAL JUSTICE AND THE POLITICAL ECONOMY OF THE ANTI-IMPUNITY TRANSNATIONAL LEGAL ORDER

*Manuel Iturralde**

8.1 INTRODUCTION

During the last three decades, the transnational legal ordering of criminal justice in the name of human rights, democracy, and the rule of law has become a salient feature of international relations and the transformation of crime control fields. The transfer of policies, practices, discourses, and institutions, particularly from the Global North to the Global South, has been a recurrent tool to uphold those ideals. The international wars against drugs and terrorism, law and order policies, international interventions in internal armed conflicts and against authoritarian regimes, international criminal tribunals, the International Criminal Court (ICC), transitional justice, peace building, among other initiatives have been sponsored and financed by Global North countries and institutions across the globe as ideal mechanisms to combat violence, disorder, transnational threats, and crimes, and to strengthen democratic institutions and the rule of law.

These transfers have transformed and conditioned crime control fields, which used to be regarded as a vital expression of a state's sovereignty and autonomy, thus giving place to a very explicit interconnection between the domestic, regional, and international dimensions of criminal justice and crime control policies, which are increasingly

* I would like to thank Gregory Shaffer, Ely Aaronson, and Máximo Langer who offered thoughtful comments to previous versions of this article. I am also grateful to the colleagues who provided useful feedback for the first version, presented at the Symposium/Book Conference on *Transnational Legal Ordering of Criminal Justice*.

interlocked. The different forms of the transnational legal ordering of criminal justice are increasingly pressuring states to recognize and enforce international norms and standards, and even to delegate public powers to supranational organizations, which push for the institutional and legal reforms that they endorse (Aaronson and Shaffer, Chapter 1).

The global expansion of liberal democracy has coincided with the rise of international criminal law and justice (including transitional justice), heralded as the most effective way to prevent violence and conflict, as well as of promoting democratic regimes, the rule of law, and development (Cravo 2014: 473; Franzki and Olarte 2014: 203; Krever 2013: 709; Urueña and Prada 2018: 400). One salient aspect of international criminal law and justice is its focus on the accountability (mainly understood as criminal responsibility) of perpetrators of serious human rights violations, which constitute war crimes and crimes against humanity.

A global apparatus aimed at putting an end to impunity regarding human rights violations through criminal justice's institutions and forms of punishment has consolidated, to the point of being considered a transnational legal order (TLO). Payne (2015: 439) refers to it as an *accountability transnational legal order* – for it meets the three criteria of a TLO specified by Halliday and Shaffer (2015). Many other authors (see Engle, Miller, and Davis 2015) have remarked that this represents an essential shift toward anti-impunity, where amnesties (and broad support for them) in post-conflict or post-authoritarian societies have given way to criminal responsibility and punishment to deal with past human rights violations and to secure peace. In this chapter, I will refer to such TLO as an *anti-impunity transnational legal order*.

Recent events in Colombia clearly illustrate the complex and multiple relationships between criminal justice, democracy, human rights, the rule of law, and the anti-impunity TLO. On October 2, 2016, Colombian voters rejected a landmark peace deal between the government and the FARC (*Fuerzas Armadas Revolucionarias de Colombia*), a Marxist guerrilla group, to put an end to the oldest armed conflict in the Western Hemisphere. This conflict has left more than 260,000 fatal victims (Centro de Memoria Histórica 2018) and more than 6.5 million violently displaced people during the last five decades (Centro de Memoria Histórica 2015: 16).[1] In an unexpected and

---

[1] The Colombian armed conflict goes back to the 1960s. Under the spell of the Cold War, from the fifties until the early eighties, the Colombian elitist and exclusionary political regime regarded communism as a threat to law and order, and linked it to social protest (particularly

extremely close result (with a difference of fewer than 54,000 votes), 50.2 percent of the electorate (6,431,376 voters) voted against it (Registraduría Nacional del Estado Civil de Colombia 2016).

One of the key, and most contested, points of the agreement was the establishment of a special jurisdiction (Special Jurisdiction for Peace – JEP for its Spanish acronym) to try war crimes and crimes against humanity committed by state agents and guerrilla fighters during the conflict. Those who fully confessed to their crimes, asked for forgiveness, and repaired the victims would have been granted more lenient sentences (five to eight years that would not be served in prison).

This kind of transitional justice, based on criminal accountability, confirmed an essential change in Colombia's legal and political tradition of dealing with illegal armed groups. Such tradition, going back to the nineteenth century, backed amnesties as the most suitable form to reach peace agreements and demobilize these groups. However, things changed as the anti-impunity TLO consolidated from the nineties, particularly in Latin America (Engle 2016); amnesties were no longer acceptable to reach peace, consolidate democracy, and deal with past human rights violations. In these circumstances, the Álvaro Uribe government (2002–2010) reached a peace agreement with the Autodefensas Unidas de Colombia (AUC), who accepted to demobilize and submit to a transitional justice that would establish criminal accountability for war crimes and crimes again humanity, but with reduced prison sentences (five to eight years) in exchange for truth, justice, and reparations. For the first time in Colombia's republican history, amnesties for such crimes were off the table (Alviar García and Engle 2015: 226–231).

Those who opposed the Special Jurisdiction for Peace, and the peace agreement itself, led by former President Uribe and his political party

---

of student, peasant, and labor movements), thus criminalizing it. The closure of the political system and its violent repression of social movements fostered the rise of leftist guerrillas in the sixties, particularly the FARC and the ELN (*Ejército de Liberación Nacional*; Iturralde 2010: 55–76). The war on drugs entered the scene in the early eighties and fueled the armed conflict. The guerrillas – as well as their deadly rivals, the paramilitary groups – found in drug trafficking a vital source of financial resources and territorial control. The eruption of extreme-right paramilitary groups further explains the escalation of violence during the eighties and nineties. Supported by narco-traffickers, landowners, industrialists, businesspeople, a sector of the military, and regional elites, the paramilitaries, unified under the umbrella group Autodefensas Unidas de Colombia (AUC), waged a dirty war against the civilian population that, according to them, supported the guerrillas (Iturralde 2010: 174–178). Between 1958 and 2017, the armed conflict left more than 215,000 dead civilians and more than 46,000 dead combatants. Paramilitary groups caused 68 percent of those deaths, the guerrillas caused 25 percent, and state security forces caused 7 percent (Centro Nacional de Memoria Histórica 2018).

(*Centro Democrático*), claimed that it was an antidemocratic expression of impunity, an insult to the victims, and violated the Colombian Constitution, as well as international standards and agreements that bind the Colombian state.[2] In other words, they claimed that the apparatus set up to deal with war crimes and crimes against humanity in Colombia was against the anti-impunity TLO.

Through the study of the Colombian case, this chapter explains how the conceptions of justice, impunity, and punishment are, to a significant degree, a construct that relies on "international standards" – on human rights, criminal justice, the rule of law, and democracy. Such standards have been devised in Global North countries and do not necessarily respond to the realities and necessities of Global South societies, but, nevertheless, have become predominant and almost uncontested. From a political economy perspective, the chapter also aims to show the ways in which the relationship between political and economic regimes, on the one hand, and the scope and forms that punishment takes (particularly penal policies, practices, and discourses), on the other, are constructed and legitimize particular forms of government, both at the national and international levels.

With the end of the Cold War and the demise of communism, liberal democracies and free markets became hegemonic, configuring what was then called a New World Order. During the 1980s and 1990s, the political economies of countries around the world, particularly in the Global South and the ex-Soviet bloc (many of them overcoming armed conflicts or authoritarian regimes), were transformed by the triumph of liberal democracy and free markets. In order to take part in the international economy and political concert of an increasingly globalized and interdependent world, these countries opened their economies and their political systems to foster the free movement of goods, services, and financial exchanges. These transformations were based on restructuring and structural adjustment policies endorsed and promoted by international financial institutions and their main donor countries (Krever 2014: 130).

---

[2] Uribe declared: "The [peace] agreement means total impunity, it violates the Constitution and international treaties, like the Statute of the International Criminal Court and the American Convention on Human Rights" (El Colombiano, September 26, 2016). As if following a script, Oscar Zuluaga, former presidential candidate of the *Centro Demcrático*, Uribe's political party, stated that the peace accord "violates the Constitution, is a fraud to international law and does not seek real peace. …Prison sentences are excluded, and the whole judicial structure is substituted" (W Radio, August 25, 2016).

These discourses have been instrumental to legitimate and enforce a thin liberal version of democracy and the rule of law (Cravo 2014: 276). Such version displays a reductionist understanding of violence and social conflict, which relies heavily on a criminal law perspective and tool-kit to solve complex social problems. This thin version of democracy has blocked attempts to reach alternative solutions that may secure compromise between justice, peace, and social stability. The latter perspectives advocate for a thicker concept of democracy and the rule of law, aimed at guaranteeing not only civil and political rights, as well as free markets, but also social and economic rights, through social justice and redistributive policies (Carvo 2014: 476; Franzki and Olarte 2014: 202; Urueña and Prada 2018: 400).

As liberal democracy and free markets globally became the norm, the anti-impunity TLO gained strength – and not by chance. Its dominant liberal narrative overlooks that its working concepts and categories, as well as its related institutions and practices, are perspectives rather than neutral descriptions of and responses to social phenomena and problems. Accordingly, different actors within the anti-impunity TLO, at different levels, strive to impose their interests within particular contexts, in light of long-standing historical and political trajectories.

Thus it is relevant to analyze and theorize the processes through which transnational rules and standards governing criminal justice practices, together with conceptions of punishment and justice, travel across borders and shape (and are shaped by) the attitudes and behavior of different actors at international, regional, national, and local levels of social organization (Aaronson and Shaffer, Chapter 1).

In the first portion of the chapter, I discuss the Colombian case, particularly the role that different actors, discourses, conceptions, and institutions of punishment (both domestic and international) played in the Peace Plebiscite. I explain how the analytic categories that have predominated in the anti-impunity TLO take their reality as the reality on which supposed universal categories are based, and how they are unable to take into account social relations that do not fall within such categories. Such conceptions, which tend to become viewed as common sense in the international and domestic orders, are used as an ideological device (Krever 2013) that naturalizes and legitimizes the status quo (both at the international and national levels), reflecting unequal power relations.

I then discuss how the predominant liberal outlook of the anti-impunity TLO fosters categories and worldviews that not only limit the autonomy of Global South societies to find responses to their problems, but that also legitimize and naturalize power relations between the Global North and south and within them. The anti-impunity TLO is a battleground where different actors (governments, national and international institutions and organizations, experts, technocrats, and scholars) clash to impose their worldviews and interests. The predominant order is an expression of the status quo that constrains the resistance – especially at the domestic level.

Finally, I argue that the experiences of Global South countries not only reveal such power relations, but also point to promising new directions of research and theorization. These will lead to better understanding of the complexity of the configuration and uses of the anti-impunity TLO, its relation to local and regional contexts, and the varied conceptions and relationships between political and economic regimes, on the one hand, and criminal justice, on the other, that underlie the TLO.

8.2 THE END OF THE ARMED CONFLICT? THE ANTI-IMPUNITY TRANSNATIONAL LEGAL ORDER AND ITS IMPACT ON THE COLOMBIAN CRIME CONTROL FIELD

The role that criminal justice practices, discourses, and institutions played, and are still playing, in the Colombian peace process is a telling example of the struggles over the normative settlement of the anti-impunity TLO, as well as its degree of concordance at the international, national, and local levels, within a particular setting.

The most important legacy of former President Juan Manuel Santos (2010–2018) is the historic peace agreement with the FARC – Colombia's most significant and oldest guerrilla movement – that put an end to more than fifty years of armed conflict, which has left more than six million victims (at least those recognized by the Colombian State since 1984). This was a transcendental achievement, one that sparked an intense political debate that has polarized Colombian society. Proof of this is the *Peace Plebiscite* as it became known. Colombian voters rejected the peace agreement; in an extremely close result, 50.2 percent voted against it.

Former president Álvaro Uribe's political party (*Centro Democrático*) was a staunch opponent of the agreement and led the political campaign to vote *No* in the plebiscite. The *No* campaign brought together a coalition of different political movements (the *Centro Democrático* and members of the Conservative Party), traditional elites (land-owners, members of the military, industrialists, and big business), and social and religious organizations that, though very diverse, shared a conservative and anti-subversive ideology. The *No* campaign's main argument was that it was not against peace but against impunity. For this coalition, justice was a precondition of peace. Moreover, justice, under this view, meant the FARC's surrender and punitive retribution. Uribe and his followers did not accept any punishment other than doing time in a State correctional facility. Uribe claimed that the peace agreement that he reached with paramilitary groups and the transitional justice it set up a decade earlier was a completely different story. Although reduced sentences were granted (five to eight years) for those who committed serious crimes, they were conceded in exchange of truth, justice, and reparations, and were served in penitentiary institutions (Alviar García and Engle 2016: 228–231).

The supporters of the retributive stance were willing to concede that violators of human rights could receive lenient prison sentences (from five to eight years for all the crimes they committed), but they were not willing to yield regarding the material and symbolic expression of punishment. According to this narrative, guerrilla fighters were nothing but terrorists, drug traffickers, kidnappers, and murderers; they were the worst of common criminals – and they should be portrayed and treated as such. Uribe and his followers have come to say that in Colombia there was no such thing as an armed conflict but rather a narco-terrorist threat. Therefore, the intensity of punishment could be negotiated, but not its quality and meaning. This strong view of punishment very consciously played into the emotions and anxieties of the population. As Juan Carlos Vélez, the manager of the *Centro Democrático* campaign against the plebiscite, declared with candour, "We appealed to people's sense of indignation, we wanted the people to vote angry"[3] (El Espectador 2016).

Such retributivist perspective of punishment took advantage of the anti-impunity TLO, particularly the Rome Statute and the ICC, on the one hand, and the American Convention on Human Rights and the Inter-American Court of Human Rights (IACHR), on the other. Both institutions, through their norms and rulings, have demanded the prosecution and effective punishment of those responsible for international crimes (Engle 2016; Hillebrecht, Huneeus, and Borda 2018;

---

[3] "Apelamos a la indignación, queríamos que la gente saliera a votar verraca."

Huneeus 2013). The IACHR, just as other human rights courts, has become an integral part of the anti-impunity TLO, acting as a quasi-criminal jurisdiction to enforce the American Convention on Human Rights and to prevent impunity, which is regarded as a violation of the victims' rights enshrined in the Convention (Huneeus 2013). The IACHR rulings over blanket amnesty laws have emphatically established that they violate the American Convention on Human Rights because they do not guarantee justice and truth to victims of human rights violations. The IACHR has ruled that, in order to adequately protect such rights, the criminal accountability of the perpetrators is required (Engle 2016).

Thus, in Colombia, the ICC and the IACHR have exerted influence through "the shadow of the law": "neither international court has an active case, yet both loom large in the domestic debate over peace" (Hillebrecht, Huneeus, and Borda 2018: 287).[4] Nevertheless, as Aaronson and Shaffer point out, the "mismatch between the actors shaping global norms of criminal justice at the international level and those implementing these scripts in national and local settings" (Chapter 1) makes it difficult to secure a stable normative settlement.

The vacuum created by the instability of normative settlement in this context is used by actors with particular interests to advance their ideological and political agendas (Payne 2015). The negotiation of the end of the Colombian armed conflict was also a negotiation over the meaning of justice and what should be expected of the Colombian democratic regime and its transformation. A maximalist view of peace, or positive peace, expected it to produce a more inclusive, egalitarian, and just democracy by addressing the deeper roots of violence (Cravo 2014: 472). Making a U-turn vis-à-vis his predecessor, Santos recognized the FARC's political status by acknowledging the existence of an armed conflict with social, political, and economic roots that need to be addressed by the Colombian state and society.

Santos took steps that were inconceivable under Uribe's administration. As part of the peace talks with the FARC, his government agreed to discuss with the group's leadership sensitive subjects, such as agrarian reform, the solution to the drugs problem, political participation and guarantees to FARC members, as well as mechanisms of transitional

---

[4] Regarding the IACHR, to date, it has ruled on eighteen cases related to Colombia, over half of which relate to massacres and other international crimes committed by the paramilitary with the support or active involvement of state actors, especially the military forces (Hillebrecht, Huneeus, and Borda 2018: 290).

and restorative justice to secure the victim's rights to truth, justice, and reparation.

The minimalist view, or negative peace (understood as the absence of direct violence and war; Cravo 2014: 472), held by the *No* campaign, thought of peace mainly in terms of the demobilization of illegal armed groups, almost a capitulation, in exchange of a more lenient punitive treatment, which was nonnegotiable. This kind of minimalist peace also meant leaving untouched political, economic, and social institutions, as well as practices, that benefit the status quo.

Punishment and the anti-impunity TLO played an essential role at this juncture. They were determinant in shaping the public debate and tipping the scale in favor of the discourse that resonated more strongly among different social groups and the media. The retributive vision of punishment was instrumental in imposing the minimalist view of peace and democracy, served status quo interests, and was in tune with popular sentiments of indignation and vengeance after a prolonged and cruel conflict that left millions of victims, within a context of entrenched economic inequality and social exclusion.

The *No* supporters in Colombia claimed to uphold international human rights law and criminal law. They used not only their legal framework, mainly provided by the American Convention on Human Rights and the Rome Statute, but also the authoritative statements and interpretations of supranational bodies. Among them, the IACHR and the ICC Prosecutor Office, and even national and international human rights NGOs (such as Amnesty International and Human Rights Watch) – even though they came from opposite ideological sides and with different agendas. Therefore, the *No* supporters argued that the international human rights and criminal justice frame demanded retributive punishment, and imprisonment as its logical consequence, as the only way to confront impunity. Former president Uribe used this line of argument to hinder peace negotiations; he submitted a petition against the peace process to the Inter-American Commission of Human Rights, a preliminary step in litigation before the IAHRC, claiming that the terms of the peace agreement violated Inter-American human rights standards (Hillebrecht, Huneeus, and Borda 2018: 286, fn. 29).

In the Latin American context, the IACHR rulings have become an essential tool for domestic actors, with different political agendas, seeking to shape government policy and domestic litigation (Hillebrecht, Huneeus, and Borda 2018: 293). In recent years, the

IACHR has ruled in five cases that the State must prosecute and punish fundamental human rights violations. Thus the Court has developed a hard line against impunity, practically outlawing, according to its critics, amnesty laws for serious crimes (Hillebrecht, Huneeus, and Borda 2018: 299–300). As Engle (2016) notes, human rights NGOs, who for decades advocated for the rights of political prisoners and their right to amnesty, turned to anti-impunity as their main banner to fight human rights violations and make those responsible accountable. Quite paradoxically, they became aligned with retributive perspectives, more common among conservative sectors of society and political forces who upheld the status quo.

As to international criminal law, the critics of the peace agreement asserted that it also violated the Rome Statute, which, according to them, establishes imprisonment as a necessary form of punishment for the crimes included in the Statute.[5] Consequently, under Statute rules, the ICC could intervene in Colombia, due to the unwillingness or inability of the Colombian State genuinely to prosecute ex-combatants.

Besides Uribe and the members of the *Centro Democrático* party, critical public figures also followed this line of argument. For instance, the ultra-Catholic and conservative former Inspector General (*Procurador General de la Nación*),[6] Alejandro Ordóñez, a staunch opponent of the peace agreement, declared the following:

> The agreement simulates a genuine process of accountability for the commission of international crimes but does not comply with international standards of justice.
>
> It establishes a complex network of institutions and procedures that in fact seek to avoid the criminal liability, specifically the handing down of prison sentences, of State agents and members of illegal armed groups who have committed crimes that fall under the jurisdiction of the International Criminal Court, as established in article 17.2 of the Rome Statute. (2016)

The possible intervention of the ICC in Colombia has been a matter of public debate and was one of the main concerns of the Colombian government and FARC's negotiators. In 2004, the Office of the Prosecutor of the ICC informed the Colombian government that it

---

[5] Genocide, war crimes, crimes against humanity, and the crime of aggression (Article 5 of the Rome Statute).

[6] According to the Colombian Constitution, the Inspector General Office is in charge of the protection of human rights, the rule of law, and the public interest.

was opening a preliminary examination (a preliminary step to activate the ICC jurisdiction), since there was evidence that international crimes, which fell under the ICC's jurisdiction, might have been committed in Colombia. After fourteen years, Colombia is still under the radar of the ICC, which has allowed it to exert influence over Colombian affairs without the need to open a criminal investigation (Hillebrecht, Huneeus, and Borda 2018: 290–291).

The former ICC Prosecutor (Luis Moreno Ocampo) and the current one (Fatou Bensouda) have made several visits to Colombia to talk to the government and Colombian State representatives, to check the situation on the ground, and to make the ICC's presence felt. During his first visit, in 2008, Ocampo declared, "with the International Criminal Court, there is a new law under which impunity is no longer an option. Either the national courts must [conduct trials] or we will." Ocampo emphasized the need to establish individual responsibility for international crimes and to remove amnesties as one of the government's possible negotiation tools (cited by Hillebrecht, Huneeus, and Borda 2018: 296).

The government and the FARC were well aware that the crimes that fell under the ICC jurisdiction, committed by both sides during the armed conflict, could not be pardoned or amnestied, according to international and Colombian law. The Colombian government's negotiators said to the FARC, "A general amnesty is not on the table. There must be a strong commitment with the truth and reparations."[7] Iván Márquez, the FARC's chief negotiator, replied, "We are not going to exchange impunities"[8] (IFIT 2018: 209). Therefore, they agreed that guerrilla fighters, who only committed political crimes (primarily rebellion) and offences directly connected to such crimes, would be pardoned or amnestied. However, those who were suspected of committing war crimes and crimes against humanity would have to submit to the JEP. In this sense, the JEP was a complex and original mechanism entrusted with guaranteeing the victims' rights to truth, justice, and reparation, while complying with international criminal law and human rights law standards (which ruled out any form of impunity) and making possible a peace agreement that would reassure both sides.

The Santos government and the FARC claimed that the JEP fulfilled all these expectations, and they made use of critical institutions of the

---

[7] "Una amnistía general no está sobre la mesa. Debe haber un compromiso fuerte con la verdad y la reparación."
[8] "No vamos a intercambiar impunidades."

anti-impunity TLO, mainly the UN and the ICC, to back their claims. Thus Santos declared that the ICC and the UN endorsed the peace agreement, and particularly the JEP. Regarding the ICC, Santos stated, "It is hard to understand the criticisms and accusations of those who claim that there will be impunity when the highest authority in the world in matters of justice against the most serious crimes backs this process" (El Tiempo 2016).

Santos was referring to the statement made by Fatou Bensouda, the Prosecutor of the International Criminal Court, after her visit to Colombia. She celebrated the fact that, under the peace agreement, war crimes and crimes against humanity could not be amnestied. However, she was cautious to fully endorse the JEP – for she also stated:

> The peace agreement acknowledges the central place of victims in the process and their legitimate aspirations for justice. These aspirations must be adequately addressed, including by ensuring that the perpetrators of serious crimes are genuinely brought to justice. The *Special Jurisdiction for Peace* to be established in Colombia is expected to perform this role and to focus on those most responsible for the most serious crimes committed during the armed conflict. The promise of such accountability must become a reality if the people of Colombia are to reap the full dividends of peace. (2016)

From the opposite political and ideological side of Uribe and his followers, but with similar arguments, Colombian and international human rights NGOs expressed their concerns about the JEP. For instance, the *Comisión Colombiana de Juristas*, one of the most well-known Colombian human rights NGOs, argued that the JEP's mandate to prosecute *mainly* those most responsible for serious crimes, and *mainly* the most serious crimes, could not guarantee truth, justice, and reparation to *all* the victims of the armed conflict, according to international standards (Comisión Colombiana de Juristas 2012). Also, José Miguel Vivanco, director of Human Rights Watch's Americas division, stated:

> Human Rights Watch has grave concerns that the justice provisions of the accord could result in confessed war criminals not receiving meaningful punishment for the grave crimes for which they were responsible. . . .
>
> A key area of concern has been the sanctions to be imposed on war criminals who fully and promptly confess to their atrocities. The original agreement stated that war criminals who fully and promptly confess their

crimes would be exempt from any time in prison and would be subjected to "effective restrictions on freedoms and rights" while carrying out community service projects. However, it provided virtually no indication of what these "restrictions" would entail nor how they would be monitored and enforced – and therefore no reason to believe they would constitute a meaningful punishment in light of the gravity of the crimes. (2017)

Thus both the backers and opponents of the peace agreement used the anti-impunity TLO to substantiate their positions, and also to delegitimize those of their antagonists. This shows that the different actors who struggle to impose their interests and worldviews within the field, use the tools it provides them to improve their positions, and, by doing so, shape the debates and possible transformations of the TLO. As Hillebrecht, Huneeus, and Borda point out, "Domestic actors are not simply recipients of international law. In addition to being constrained by international courts and using international judicialization to try to constrain their domestic opposition, domestic actors are also trying to reign in those very same adjudicative bodies" (2018: 310).

Despite the stark opposition they confronted, the Colombian government and the FARC managed to reach a deal that, even if it focused on criminal responsibility and ruled out amnesties for international crimes, distanced itself from mere retribution, as the government's opposition wanted. Notably, the agreement avoided the term "jail" as the form of punishment to be applied by the JEP. It spoke, in rather vague terms, about "effective restriction of freedom." This was a point of honor for the FARC, as the FARC's negotiators repeatedly said, "We are not going to be the first guerrilla on the planet that signs a peace agreement to go to jail"[9] (IFIT 2018: 238). This happened, at least, with the acquiescence of key actors in the anti-impunity TLO, such as the ICC, the UN Secretary-General, and the Security Council, and global powers, such as the United States and the EU. It is also an innovative approach, which has not been experienced or tested, within the anti-impunity TLO. Hence, it may open new possibilities to understand critical aspects of the field, such as the meaning and reach of retribution and punishment, and their relationship to other fundamental values, like peace building.

However, as the legal and political debates in Colombia show, even though there is room for interpretation and different kinds of enforcement, the legal and institutional framework of the anti-impunity TLO still tends to promote a retributive idea of punishment and justice that focuses

---

[9] "No vamos a ser la primera guerrilla del planeta que firme un acuerdo de paz para irse a la cárcel."

on individual responsibility. Being an end in itself, the justification of retributivism is a normative one; it claims to be "fair," "good in itself," "universal," and therefore does not have to deal with the social consequences of its application in a particular context. This legitimation mechanism eases the expansion and enforcement of the anti-impunity TLO – and retributivist punishment – at a national level in different types of contexts, without assuming the political costs of dealing with the consequences, and without addressing the more complex demands of social and economic justice.

8.3   THE AFTERMATH OF THE PEACE PLEBISCITE

As the Peace Plebiscite showed, the opposition's appropriation of the most punitive aspects of the legal categories and framework of international criminal law prevailed. After a shocking defeat, the Santos government and the FARC were forced to renegotiate critical aspects of the agreement. Regarding transitional justice and the JEP, some modifications, precisions, and concessions (especially to the state armed forces) were made, though no significant changes to its basic structure. Even though the *No* supporters claimed that these changes were not enough and that the new agreement betrayed the democratic decision of the Colombian people, Santos went ahead and signed, on November 24, 2016, the agreement with Timoleón Jiménez, *Timochenko*, the FARC's leader, with the support of the Colombian Congress.

The Santos government came to an end on August 7, 2018. The new elected President, Iván Duque, is a young politician and former Senator, almost unknown to Colombian voters, until former President Uribe and their political party, *Centro Democrático*, supported Duque. Not surprisingly, Duque assured that the peace agreement had to be modified in order to avoid impunity and guarantee the victims' rights. Compared to some of the members of his party, he presented himself as a conciliatory person who wanted to unite all Colombians. However, the political campaign was ruthless. Fernando Londoño, former Minister of Justice and the Interior of the Uribe government, and one of the most radical members of *Centro Democrático*, promised voters that if Duque came to power, the first challenge of his party would be to tear to pieces the peace agreement.[10] This kind of rhetoric still persuaded Colombian voters and

---

[10] Giving a public speech at the National Convention of his party, Londoño declared "the first challenge of *Centro Democrático* will be to tear to pieces that damn paper that they call final

Duque won the election by a comfortable margin – 54 percent of the vote, against leftist candidate Gustavo Petro's 42 percent.

Duque has not made shreds of the peace agreement, in part because Santos and the FARC made sure that it was armored through several constitutional reforms and laws. Nonetheless, the negative concept of peace, as lack of a declared armed conflict, seems to be the primary objective of the current government. It does not seem to want to upset the status quo, which backs it. Many of the promises made to the FARC have not been fulfilled; the government has appointed in critical positions to implement the agreement unknown, inexperienced, mediocre, and even shady characters; the budget for various peace programs has been cut, with the argument that the previous government left no funds and that the current one has nowhere to find them. This suggests that the Duque administration does not have the political will to implement the peace accords fully. Thus it seems that the peace agreement will not be shredded to pieces, but it does look like the government, and the establishment, will let it wither away.

Even more concerning, the structural problems at the root of the armed conflict are not being addressed; drug trafficking is still a significant security problem that involves thousands of poor peasants who do not have other legal ways to make a living; there is no land reform in sight, and powerful illegal armed groups are still at large. Many dissatisfied ex-paramilitary and FARC members regrouped and formed new organizations that fight each other for territorial domination and economic control of legal and illegal resources (especially drugs and natural resources). They are waging a low-intensity war that still victimizes many civilians. During the Santos government, while peace talks were taking place, 609 social leaders were killed, and 2,646 were threatened (El Espectador 2018). In many cases, such attacks against the civilian population were related to land conflicts, and opposition to the extraction of natural resources; local social and political elites are involved in such conflicts. The Colombian Ombudsman Office (*Defensoría del Pueblo*) has reported 331 killings of social leaders between January 2016 and August 2018 (El Espectador 2018). Finally, the Constitutional Court ruled that third parties (such as landowners, politicians, businesspeople, industrialists) that were not actors in the armed conflict, for they did not participate directly in it,

agreement with the FARC" ("el primer desafío del Centro Democrático será el de volver trizas ese maldito papel que llaman el acuerdo con las FARC"; Semana 2017).

even though they may have benefited or profited from it, could not be subjected to the JEP jurisdiction, unless they voluntarily decide to do so. Considering all this, it may be concluded that peace, especially positive peace, is far from being achieved in Colombia, despite the peace agreement.

8.4 THE ANTI-IMPUNITY TRANSNATIONAL LEGAL ORDER: WHAT LIES BEHIND IT?

As the Colombian case shows, many Global South societies are still struggling with conflict, violence, inequality, and poverty, not merely because they are "shallow" or "dysfunctional" democracies, but precisely because this is the only kind of democracy available to vast sectors of their populations. Moreover, this has happened to a significant degree because the interests of well-situated actors with political, economic, and cultural leverage, both at the domestic and international levels, concur in positioning a limited form of democracy that works to their benefit.

The anti-impunity TLO plays a vital role in the legitimation of a limited version of liberal democracy and the rule of law, as well as the interests that underlie it. Such limited vision, presented by the anti-impunity TLO and its advocates as if it were a standard, technical definition of neutral concepts, works ideologically as a legitimizing device, which depicts it as the natural, commonsense set of institutions, norms, discourses, and practices to confront international crimes, conflicts, and violence, while also achieving peace and social order. However, by focusing on individual offenders and crimes, and by adjudicating individual criminal responsibility, the anti-impunity TLO obscures or ignores the structural forms of violence and conflict in which specific crimes are rooted.

Of course, to assert that crime and atrocities are rooted in structural, political, and economic forces does not mean to deny the existence and relevance of agency and individual responsibility (Krever 2015: 303). The point is that the background contexts of massive violence and conflict, which characterize international crimes, are essential to understanding the decisions made by individuals and, hence, to avoid their repetition (Krever 2013: 719) – something that the criminal trial is in no position to guarantee.

The anti-impunity TLO plays a crucial political role in global and local contexts. As Krever notes, the most common debate on the political nature of international criminal law displays two sides. Its critics claim that it is a politicized tool, used by global powers to protect their interests. Meanwhile, the anti-impunity TLO advocates argue that its norms and institutions are neutral vehicles for the promotion of international justice and the rule of law. Politics may get involved and manipulate the discourse, but there is a faith that the TLO can and should transcend politics to do its job. Both positions are reductionist, for they depict politics as an instrument foreign to the anti-impunity TLO and, by doing this, reproduce its image as a neutral, apolitical institution. They mask and put beyond scrutiny, its inherently deeper, political character (2014: 118; Moyn 2016).

From a political economy perspective, it is clear that politics is inherent to the anti-impunity TLO, for it is embedded in broader political and social relations, which shape it, and are shaped by it. The actors in the field may not be aware of such relations and how they condition their decisions, but the power relations of which they are part, and through which they act, shape their perceptions and preferences. Thus they accept, and reproduce, their role in the existing order of things, which is taken for granted (Krever 2014: 127).

In Latin America, during the 1980s and 1990s, many countries were suffering military dictatorships (backed by the United States in its fight against the communist threat) or internal armed conflicts, which were also a by-product of the Cold War. This was also the period of structural adjustment programs promoted the World Bank and the International Monetary Fund, which conditioned financial aid, in a time of economic crisis, on compliance with their recommendations. These were ideologically inspired by neoliberal institutions, practices, and discourses, which began to play a leading role in the region (Dezalay and Garth 2002), and which also impacted crime control policies (Iturralde 2018). Such traumatic changes resulted in a highly inequitable distribution of land, wealth, resources, and political power, in a region that already featured extremely high levels of inequality. These structural changes laid the foundations for recurring cycles of conflict and violence, making Latin America the most violent region of the world (UNODC 2008: 3; Muggah and Aguirre Tobón 2018: 2–9).

The political economy of the anti-impunity TLO is not crude economic determinism. The agency and interests of specific actors in the field, located in different positions, are also crucial in shaping and transforming it. Turning back to the Latin American case, Dezalay and Garth (2002) rightly note that neoliberal ideas, practices, and discourses, which included economic policies, human rights and the rule of law, traveled from the United States to advance the worldviews and interests of particular US and international actors and institutions. However, at the same time, local actors from Latin American countries introduced, adapted, and transformed these ideas, practices, and discourses to fit their interests and to wage their palace wars (such as economists and technocrats against lawyers, the traditional political elite in the region) to gain predominance.

This does not imply that the anti-impunity TLO merely is a blunt tool that is used at will by the powerful, or by Global North countries against their southern counterparts. Instead, such ordering involves a complex web of institutions, ideas, discourses, strategies, beliefs, and practices that travel in different directions. It is a social field where diverse actors interact and struggle to impose their views and interests in the international scene and domestic contexts, both in the Global South and north. Nevertheless, the predominant framework ideologically restricts legal and political consciousness (Krever 2013: 703), thus setting the scenario and limits of discussions and struggles, constraining political and legal imagination, to the benefit of the status quo.

8.5 THE INTERNATIONAL CRIMINAL COURT AND THE IDEOLOGICAL FUNCTION OF THE ANTI-IMPUNITY TRANSNATIONAL LEGAL ORDER

The emergence of the ICC provides a telling example of how the ideological function of the anti-impunity TLO is not about enforcing power relations, but rather about legitimizing them – that is, to get social and political actors to accept the legitimacy and inevitability of the status quo (Krever 2013: 707) as a way of advancing their agendas. As the Colombian case showed, the ICC is a key player of the anti-impunity TLO, particularly at the national level where different social actors use and appropriate its discourse and norms to defend their interests and political agendas. Different groups take advantage of the unsettled character of the TLO, especially at the domestic level, by interpreting its norms and practices to their benefit.

The ICC is celebrated as a success story of the anti-impunity TLO. A total of 123 countries are States Parties to the Rome Statute of the International Criminal Court: 33 are African States, 19 are Asia-Pacific States, 18 are Eastern Europe States, 28 are Latin American and Caribbean States, and 25 are Western European and other States (ICC 2018). Nonetheless, in recent years the ICC has come under attack, especially from African countries, which regard it as biased. To confront these complaints, defenders of the ICC affirm that it is preposterous to claim that it is biased and that it functions as a new form of colonialism and interventionism of Global North countries in Global South countries' affairs. After all, the vast majority of Parties to the ICC come from the Global South, and an essential part of its bureaucracy (starting with its Prosecutor, Fatou Bensouda, from the Gambia) comes as well from Global South countries (Krever 2016).

Nonetheless, suspicions of the ICC's bias are not groundless and should be taken into account. The absence of many of the world's major powers, or their allies, in the ICC, poses a real legitimacy problem for an allegedly global court[11] (Krever 2016). Furthermore, most of the cases under the ICC involve African states and citizens. Hence, it is not surprising that a Gambian Information Minister claimed that the ICC actually means "International Caucasian Court" (Krever 2016).

Even though many of the armed conflicts and situations of mass violence that involve international crimes affect African States, they also include different countries and parts of the world where Global North countries and their allies are deeply involved. These cases also fall under the ICC's jurisdiction, either because the countries where violence is taking place are State parties to the treaty (for instance, Palestine and Afghanistan) or because nationals of State parties, many of them Global North countries (such as the United Kingdom, France, and Australia) are directly involved.

As Krever (2016) acknowledges, maybe there is not a conscious agenda to target Africans or Global South countries, but the institutional design of the ICC, together with the fact that many global powers and their allies are excluded from its jurisdiction, as well as the decisions it has taken so far, do point to an institutional, even if unconscious, bias. Also, the ICC, like any institution of the anti-impunity TLO, is subject to political pressures, probably not to target Global South countries, but to turn a blind eye to the crimes in which the major global powers may be involved. Thus, even if unwillingly, the ICC, so far, has tended to align with powerful interests.

---

[11] For instance, the United States, Israel, and Russia signed the treaty but did not ratify it. China, India, Saudi Arabia, and Turkey, among others, did not sign the treaty (ICC 2018).

Not everything is bleak. Like the African countries that are complaining about a possible institutional bias of the ICC show, contestation and resistance against the institutionalization and normalization of global scripts of criminal legislation and enforcement (Aaranson and Shaffer, Chapter 1 this volume) are possible and are also a significant part of the anti-impunity TLO. Therefore, though there may be a *normative settlement* (Halliday and Shaffer 2015: 42, 43) that gives shape to a particular TLO, there is also an unrelenting struggle to appropriate it, adapt it, change it, or oppose it.

Such struggle also reveals that the *concordance* – that is, the degree of convergence of the settled meaning of the international legal framework of criminal justice at the international, regional, national, and local levels (Halliday and Shaffer 2015) – is unstable and continuously changing. The Colombian case reveals how, in the context of the anti-impunity TLO, discourses, practices, and institutions that shape domestic crime control fields travel, affecting the debates and power struggles that take place within them. However, it also reveals how social actors who engage in those discussions and struggles use the TLO, and also transform it, with different, at times unexpected, results.

8.6   IN SEARCH OF A BROADER NARRATIVE

The peace negotiations and the JEP were significant battlefields in the political struggle between social actors that have confronted each other over decades in Colombia, quite often through violent means. The dynamics and configuration of the domestic crime control field conditioned this struggle, as did the anti-impunity TLO. The interaction between different conceptions and interests regarding punishment and democracy in Colombian society became apparent in the public and political debate that the Peace Plebiscite elicited. The outcome was a hybrid conception of punishment and democracy, based on individual penal responsibility, but with a higher, though limited, commitment to political inclusion and social transformation – forward looking and more centered on the recognition and reparation of victims.

It was these different conceptions of punishment that in the end played a significant role in defining voters' opinions regarding the peace agreement. However, what is striking is that both worldviews, even though they clashed, were based mainly on the same principles, values, and legal framework of the anti-impunity TLO.

Democracy, justice, human rights, and the rule of law were critical components of the narratives of both sides. Different actors in such transitional ordering (the ICC, the UN, governments from the Global South and North, human rights NGOs) played a significant part in peace negotiations and the design of the JEP. They provided expertise and financial and human resources, and they exerted political pressure, to influence the outcome. This shows that the anti-impunity TLO, although being liberal, is not monolithic nor static. It is riddled with tensions, struggles, and contradictions, and it is transformed by them.

As the Colombian case shows, these struggles take place within a specific legal and political framework – that of liberal democracy, mainly forged in Global North countries. Such a framework has captured the center of the debates and the political imagination, pulling the extremes toward it. This may be considered as a positive outcome – for political and social conflicts must be addressed using the grammar of human rights, democracy, and the rule of law, which are deeply shared values.

The anti-impunity TLO has provided a vocabulary, a set of values and norms, a political and legal framework that are worthy of admiration – for they strive to protect the freedoms and dignity of human beings. However, by concealing and ignoring the historically, politically, and socially situated dimensions of the categories it uses, and the interests they reflect, by failing to account for the local contexts where the TLO's norms are enforced, such ordering limits the political and legal imagination to deal with law breaking through alternative, more inclusive, and far-reaching forms of justice. As a result, it favors unequal power relations, both at the national and international levels.

The Colombian case reveals that a more comprehensive narrative is needed if the anti-impunity TLO wants to fulfil its promise of not only punishing war criminals but also effectively contributing to peacebuilding and justice, as it claims. A broader narrative, one that seriously considers experiences that do not fit the Global North archetype, is needed to identify new strands, patterns, and points of comparison in order to better understand the relationship between political regimes, political economies, and different conceptions of democracy and the rule of law, on the one hand, and diverse constructions of punishment, on the other.

Instead of talking of consolidated, young, or transitional democracies, which implies a progressive narrative where Global North democracies are always more developed than their Global South counterparts, it may be useful to attempt a broader, less pure, and more hybrid perspective – a narrative that takes seriously the peculiarities, power relations, struggles, and needs of different contexts, and that considers other parameters of comparison and action, present in different societies, both from the Global North and South. Only then will it be possible to talk about a global, pluralistic justice.

REFERENCES

Alviar García, Helena, and Karen Engle. 2016. The Distributive Politics of Impunity and Anti-impunity: Lessons from Four Decades of Colombian Peace Negotiations. Pp. 216–254 in *Anti-Impunity and the Human Rights Agenda*, edited by K. Engle, Z. Miller, and D. M. Davis. New York: Cambridge University Press.

Bensouda, Fatou. 2016. Statement of ICC Prosecutor, Fatou Bensouda, on the Conclusion of the Peace Negotiations between the Government of Colombia and the Revolutionary Armed Forces of Colombia – People's Army. www.icc-cpi.int/Pages/item.aspx?name=160901-otp-stat-colombia (accessed September 4, 2018).

Carrington, Kerry, and Russell Hogg. 2017. "Deconstructing Criminology's Origin Stories." *Asian Journal of Criminology* 12(3): 181–197.

Carrington, Kerry, Russell Hogg, and Máximo Sozzo. 2016. "Southern Criminology." *British Journal of Criminology* 56(1): 1–20.

Centro de Memoria Histórica. 2015. *Una nación desplazada.Informe nacional del desplazamiento forzado en Colombia*. www.centrodememoriahistorica.gov.co/d escargas/informes2015/nacion-desplazada/una-nacion-desplazada.pdf (accessed August 15, 2018).

Centro de Memoria Histórica. 2018. *Observatorio de Memoria y Conflicto. Contando la guerra en Colombia*. http://centrodememoriahistorica.gov.co/o bservatorio/ (accessed August 15, 2018).

Comisión Colombiana de Juristas. 2012. Demanda de Inconstitucionalidad contra el acto legislativo 01 de 2012. www.corteconstitucional.gov.co/rela toria/2014/C-577-14.htm (accessed September 4, 2018).

Cravo, Teresa Almeida. 2014. Post-conflict Peacebuilding and the Rule of Law. Pp. 471–489 in *Handbook on the Rule of Law*, edited by C. May and Winchester A. Cheltenham: Edward Elgar Publishing.

Dezalay, Yves, and Bryant Garth. 2002. *The Internationalization of Palace Wars: Lawyers, Economists, and the Contest to Transform Latin American States*. Chicago: University of Chicago Press.

El Colombiano. 2016. Manuscrito de Uribe frente al Acuerdo que se firma hoy. September 26. www.elcolombiano.com/colombia/acuerdos-de-gobierno-y-farc/acuerdo-de-paz-manuscrito-de-alvaro-uribe-DF5052072 (accessed August 29, 2018).

El Espectador. 2014. Acuerdo entre Colombia y Farc sobre drogas es un "paso hacia la paz": UE. May 19, 2014. www.elespectador.com/noticias/paz/acuerd o-entre-colombia-y-farc-sobre-drogas-un-paso-paz-articulo-493201 (accessed December 11, 2018).

El Espectador. 2016. La cuestionable estrategia de campaña del No. October 6. www.elespectador.com/noticias/politica/cuestionable-estrategia-de-campana-del-no-articulo-658862 (accessed June 17, 2017).

El Espectador. 2018. Agresiones contra líderes sociales antes y después del acuerdo de paz. September 24, 2018. https://colombia2020.elespectador.com/ pais/agresiones-contra-lideres-sociales-antes-y-despues-del-acuerdo-de-paz (accessed December 11, 2018).

El Tiempo. 2016. CPI destaca que en paz con Farc no haya amnistía en crímenes de guerra. September 1. www.eltiempo.com/politica/proceso-de-paz/respaldo-de-la-corte-penal-internacional-al-acuerdo-de-paz-con-las-farc-43107 (accessed September 4, 2018).

Engle, Karen. 2016. A Genealogy of the Criminal Turn in Human Rights. Pp. 15–67 in *Anti-impunity and the Human Rights Agenda*, edited by K. Engle, Z. Miller, and D. M. Davis. New York: Cambridge University Press.

Engle, Karen, Zinaida Miller, and Denys Mathias Davis, eds. 2016. *Anti-impunity and the Human Rights Agenda*. New York: Cambridge University Press.

Franzki, Hanna, and María Carolina Olarte. 2014. Understanding the Political Economy of Transitional Justice. Pp. 201–221 in *Transitional Justice Theories: A Critical Theory Perspective*, edited by S. Buckley-Zistel, T. Koloma Beck, C. Braun, and F. Mieth. Abingdon: Routledge.

Halliday, Terence C., and Gregory Shaffer, eds. 2015. *Transnational Legal Orders*. New York: Cambridge University Press.

Hillebrecht, Courtney, Alexandra Huneeus, and Sandra Borda. 2018. "The Judicialization of Peace." *Harvard International Law Journal* 59(2): 279–330.

Huneeus, Alexandra. 2013. "Law by Other Means: The Quasi-Criminal Jurisdiction of the Human Rights Courts." *The American Journal of International Law* 107(1): 1–44.

Institute for Integrated Transitions (IFIT). 2018. Los debates de La Habana: una Mirada desde adentro. Bogotá: Fondo de Capital Humano para la Transición Colombiana, Instituto para las Transiciones Integrales (IFIT).

International Criminal Court (ICC). 2018. *The States Parties to the Rome Statute*. https://asp.icc-cpi.int/en_menus/asp/states%20parties/pages/the%20states%20 parties%20to%20the%20rome%20statute.aspx (accessed December 10, 2018).

Iturralde, Manuel. 2008. "Emergency Penalty and Authoritarian Liberalism: Recent Trends in Colombian Criminal Policy." *Theoretical Criminology* 12 (3): 377–397.

Iturralde, Manuel. 2010. *Castigo, liberalismo autoritario y justicia penal de excepción*. Bogotá: Siglo del Hombre Editores, Universidad de los Andes, Instituto Pensar-Pontificia Universidad Javeriana.

Iturralde, Manuel. 2018. Neoliberalism and Its Impact on Latin American Crime Control Fields. *Theoretical Criminology*. http://journals.sagepub.com /doi/full/10.1177/1362480618756362, 1–20.

Krever, Tor. 2013. "International Criminal Law: An Ideology Critique." *Leiden Journal of International Law* 26: 701–723.

Krever, Tor. 2014. Unveiling (and Veiling) Politics in International Criminal Trials. Pp. 117–137 in *Critical Approaches to International Criminal Law*, edited by C. Schwöbel. Abingdon: Routledge.

Krever, Tor. 2015. Ending Impunity? Eliding Political Economy in International Criminal Law. Pp. 298–314 in *Research Handbook on Political Economy and Law*, edited by U. Mattei and J. D. Haskell. Cheltenham: Edward Elgar Publishing.

Krever, Tor. 2016. Africa in the Dock: On ICC Bias. In Critical Legal Thinking. Law and the Political. http://criticallegalthinking.com/2016/10/ 30/africa-in-the-dock-icc-bias/ (accessed December 10, 2018).

Moyn, Samuel. 2016. Anti-impunity as Deflection of Argument. In *Anti-impunity and the Human Rights Agenda*, edited by K. Engle, Z. Miller, and D. M. Davis. New York: Cambridge University Press.

Muggah, Robert, and Katherine Aguirre Tobón. 2018. *Citizen Security in Latin America: Facts and Figures*. Igarapé Institute Strategic Paper 33. https://igarape .org.br/wp-content/uploads/2018/04/Citizen-Security-in-Latin-America-Facts -and-Figures.pdf?utm_campaign=2018_newsletter_10&utm_medium=emai l&utm_source=RD+Station (accessed January 2019).

Ordóñez, Alejandro. 2016. *Víctimas, justicia y lucha contra la impunidad*. https:// es.scribd.com/document/327405587/Victimas-Justicia-Lucha-Contra-La- Impunidad-Punto-1 (accessed September 4, 2018).

Payne, Leigh. 2015. The Justice Paradox? Transnational Legal Orders and Accountability for Past Human Rights Violations. Pp. 439–474 in *Transnational Legal Orders*, edited by T. Halliday and G. Shaffer. New York: Cambridge University Press.

Registraduría Nacional del Estado Civil de Colombia. 2016. Plebiscito 2 de octubre 2016 Colombia. https://elecciones.registraduria.gov.co/pre_ple bis_2016/99PL/DPLZZZZZZZZZZZZZZZZZZ_L1.htm (accessed June 16, 2017).

Semana. 2017. "Hacer trizas" el acuerdo con las FARC: ¿es posible? August 5, 2017. www.semana.com/nacion/articulo/uribismo-hara-trizas-acuerdo- acuerdo-con-farc-esta-blindado/524529 (accessed December 11, 2018).

United Nations Office on Drugs and Crime (UNODC). 2008. La amenaza del narcotráfico en América. www.unodc.org/documents/data-and-analysis/St udies/Reporte_OEA_2008.pdf (accessed September 10, 2018).

United Nations Office on Drugs and Crime (UNODC). 2017. Histórico acuerdo entre Colombia y la UNODC para ayudar a campesinos a adoptar alternativas a la cultivación de coca. www.unodc.org/unodc/es/frontpage/2017/November/

historic-agreement-between-colombia-and-unodc-can-help-farmers-embrace-alternatives-to-coca-cultivation.html (accessed December 11, 2018).

Urueña, René, and Prada María Angélica. 2018. "Transitional Justice and Economic Policy." *Annual Review of Law and Social Science* 14: 397–410.

Vivanco, José Miguel. 2017. Colombia: Fix Flaws in Transitional Justice Law. www.hrw.org/news/2017/10/09/colombia-fix-flaws-transitional-justice-law (accessed September 4, 2018).

W Radio. 2016. Óscar Iván Zuluaga dijo que el acuerdo de paz viola la Constitución. August 25. www.wradio.com.co/noticias/actualidad/oscar-ivan-zuluaga-dijo-que-el-acuerdo-de-paz-viola-la-constitucion/20160825/nota/3226933.aspx (accessed August 29, 2018).

PART IV

TRANSNATIONAL LEGAL
ORDERING AND HUMAN RIGHTS
STANDARDS IN CRIMINAL
JUSTICE

CHAPTER NINE

INTERNATIONAL PRISON STANDARDS AND TRANSNATIONAL CRIMINAL JUSTICE

Dirk van Zyl Smit[*]

Are prison conditions a subject of relevance to the transnational legal ordering of criminal justice? The concept of transnational legal ordering is a fresh way of understanding the complex interactions between international law and the creation of international and regional institutions that have a real impact, not only on legal rules but on social reality at the national level.[1]

The question of whether prison conditions are influenced by transnational legal ordering presents a particular challenge. Unlike some specific criminal justice areas, such as money laundering, human trafficking, or drug trade across borders, where national legal frameworks are shaped directly by international instruments, it is not obvious that prison conditions are influenced by forces beyond national borders. If it can be demonstrated that prison conditions are subject to transnational legal ordering, this will be an important contribution to understanding transnational legal orders in general, as the practical implementation of prison sentences has not previously been studied from this perspective.

The elements of "legal," "ordering," and transnational" all have to be present for a topic to be relevant to this form of analysis. The answer to the primary question begins by first considering briefly whether prison conditions are subject to law and are therefore "legal." Second, one must

[*] Thank you to Gregory Shaffer and Ely Aaronson, and to the participants at the Conference on Transnational Legal Ordering of Criminal Justice, University of California Irvine, School of Law, for stimulating my thinking on this topic. Special thanks to Keramet Reiter for her comments and to Julia Anderson for her excellent research assistance.
[1] The terms "transnational," "legal," and "order" are used here as defined in Halliday and Shaffer 2015.

decide whether prison conditions are subject to a process of "ordering," which results in their developing a particular way. And third, one must evaluate any process of legal ordering to which prison conditions may be subject to determine whether it is really "transnational."

Before considering these issues directly, one should observe that virtually every nation-state in the modern world has at least one prison. The universal relevance of prisons to modern criminal justice is obvious: At their core, prisons are institutions where individuals are held against their will, either because they are alleged to have committed a criminal offense or because they have been sentenced to a term of imprisonment as a punishment resulting from their having been found to have committed a criminal offense.[2] The principle of the use of imprisonment for purposes of crime prevention and punishment is not seriously challenged. In that sense, abolitionist movements notwithstanding, prisons worldwide enjoy a great deal of legitimacy.

On the question about the role of law in shaping prison conditions, it is noteworthy that, in each modern nation-state, there is law governing the external and internal aspects of imprisonment. *Legal* rules govern, respectively, both who should be admitted to or released from prison (external) and how they should be treated while they are in prison (internal). Internal and external aspects of imprisonment are closely related, for the internal regime not only determines the day-to-day running of the prison but also whether prisoners are offered opportunities for self-improvement, which will influence decisions about their release (Kelk 1978). Prison conditions are therefore dependent on both the internal and external aspects of imprisonment. Both are subjects of a national *legal* order, in that in all modern states they are governed by law, both statutory and as developed in the jurisprudence of the national courts.

On the question of ordering, it is noteworthy that, in almost all countries, this law is underpinned by a national or, in federal countries, a state-based prison bureaucracy that operates within the wider administrative structures of the state to normalize the notion of a state prison system. It seems, therefore, to be beyond dispute that prisons and the conditions that pertain in them are part of a legal *order*. The nature of this legal order and its impact on prison conditions is, however, open to dispute.

---

[2] The focus of this chapter is on prisons as institutions that primarily perform these two functions. This chapter does not investigate directly the transnational legal ordering of other carceral institutions that have as their primary function the detention of migrants, prisoners of war, or mentally ill persons.

The key remaining question is whether the ubiquity of imprisonment makes the legal rules governing prison conditions into elements of a *transnational* legal order? Clearly not automatically or necessarily. It is possible that the law governing national prison systems developed quite independently of international standards and that national prison systems operate quite independently of any constraints, other than those of the national legal and bureaucratic frameworks.

Notwithstanding the possibility that prison conditions are an entirely national question, this chapter argues that there is evidence that modern prison law, including the part of it that governs prison conditions, has a key *transnational* component. Moreover, it seeks to demonstrate that the way in which transnational prison law impacts on national prison systems is evidence of the emergence of a legal ordering of prison conditions that is specifically transnational.

The substance of this chapter is divided into three parts: The first part considers how legal standards governing prison conditions have emerged at the international and regional levels and how, increasingly, they have gained legitimacy. The second part describes how these standards are applied in a way that contributes to a recognizable transnational legal order in respect of prison conditions. In the third part, close attention is paid to the transfer of prisoners between states, as a mechanism that *operates transnationally* and in the process enhances the importance of international prison standards. The conclusion returns to the primary questions about the impact of legal ordering and what it reveals about transnational legal ordering as a conceptual framework for understanding the evolution of prison conditions.

9.1 EMERGENCE

Rudimentary forms of imprisonment have existed ever since people developed the technical skills to build securely enough to incarcerate others. However, only from the Enlightenment onward were movements for improving prison conditions routinely accompanied by legal reforms. In England, for example, exposure of the vile prison conditions common in the late eighteenth century by the great prison reformer, John Howard, was followed by legislation.[3] Initially, the legislation did not deal directly with prison conditions. Instead, it concentrated on

---

[3] Gaols Act, 1791: 31 Geo. III, c. 46. For details of this and subsequent English legislation, see Owen and MacDonald 2015.

creating a national institutional order, which would fix the disorder in the prisons of the old system and in the process improve prison conditions. Revisionist historians of punishment, as different as Michel Foucault (1977) and Michael Ignatieff (1981), have noted the impact of these changes. The new order, in Ignatieff's words, "substituted the rule of rules for the rule of custom" with profound consequences for the way order was maintained in prisons and for the way in which prisoners interacted with the prison authorities (Ignatieff 1981: 161).

The gradual systemization of imprisonment by national law did not bring an end to concerns about prison conditions. On the contrary, these concerns remained, and from a very early stage, they transcended national boundaries. This is epitomized in the life of John Howard, who, from his English base, broadened his work to include the rest of the United Kingdom and subsequently to large areas of the European continent (Howard 1792). Indeed, on his last prison visit, which took him as far as modern-day Ukraine, Howard died of an illness contracted while visiting a prison (Wilson 2014).

A similar reformist tendency, which combined concern with prison conditions with the crystallization of prison law, emerged throughout Europe as ideas on prison policies were widely shared. In the course of the nineteenth century, as the prison historian, Patricia O'Brien, has noted,

> Each European nation formed and maintained its own prison system. In spite of distinct, national institutions, however, the prison systems that developed throughout Europe in the nineteenth century were remarkably similar, reflecting a commonly held penal philosophy. Shared ideas about how to create prisons that were secure, sanitary, and rehabilitative produced similar prison populations, architecture, work systems, and inmate subcultures. (O'Brien 1995: 178)

Shared ideas about what prison conditions should ideally be like were internationalized at a surprisingly early stage. Americans visited European prisons to see the newest prisons that had been praised by John Howard. Traffic in the opposite direction was even more pronounced. The most famous transatlantic visitor to the United States of this period was Alexandre de Tocqueville, who was sent by the French government to study US prisons in 1831 and who came back with sharp insights about the latest prison regimes. Delegations from the British and Prussian governments followed in his footsteps (van Zyl Smit and Snacken 2009).

The early International Penitentiary Congresses, first held in Frankfurt in 1846 and Brussels in 1847, attracted expert delegates – scholars and practitioners – from throughout what was then known as the civilized world: These congresses played an influential role well into the early twentieth century. They adopted solemn resolutions, describing the emerging international consensus on the conditions under which prisoners should be held and the regimes with which they should best be treated. The idea that there should be international prison standards had its roots in these transnational scientific conferences (Leonards 2015; Leonards and Randeraad 2010).

9.1.1 The Emergence of International Legal Standards on Prison Conditions

After the First World War, the focus gradually shifted to the development of standards that would have the imprimatur of an international organization. In 1926 the International Penological and Penitentiary Council (IPPC), in some ways the successor body to the earlier international penitentiary congresses, and consisting of a mixture of governmental and independent expert members, began drafting a set of standard minimum rules for the treatment of prisoners (Radzinowicz 1999). In 1934 the IPPC draft received the endorsement of the League of Nations (Clifford 1972). However, the League of Nations was a relatively weak international organization. Moreover, the rise of fascism not only disrupted the system of international conferences but also contributed strongly to the demise of the League of Nations as a body that could lend much legitimacy to international standards on prison conditions.

The growing worldwide recognition of human rights in the post-second world war period, as reflected initially in the establishment of the United Nations and its adoption of the Universal Declaration of Human Rights (UDHR), provided a more secure anchor for international standard-setting on prison conditions (van Zyl Smit 2013b). The recognition of a general right to human dignity, together with the prohibition not only of torture but also of cruel, inhuman, or degrading treatment or punishment in Article 5 of the UDHR, was of obvious relevance to prison conditions, for it provided a basis for specifying which conditions were unacceptable and therefore potentially in conflict with this prohibition.

Prison conditions were also the first criminal justice issue that the United Nations addressed when it came to setting international standards. Earlier developments had provided it with a useful head start in this regard: there was already an established body of knowledge, legitimated by international experts, on what prison conditions such standards should support. Equally important was that a dialogue had begun between the purveyors of penological expertise and the makers of international law. The initial link between the IPPC and the League of Nations provided a foundation for this dialogue on which the United Nations could build by providing a forum for its continuation. This forum was provided by the First United Nations Congress on Crime Prevention and Criminal Justice in Geneva in 1955 which allowed for a further mixture of official and "expert" knowledge (Radzinowicz 1999), and at which UN member states could assent to the first inter-national set of standards that governed prison conditions in any detail, the United Nations Standard Minimum Rules for the Treatment of Prisoners (UNSMR). After the Congress, the UNSMR were given the further imprimatur of the UN Economic and Social Council in 1957 and finally of the UN General Assembly in 1971 (Clark 1994).

A notable feature of the UNSMR was that its legal status was initially very limited. The Rules themselves have an almost apologetic tone. The preliminary comments to the 1955 UNSMR indicated that they were

> not intended to describe in detail a model system of penal institutions. They seek only, on the basis of the general consensus of contemporary thought and the essential elements of the most adequate systems of today, to set out what is generally accepted as being good principle and practice in the treatment of prisoners and the management of institutions.

This is not the wording of a binding treaty. International lawyers of the time would have had no difficulty denying that the UNSMR was an instrument of any legal significance, a self-limiting reassurance that undoubtedly initially made it easier for diverse states to accede to it. Gradually, however, the legal standing of the UNSMR increased. One reason was that, at both the international and regional levels, provi-sions relating to the human dignity of prisoners and the primary prohibitions on torture and on inhuman and degrading punishment or treatment were increasingly incorporated into binding treaties. At the international level, the most important provisions were the require-ments of the 1966 International Covenant on Civil and Political Rights (ICCPR) that all persons deprived of their liberty should be treated with humanity and respect for their human dignity, and that cruel, inhuman, or degrading punishment and treatment were prohibited. The Human Rights Committee (HRC), which was charged with interpreting the provisions of the ICCPR, began to regularly make use of the UNSMR when applying the ICCPR to prison conditions. In the process, specific rules of the UNSMR were given increased legal status. By 1987 Nigel Rodley was able to quote several references by the HRC to rules in the UNSMR pertaining to diverse prison conditions ranging from cell size to use of dark cells and handcuffs as punishment, which the HRC now regard as embodying direct legal obligations of states (Rodley 1987).

The increase in the legal status of the UNSMR was uneven, however. In the first sixty years after their initial adoption, the 1955 UNSMR were subject to only one relatively minor amendment – in 1979 – and for a long time there was considerable resistance to updating these rules, lest they be given even more weight. However, the United Nations reinforced the UNSMR by adopting additional instruments that collectively supported the process of hardening what had initially been regarded as a soft law instrument. These included the 1985 UN Standard Minimum Rules for the Administration of Juvenile Justice (the Beijing Rules), the 1988 UN Body of Principles for the Protection of All Persons under Any Form of Detention or Imprisonment, the 1990 UN Rules for the Protection of Juveniles Deprived of Their Liberty (the Havana Rules), the 1990 UN Guidelines for the Prevention of Juvenile Delinquency (the Riyadh Guidelines), the 2007 Istanbul statement on the use and effects of solitary confinement,[4] and the 2010 UN Rules for the Treatment of Women Prisoners and Non-custodial Sanctions for Women Offenders (the Bangkok Rules).

Of these, the Bangkok Rules have been particularly important in the process of upgrading the international requirements for prisons. The individual provisions of the Bangkok Rules systematically referred back to the UNSMR and in the process indicated the detailed developments that would create prison conditions suitable for women prisoners in the twenty-first century. The Bangkok Rules may have been relatively easy to adopt, for they drew on the legitimacy that the development of

---

[4] It was annexed to the interim report of the UN Special Rapporteur on Torture and Other Cruel, Inhuman or Degrading Treatment or Punishment, Manfred Nowak, of July 28, 2008. The Special Rapporteur considered it "a useful tool to promote the respect and protection of the rights of detainees."

women's rights has accumulated in modern international human rights law. No state would want to be seen to oppose them and thus appear to be against women's rights (Tiefenbrun 2012). The Bangkok Rules were undoubtedly also important as a practical indication that development of the UNSMR could be possible within the UN framework. International nongovernmental organizations, such as Penal Reform International, used this momentum to press for reform of the UNSMR (van Zyl Smit 2013a).

Eventually in 2015, with significant support from the United States, the UN General Assembly adopted a revised and updated version of the UNSMR, officially also to be known as the Nelson Mandela Rules. When adopting the Nelson Mandela Rules, the General Assembly observed that the Rules sought "on the basis of the general consensus of contemporary thought and the essential elements of the most adequate systems of today, to set out what is generally accepted as being good principles and practice in the treatment of inmates and prison management" (General Assembly resolution 70/175, annex, adopted on December 17, 2015, Preliminary Observation 1).

At the international level, a firm seal of approval was quickly placed on the revised UNSMR. Since 2015, the HRC has quoted them with strong approval in at least six instances.[5] The recent language of the HRC has often been peremptory. Thus, for example, in two of these cases, one in 2016 and one 2017, in a matter that turned on the adequacy of medical treatment for prisoners, the HRC commented pointedly and in identical words that the state party to the ICCPR was "under an obligation to observe certain minimum standards of detention, which include the provision of medical care and treatment for sick prisoners, in accordance with Rule 24 of the Nelson Mandela Rules but that it had failed to do so."[6]

Other international developments have also contributed to the emergence of international legal standards on prison conditions. Prominent among these is the increasing role played by the International Committee of the Red Cross (ICRC) with regard to prisons generally. The initial focus of the ICRC was on the prisoners

---

[5] *Mukhtar v. Kazakhstan*, CCPR/C/115/D/2304/2013, December, 9, 2015; *Askarov v. Kyrgyzstan* CCPR/C/116/D/2231/2012, May 11, 2016; *Matyakubov v. Turkmenistan* CCPR/C/117/D/2224/2012, September 26, 2016; *Uchetov v. Turkmenistan*, CCPR/C/117/D/2226/2012, September 26, 2016; *Samathanam v. Sri Lanka*, CCPR/C/118/D/2412/2014, December 7, 2016; *Suleimenov v. Kazakhstan* CCPR/C/119/D/2146/2012, May 12, 2017.

[6] *Askarov v. Kyrgyzstan*, May 11, 2016, para. 8.5; *Suleimenov v. Kazakhstan*, May 12, 2017, para. 8.7.

of war, who are not normally held in civilian prisons, which are primarily for untried or sentenced persons, but in special POW camps. However, the ICRC explained in 2016: "The ICRC's detention-related activities have progressively evolved from a monitoring role during armed conflicts to a broader range of activities that seek to help individuals deprived of their liberty in a variety of situations and places of detention" (ICRC 2016). The situations include not only detention in facilities, such as Guantanamo Bay, where the POW status of the detainees is in dispute, but also instances where detainees held in relation to a non-international armed conflict or another situation of violence are often mixed with prisoners held for other reasons (ICRC 2016; van Zyl Smit 2005). In recent years the ICRC has begun to publish guidelines that can be applied in prisons of all kinds. These include specific guidance on water, sanitation, hygiene and habitat in 2012 and health care in 2017 (ICRC 2012; 2017; 2018). This guidance is highly detailed and practical, going beyond that offered in the international standards.

Finally, it is now generally recognized that persons imprisoned by international tribunals and courts, such as the International Criminal Court (ICC), have to be held in conditions that meet the requirements of international law. This was not always the case: the regime governing the prison at Spandau holding prisoners sentenced by the International Military Tribunal that sat in Nuremburg was not clearly specified in law and varied according to which allied power was managing the prison in a particular month (Goda 2007). However, when the International Criminal Tribunal for the former Yugoslavia (ICTY) was established in the 1990s, one of its first judgments stipulated that all prisoners sentenced by it had to be treated in a way that met "principles of humanity and dignity which constitute the inspiration for the international standards governing the protection of the rights of convicted persons."[7] In this regard, it listed a range of international treaties and other instruments, which included both the ICCPR and the UNSMR.

The ICC has adopted the same approach. Art. 103 of the Rome Statute, which governs the ICC, provides directly that conditions in prisons where its sentences are enforced "shall be consistent with widely accepted international treaty standards governing treatment of prisoners." In practice, this also includes taking into account standards such as the UNSMR (van Zyl Smit 2005). Only a very small percentage

---

[7] *Prosecutor v. Erdomović* IT-96–22-T Trial Chamber, November 29, 1996.

of the world's prisoners are detained as a result of the activities of international courts and tribunals, either in the detention centers attached to these bodies or in national prisons to which they send their convicts to serve their sentences. However, their impact on the emergence of a transnational prison ordering is significant. Such impact is not only symbolic. Where prisoners sentenced by an international court or tribunal are held in a national prison, the requirement that their treatment must meet international standards puts considerable pressure on the national prison system to conform to the same standards.[8]

9.1.2 The Emergence of Regional Legal Standards on Prison Conditions

Regional standards on prison conditions emerged in much the same way as they did on the international level. Typically, a regional human rights treaty would recognize human dignity and prohibit, with minor variations of language, inhuman or degrading punishment, or treatment. This would then be followed by specific instruments that spelled out for the region what prison conditions should be like and how prisoners should be treated. In the Americas, the key treaty is the 1969 American Convention on Human Rights, applied to prisoners by the 2008 Principles and Best Practices on the Protection of Persons Deprived of Liberty in the Americas. In Africa, the 1981 African Charter on Human and Peoples Rights has been underpinned for prisoners by the 1996 Kampala Declaration on Prison Conditions in Africa,[9] the 1999 Arusha Declaration on Good Prison Practice, and the 2002 Ouagadougou Declaration and Plan of Action on Accelerating Prisons and Penal Reforms in Africa.

In Europe, this regional pattern emerged the earliest and has developed the furthest. It will therefore be treated as an example of the transnational legal order that can emerge from such regional standards. The initial treaty was the 1953 European Convention on Human Rights (ECHR). In 1973 the Committee of Ministers of the Council of Europe adopted the European Standard Minimum Rules on the Treatment of Prisoners (ESMR). These Rules were modeled on the

---

[8] For further analysis of these questions, see Abels 2012; Mulgrew 2013.

[9] Adopted by consensus in September 1996 by 133 delegates from 47 countries, including 40 African countries, which met in Kampala, Uganda. The president of the African Commission on Human and Peoples' Rights, ministers of state, prison commissioners, judges, and international, regional, and national nongovernmental organizations concerned with prison conditions took part in the meeting.

1955 UNSMR but designed also to emphasize a specifically European approach to prison conditions. In 1987 the ESMR were replaced by a more comprehensive set of rules, known simply as the European Prison Rules (EPR).

In 2006 the 1987 EPR were restructured comprehensively. The 2006 EPR reflect in considerable detail an "expert" view of what minimum standards prison conditions should meet throughout Europe: one that has been endorsed by all member states of the Council of Europe – that is, by all countries in geographic Europe except Belarus. In his powerful, analytical dissenting opinion in the 2016 decision of the Grand Chamber of the European Court of Human Rights (ECtHR) in *Muršić v. Croatia*, Judge Pinto de Albuquerque makes much of these factors in arguing that the 2006 EPR have developed from being soft law into the type of hard law that requires formal recognition by the ECtHR as a binding part of the overall European human rights framework.[10] Detailed analysis of the whole process of standard setting for detention conditions in Europe concludes that it is a product of a conscious, cosmopolitan commitment to human rights by key policy makers and penological experts (Deruiter 2018).

9.2   APPLICATION

International and regional interventions may have developed legal rules on prison conditions that have the status of transnational law, but for them to be part of a transnational legal order they must be applied across national boundaries. This may be done by courts and tribunals and by inspecting bodies of various kinds.

9.2.1   Direct Application by International and Regional Courts and Tribunals

In discussing the development of international and regional prison rules we have already given some examples of where international and regional courts and tribunals have upheld rules on prison conditions and found against nation-states that did not conform to these rules. The contribution that these findings make toward establishing a transnational legal order is uneven.

---

[10] *Muršić v. Croatia* ECtHR (app. 7334/13), October 20, 2016, dissenting opinion of Judge Pinto de Alburquerque, paras 41–42. See also van Zyl Smit 2013a, for further reflections on the legitimacy of the EPR, including evidence of the specific application of the 2006 EPR by European states.

At the European level, the ECtHR plays a significant role in applying standards that govern prison conditions. State parties to the ECHR undertake to enforce the judgments of the ECtHR and generally do so by improving the prison conditions of individual prisoners who can demonstrate that their treatment infringes the ECHR. The ECtHR can also award costs and damages to individual complainants, and these too are generally paid by the state parties against whom they are awarded. In addition, so-called pilot judgments are a further useful remedy, as they allow the Court to order a government to make systemic changes rather than merely to provide relief to an individual applicant. For example, where lack of space in a cell or poor medical services has led to findings that prisoners in a particular state are persistently being treated in an inhuman or degrading way, the Court has ordered the government of the state concerned to reduce prison overcrowding, so that all prisoners in the system have adequate space, or to remedy shortcomings of the prison medical system as a whole, so that all prisoners have better health care.[11] Recent research findings have shown that, while some European states resist supervision of their prison systems by the ECtHR or claim that for economic reasons they are unable to implement them, the Court's judgments have had a systematic impact on how prisoners are treated throughout Europe.[12]

At the international level, the HRC has less power to issue binding judgments, even where states have acceded to the Optional Protocol to the ICCPR that allows individuals to bring complaints, (called "communications") against them (Art. 1 Optional Protocol to ICCPR). States that accede to the Optional Protocol undertake to provide the complainants with an effective remedy, including compensation, if required. They are also under an obligation to take steps to prevent similar violations in the future (Art. 2 ICCPR). In practice, however, these obligations are not always met. Thus, for example, in 2006 the HRC found that Australia had sentenced two juveniles to what was effectively a term of life imprisonment without parole (LWOP), which, the HRC concluded, created prison conditions that infringed the ICCPR.[13] The

---

[11] *Orchowski* v. *Poland* (App. 17885/04), October 22, 2009; *Torreggiani and Others* v. *Italy*, ECtHR (Apps. 43517/09, 46882/09, 55400/09, 57875/09, 61535/09, 35315/10, and 37818/10), January 8, 2013.

[12] See the accounts of the role of the ECtHR in Germany, France, the Netherlands, Italy, Greece, the Nordic countries, England and Wales, and Spain in Cliquennois and Hugues de Suremain 2018.

[13] *Blessington and Elliot* v. *Australia*, HRC Communication No. 1968/2010, U.N. Doc. CCPR/C/112/D/1968/2010, November 17, 2014.

Australian government, however, in what has been described as a "contemptuous response," simply reiterated its view that the sentence allowed the complainants a reasonable possibility of being released and did take not any remedial action, either in respect of the complainants or by amending the law (Dyer 2016; Government of Australia 2014).

9.2.2 Application by Regional and International Inspection Bodies

A second indication that international rules on prison conditions are applied in a way that indicates that they are part of a transnational legal order is to be found in the activities of regional and international bodies, other than courts and tribunals, which attempt to enforce the application of standards governing prison conditions.

The European Committee on the Prevention of Torture (the CPT) is a regional example of such a body. It was established by a treaty, the 1987 European Convention for the Prevention of Torture and Inhuman or Degrading Treatment or Punishment, Article 1 of which provides that the CPT "shall, by means of visits, examine the treatment of persons deprived of their liberty with a view to strengthening, if necessary, the protection of such persons from torture and from inhuman or degrading treatment or punishment." Although the brief of the CPT extends beyond prisons, prison conditions are a key focus of its work. Today, all European states except Belarus are parties to the Convention and have a treaty-based duty to cooperate with the CPT (Art. 3). States parties must help the CPT to perform its tasks, by granting access to all places of detention and providing all relevant information. In addition, they must respond to the CPT country visit reports within six months, and in a final response after one year must set out how they will take into account its recommendations (Art. 8).

The reports on the visits are confidential, but they can be published at the request or with the consent of the country concerned. If a state does not cooperate with the CPT or systematically does not follow its recommendations, the CPT may publish a statement about its key findings and recommendations without the consent of the state concerned. As a result, most countries consent to publication of the full CPT reports, which are published together with the responses of the member states (Cassese 1996). This publicity is a powerful incentive for them to change their practices. At the regional level, the CPT has played a further role by inspecting the detention facility in the

Netherlands where prisoners standing trial before the ICTY are housed, as well as prisons in other European countries that hold prisoners sentenced by the Tribunal (Snacken and Kiefer 2016).

At the international level, there is an interesting variation on the CPT's methods of work. The explicit objective of the 2006 Optional Protocol to the United Nations Convention against Torture and other Cruel Inhuman or Degrading Treatment or Punishment (OPCAT) is to "establish a system of regular visits undertaken by independent *international and national* bodies to places where people are deprived of their liberty, in order to prevent torture and other cruel, inhuman or degrading treatment or punishment" (emphasis added).

For this purpose, OPCAT requires the creation of two types of bodies. First, there is the Subcommittee on Prevention of Torture (SPT), an international body that undertakes visits (Arts. 5–8). The SPT conducts its visits in much the same way the CPT does (Art. 11 (a)), and since 2007 has undertaken a number of visits worldwide.

Second, national states that accede to OPCAT have to set up National Preventive Mechanisms (NPMs), which must have "functional independence" (Art. 18), access to information, and wide powers of investigation (Art. 19) in respect of all persons deprived of their liberty. OPCAT also provides that NPMs may publish their findings (Art. 23). In terms of OPCAT, national authorities undertake to enter into a dialogue with the NPMs about the implementation of any recommendations they may make (Art. 20). Working with NPMs is a major function of the SPT (Art. 11(b)). Much of the SPT's energy is focused on strengthening NPMs rather than on only undertaking investigations. States parties have considerable flexibility on how they constitute their NPMs and many of them seek to rely on their existing prison monitoring systems as key elements of their NPMs.[14] Nevertheless, OPCAT, through the SPT, has had an impact on the development of national monitoring bodies to ensure that they meet the commitments that states parties have entered into. The substance of these commitments include the implementation of the UNSMR and other international instruments that refer to prison conditions.

The ratification of OPCAT and the establishment of NPMs has been a slow process. Currently there are eighty-eight states parties, of whom sixty-seven have designated their NPMs (Association for the Prevention of Torture 2018). A 2016 report by the Association of the

---

[14] Slovenia spelled this out in its reservation to its ratification of OPCAT.

Prevention of Torture, an International NGO that has sought to propagate OPCAT, points to a direct impact of NPMs on prison conditions in several countries (Association of the Prevention of Torture 2016). These range widely, with reports of positive changes in Costa Rica, Indonesia, Georgia, Mali, and Morocco.

A more critical literature, which points out that NPMs are not a panacea to all problems of imprisonment, is gradually emerging (McGregor 2017; Steinerte 2014). The powers and influence of NPMs vary from country to country. Moreover, some key countries, including the United States, have not ratified OPCAT at all.[15] However, OPCAT remains important as a potentially worldwide mechanism that is concerned with improving the detail of prison conditions.

Finally, there are various other international processes that also contribute to monitoring prisons and thus have some impact on the recognition of prison conditions as something of more than local significance. A whole range of UN committees, including the Human Rights Committee, the Committee against Torture, the Committee on the Rights of the Child, the Committee on the Rights of Persons with Disabilities, and the Committee on the Elimination of Discrimination against Women, all receive reports from state parties on whether they are meeting the standards set by the underlying treaties. In as far as these treaties are relevant to the treatment of prisoners, these reports regularly include accounts of prison conditions. The evaluations of these reports by the relevant committees produce further international understandings of what prison conditions should be like. Similarly, the reports of UN special rapporteurs, particularly the Special Rapporteur on Torture, often contain both information on abusive prison conditions and recommendations on what should be done to combat them.[16] Inspections by the ICRC play largely the same role, although ICRC reports are usually confidential to the government concerned (Rodley and Pollard 2009).

9.2.2.1 Application by Professional Associations

Professional associations play an important part in encouraging the implementation of regional and international prison standards. In

---

[15] For an argument supporting the ratification of OPCAT by the United States, see Simon 2018.

[16] For the introduction of prison conditions to the remit of the Special Rapporteur on Torture and Other Cruel, Inhuman or Degrading Treatment or Punishment, see Rodley and Pollard 2009, at 400–401 (for the nature and function of the Special Rapporteur on Torture more broadly, see 204).

Europe, the Penological Council of the Council of Europe organizes Annual Conferences for Directors of Prison and Probation Services at which European prison standards are given considerable prominence.[17] In addition, the European Union has supported the establishment of EuroPris, the umbrella organization of prison services throughout Europe, which represents the interests of prison administrations and prison officers before the various European bodies in the EU and the Council of Europe. EuroPris describes its primary function as "bringing together practitioners in the prisons' arena with the specific intention of promoting ethical and rights-based imprisonment, exchanging information and providing expert assistance to support this agenda" (EuroPris website n.d.).

In other regions, there are similar organizations. In Africa, for example, the African Correctional Services Association represents the interests of correctional professionals and at the same time places emphasis on the recognition of the rights that prisoners have to humane prison conditions.[18]

At the international level, the International Corrections and Prisons Association (ICPA) has developed into the leading professional organization for prison officers worldwide. The stated mission of the ICPA is "to promote and share ethical and effective correctional practices to enhance public safety and healthier communities world-wide" (ICPA website). Much of its work aims to improve technical aspects of prison administration. However, it has involved itself in developing regional and national prison standards[19] and in propagating the Nelson Mandela Rules.[20]

---

[17] For example, see Kleijssen 2018, discussing ECtHR judgments and CPT reports relating to prison overcrowding; Frøysnes 2013, outlining the importance of ECtHR case law and pilot judgments (para. 5) and emphasizing the aim of improving implementation of CoE standards and ECtHR judgments (para. 6); and Das Neves 2018.

[18] "The Association aims to become the front runner and nucleus of Correctional professional development on the African continent and one of the leading Correctional development organizations in the world." ACSA 2018. The Fourth ACSA Biennial Conference held in Kigali, Rwanda, in May 2017 included a presentation from Penal Reform International, titled *Implementation of the Nelson Mandela Rules in Africa: Challenges and Opportunities*.

[19] The introductory text of the ICPA states, "The ICPA has collaborated and formed agreements with partner organizations for standards-setting in both Africa (the Abuja Declaration) and in Latin America (the Barbados Declaration), and has pledged to work together with the United Nations Department of Peacekeeping in a concerted manner to address the many challenges facing prison systems, particularly in developing and post-conflict environments (the UNDPKO Declaration)." ICPA website.

[20] See, for example, Irish Prisons 2017.

9.2.2.2 Application by International Nongovernmental Organizations
Specialist international nongovernmental organizations (INGOs) rely heavily on international prison standards to justify and legitimate their initiatives to improve prison conditions. Prominent among these is Penal Reform International, which specifically refers to the Bangkok Rules when seeking the reform of prison conditions for women in the Middle East and North Africa region (Swedish International Development Agency 2014). Penal Reform International also mentions the Nelson Mandela Rules more generally when campaigning for reforms, ranging from a worldwide limit on the use of solitary confinement to the treatment of life-sentenced prisoners (Rope and Sheahan 2018). The Association for the Prevention of Torture campaigns for the ratification of OPCAT and trains bodies acting as National Preventive Mechanisms in international human rights standards (Association for the Prevention of Torture 2017). Human Rights Watch, which regularly produces reports on prison conditions in various countries, refers to UN standards when justifying its recommendations for improving these conditions (Human Rights Watch 2016a; 2016b; 2018a; 2018b). Amnesty International also makes use of these instruments. For example, a recent report by Amnesty International, *Punished for Being Poor: Unjustified, Excessive and Prolonged Pre-Trial Detention in Madagascar*, relied heavily on the Bangkok Rules and the Nelson Mandela Rules in its call for action to set right prison conditions that amount to serious human rights abuses (Amnesty International 2018).

9.2.3 National Applications
In Europe, there is evidence that initiatives taken at the European level to improve prison conditions have been reflected in changed national practices. In 2011 the Penological Council of the Council of Europe conducted a survey of what European states have done to implement the 2006 EPR (Council of Europe 2011). Of the thirty-four states that replied, only the United Kingdom answered that the EPR had had no impact on its prison legislation or practices. Evidence of the practical effect of CPT interventions on prison conditions at the national level has also increased in recent years. Scholarly research shows that several states do make some efforts to conform to the recommendations of the CPT.[21]

---

[21] For example, the Netherlands (de Lange 2008); Germany (Cernko 2014); and the Nordic countries (Lappi-Seppälä and Lauri Koskenniemi 2018). Greece is an exception; Xenakis and Chelioliotis (2017) comment that "Greek governments have long responded to critical CPT

A good example of how these various European developments could combine to have practical impact on prison conditions occurred in 2004 when a Scottish prisoner sued the authorities on the grounds that his human rights had been breached by his suffering from severe eczema because of the conditions in which he had been forced to live. A Scottish court found that the conditions under which the prisoner had been held, which included the practice of "slopping out" (i.e., using a bucket that had to be emptied in the morning as a lavatory during the night), breached his right not to be subject to inhuman or degrading treatment.[22] In coming to this conclusion, the Scottish court referred both to judgments of the ECtHR and to the EPR. In addition, it placed considerable weight on the reports of the CPT that had condemned the practice of slopping out and noted the failure of the Scottish executive to abide by earlier government undertakings to rectify the problem. The practical effect on prison conditions was that the Scottish authorities abolished the practice of slopping out throughout the Scottish prison system, by building extra facilities that give all prisoners direct access to lavatories (Armstrong 2018).

International prison standards were initially paid relatively little attention by national courts (van Zyl Smit 2003). However, the revised Nelson Mandela Rules were relied on shortly after their adoption in some pathbreaking national decisions on the controversial subject of solitary confinement. For example, in 2016 this happened in the Federal District Court in New York where Judge Shira Schneidlin justified a consent decree drastically reducing the use of solitary confinement with reference to Rule 45 of the Nelson Mandela Rules, which provides that "solitary confinement shall be used only in exceptional cases, for a last resort, and subject to independent review."[23] An even more specific example arose in Canada in early 2018: a judge of the Supreme Court of British Columbia relied heavily on the Nelson Mandela Rules to define administrative segregation as solitary confinement and to prohibit it when continued for longer than 15 days, the maximum period that the Rules allow for solitary confinement.[24] These decisions are an indication that international

---

reports with a combination of denial and defiance." The same may be said of Russia, which has been the subject of number of highly critical public statements by the CPT.

[22] *Napier* v. *Scottish Ministers* [2004] SLT 555, [2004] UKHRR 881.

[23] *People* v. *Annucci* No. 1:2011cv02694 – Document 329 (S.D.N.Y. 2016).

[24] *British Columbia Civil Liberties Association* v. *Canada (Attorney General)*, 2018.

standards on prison conditions may play an increasing role in the future.

9.3 MUTUAL ASSISTANCE

Mutual assistance in criminal matters is widely recognized as an element of transnational criminal law (Boister 2018). The extradition of suspects from one state to stand trial in another state and, to a lesser extent, the transfer of sentenced prisoners from the state where they committed their offenses to serve their sentences in the states of which they are nationals, have long been accepted as key elements of mutual assistance.

Making such assistance dependent on the prison conditions, to which the person to be extradited or transferred will be subject in the receiving state, is a much more recent development. This issue first came to international attention in 1989 in the case of Jens Soering, whose extradition from the United Kingdom to the United States was challenged before the ECtHR on the basis that it would infringe his human rights as he would face the death penalty in the United States. The ECtHR agreed, not because it regarded the death penalty as inherently contrary to the ECHR, but because the long period of detention on death row to which Soering might be subject would be inhuman and degrading treatment that would infringe the prohibition of such treatment in Article 3 of the ECHR.[25] Therefore, Soering could not be extradited to the United States if there was a possibility that he would be sentenced to death. The United States responded to this decision by giving a guarantee that Soering would not face the death sentence, and on this basis, the British government allowed his extradition. Subsequently, such guarantees have routinely been given in all cases where extradition is sought from abolitionist countries. The *Soering* judgment, however, was of international significance beyond the question of the death penalty – for it raised the wider question of whether the possibility that persons sent abroad against their will would potentially face human rights violations in prison, could also be a ground for refusing extradition.

National courts were initially hostile to considering these wider implications and sought to relativize the human rights standards relating to prison conditions by arguing that strict national and regional standards should not be applied when someone was to be sent outside the region. In 2008 the House of Lords (then still the apex court in the

---

[25] *Soering* v. *The United Kingdom* ECtHR (App.14038/88), July 7, 1989.

United Kingdom) specifically declined to apply an absolute standard in cases where someone would face life imprisonment outside Europe.[26] An absolute standard would mean, Lord Hoffmann suggested sarcastically, that a suspect could not be extradited to a country where prisons did not have flush lavatories, since it had been held in the UK that a failure to provide such facilities for domestic prisoners was inhuman and degrading.

Even the German Federal Constitutional Court equivocated on whether prisoners should have the same human rights following extradition as they would in the country in which they had initially been arrested. In 2005 it allowed the extradition from Germany to California of two murder suspects where they would face LWOP sentences. In Germany such a sentence would be regarded as contrary to the constitutional right to human dignity, because imprisonment without a clear procedure for considering release after a fixed period is regarded as denying the fundamental humanity of the prisoner concerned. However, in an extradition case that was important for purposes of mutual assistance, the German Court explained, a less strict standard could be applied.[27]

Nevertheless, in 2010, in a case involving a request from Turkey for the extradition of someone who, on conviction, would also face an LWOP sentence, the Federal Constitutional Court changed its position. It found that, notwithstanding the requirement of international law that foreign legal orders were to be respected, if someone had no practical prospect of release such punishment would be cruel and degrading (*grausam und erniedrigend*).[28]

European human rights law has developed in the same way as that in Germany. Since the beginning of the current decade, the ECtHR has repeatedly recognized in principle that suspects facing extradition should have their human rights as prisoners – both to the internal conditions of imprisonment that meet human rights standards and, in the case of persons facing a life sentence, to appropriate consideration for release – recognized before extradition would be allowed. In principle, therefore, the ECHR standards are absolute – to be applied whenever a European state wishes to send someone abroad to be incarcerated there.

---

[26] *Regina (Wellington)* v. *Secretary of State for the Home Department* [2008] UKHL 72, [2009] 1 A.C. 335 (HL) (Eng.).
[27] Bundesverfassungsgericht [BVerfG] [Federal Constitutional Court], July 6, 2005 (Ger.).
[28] Bundesverfassungsgericht [BVerfG] [Federal Constitutional Court], January 16, 2010 (Ger.).

The difficulty for persons facing extradition has been to prove that in practice their imprisonment abroad would not meet these human rights criteria. There are a few examples where extradition has been resisted successfully on the grounds of the treatment that they may face if they were to be imprisoned in the country seeking their extradition. In the important 2015 case of *Trabelsi v. Belgium*, the ECtHR did find that the highly restrictive prospects of release that Trabelsi, who was wanted for terrorism in the United States, would face if he were convicted and sentenced to life imprisonment would be inhuman and degrading, and that his extradition should be prohibited. Even this was something of a Pyrrhic victory, as Belgium sent Trabelsi back to the United States before the ECtHR could give its judgment.[29]

In most extradition cases, however, allegations that prison conditions would be so bad that prisoners would inevitably be subject to inhuman or degrading treatment have rarely succeeded on the facts. For example, in 2012 a high-profile group of alleged terrorism offenders argued that their detention in the supermax prison, ADX Florence, where they might well be held in solitary confinement following their extradition to the United States, would be a form of inhuman and degrading treatment that would contravene Article 3 of the ECHR. In spite of being able to present considerable evidence of the shortcomings of the regime at ADX Florence, they were unable to convince the ECtHR that the ill treatment that they could suffer there was likely to reach the minimum level of severity that would justify a finding that Article 3 of the ECHR would be contravened.[30]

Within the European Union, mutual assistance has developed a more streamlined alternative to the cumbersome procedures of worldwide extradition. Member states of the EU have made provision for a European Arrest Warrant, which entitles an EU member state to issue a warrant requesting that a person be sent to them from another member state to attend trial or serve a sentence of imprisonment (European Union 2002). If certain formal requirements relating primarily to the seriousness of the offense and the nationality of the person whose arrest is sought are met, such warrant must be implemented more

---

[29] *Trabelsi v. Belgium*, ECtHR (app. 140/10), September 4, 2014; Eeckhaut and Temmerman 2013. The Belgian government relied on a decision of the Belgian Conseil d'Etat (L'arrêt n° 224.770 du September 23, 2013) and ignored its obligations under the European Convention on Human Rights. For this reason, perhaps, Belgium did not seek to take the case of Trabelsi to the Grand Chamber of the ECtHR.

[30] *Babar Ahmad and Others v. United Kingdom*, ECtHR (apps. 24027/07, 11949/08, 36742/08, 66911/09, and 67354/09), April 10, 2012.

or less automatically by the executing state, without an enquiry into the substantive grounds for the request that is necessary before traditional extradition could be allowed. A further EU instrument makes provision for executing member states to send sentenced prisoners without their consent to serve their sentences in the countries of which they are nationals (European Union 2008). Again, if certain formal require-ments are met, this may happen also without the consent of the state to which the prisoners are to be returned.

The (unintended?) result of these tighter regulations has been that one of the few grounds on which a cross-border transfer of prisoners can be challenged is that prison conditions in the issuing state, where they will be held, as either awaiting trial or sentenced prisoners, do not meet human rights standards. This is paradoxical, for the assumption of these EU instruments, as the Luxembourg based Court of Justice of the European Union (CJEU) has recently again emphasized, is that there is a strong presumption that all member states comply with the funda-mental rights recognized by the EU as a whole (Mitsilegas 2015).[31] However, in exceptional circumstances, the CJEU has held there may be a departure from the principle of mutual assistance based on mutual trust. As the CJEU has explained:

> [W]here the judicial authority of the executing Member State is in possession of evidence of a real risk of inhuman or degrading treatment of individuals detained in the issuing Member State, having regard to the standard of protection of fundamental rights guaranteed by EU law and, in particular, by Article 4 of the Charter, that judicial authority is bound to assess the existence of that risk when it is called upon to decide on the surrender to the authorities of the issuing Member State of the indivi-dual sought by a European arrest warrant. The consequence of the execution of such a warrant must not be that that individual suffers inhuman or degrading treatment.[32]

This principle is a vivid example of how the transnational recogni-tion of standards for prison conditions can influence decisively how a key "moving part" of the transnational legal order operates, or even whether it operates at all.

A further question is, how should an executing state decide whether there is a risk that a particular prisoner who is to be transferred might

---

[31] For a recent statement of this principle by the Grand Chamber of CJEU, see *Minister for Justice and Equality* v. *LM* (C-216/18 PPU), July 25, 2018, para. 40.
[32] *Aranyosi and Căldăraru* CJEU (C-404/15 and C-659/15 PPU Pdl, EU:C:2016:198), April 5, 2016, para. 88.

suffer inhuman or degrading treatment? In two important cases, both involving a request following from a European arrest warrant to transfer a prisoner from Germany to Hungary, the CJEU has given some important guidance in this regard. The process has two steps. First, the court in the executing state must, in the words of the CJEU,

> initially, rely on information that is objective, reliable, specific and properly updated on the detention conditions prevailing in the issuing Member State and that demonstrates that there are deficiencies, which may be systemic or generalized, or which may affect certain groups of people, or which may affect certain places of detention. That information may be obtained from, inter alia, judgments of international courts, such as judgments of the ECtHR, judgments of courts of the issuing Member State, and also decisions, reports and other documents produced by bodies of the Council of Europe or under the aegis of the UN.[33]

This technique itself is of significance for the recognition of the transnational aspect of the law governing prison conditions, as the sources mentioned here are also the sources of information on which, as we have seen, transnational insights into prison conditions rely. In this particular case, much was made by the CJEU of a decision of the ECtHR that had held that prisons in the Hungarian system as a whole were overcrowded.[34] This was coupled with other key decisions of the ECtHR indicating that overcrowding resulted in conditions that infringed the prohibition on inhuman and degrading treatment.[35] The fact that the CJEU also allows consideration of other documents produced by the Council of Europe opens the way for courts to consider CPT reports on conditions in the requesting state, while the reference to UN reports would allow reports by, for example, a special rapporteur to be considered in appropriate cases.

If the court in the executing state considers that it is in possession of information that shows that there are systemic or generalized deficiencies in detention conditions in the receiving state, the second step commences. The court in the executing state must determine whether the particular individual who is the subject of a European Arrest Warrant is likely to be detained in a prison where he or she is likely to be subjected to inhuman or degrading treatment. Guidance

---

[33] *Aranyosi and Căldăraru* CJEU (C-404/15 and C-659/15 PPU Pdl, EU:C:2016:198), April 5, 2016, para. 89.
[34] *Varga and Others v. Hungary*, ECtHR (Apps. 14097/12, 45135/12, 73712/12, 34001/13, 44055/13, and 64586/13), March 10, 2015.
[35] *Torreggiani and Others v. Italy*, ECtHR January 8, 2013, para. 65.

issued by the CJEU in a recent judgment suggests that in such a case the court in the executing state must also rely on official material from international and regional sources and cannot rely only on the undertakings given by the issuing state.[36] The executing judicial authorities are still bound to undertake an individual assessment of the situation of each person concerned, in order to satisfy themselves that their decision on the surrender of that person will not expose him, on account of those conditions, to a real risk of inhuman or degrading treatment.

Finally, with regard to mutual assistance more generally, insistence on international standards may result in states that wish to transfer prisoners out of their territory seeking to intervene in the prison systems of foreign states to ensure that the conditions in their prisons are human rights compliant.[37] A striking example of this tendency is to be found in interactions between the United Kingdom and Nigeria in this respect. In 2014 the British government concluded an agreement with Nigeria, which allows the United Kingdom to return Nigerian nationals, who are serving prison sentences in the United Kingdom, to Nigeria to serve the remainder of their sentences (British High Commission Abuja 2014).[38] Contrary to what had been the general practice in international agreements outside Europe up to this point, the agreement provides that such prisoners may be returned without their consent. The British government, fearing, not without reason, that prisoners, facing being sent to Nigeria against their will, would object on the grounds that Nigerian prison conditions would infringe their human rights, provided Nigeria with a significant amount of aid money that would enable the Nigerians to build and run human rights compliant prisons where returning prisoners could be housed. In March 2018 the Foreign Secretary informed Parliament that the British Government had agreed to build a "UN compliant" 112 bed wing in KiriKiri Prison, in Lagos in Nigeria, at a cost of almost £700,000 (Johnson 2018).[39] The small phrase, "UN compliant," is a further indicator of the extent to

---

[36] ML intervener: Generalstaatsanwaltschaft Bremen CJEU (C-220/18 PPU), July 25, 2018.

[37] Austria, for example, has sought to do so since 2003, when it announced that it would build a prison in Romania to house the many Romanians currently held in Austrian prisons. Hitherto, however, these efforts have been unsuccessful; see Seeh 2018.

[38] For a background, see Mulgrew 2011.

[39] The British government sought to make a similar arrangement with Jamaica, but it was rejected by the Jamaican government; see Corporate Watch 2018.

which international standards have become an accepted part of this transnational process.

9.4 CONCLUSION

The transnational ordering of prison conditions has a long history. Ideas about how all prisons should be managed have been formulated over more than the last two centuries. That international and regional standards should embody these ideas is largely a product of the emphasis on human rights in the post–Second World War period.

As this chapter has demonstrated, the mechanisms for articulating and enforcing these standards have continued to develop at the international and regional levels, thus enabling the ordering of this area of law and practice. Since the earliest times, the ordering process has been driven by a mixture of theorists and practitioners. In more recent times, these theorists have tended to be academics and judges, inspired by rights-driven ideals of human dignity. The human rights discourse has contributed to the legitimacy of the ordering process. However, its success has always depended on engaging with prison officials who have the immediate power to improve prison conditions. This engagement has been deliberately sought, with varying degrees of success, in different parts of the world.

More research is required to show the impact the discourse about prisoners' rights has on prison conditions in individual countries, particularly in the developing world.[40] There can be little doubt, however, that an element of transnational legal ordering of prison conditions is a factor in all modern prison systems.

In many ways, the growing attention paid to the international and regional standards governing prison conditions is a positive aspect of the transnational legal ordering of imprisonment. The 2015 Nelson Mandela Rules and 2006 European Prison Rules exemplify this renewed emphasis. Among the benefits of rules of this kind are the additional rights and legal protections they offer prisoners worldwide.

---

[40] See, for example, the analyses of imprisonment in Sierra Leone by Andrew Jefferson, who argues that, in societies where there is "exorbitant poverty," the relationship between institutions, such as a prison service, and legal rules and structures is weaker and less legitimate than it might be in the Global North (Jefferson 2013; 2014). In these societies, personal links and patronage may be more important than elsewhere. However, law and legal structures continue to play some role. The manner and extent to which the latter are subject specifically to transnational ordering need to be investigated more fully.

At the same time, the existence of common standards underpins transnational cooperation in prosecuting crime and enforcing sentences of imprisonment. The mutual recognition of common standards facilitates the extradition of accused persons and sentenced prisoners between states that apply these standards in their prisons. It also has the potential to give states that are responding to requests for extradition, or the transfer of sentenced prisoners, leverage to demand the improvement of prison conditions in the receiving states where the prisons may not be up to standard.

The overall impact of human rights-based standards on actual prison conditions has been subject of much debate. One position is out-and-out skepticism about whether they have any impact at all. This is relatively easy to dismiss for, as we have seen, there is empirical evidence of specific changes for the better in prison conditions flowing directly from such interventions. At very least, there is some impact on national law and practice in respect of prison conditions some of the time.

A variation on out-and-out skepticism would hold that human rights interventions in the form of international standards may be of very limited direct significance in their own right, but that they provide stimulus to NGOs, which can use them to legitimize their own interventionist strategies (Hafner-Burton and Tsutsui 2005). As we have seen, there is certainly convincing evidence that INGOs in particular are empowered by the legitimacy of regional and international instruments that set standards in relation to prison conditions.

Finally, there is a more sophisticated argument that recognizes that a human rights approach to prisoners' rights may lead to bureaucratic reforms – that is, to increased legal ordering of prison services. However, the unintended consequence may be to increase not only the legitimacy of "human-rights-compliant" prison services but to provide them with more resources – for example, to build new (and larger) facilities in order to fulfil a mandate of providing better prison conditions. For example, it has been argued that abolition of "slopping out in Scotland led to resources being made available to expand the prison system as a whole" (Armstrong 2018).

The risk is that, while transnational legal ordering of prison conditions will pay lip service to having acceptable conditions worldwide, it will contribute to a growth in imprisonment. For example, it may be argued that prisoners will be rehabilitated more effectively if they are returned to their countries of origin, but the real motivation may be that wealthier states are keen to facilitate such transfers in order to rid themselves of troublesome offenders. Even allowing for the cost of improving prisons abroad, it is often cheaper to have them serving their sentences there than in the countries that seek to send them. The paradoxical effect may be that a focus sign improving prison conditions in developing countries may lead to foreign aid being directed to building prisons to house expelled prisoners rather than to development programs that will benefit those countries more directly.

The recognition of paradoxes of this kind illustrates the utility of seeing human rights-driven reforms through the critical lens of transnational legal ordering, which considers law and practice at the same time. It also illustrates how carefully analyzing prisons conditions as a product of transnational legal ordering can provide insights that go beyond claims that setting international standards for prison conditions is necessarily desirable, while at the same time not denying the positive impact such standards can have.

REFERENCES

Abels, Denis. 2012. *Prisoners of the International Community*. The Hague: TMC Asser Press.

African Correctional Services Association. 2017. Home Page. http://acsa-ps.org/index.php.

Amnesty International. 2018. *Punished for Being Poor: Unjustified, Excessive and Prolonged Pre-trial Detention in Madagascar*. London: Amnesty International.

Armstrong, Sarah. 2018. "Securing Prison through Human Rights: Unanticipated Implications of Rights-Based Penal Governance." *The Howard Journal of Crime and Justice* 57(3): 401–421.

Association for the Prevention of Torture. 2016. *Putting Prevention into Practice 10 Years On: The Optional Protocol to the UN Convention against Torture*. Geneva: APT.

Association for the Prevention of Torture. 2017. *Annual Report 2017: 40 Years of Torture Prevention*. Geneva: APT.

Association for the Prevention of Torture. 2018. *OPCAT Database*. https://apt.ch/en/opcat-database/.

Boister, Neil. 2018. *An Introduction to Transnational Criminal Law*, 2nd ed. Oxford: Oxford University Press.

British High Commission Abuja. 2014. *UK–Nigeria Sign Compulsory Prisoner Transfer Agreement*. www.gov.uk/government/news/uk-nigeria-sign-compulsory-prisoner-transfer-agreement.

Cassese, Antonio. 1996. *Inhuman States: Imprisonment, Detention and Torture in Europe Today*. Cambridge: Polity Press.

Cernko, Daniela. 2014. *Die Umsetzung der CPT-Empfehlungen im deutschen Strafvollzug*. Berlin: Duncker und Humblot.

Clark, Roger. 1994. *The United Nations Crime Prevention and Criminal Justice Program*. Philadelphia: University of Pennsylvania Press.

Clifford, William. 1972. "The Standard Minimum Rules for the Treatment of Prisoners." *American Society of International Law Proceedings* 66: 232–236.

Cliquennois, Gaëtan, and Hugues de Suremain, eds. 2017. *Monitoring Penal Policy in Europe*. London: Routledge.

Corporate Watch. 2018. *Carceral Colonialism: Britain Plans to Build a Prison Wing in Nigeria*. https://corporatewatch.org/carceral-colonialism-britains-plan-to-build-a-prison-wing-in-nigeria/.

Council of Europe. 2011. *Report Presented to the Sixteenth Conference of Directors of Prison Administration: Summary of the Replies Given to the Questionnaire Regarding the Implementation of the Most Recent Council of Europe Standards Related to the Treatment of Offenders While in Custody as Well as in the Community*. Strasbourg: Council of Europe.

Das Neves, Pedro. 2018. The "Low Cost" Prison: Minimum Design for Minimum Results. Presentation to the 18th Conference of Directors of Prison Administration, Brussels, November 27, 2018. https://rm.coe .int/CoERMPublicCommonSearchServices/DisplayDCTMContent? documentId=09000016806f4fc2.

de Lange, Jan. 2008. *Detentie genormeerd: Een onderzoek naar de betekenis van het CPT voor de inrichting van vrijheidsbeneming in Nederlandse penitentiaire inrichtingen*. Oisterwijk: Wolf.

Deruiter, Rebecca. 2018. *Detention Conditions in a Cosmopolitan Europe*. PhD thesis, Ghent University, Belgium.

Dyer, Andrew. 2016. "Irreducible Life Sentences: What Difference Have the European Convention on Human Rights and the United Kingdom Human Rights Act Made?" *Human Rights Law Review* 16: 541–584.

Eeckhaut, Mark, and Jan Temmerman. 2013. "Nizar Trabelsi uitgeleverd aan de VS." *De Standaard* (Belgium), October 3, 2013.

European Union. 2002. *Framework Decision 2002/584/JHA of June 13, 2002, on the European Arrest Warrant and the Surrender Procedures between Member States*.

European Union. 2008. *Framework Decision 2008/909/JHA, of November 27, 2008, on the Application of the Principle of Mutual Recognition to Judgments in Criminal Matters Imposing Custodial Sentences or Measures Involving Deprivation of Liberty for the Purpose of Their Enforcement in the European Union*.

EuroPris. n.d. www.europris.org/about/.

Foucault, Michel. 1977. *Discipline and Punish: The Birth of the Prison*. Trans. A. Sheridan. Harmondsworth: Penguin.

Frøysnes, Torbjørn. 2013. *Head of the Council of Europe Office to the EU, Opening Speech at the Eighteenth Conference of Directors of Prison Administration, Brussels, November 27–29, 2013*. https://rm.coe.int/CoERMPublicCommon SearchServices/DisplayDCTMContent?documentId=09000016806f5088.

Goda, Norman. 2007. *Tales from Spandau: Nazi Criminals and the Cold War*. Cambridge: Cambridge University Press.

Government of Australia. *Response of Australia to the Views of the Human Rights Committee in Communication No. 1968/2010 (Blessington and Elliot v. Australia)* www.ag.gov.au/RightsandProtections/HumanRights/Docume nts/Blessington&ElliotVAustralia-AustralianGovernmentResponse.pdf.

Hafner-Burton, Emilie M., and Kiyoteru Tsutsui. 2005. "Human Rights in a Globalizing World: The Paradox of Empty Promises." *American Journal of Sociology* 110(5): 1373–1411.

Howard, John. 1792. *The State of the Prisons in England and Wales, with Preliminary Observations, and an Account of Some Foreign Prisons and Hospitals*. London: Johnson, Dilly, and Cadell.

Human Rights Watch. 2016a. *We Are in Tombs: Abuses in Egypt's Scorpion Prison*. Washington, DC: Human Rights Watch.

Human Rights Watch. 2016b. *Double Punishment: Inadequate Conditions for Prisoners with Psychosocial Disabilities in France*. Washington, DC: Human Rights Watch.

Human Rights Watch. 2018a. *I Needed Help, Instead I Was Punished: Abuse and Neglect of Prisoners with Disabilities in Australia*. Washington, DC: Human Rights Watch.

Human Rights Watch. 2018b. *We Are Like The Dead: Torture and Other Human Rights Abuses in Jail Ogaden, Somali Regional State, Ethiopia*. Washington, DC.: Human Rights Watch.

ICPA. *Mission, Vision and Values*. https://icpa.ca/about-us/mission-vision-and-values/.

Ignatieff, Michael. 1981. "State, Civil Society, and Total Institutions: A Critique of Recent Social Histories of Punishment." *Crime and Justice* 3: 153–191.

International Committee of the Red Cross. 2012. *Water, Sanitation, Hygiene and Habitat in Prisons*. Geneva: ICRC.

International Committee of the Red Cross. 2016. *Protecting People Deprived of Their Liberty*. Geneva: ICRC.

International Committee of the Red Cross. 2017. *Health Care in Detention*. Geneva: ICRC.

International Committee of the Red Cross. 2018. *Toward Humane Prisons: A Principled and Participatory Approach to Prison Planning and Design*. Geneva: ICRC.

Irish Prisons. 2017. *Director General Michael Donnellan Awarded Head of Service Award*. www.irishprisons.ie/director-general-michael-donnellan-awarded-head-service-award-icpa-conference-london-25th-october–2017/.

Jefferson, Andrew. 2013. The Situated Production of Legitimacy: Perspectives from the Global South. Pp. 267–292 in *Legitimacy and Criminal Justice*, edited by Justice Tankebe and Alison Liebling. Oxford: Oxford University Press.

Jefferson, Andrew. 2014. "Conceptualizing Confinement: Prisons and Poverty in Sierra Leone." *Punishment and Society* 14: 41–60.

Johnson, Boris MP. 2018. Secretary of State for Foreign and Commonwealth Affairs. *Provision of Prison Accommodation to Nigeria: Written Statement – HCWS518*. March 7. www.parliament.uk/business/publications/written-questions-answers-statements/written-statement/Commons/2018–03-07/H CWS518/.

Kelk, Constantijn. 1978. *Recht Voor Gedetineerden: Een Onderzoek Naar De Beginselen Van Het Detentierecht*. Alphen aan de Rijn: Samsom.

Kleijssen, Jan. 2018. *Opening Speech at the Twenty-Third Council of Europe Conference of Directors of Prison and Probation Services, Working Together Effectively: Management and Co-operation Models between Prison and Probation Services*. June 19, 2018. Jõhvi, Estonia. https://rm.coe.int/jan-kleijssen-opening-speech-23rd-cdpps-estonia-2018-doc/16808b7dfe.

Lappi-Seppälä, Tapio, and Lauri Koskenniemi. 2018. "National and Regional Instruments in Securing the Rule of Law and Human Rights in the Nordic Prisons." *Crime, Law and Social Change* 70: 135–159.

Leonards, Chris. 2015. "Visitors to the International Penitentiary Congress: A Transnational Platform Dealing with Penitentiary Care." *Österreichische Zeitschrift für Geschichtswissenschaften* 26: 80–101.

Leonards, Chris, and Nico Randeraad. 2010. "Transnational Experts in Social Reform, 1840–1880." *International Review of Social History* 55: 215–239.

McGregor, Judy. 2017. "The Challenges and Limitations of OPCAT National Preventive Mechanisms: Lessons from New Zealand." *Australian Journal of Human Rights* 23: 351–367.

Mitsilegas, Valsamis. 2015. "The Symbiotic Relationship between Mutual Trust and Fundamental Rights in Europe's Area of Criminal Justice." *New Journal of European Criminal Law* 4: 457–480.

Mulgrew, Róisín. 2011. "The International Movement of Prisoners." *Criminal Law Forum* 22: 103–143.

Mulgrew, Róisín. 2013. *Toward the Development of the International Penal System*. Cambridge: Cambridge University Press.

O'Brien, Patricia. 1995. The Prison on the Continent Europe 1865–1965. Pp. 178–201 in *The Oxford History of the Prison*, edited by Norval Morris and David Rothman. Oxford: Oxford University Press.

Owen, Tim, and Alison MacDonald, eds. 2015. *Livingstone, Owen and MacDonald on Prison Law*, 5th ed. Oxford: Oxford University Press.

Penal Reform International. 2017. *Implementation of the Nelson Mandela Rules in Africa: Challenges and Opportunities*. Presentation at the Fourth ACSA

Biennial Conference, May 16, 2017; conference program available at http://acsa-ps.org/4th%20conference%20program%20Day2.php.

Radzinowicz, Leon. 1999. *Adventures in Criminology*. New York: Routledge.

Rodley, Nigel. 1987. *The Treatment of Prisoners under International Law* Oxford: Clarendon Press.

Rodley, Nigel, and Matt Pollard. 2009. *The Treatment of Prisoners under International Law*, 3rd ed. Oxford: Oxford University Press.

Rope, Olivia, and Frances Sheahan. 2018. *Global Prison Trends 2018*. London: Penal Reform International and Thailand Institute of Justice.

Seeh, Manfred. 2018. *Häftlinge in Heimatländer bringen*. June 25, 2018. *Die Presse*.

Simon, Jonathan. 2018. "Penal Monitoring in the United States: Lessons from the American Experience and Prospects for Change." *Crime, Law and Social Change* 70: 161–173.

Snacken, Sonia, and Nik Kiefer. 2016. Oversight of International Imprisonment: The Committee for the Prevention of Torture. Pp. 322–344 in *Research Handbook on the International Penal System*, edited by Róisín Mulgrew and Denis Abels. Cheltenham: Edward Elgar.

Steinerte, Elina. 2014. "The Jewel in the Crown and Its Three Guardians: Independence of National Preventive Mechanisms under the Optional Protocol to the UN Torture Convention." *Human Rights Law Review* 14: 1–29.

Swedish International Development Agency. 2014. *Promoting Human-Rights Based Approach Toward Vulnerable Groups in Detention in the Middle East and North Africa Region: Impact Evaluation*. London: Penal Reform International.

Tiefenbrun, Susan. 2012. *Women's International and Comparative Human Rights*. Durham: Carolina Academic Press.

van Zyl Smit, Dirk. 2003. The Impact of United Nations Crime Prevention and Criminal Justice Standards on Domestic Legislation and Criminal Justice Operations. In *The Application of United Nations Standards and Norms in Crime Prevention and Criminal Justice*, edited by United Nations Office on Drugs and Crime. New York: United Nations.

van Zyl Smit, Dirk. 2005. "International Imprisonment." *International & Comparative Law Quarterly* 54: 357–386.

van Zyl Smit, Dirk. 2013a. Legitimacy and the Development of International Standards for Punishment. Pp. 267–292 in *Legitimacy and Criminal Justice*, edited by Justice Tankebe and Alison Liebling. Oxford: Oxford University Press.

van Zyl Smit, Dirk. 2013b. Punishment and Human Rights. Pp. 395–414 in *The Sage Handbook of Punishment and Society*, edited by Jonathan Simon and Richard Sparks. London: Sage.

van Zyl Smit, Dirk, and Sonja Snacken. 2009. *Principles of European Prison Law and Policy: Penology and Human Rights*. Oxford: Oxford University Press.

Wilson, David. 2014. *Pain and Retribution: A Short History of British Prisons, 1066 to the Present*. London: Reaktion Books.

Xenakis, Sappho, and Leonidas Chelioliotis. 2017. International Pressure and Carceral Moderation: Greece and the European Convention on Human Rights. In *Monitoring Penal Policy in Europe*, 1st ed., edited by Gaëtan Cliquennois and Hugues de Suremain. London: Routledge.

CHAPTER TEN

THE TRANSNATIONAL LEGAL ORDERING OF THE DEATH PENALTY

Stefanie Neumeier and Wayne Sandholtz

A transnational legal order (TLO) has emerged since 1945 around capital punishment. The TLO is clearly *transnational*: as of 2017, 105 countries had abolished the death penalty for all crimes. A further eight countries had prohibited it for ordinary crimes, and forty-six had abolished it in practice (by not carrying out any executions for at least ten years).[1] The death penalty TLO is *legal*, at both the national and international levels. In national law, the prohibition on the death penalty can be written into the constitution itself, established by judicial interpretation, or implemented via legislation. At the global level, core human rights treaties do not prohibit the death penalty but envision its "progressive restriction" (Hood and Hoyle 2015: 26). The death penalty is explicitly excluded as a punishment in the international criminal tribunals established in the 1990s and since.[2] Regional treaties aim directly at its abolition, including the Protocol to the American Convention on Human Rights to Abolish the Death Penalty, and especially Protocol No. 6 and Protocol No. 13 to the European Convention on Human Rights (ECHR). Finally, the interconnected domestic, regional, and international legal rules related to capital punishment constitute an *order*: they authoritatively shape "the understanding and practice of law" in a specific area of social activity (Halliday and Shaffer 2015: 5, 20).

---

[1] Data compiled by the authors.
[2] Including the International Criminal Tribunal for the former Yugoslavia (ICTY), the International Criminal Tribunal for Rwanda (ICTR), and the International Criminal Court (ICC).

The death penalty TLO differs from transnational legal orders that have emerged in other areas of criminal justice. In areas like money laundering, the financing of terrorism, human trafficking, or drug smuggling, the objective of transnational legal ordering is to regulate criminal activity that crosses borders. In contrast, the death penalty TLO regulates a national or local activity. Other studies usefully place the death penalty within the broader context of a national criminal justice system.[3] Our goal is different: to explain the development of transnational regulation of the death penalty. Instead of providing fine-grained background on national criminal justice systems, we focus on themes that are central to the TLO framework, including normative settlement, concordance, institutionalization, and recursivity (Halliday and Shaffer 2015). We will show that the death penalty TLO has attained partial normative settling, uneven concordance, and patchy institutionalization. The explanation for this set of mixed outcomes builds on the TLO insight that transnational legal orders are almost invariably interconnected. In the case of capital punishment, the key linkage is to the broader international human rights regime. The consolidation of international standards for criminal law, as well as the movement for death penalty abolition, were shaped by the larger post–World War II human rights movement; indeed, both the Universal Declaration of Human Rights (UDHR) and the ICCPR delineate basic rights of those subject to criminal proceedings. The cause of death penalty abolition advanced under a banner of rights: the fundamental right to life, and the right to be free from cruel, inhuman, or degrading punishment.

Our analysis of the death penalty TLO incorporates core features of the TLO framework. It assesses the creation of legal order at both national and international levels, and emphasizes the recursivity linking developments at both levels (Halliday and Shaffer 2015: 3, 5). We directly confront several of the questions posed in the introduction. We

---

[3] A rich body of research assesses the death penalty, with close attention to its broader domestic social, cultural, political, legal, and criminal justice settings. That literature is too plentiful to cite thoroughly, but excellent examples include Garland (2010); Gottschalk, Blumstein, and Farrington (2006); Hodgkinson and Rutherford (1996); Sarat and Martschukat (2011); Steiker (2002); and Zimring (2003). In contrast with most US-based research on the death penalty, we treat the United States simply as one case among approximately 150. We recognize that death penalty law varies across the US fifty states and that death penalty practices vary across counties within states. Our goal is not to explain that heterogeneity. Following Hood and Hoyle (2015), we code the United States as retentionist because the death penalty has not been abolished by law for the country as a whole. The US Supreme Court's decision in *Furman* v. *Georgia* (1972) instituted a de facto nationwide moratorium on executions. That pause ended in 1976 when the Supreme Court ruled in favor of allowing the death penalty (*Gregg* v. *Georgia*).

return to some of them more specifically in our conclusion, but the core of our argument is that the death penalty TLO has attained *partial* settling, concordance, and implementation in large part because the global human rights framing has been at odds with domestic framings that see the death penalty not just as congruent with local values but as necessary to protect them. In fact, death penalty abolition at the national level has generally occurred not in response to public demands but despite public support for retention. The story at the global and regional levels is relatively straightforward: treaties limiting or abolishing the death penalty were agreed upon by political elites who worked at one remove from mass political opinion.

Abolition of the death penalty has practical effect only at the domestic level, which is also where the primary puzzle resides. The core of our analysis therefore analyzes abolition in domestic law, where we confront the question of how abolition can occur domestically when publics almost universally favor retention. We argue that specific types of domestic institutions can make non-majoritarian policy making more likely – specifically, (1) proportional representation in the legislature and (2) courts that are independent of the political branches. These institutions make more likely, respectively, abolition through legislation and abolition via judicial decision. We additionally hypothesize that transnational influences can enhance the likelihood of abolition – in particular, (1) the incentive of membership in regional organizations, and (2) the persuasive and socializing influence of international nongovernmental organizations (INGOs). We offer a novel means of measuring INGO influence and incorporate it in the analysis of data from about 150 countries.

The first two sections describe the death penalty TLO and the broad outlines of its emergence at both national and international levels. The third section presents our data and analysis of abolition in national law. A fourth section offers brief case studies to illustrate the mechanisms highlighted by the broader analysis, including instances of both abolishers and non-abolishers. In the conclusion, we return to the broader questions posed by the overall project.

10.1 ABOLITION: THE BIG PICTURE

Punishment of death has existed since antiquity and is still seen in some parts of the world as a natural, or even necessary, part of penal law. The death penalty served simultaneously as a public spectacle, an exemplar of the wages of crime (or of sin), and a tool of social control and repression. Enlightenment thinkers sought to demolish the assumptions and myths that accumulated over the centuries surrounding capital punishment. Cesare Beccaria argued that punishment, instead of seeking to terrorize the populace into compliance with the laws, should be proportionate to the nature of the offense. He contended, in his famous treatise *On Crimes and Punishments* of 1763, that capital punishment had no place in a modern society because it was inhumane and ineffective (Beccaria 2008).

The first laws to abolish capital punishment were enacted in US states, perhaps ironically given the continued retention of the death penalty in much of the United States. Pennsylvania in 1794 abolished it for all crimes except premeditated murder; Michigan became the first state to abolish the death penalty for murder in 1846. A few countries banned capital punishment for peacetime offenses in the nineteenth century and early twentieth century (though some would later reinstate it for periods of time). These were clustered in Europe (Portugal, San Marino, the Netherlands, Italy, Austria, Romania, and Switzerland) and Latin America (Venezuela, Costa Rica, Ecuador, and Uruguay). The Latin American countries banned the death penalty for all crimes, in peacetime and in war. The Nordic countries (Denmark, Finland, Iceland, Norway, Sweden) abolished the death penalty for ordinary crimes (excluding treason and certain wartime offenses) in the first decades of the twentieth century (Hood and Hoyle 2015: 13). After World War II, a global movement to ban capital punishment developed, aiming to prohibit its use under both national and international law. As Figure 10.1 shows, the majority of acts abolishing the death penalty have occurred since about 1950.

Of course, states can abolish capital punishment through various legal means, by constitutional enactment or amendment, by judicial interpretation, and by legislation. Constitutional revision represents a more fundamental commitment, as constitutions are in principle less subject to subsequent revision than are legislation and case law. Abolition at the constitutional level has, like abolition overall, taken off after World War II. Figure 10.2 displays the cumulative number of constitutions that abolish the death penalty, based on data from the Comparative Constitutions Project (Elkins, Ginsburg et al. 2014).

As the preceding figures show, the momentum for abolition gathered after World War II and peaked in the 1990s and the first decade of the twenty-first century (Table 10.1). Figure 10.3 depicts the global

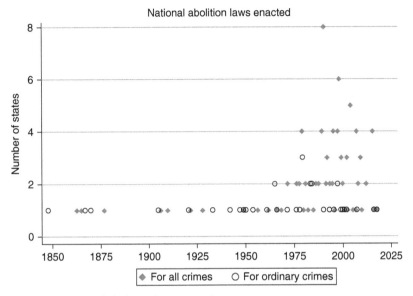

Figure 10.1 National abolition laws enacted

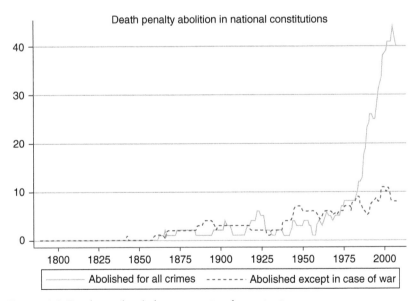

Figure 10.2 Death penalty abolition in national constitutions

TABLE 10.1 Abolition in law, by decade

	Abolished for all crimes	Abolished for ordinary crimes	Total
Before 1950s	9	9	18
1950s	1	2	3
1960s	4	4	8
1970s	10	6	16
1980s	14	4	18
1990s	35	6	41
2000–2009	23	4	27
2010–2017	9	2	11
Total	105	37	142

Note: a number of states first abolished for ordinary crimes and later for all crimes; the table counts both. The overall total is greater than the sum of abolitionist countries as of 2017 because some states appear twice – once in the column for all crimes and once in the column for ordinary crimes.

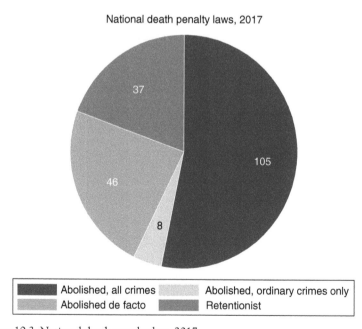

National death penalty laws, 2017

Figure 10.3 National death penalty law, 2017

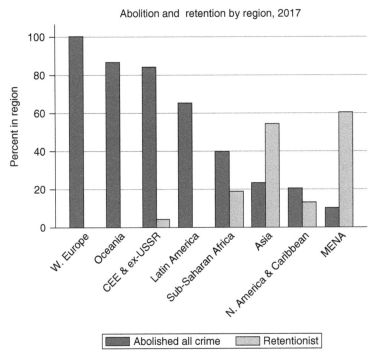

Figure 10.4 Abolition and retention by region, 2017

situation as of 2017. "De facto abolition" refers to countries that retain capital punishment in the law but that have not carried out an execution in the previous ten years (Hood and Hoyle 2015).

Finally, the extent of abolition varies dramatically across regions. Figure 10.4 depicts the regional picture as of 2017. Note that all Western European countries have abolished the death penalty for all crimes, as have most post-Soviet states and the countries of Oceania (Australia, New Zealand, and the Pacific Island states). In contrast, abolition has made little headway in Asia and the Middle East and North Africa (MENA), where more than half of states retain the death penalty.

10.2 ABOLITION AND LEGAL ORDERING: INTERNATIONAL

The construction of the death penalty TLO proceeded in parallel at the domestic and international levels, with both processes drawing force from the emerging global human rights movement. We begin with the international level. Empirical research has demonstrated the influence of international instruments like the UDHR and the core international human rights treaties on the incorporation of human rights in national constitutions (Beck, Meyer et al. 2017; Elkins, Ginsburg et al. 2013; Law and Versteeg 2011; Sloss and Sandholtz 2018; Versteeg 2015).

10.2.1 Global Ordering

Though a number of countries abolished capital punishment in the nineteenth and early twentieth centuries, a genuine transnational drive to prohibit executions began only after World War II. The campaign to abolish the death penalty was, in large part, a reaction to the horrible excesses that had occurred during the war. Fascist regimes had used widespread executions, judicial and extrajudicial, as a tool of political repression. The Nazi Reich, for example, had issued "some 16,500 death sentences" (Evans 1996: 795). Thus the "right to life" language that appeared in post–World War II international human rights documents was aimed at the death penalty. The UDHR, which was adopted by the United Nations General Assembly on December 10, 1948, declares in Article 3, "Everyone has the right to life, liberty and security of person" (UN General Assembly, December 10, 1948). As Schabas relates, in the discussions that accompanied the drafting of the UDHR, the right to life provision triggered debate on two issues, abortion and the death penalty. In the end, the Declaration affirmed the right to life without qualification and omitted any statement for or against the death penalty (Schabas 1997: 24–25).

The UDHR was a statement of common aspirations, but its authors were simultaneously beginning work on a document that would take the form of a binding convention – namely, the *International Covenant on Civil and Political Rights* (ICCPR). Capital punishment was intensely debated at each stage of the drafting of the Covenant (Schabas 1997: 44, 48). As adopted by the General Assembly in 1966, the ICCPR included the following in Article 6:

1. Every human being has the inherent right to life. This right shall be protected by law. No one shall be arbitrarily deprived of his life.
2. In countries which have not abolished the death penalty, sentence of death may be imposed only for the most serious crimes in accordance with the law in force at the time of the commission of the crime and not contrary to the provisions of the present Covenant

and to the Convention on the Prevention and Punishment of the Crime of Genocide. This penalty can only be carried out pursuant to a final judgement rendered by a competent court. . . .

3. Anyone sentenced to death shall have the right to seek pardon or commutation of the sentence. Amnesty, pardon or commutation of the sentence of death may be granted in all cases.

4. Sentence of death shall not be imposed for crimes committed by persons below eighteen years of age and shall not be carried out on pregnant women.

5. Nothing in this article shall be invoked to delay or to prevent the abolition of capital punishment by any State Party to the present Covenant. (UN General Assembly, December 10, 1948)

In addition, Article 4 prohibits any derogation from Article 6, even in "time of public emergency which threatens the life of the nation." Article 4 thus forbids states from compromising the procedural safeguards that must accompany imposition of the death penalty (Articles 6(2) and 6(4)) or the prohibition on applying it to specific categories of persons (Article 6(5)), even during the most critical national emergencies. In other words, the ICCPR signaled that the direction of development of human rights law was to the "progressive restriction" of capital punishment (UN General Assembly, December 10, 1948).

In 1980 a set of Latin American and European countries introduced in the General Assembly a draft Second Optional Protocol to the ICCPR.[4] The Protocol would both require abolition of the death penalty and prohibit its reintroduction by any state that abolished it. The *Second Optional Protocol to the International Covenant on Civil and Political Rights Aiming at the Abolition of the Death Penalty* passed in the General Assembly in December 1989; fifty-nine states voted in favor, twenty-six against, and forty-eight abstained (Schabas 1997: 168–175). The key provisions appear in Article 1:

1. No one within the jurisdiction of a State Party to the present Protocol shall be executed.

2. Each State Party shall take all necessary measures to abolish the death penalty within its jurisdiction.

The *Second Optional Protocol* also prohibits any reservations except for those that retain the death penalty for serious military crimes in

---

[4] The sponsors were Austria, Costa Rica, the Dominican Republic, the Federal Republic of Germany, Italy, Portugal, and Sweden.

wartime (Article 2) and renews the ICCPR's ban on derogations (Article 6). As of March 2019, 86 states were parties to the Second Optional Protocol and another two had signed the Protocol but not ratified it (United Nations 2018).[5]

10.2.2 Regional Ordering

The international movement to end capital punishment also has a powerful regional dimension. Regional bodies in Europe and Latin America began preparing their own international human rights instruments in parallel with the United Nations in the late 1940s.

A special Inter-American Conference in 1969 considered a draft *American Convention on Human Rights* (ACHR). Though several states favored an all-out ban on capital punishment, the final text contained a number of restrictions on the death penalty, without prohibiting it. The ACHR was signed in November 1969 and entered into effect in July 1978. Fourteen out of nineteen national delegations issued a declaration of their "firm hope of seeing the application of the death penalty eradicated from the American environment" and called for an abolitionist additional protocol (Schabas 1997: 278–280). The *American Convention* follows the lead of the ICCPR in limiting the application of the death penalty and pointing toward abolition, but is more restrictive than the UN document. For instance, under Article 4(2), the death penalty may "not be extended to crimes to which it does not presently apply."[6] Furthermore, states that have abolished the death penalty may not reinstate it (Article 4(3)). The ACHR also expands the categories of persons to whom the death penalty cannot be applied to include those over seventy years of age (Article 4(5)), and prohibits capital punishment for "political offenses" (Article 4(4)).

The Inter-American Commission on Human Rights, created by the *American Convention*, became concerned in the mid-1980s with the extension of the death penalty to new crimes in some states. At the urging of Uruguay, the Commission proposed in 1987 a protocol to the ACHR to ban the death penalty. Only four of the nineteen states parties to the Convention had retained capital punishment, and in June 1990 the OAS General Assembly approved the optional protocol (Schabas 1997: 290–292). The Protocol to the ACHR abolishes the

---

[5] *Second Optional Protocol to the International Covenant on Civil and Political Rights, Aiming at the Abolition of the Death Penalty.* 2018. https://treaties.un.org/Pages/ViewDetails.aspx?src=TREA TY&mtdsg_no=IV-12&chapter=4&clang=_en.

[6] *American Convention on Human Rights.* 1969. www.oas.org/juridico/english/Treaties/b-32.htm.

death penalty directly: "the States Parties to this Protocol shall not apply the death penalty in their territory to any person subject to their jurisdiction."[7] Thirteen states are parties to the ACHR Protocol to Abolish the Death Penalty (Organization of American States 2018).

The abolition movement in Europe has been even more far-reaching. Western European countries were among the first to prohibit capital punishment. A number of them, including Austria, Germany, the Netherlands, Sweden, Norway, Denmark, Spain, Portugal, and Italy, were leading promoters of abolition in the UN and sponsored many of the General Assembly resolutions on the subject. International institutions in Europe reflected the abolitionist commitments of a growing number of European states. For instance, the Council of Europe's *European Convention on Human Rights* (ECHR), the first general international human rights treaty, defines capital punishment as an exception to the right to life.[8] But by the 1980s, most member states of the Council of Europe had abolished capital punishment in national law.

In order to bring the ECHR up to date with respect to European practice, the Council of Europe prepared Protocol No. 6 to the ECHR, which twelve states signed in April 1983. Protocol No. 6 bans the death penalty directly: "The death penalty shall be abolished. No-one shall be condemned to such penalty or executed."[9] Under Protocol No. 6, states may retain capital punishment provisions for wartime or imminent threat of war (Article 2). In May 2002, the Council of Europe passed Protocol No. 13 to the ECHR. Protocol No. 13 directly and completely abolishes the death penalty, with no reservations or derogations permitted.[10] As of May 2018, forty-four states had ratified or acceded to Protocol No. 13 and one had signed but not ratified (Russia; Council of Europe 2018).

The European Union has similarly embraced death penalty abolition. Of course, all EU states are also members of the Council of Europe and therefore potential parties to Protocol No. 6 and Protocol No. 13. By 2000, all twenty-seven of the current EU member states had ratified Protocol No. 6. That same year, the EU bodies with legislative roles – the

[7] *Protocol to the American Convention on Human Rights to Abolish the Death Penalty*. 1990. www .oas.org/main/main.asp?sLang=E&sLink=http://www.oas.org/dil/.

[8] *Convention for the Protection of Human Rights and Fundamental Freedoms*. 1950. www.echr.coe .int/NR/rdonlyres/D5CC24A7-DC13-4318-B457-5C9014916D7A/0/EnglishAnglais.pdf.

[9] *Protocol No. 6 to the Convention for the Protection of Human Rights and Fundamental Freedoms Concerning the Abolition of the Death Penalty*. 1983. www.echr.coe.int/NR/rdonlyres/D5CC24 A7-DC13-4318-B457-5C9014916D7A/0/EnglishAnglais.pdf.

[10] *Protocol No. 13 to the Convention for the Protection of Human Rights and Fundamental Freedoms Concerning the Abolition of the Death Penalty in All Circumstances*. 2002. www.echr.coe.int/NR/ rdonlyres/D5CC24A7-DC13-4318-B457-5C9014916D7A/0/EnglishAnglais.pdf, Articles 1–3.

European Council, the European Parliament, and the Commission – all approved a Charter of Fundamental Rights. Article 2 of the Charter, titled "Right to Life," declares, "No one shall be condemned to the death penalty, or executed."[11] The Charter was incorporated as Part II of the Treaty Establishing a Constitution for Europe.[12]

To illuminate the influence of regional institutions, we take a closer look at how the Council of Europe (COE) and the European Union (EU) actively promoted abolition in newly independent states of Central and Eastern Europe. The COE and the EU exercised considerable influence because the transition states were eager to consolidate their fledgling democracies and market economies by joining these key European institutions. The COE did not initially make death penalty abolition an explicit requirement for the early applicants, like Hungary in 1990 or Estonia and Lithuania in 1993. But by the mid-1990s, the Council of Europe had made signature and ratification of Protocol No. 6 to the ECHR a condition of joining (Parliamentary Assembly of the Council of Europe 1994: para. 6; Parliamentary Assembly of the Council of Europe 1996: para. 6).

In a few cases, when new members failed to fulfill their obligations related to abolition of capital punishment, the COE increased the pressure for them to comply. For instance, Armenia came in for strong criticism from the Parliamentary Assembly in 2002 for having failed to ratify Protocol No. 6 and having failed to abolish the death penalty in its criminal code, contrary to commitments made at accession (Parliamentary Assembly of the Council of Europe 2000). By September 2003, Armenia had both ratified Protocol No. 6 and eliminated capital punishment from its domestic statutes (Organization for Security and Cooperation in Europe 2003: 18, 19). In general, the Council of Europe requirement has been effective in spreading abolition to the former communist countries. By 2002, "16 East European countries had abolished capital punishment and ratified the Sixth Optional Protocol to the ECHR, and three had signed it"; all had been retentionist in 1989 (Hood 2002: 16–18).

The European Union has similarly promoted abolition through its enlargement process. By the early 1990s, as the newly independent states of Central and Eastern Europe began to apply for EU

---

[11] *Charter of Fundamental Rights.* 2000. http://eur-lex.europa.eu/LexUriServ/site/en/oj/2000/c_3 64/c_36420001218en00010022.pdf.
[12] *Treaty Establishing a Constitution for Europe.* 2004. http://eur-lex.europa.eu/JOHtml.do?uri=OJ: C:2004:310:SOM:EN:HTML.

membership, all of the existing fifteen EU member states had ratified Protocol No. 6 except Belgium, Greece, and the United Kingdom. All three ratified by 1999. The European Council established in 1993 the "Copenhagen Criteria," political, economic, and legislative conditions that applicant states would have to meet before accession. The political criteria included "democracy, the rule of law, human rights and respect for and protection of minorities" (European Council 1993: 13). The European Commission translated those general ideals into detailed series of specific standards, which it published in "Enlargement Strategy" papers. With respect to the death penalty, the Commission's initial "opinions" reported on the status of capital punishment in each applicant country.[13]

Succeeding annual reports on each applicant country monitored the status of the death penalty and ratification of Protocol No. 6.[14] In its overall reports, the Commission included tables on the ratification of human rights treaties by all of the candidate countries. The June 1999 report showed that of the ten applicant states – only Bulgaria, Cyprus, and Poland had not yet ratified ECHR Protocol No. 6 (European Commission 1999). But by the 2001 report, all had ratified (European Commission 2001), and in 2005 the ten became EU members. The death penalty criterion applied to the 2007 entrants (Bulgaria and Romania) and will apply in any subsequent enlargements.

In short, European institutions have played an active role in pushing new democracies in Eastern and Central Europe toward abolition of the death penalty. The lure of the Council of Europe and the European Union was so great that post–Cold War, democratizing countries were willing to give up capital punishment in order to gain the political and economic benefits of membership in Europe's core institutions.

10.2.3 Transnational Actors
Efforts to craft international and regional legal instruments abolishing the death penalty began in intergovernmental fora immediately after World War II and continue to the present. The effort to ban capital punishment thus predates the emergence of transnational human rights NGOs and the expansion of their influence. The most prominent international human-rights NGOs, Amnesty International (AI) and

---

[13] See the response to Bulgaria's application in European Commission 1997: 16; and the response to Estonia's application in European Commission 1997: 16.

[14] For instance, the 1999 report on Poland noted that Protocol No. 6 had not yet been ratified (European Commission 1998: 11).

Human Rights Watch (HRW), have become consistent and vocal advocates of death penalty abolition. AI (founded in 1961) has made death penalty abolition one of its main themes. Amnesty's concern with executions arose in connection with its primary initial mission on behalf of political prisoners. The organization subsequently came to oppose capital punishment in general and in 1971 called for its universal abolition. Amnesty launched a global anti-death penalty campaign in 1989; since then it has monitored and reported on the status of capital punishment around the world and pushed for abolition (Amnesty International 2018). HRW was founded in 1978 as Helsinki Watch; in 1988 it joined with the other regional "Watch Committees" to form the current global organization. The organization focuses on the death penalty in specific countries rather than on a general campaign for abolition. It publicizes and condemns executions, and reports on the status of capital punishment in specific countries in its annual *World Report*.

HRW and AI both began to campaign actively for death penalty abolition in the 1980s, just before the burst of abolition in national law after 1990. The NGOs did not cause that surge. The collapse of the Soviet Union, democratization in the successor states, and the subsequent inclusion of former Soviet states and satellites in the main European institutions – the EU and the Council of Europe – were clearly the key proximate cause. We argue that the international nongovernmental organizations (INGOs) added political and normative force to the abolitionist movement. Researchers in the world society tradition have shown in a variety of substantive contexts that INGOs are effective carriers of international norms and institutional forms into national contexts (Boli 1987; Boli-Bennett and Meyer 1978; Cole 2009; Meyer, Boli et al. 1997; Tsutsui and Wotipka 2004; Wotipka and Tsutsui 2008). With respect to death penalty abolition, Kim argues that

> human rights INGOs can empower pro-abolition constituencies and influence governments' calculations and deliberations toward abolition. Specifically, they do so by framing capital punishment as a human rights violation through abolitionist campaigns and lobbying parliamentarians to repeal death penalty laws. Through their anti-death penalty activism, human rights INGOs tip the domestic political balance between pro- and anti-death penalty constituencies in favor of complete abolition.
>
> (Kim 2016: 597)

Kim's empirical analysis demonstrates a strong link between the presence of human rights INGOs in a country and the likelihood that it abolishes the death penalty for all crimes (Kim 2016).

We offer a similar argument and find support for it using a new method for gauging INGO influence. As a first cut, we present a descriptive picture of the scale of INGO death penalty activism. Instead of measuring the number of human rights INGOs present in a country, we assessed the documents (world reports, country reports) produced by AI and HRW. We classified the documents as to whether they address a specific country or are global in coverage. Using textual analysis tools, we counted the number of occurrences in each document of three key phrases: "death penalty," "death sentence," and "capital punishment," coding each such reference as a "hit."[15] The number of documents addressing a specific country in any given year is small, usually one or two. For specific countries, we therefore use the number of "hits" (death penalty references) in country-specific documents in a given year as a measure of INGO activity regarding the death penalty. We likewise counted the number of general INGO documents (not country-specific) that include the death penalty phrases. The year coverage for the two organizations differs because AI was created fifteen years before HRW. Figure 10.5 depicts the total number of documents, both general and country-specific, referring to the death penalty. The highest levels are reached during the 1990s and after 2000. The following figure (Figure 10.6) shows the number of hits (occurrences of death penalty phrases) in all INGO documents; these also peak at nearly one thousand per year after 2000. Clearly, death penalty abolition was the subject of vigorous INGO campaigning during the key period.

10.3 DATA AND ANALYSIS

The analysis now focuses on abolition of the death penalty in national law. Because penal law and the carrying out of punishments is a matter of domestic law and practice, the settling of a death penalty TLO must be visible at the national level. We model the most comprehensive form of abolition (for all crimes) in domestic law. We utilize a technique – Cox proportional hazard models – that allows us to estimate the extent to which various domestic and international factors

---

[15] The term "execution" or its stem ("execute") could not be used because they collected too many unrelated terms related to, for example, the executive branch, an executive summary, and so on.

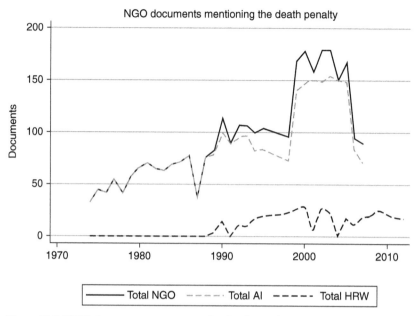

Figure 10.5 NGO documents mentioning the death penalty

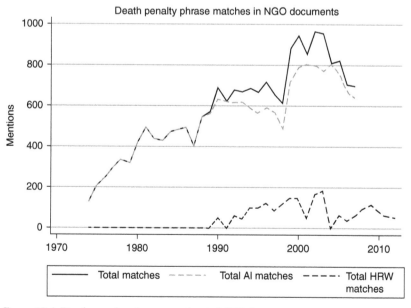

Figure 10.6 Death penalty phrase matches in NGO documents

affect (a) the likelihood that a country will abolish the death penalty and, if it does, (b) how long it takes to do so. The period covered by our analyses begins in 1960 and ends in 2012;[16] the models include at least 150 countries.

Our central puzzle is that death penalty abolition virtually always occurs despite majority public support for retention. Hood and Hoyle, in their comprehensive global analysis, state unequivocally, "[W]here abolition has come about it has not been as a result of the majority of the general public supporting it" (Hood and Hoyle 2008: 350). Indeed, abolition has generally occurred despite public opposition. Steiker declares that "there are no examples of abolition occurring at a time when public opinion supported the measure" (Steiker 2002: 108). As Neumayer puts it, "leadership by the political elite is important since in many countries abolition has been achieved against the majority opinion of the people" (Neumayer 2008, 9). Regarding Western Europe, as Gottschalk et al. note, "Leading European countries abolished the death penalty [after World War II] in the face of strong, sometimes overwhelming, public support for its retention" (Gottschalk, Blumstein et al. 2006: 227). This was the case in Germany (abolished 1949), the United Kingdom (abolished 1969), France (1981), as well as Canada (1998) (Hood and Hoyle 2015: 428). As we report in our brief case studies of Lithuania and South Africa, abolition there followed the same pattern. The absence of comprehensive cross-national public opinion data makes it impossible to demonstrate conclusively that no state has ever abolished the death penalty at a time when the public supported such a change. However, in our review of country studies, we have yet to find an instance of supportive public opinion at the time of abolition.[17]

In many, perhaps most, countries (including some that have already abolished), capital punishment is regarded as not just appropriate for certain crimes but as necessary for upholding social morality and values. We therefore theorize institutional arrangements under which it is possible for a polity to overcome majoritarian opposition to abolition. We suggest one contextual variable that could facilitate abolition

---

[16] The analysis loses little by not starting before 1960, as only two countries (Honduras and the Federal Republic of Germany) abolished the death penalty for all crimes between 1945 and 1959. Data for some key variables are not available for years prior to 1960.

[17] Other abolishing countries in which public opinion favored retention include Czechoslovakia (Frankowski 1996: 227) and Poland (Frankowski 1996: 229).

(transition to democracy) and two institutional mechanisms – one legislative and one judicial – that could make abolition more likely.

1. **Democracy:** We expect democratic institutions to play an ambiguous role. Our models include a variety of variables that capture democracy to account for regime type, electoral years, and democratic transition periods.[18] We expect that regime type (democracy) is negatively associated with abolition (due to public retentionist pressure). Both post-electoral years and democratic transitions should have a positive effect on abolition.

2. **Proportional representation (PR):** We anticipate that parliamentary systems with proportional representation will be more likely to abolish than other systems because accountability is more diffused, and parties are less constrained by voters.

3. **Judicial independence:** As non-majoritarian institutions, courts are less constrained by mass public opinion and have the authority to find the death penalty unconstitutional. We include judicial independence and anticipate that it has a positive effect on abolition. We also argue that transnational influences can affect public and elite opinion regarding the death penalty. Those influences can operate in at least two important ways, through persuasion and socialization, and through material incentives.

4. **INGO influence:** We include two measures of the effects of INGO pressure and persuasion on national abolition. We expect that higher values of the INGO measures are associated with an increased likelihood of abolition.

5. **Regional organization incentives:** The regional ordering of the death penalty in the key European institutions (described above) has been decisive for many states that gained independence after 1990. We thus include a binary variable that captures whether a state joined the Council of Europe during the current year or in the next two years.

Finally, we include a number of control variables to capture the influence of additional factors that could affect a country's likelihood of abolishing.[19] Some additional variables that might seem logical

---

[18] For this and the following paragraphs, a more detailed discussion is offered in Sandholtz and Neumeier 2019.

[19] Controls: prior abolition for ordinary crimes, country size, neighborhood, religion, ethnic fractionalization/conflict, and repression. A more detailed discussion is offered in Sandholtz and Neumeier 2019.

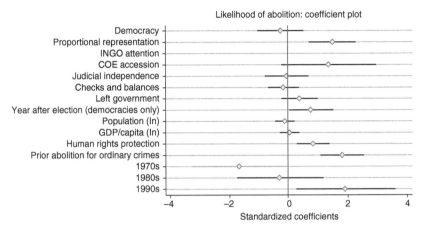

Figure 10.7 Likelihood of abolition: coefficient plot

candidates for inclusion were not included because of constraints imposed by data availability or reliability.[20]

Figure 10.7 presents the results of the main regression (model 8 in Table 10.2, re-estimated with standardized variables). It depicts the estimated effect of each variable, with 95 percent confidence intervals, on the likelihood that a country will abolish the death penalty for all crimes in any given year. Estimates to the left of the zero line decrease the likelihood of abolition; markers to the right of zero mean that the variable increases the likelihood of abolition. If the confidence interval lines overlap zero, we cannot be confident that the effect of the variable is not due to chance (it is not significant at the conventional five percent level). In addition, because the graph represents standardized coefficients (for the nonbinary variables), we can compare the relative size of the effects of the variables.

A few findings stand out. Aside from the variables indicating the various decades, the variables having the largest (positive) effect on the likelihood of abolition were (starting with the greatest) *Prior abolition for ordinary crimes*, *Proportional representation*, *COE accession*, *Human rights protection*, *Year after election*, and *INGO attention*. We were particularly interested in (1) institutional arrangements that could make

---

[20] Please refer to the article for a more detailed discussion on data availability and variables that were not included due to data constraints: Wayne Sandholtz and Stefanie Neumeier, "The Transnational Legal Ordering of the Death Penalty."

non-majoritarian death-penalty abolition more likely, and (2) transnational influences. As expected, the results for democracy are somewhat ambiguous. While democracy in itself and democratic transitions do not have a significant effect on the likelihood of abolition, postelection years and proportional representation are positively correlated with abolition (see Table 10.3).

We also hypothesized that country-specific attention from international human rights NGOs would increase the likelihood of abolition. The models show the hypothesized effect: each one-unit increase in the number of country-specific INGO references raises the likelihood of abolition by about 12–20 percent (see the results reported in Table 10.2). One potential concern with the INGO variable is that reverse causation might account for the significant relationship with death penalty abolition. INGOs (in this case, AI and HRW) might devote greater attention in their documents to countries where they think it can have the greatest effect – that is, in countries where abolition appears to be possible or imminent. We control for that by examining the countries that receive most attention and find that INGOs do not simply focus on easy cases but instead devote significant attention to countries that are rather unlikely to abolish.[21]

Imminent accession to the Council of Europe (COE) increases the likelihood of abolition. In the model graphed in Figure 10.7, COE accession is significant only at the 0.10 level. However, in most of the models, it is significant at the 0.05 level (see Table 10.2). Among the political variables, a larger number of legislative veto points (*Checks and balances*) has no significant effect, nor does having a left-leaning government in power. We also suggested that independent courts would be more likely to rule the death penalty incompatible with constitutional law or treaty obligations. We did not find support for that proposition. Higher levels of respect for physical integrity rights are associated with a greater likelihood of abolition. Prior abolition for ordinary crimes makes abolition for all crimes more likely. The decade variables confirm what we presented in Figures 10.1 and 10.2, namely, that the 1990s – following the end of the Cold War and the

---

[21] Most attention is given to countries that are "hard cases" and continue to carry out executions: the United States, Russia, Jamaica, Trinidad and Tobago (like several other Caribbean countries that remain strongly retentionist), Nigeria, Sierra Leone, Somalia, Mali, Sudan, Uganda, China, Singapore, Vietnam, Pakistan, Tajikistan, Kazakhstan, Belarus, Libya, Kuwait, United Arab Emirates, Iran, Iraq, and Cuba. For a list of country years with the largest number of INGO death penalty references, see Table 10.4.

collapse of the Soviet Union – were propitious for ending capital punishment.[22]

10.4 CASE STUDIES

In the following brief case studies, we seek to illustrate the main arguments. We selected two countries that fit the account of TLO development supported by the data analysis (Lithuania and South Africa) and two countries that could be seen as "off the regression line" and did not abolish (Belarus and Japan).

10.4.1 Lithuania

Lithuania displays several of the factors that we have argued make it possible to abolish capital punishment despite majority public opinion in favor of retention. Particularly crucial were democratization and the strong motivation to join the EU and the Council of Europe. Lithuania also illustrates that courts offer a mechanism for overcoming popular support for retention.

Lithuania made use of capital punishment during the Soviet era (1940–1990) but began to shift away from after regaining independence in 1990. The new constitution established a semi-presidential multiparty system, with the president as the head of state and the prime minister as the head of government. Lithuania's democratic transition included judicial and penal reforms, and it was in that context that the death penalty became a central issue (Hood and Hoyle 2015: 234). In the early 1990s, Lithuania revised its Criminal Code to limit gradually the use of the death penalty.

Joining European institutions – the Council of Europe and eventually the European Union – was also a central element of Lithuania's transition (Hood and Hoyle 2015: 64). When Lithuania joined the Council of Europe, it was exposed to continuous debates on the abolition of the death penalty and pressure to halt executions. However, due to sustained political and public pressures, Lithuania remained retentionist.

Human rights organizations and the Council of Europe introduced various projects in 1996–1999 in an effort to increase public awareness about capital punishment and promote a pro-abolitionist

---

[22] For a more detailed discussion of the empirical results and additional covariates, see Sandholtz and Neumeier 2019.

viewpoint across society (Hood and Hoyle 2015: 237). Faced with the dilemma of overwhelming constituent support for retention, but strongly desiring to join the EU, Lithuanian legislators passed the matter to the Constitutional Court, in essence asking the Court to take the abolitionist step for them (Hodgkinson 2000: 637–638). The Constitutional Court investigated the matter and ruled the death penalty unconstitutional in December 1998 (Hood and Hoyle 2015: 64–65). Within weeks the Lithuanian Parliament had modified the criminal Code, and the following month it ratified Protocol No. 6, officially abolishing the death penalty for all crimes.

10.4.2 South Africa

South Africa displays several of the factors that make abolition more likely, including a democratic transition, international influences, and NGO activism. The apartheid regime of South Africa relied heavily on death sentences as this form of punishment was considered a means of controlling violent crime and protecting the white minority from the majority African population (Bouckaert 1996: 292–293). The apartheid government also cited public opinion as a source for retention (Hodgkinson and Rutherford 1996: 161). However, the political apartheid system started to crumble in the late 1980s, giving way to constitutional change and social reforms.

Even before the abandonment of apartheid, domestic and international pressure, from states and non-state organizations, fueled reforms and revitalized the cause for abolition. Various organizations such as the Institute for Race Relations, the Association of Law Societies, the Society of University Teachers of Law, the General Council of the Bar, the Medical Association on South Africa, and especially Black Sash, as well as Lawyers for Human Rights, pressed the government to reopen the discussion on the death penalty (Bouckaert 1996: 296). In 1986 AI announced a campaign to end human rights abuses in South Africa, calling attention to the death penalty. The organization also sent an open letter to President Botha condemning the death penalty for political prisoners. UN General Assembly resolutions in 1986, 1987, and 1988 denounced apartheid, opposed the death penalty, and called for a halt to executions.

In February 1990 President F. W. De Klerk gave in to the increasing domestic and international pressures and set the path to democratic reform (Bouckaert 1996: 296–297; Hood and Hoyle 2015: 89). The president also announced a death penalty moratorium, stating that "no executions will take place until Parliament has taken a final decision on the new proposals" (Bouckaert 1996: 296–297; Hodgkinson and Rutherford 1996: 161). One year later, De Klerk's proposals were adapted, greatly reducing the applicability of the death penalty (Bouckaert 1996: 297).

Following democratic elections in 1994, the new Minister of Justice saw the death penalty as contrary to the human rights regime and a resumption of executions as undermining fundamental rights given by the 1994 Constitution (Bouckaert 1996: 301). In June 1995 the Constitutional Court decided unanimously that the death penalty was unconstitutional (Bouckaert 1996: 304; Hodgkinson and Rutherford 1996: 161). The Court's decision was endorsed by the South African Parliament and with the Criminal Law Amendment Act of 1997, all references to capital punishment were removed from the statute book (Hood and Hoyle 2015: 89).

10.4.3 Belarus

Belarus is the only country in Europe that actively applies the death penalty, though Criminal Code revisions in 1999 limited the scope and applicability of capital punishment and reduced the number of executions.[23] The Belarussian government has claimed that the reason to retain the death penalty is public support for it, pointing to a 1996 referendum that produced 85 percent of the votes in favor of retaining capital punishment. Abolition generally occurs despite public support for retention, but Belarus lacked several of the factors that are associated with abolition: democratic government, robust INGO activity, the incentive of membership in the EU and the Council of Europe, and independent courts.

Belarus has been ruled autocratically since independence. It has lacked a developed parliament, separation of powers, a real opposition, and fair and secret elections. The Venice Commission of the Council of Europe stated that Belarus's constitution was "illegal and ... does not respect minimum democratic standards and thus violates the principles of separation of powers and the rule of law" (Shelton 2010: 21). Another major concern is the lack of judicial independence and its effect on the criminal justice system. AI has criticized the country's judicial system, pointing to unfair trials, no presumption of innocence,

---

[23] While there were forty-seven executions in 1998, this number decreased to an average of two per year since 2008 (Sergeyeva and Pokras 2012: 8).

torture and ill treatment of prisoners, lack of confidential communications with lawyers, and lack of independent investigations.

We have argued that INGOs can be carriers of anti-death-penalty
norms. Though AI has criticized Belarus, NGOs are often unable to
operate there effectively and without government interference.[24]
Unregistered organizations are not allowed to receive or spend funding,
and any activities carried out are punishable with imprisonment. While
INGOs such as AI and HRW have been reporting human rights abuses
and have campaigned against Belarus's death penalty practices, they
have also decried the lack of public information on executions as
hindering abolitionist efforts.

The absence of democratic, rule-of-law institutions bears directly on
another pro-abolition factor: European regional organizations. The
Council of Europe and the European Union made democratization
and respect for rights prerequisites for membership, creating powerful
incentives for newly independent states in Central and Eastern Europe
to (among other steps) abolish capital punishment. However, the
Belorussian regime under President Lukashenko has embraced
a conservative Stalinist ideology and has oriented itself away from
Europe. A report issued by the European Parliament described EU-
Belarus relations as "hav[ing] always been difficult and hav[ing] developed at a much slower pace" compared to other countries (Bosse and
Vieira 2018: 8). This outcome was mainly a result of Belarus's continued reluctance to meet human rights standards, including the continuation of the death penalty (Bosse and Vieira 2018: 21).

The Parliamentary Assembly of the Council of Europe agreed in
2009 to restore Belarus's guest status if the country introduced an
official moratorium on executions, reviving the abolition debate within
the country. Belarus acknowledged to the UN Human Rights Council
the importance of shifting public opinion on the death penalty and of
eventually abolishing it. However, after the disputed presidential elections of December 2010, President Lukashenko halted progress toward
abolition. The main argument for this development was the terrorist
attack on the Minsk subway in 2011; the two men responsible for the
attack were sentenced to death by the Supreme Court in 2011 and
executed in 2012. The latest human rights dialogue between Belarus
and the EU occurred in July 2017 and specifically addressed freedoms of

---

[24] For instance, Viasna, a leading local human rights organization, was not allowed to register in
2003, although such denial is a violation of the ICCPR (Sergeyeva and Pokras 2012: 22).

expression, assembly, and association, as well as electoral rights, and the death penalty.

10.4.4 Japan

Besides the United States, Japan is now the only highly developed democratic country that retains the death penalty in legal and practical terms (Johnson 2014: 166; Sato 2014: 21). However, compared to the United States and other Asian countries, where executions have been decreasing in recent years, Japan presents a unique case with its increasing numbers in death penalty sentences and executions (Hood and Hoyle 2015: 112; Johnson 2014: 166). Historically, except for a brief period in the late 1980s, where the country had implemented a moratorium on capital punishment for three years, Japan has been consistently retentionist since the end of Second World War (Sato 2014: 22). The Japanese government grounds the decision for maintaining the death penalty in public support for retention.[25] Why has Japan not followed the path of most other wealthy democracies, abolishing the death penalty despite retentionist public opinion? We argued that proportional representation increases the likelihood of legislative bargains that include abolition. Japan's political system has prevented those kinds of coalitional log-rolling agreements.

Though Japan has a multiparty system, the conservative Liberal Democratic Party (LDC) has been the dominant ruling party since it was founded in 1955. During the brief ruling period of Democratic Party (DPJ; 2009–2012), executions were in the decline (Johnson 2014: 170; Sato 2014: 22). However, with the LDC regaining power in 2013, executions have been steadily increasing (Sato 2014: 22). Japan's judiciary has also referenced the majority public support for retention to justify continued application of death penalty sentences and executions (Jiang, Lambert et al. 2010: 863; Sato 2014: 23).[26] Interestingly, the Supreme Court stated that abolishing the death penalty is a "legislative policy decision rather than a judicial action" (Sato 2014: 24).

In terms of domestic and international pressure, thus far Japan has successfully resisted abolition demands. Overall, domestic NGOs face

---

[25] A government survey in 2009 found that 86 percent participants favored retention (Hood and Hoyle 2015: 113; Sato 2014: 25).

[26] One Minister of Justice claimed it was a "duty to order executions" (Johnson 2014: 171). The Supreme Court has acknowledged the global trend of abolition but has also referred to government surveys on public attitudes favoring retention for its reluctance to challenge the constitutionality of the death penalty (Sato 2014: 24).

a variety of regulations and restrictions. Further, human rights NGOs lack consultation status, do not participate in the drafting of official human rights reports in Japan, and only have access to the reports after they are published (Neary 2002: 66). In terms of INGO activity, AI has consistently criticized Japan's retentionist position and the questionable procedures surrounding the practice. The EU in 2001 threatened to withdraw Japan's observer status. Though Japan did not respond, the EU has yet to follow through with this threat (Hood and Hoyle 2009: 29; Obara-Minnitt 2016: 110).

10.5 CONCLUSION

In concluding, we return to the questions posed in the introductory chapter.

Framing. The death penalty TLO is not about enhancing the power of state officials to combat transnational crime. The death penalty is situated at the punishment end of the criminal justice spectrum, and the death penalty TLO is about establishing limits to what the state can do in punishing the guilty. Capital punishment is framed by advocates and policy entrepreneurs as a global human rights problem. In this sense, domestic processes of enforcement have "become more enmeshed in transnational frameworks."[27] The post–World War II context was propitious for advancing a human rights framing of the death penalty, in reaction to the massive abuses of execution as a tool of political repression and genocide. But the success of the human rights framing has been partial because normative counter-narratives are available, even within the expanding international human rights regime. The right to life is not absolute; taking human life is permissible in war and in personal self-defense, for example. The right to life, in some constructions, can be forfeited. Divergent national frameworks regarding capital punishment could therefore be asserted and retained even while retentionist states accept the broader international human rights system.

Settling. What inhibits the settling of TLO norms? In the case of the death penalty, transnational norms are neither ambiguous nor indeterminate: capital punishment is framed as a violation of the most fundamental human right, the right to life. Settling of this norm is incomplete because it is in direct collision with

---

[27] Aaronson and Shaffer, Chapter 1.

national or local norms that see capital punishment as justified or even necessary to defend social order or national security. The norm of abolition has settled in much of the world, but it remains contested, especially in some regions (Middle East and North Africa, Asia).

Concordance. We observe considerable concordance at the regional and domestic levels in some parts of the world (Europe, Oceania, and Latin America) but with continuing gaps in others. The variation is mainly across countries and regions.

State power. The death penalty TLO has not been driven by powerful states seeking to impose their conceptions of criminal justice on others. In fact, several of the most powerful states (the United States, China) remain among the leading resisters to the TLO. At the international level, in the drafting of key instruments like the Universal Declaration of Human Rights, the ICCPR, and its Optional Protocol on Abolition of the Death Penalty, the policy entrepreneurs tended to represent small and mid-sized states, often from Latin America and Western Europe.

Data power. Data and information on the death penalty have been collected and disseminated largely by NGOs at the heart of transnational human rights networks: Amnesty International and Human Rights Watch. Even so, the ongoing dynamics of abolition and resistance are not driven primarily by differing quantitative or qualitative assessments of capital punishment, but rather by divergent underlying values.

Recursivity. The TLO framework posits constant recursivity, that is, influences flowing in both directions across levels (national and international) and between law and practices (Halliday and Shaffer 2015). Thus changes in law can affect attitudes and beliefs. There is evidence of that effect in death penalty abolition. Though abolition occurs in spite of retentionist public opinion, TLO theory would lead us to expect that after death penalty abolition takes effect, public beliefs and values should shift to align with the new norm. That is, following abolition, an increasing share of the public will begin to view capital punishment not just as illegal but as obsolete, inappropriate, immoral, or inhumane (Hood and Hoyle 2008: 376). In some countries where public opinion supported retention of capital punishment pre-abolition, that support declined steadily – and dramatically – post-abolition, including in Britain, France, Germany, Italy, Norway, Australia, and New Zealand (Hood and Hoyle 2008: 376–377).

Hood and Hoyle note that Robert Badinter, who played a central role in France's 1981 death penalty abolition, "has often suggested that it usually takes about 10 to 15 years following abolition for the public to stop thinking of it as useful and to realize that it makes no difference to the level of homicide." Hood and Hoyle also point out that experience has often supported Badinter's speculation (Hood and Hoyle 2015: 464). In an empirical study of seventeen countries, Stack found that "[r]esidents of abolitionist nations, especially if they resided in nations with a long history of abolition, were significantly less supportive of the death penalty than residents of retentionist nations" (Stack 2004: 69). Unnever's subsequent study of public attitudes in fifty-nine countries found that 58.0 percent of those surveyed in retentionist countries supported the death penalty, as opposed to 41.9 percent of those in abolitionist countries. Unnever concludes that the gap in opinion is most likely due to "a significant decline in support among people living in countries that have abolished the death penalty" and that, as of 1999, "the majority of people living in a state that has abolished capital punishment now oppose its use" (Unnever 2010: 477). As the TLO framework leads us to expect, death penalty abolition produces a supportive change in public opinion.

The transnational legal ordering of capital punishment remains uneven, with significant parts of the world remaining outside its reach. As shown above, countries in the Middle East, North Africa, and much of Asia have largely retained the death penalty. Moreover, some of the world's largest countries continue not just to keep the death penalty on the books but to carry it out: China (the world leader in executions), the United States, Egypt, India, Indonesia, Iran, Japan, and Nigeria. In this light, the transnational legal ordering of the death penalty may well have reached a point at which its further extension will be slow, or perhaps unlikely. In the current climate of populist authoritarianism, some retreat may even be possible.

APPENDIX

TABLE 10.2 Death penalty abolition for all crimes: main models

Cox proportional hazard regressions

	1	2	3	4	5	6	7	8
Democracy	6.547***	3.472	6.398*	4.486	3.830	3.738	1.493	0.391
	(3.771)	(3.365)	(7.195)	(5.060)	(4.400)	(4.481)	(1.883)	(0.543)
Proportional representation	3.256***	3.373***	3.255***	3.563***	3.500***	3.640***	4.281***	4.366***
	(1.092)	(1.157)	(1.236)	(1.408)	(1.387)	(1.579)	(1.800)	(1.659)
INGO attention	1.122***	1.119***	1.133***	1.135***	1.137***	1.161***	1.170***	1.216***
	(0.043)	(0.044)	(0.048)	(0.050)	(0.051)	(0.056)	(0.058)	(0.059)
COE accession, this year or in next two	4.981**	5.126**	4.398**	4.751***	4.677**	4.648**	4.319**	3.856*
	(3.569)	(3.689)	(3.297)	(2.791)	(3.053)	(2.933)	(2.521)	(3.118)
Judicial independence		1.893	2.405	2.639	2.183	0.724	0.449	0.810
		(1.614)	(2.139)	(2.350)	(1.922)	(0.884)	(0.612)	(0.998)
Checks			0.799*	0.834	0.832	0.865	0.880	0.904
			(0.098)	(0.105)	(0.103)	(0.117)	(0.128)	(0.139)
Left government (executive and legislative)				1.527	1.511	1.641	1.491	1.437
				(0.444)	(0.441)	(0.502)	(0.472)	(0.448)
Year after election (democracies)					2.060**	1.949*	2.046*	2.105*
					(0.755)	(0.715)	(0.769)	(0.805)
Population (ln)						0.798*	0.867	0.917
						(0.094)	(0.100)	(0.102)
GDP/capita (ln)							1.234	1.032
							(0.219)	(0.190)
Human rights protection							1.640**	1.929***
							(0.340)	(0.437)

TABLE 10.2 (cont.)

Cox proportional hazard regressions

	1	2	3	4	5	6	7	8
Prior abolition for ordinary crimes								6.043*** (2.231)
1970s	0.673 (0.685)	0.702 (0.710)	0.228** (0.169)	0.184** (0.150)	0.185*** (0.147)	0.224* (0.184)	0.325 (0.271)	0.188** (0.155)
1980s	1.511 (1.571)	1.569 (1.618)	0.554 (0.413)	0.554 (0.409)	0.539 (0.395)	0.677 (0.533)	0.958 (0.812)	0.729 (0.544)
1990s	11.576*** (10.695)	12.085*** (11.182)	3.923** (2.688)	3.617* (2.491)	3.799* (2.598)	5.437** (4.367)	7.654** (6.952)	6.731** (5.692)
2000s	1.987 (1.953)	2.188 (2.165)	–	–	–	–	–	–
Observations	5,895	5,871	4,053	3,833	3,833	3,686	3,686	3,686
Countries	150	148	142	140	140	135	135	135
Abolition events	62	62	53	50	50	49	49	49
Log likelihood	–241.8	–241.3	–200.6	–188.8	–187.0	–178.2	–175.2	–164.2
Chi^2	96.51	95.90	56.04	66.86	76.12	92.67	81.22	131.1

Hazard ratios with robust standard errors in parentheses
*** p<0.01, ** p<0.05, * p<0.1

TABLE 10.3 Death penalty abolition for all crimes: additional variables

Cox proportional hazard regressions

	1	2	3	4	5	6	7	8	9
Democracy	0.076 (0.151)	0.310 (0.434)	0.337 (0.466)	0.194 (0.271)	0.179 (0.252)	0.339 (0.498)	0.343 (0.484)	0.191 (0.292)	0.405 (0.580)
Proportional representation	7.206*** (3.975)	4.504*** (1.792)	4.572*** (1.908)	6.208*** (3.213)	6.114*** (3.098)	3.866*** (1.518)	4.093*** (1.689)	4.877*** (2.235)	4.514*** (1.732)
INGO attention	1.219*** (0.073)	1.209*** (0.059)	1.219*** (0.059)	1.259*** (0.072)	1.255*** (0.073)	1.221*** (0.064)	1.222*** (0.059)	1.221*** (0.063)	1.219*** (0.060)
COE accession, this year or in next two	6.910* (7.783)	3.897* (3.174)	3.652 (3.010)	4.734 (5.537)	4.657 (5.452)	4.294** (2.963)	3.928 (3.513)	3.443 (3.118)	7.584*** (5.955)
Judicial independence	4.878 (7.403)	0.911 (1.135)	0.880 (1.120)	2.813 (3.708)	4.072 (6.171)	0.942 (1.141)	1.091 (1.333)	1.599 (2.034)	0.877 (1.126)
Checks	0.797 (0.209)	0.914 (0.140)	0.894 (0.136)	0.884 (0.161)	0.882 (0.164)	0.882 (0.135)	0.892 (0.150)	0.857 (0.156)	0.903 (0.137)
Left government (executive and legislative)	1.167 (0.657)	1.415 (0.435)	1.474 (0.447)	0.995 (0.370)	0.995 (0.369)	1.441 (0.472)	1.268 (0.414)	1.138 (0.423)	1.433 (0.445)
Year after election (democracies)	1.370 (0.714)	2.065* (0.786)	2.188** (0.849)	2.028 (0.975)	2.030 (0.949)	2.040* (0.778)	2.257** (0.874)	2.097* (0.888)	2.124** (0.812)
Population (ln)	0.961 (0.176)	0.937 (0.104)	0.981 (0.118)	0.888 (0.122)	0.900 (0.127)	0.896 (0.103)	0.904 (0.099)	0.861 (0.109)	0.912 (0.102)
GDP/capita (ln)	0.985 (0.218)	1.040 (0.208)	0.961 (0.197)	0.892 (0.186)	0.886 (0.181)	1.032 (0.188)	1.013 (0.186)	1.071 (0.209)	1.017 (0.190)

TABLE 10.3 (cont.)

Cox proportional hazard regressions

	1	2	3	4	5	6	7	8	9
Human rights protection	1.845*	1.983***	2.055***	1.929**	1.698	1.807***	1.831***	1.923***	1.859***
	(0.588)	(0.455)	(0.468)	(0.553)	(0.569)	(0.410)	(0.426)	(0.459)	(0.432)
Prior abolition for ordinary crimes	7.039***	5.892***	6.377***	6.768***	6.718***	6.084***	6.331***	6.173***	6.264***
	(2.984)	(2.166)	(2.411)	(2.885)	(2.894)	(2.219)	(2.392)	(2.495)	(2.421)
Inequality (GINI)	0.975								
	(0.026)								
Ethnic fractionalization		0.990							
		(0.671)							
Ethno-linguistic fractionalization			0.764						
			(0.477)						
Ethnic violence				1.328					
				(0.400)					
Ethnic war					0.783				
					(0.338)				
Protestantism						1.010			
						(0.009)			
Catholicism						1.009			
						(0.007)			
Islam						1.000			
						(0.007)			

	(1)	(2)	(3)	(4)	(5)	(6)	(7)	(8)	(9)
Proportion of neighbors that have abolished (COW)	1.372 (2.045)						1.228 (0.721)		
Proportion of neighbors that have abolished (CEPII)								0.895 (0.590)	
Democratic transition this year or previous two									0.223 (0.225)
1970s	–	0.187** (0.155)	0.165** (0.137)	–	–	0.137** (0.114)	0.216* (0.191)	0.190* (0.166)	0.194** (0.160)
1980s		0.732 (0.565)	0.786 (0.615)	–	–	0.630 (0.459)	0.670 (0.534)	0.608 (0.505)	0.708 (0.537)
1990s	9.629* (11.334)	6.880** (6.170)	9.671** (8.837)	9.344** (8.713)	8.078** (7.215)	6.279*** (4.988)	8.604** (7.629)	8.488** (7.773)	6.719*** (5.714)
2000s	–	–	–	–	–	–	–	–	–
Observations	1,506	3,654	3,641	2,129	2,129	3,649	3,648	3,338	3,686
Countries	104	134	133	126	126	133	134	123	135
Abolition events	28	49	49	40	40	48	48	44	49
Log likelihood	−74.20	−163.6	−162.7	−118.7	−118.6	−160.0	−159.5	−142.9	−163.0
Chi^2	52.18	138.4	129.4	119.4	116.5	152.5	133.2	106.3	135.2

Hazard ratios with robust standard errors in parentheses
*** $p<0.01$, ** $p<0.05$, * $p<0.1$

TABLE 10.4 Top country-specific INGO death penalty references (country year)

Rank	Country	Year	Year of abolition for all crimes	INGO references to this country	Rank	Country	Year	Year of abolition for all crimes	INGO references to this country
1	United States	2003		35	54	Russia	1998		10
2	United States	2002		27	55	Jamaica	1984		10
3	United States	2001		26	56	China	2000		10
4	United States	1996		24	57	Kuwait	1995		10
5	United States	1999		23	58	Nigeria	1986		10
6	United States	2000		22	59	India	2012		10
7	United States	1989		22	60	Iran, Islamic Republic of	2010		10
8	United States	1995		20	61	United Arab Emirates	1999		10
9	United States	1998		20	62	Mauritius	1992	1995	10
10	Russia	1990		18	63	Iraq	2005		10
11	United States	1988		17	64	China	1985		10
12	United States	1983		17	65	Kuwait	1994		10
13	Korea, Republic of	1980		16	66	Korea, Republic of	1983		10
14	Jamaica	1992		15	67	Nigeria	2001		10
15	United States	1987		15	68	Pakistan	1991		10
16	Nigeria	2003		15	69	Pakistan	1978		10
17	China	1999		14	70	Libya	1976		10
18	Russia	1992		14	71	Libya	2004		10
19	Tajikistan	2003		14	72	China	2007		10
20	Libya	1988		14	73	Cuba	2002		10
21	Uzbekistan	2003	2008	14	74	Russia	1999		10

Rank	Country	Year	Year	No.
22	Russia	1993		14
23	China	2002		14
24	Uzbekistan	2000	2008	13
25	United States	1990		13
26	United States	2009		13
27	Tajikistan	2002		13
28	Russia	1991		13
29	Azerbaijan	1994	1998	13
30	Nigeria	2005		13
31	Kuwait	1992		13
32	China	2003		12
33	Russia	2000		12
34	China	1990		12
35	China	1984		12
36	Korea, Democratic Republic of	1993		12
37	Pakistan	2009		12
38	Kazakhstan	1997		11
39	United States	1986		11
40	Ukraine	1995	1999	11
41	Vietnam	2003		11
42	United Arab Emirates	2000		11
43	Armenia	2001	2003	11
44	Somalia	1986		11
45	Georgia	1995	1997	11

Rank	Country	Year	Year	No.
75	South Africa	1995	1997	10
76	United Arab Emirates	1986		10
77	Armenia	2002	2003	10
78	China	2012		10
79	Singapore	2011		10
80	Hungary	1976	1990	9
81	Uganda	2009		9
82	Cuba	2000		9
83	Belarus	2009		9
84	Tanzania	2002		9
85	Iran, Islamic Republic of	2008		9
86	South Africa	1990	1997	9
87	Russia	1989		9
88	Turkey	1980	2004	9
89	United States	1994		9
90	Lebanon	2001		9
91	Nigeria	2002		9
92	Egypt, Arab Republic of	1985		9
93	Cuba	1999		9
94	Sudan	1989		9
95	United States	1997		9
96	Turkey	1984	2004	9
97	Jamaica	1983		9
98	Mali	1988		9

TABLE 10.4 (*cont.*)

Rank	Country	Year	Year of abolition for all crimes	INGO references to this country
46	United States	2007		11
47	Romania	1983	1989	11
48	Turkey	1985	2004	11
49	Nigeria	1992		11
50	Russia	1988		11
51	Kazakhstan	1998		11
52	Turkey	2000	2004	10
53	Belarus	2010		10
99	Libya	2007		9
100	Uzbekistan	2005	2008	9
101	India	2002		9
102	Somalia	1987		9
103	Azerbaijan	1996	1998	9
104	Iran, Islamic Republic of	1997		9
105	Vietnam	2009		9
106	Armenia	1999	2003	9

Note: This table includes only those country years in that received nine or more INGO references. These 106 observations account for about 2 percent of the total of 5,575 observations. Approximately 56 percent of country-years received no INGO references, and an additional 20 percent received one or two.

REFERENCES

Amnesty International. 2018. *Death Sentences and Executions 2017*. London: Amnesty International.

Beccaria, Cesare. 2008. *On Crimes and Punishments and Other Writings*. Toronto: University of Toronto Press.

Beck, Colin J., John W. Meyer, et al. 2017. "Constitutions in World Society: A New Measure of Human Rights." Unpublished manuscript. January 27, 2017. https://ssrn.com/abstract=2906946 (accessed April 29, 2018).

Boli, John. 1987. "Human Rights or State Expansion? Cross-National Definitions of Constitutional Rights, 1870–1970." Pp. 71–91 in *Institutional Structure*, edited by George Thomas, John Meyer, Francisco Ramirez, and John Boli. Newbury Park, CA: Sage.

Boli-Bennett, John, and John Meyer. 1978. "The Ideology of Childhood and the State: Rules Distinguishing Children in National Constitutions, 1870–1970." *American Sociological Review* 43(6): 797–812.

Bosse, Giselle, and Alena Vieira. 2018. "Human Rights in Belarus: The EU's Role since 2016." European Parliament Think Tank. www.europarl.europa.eu/thinktank/en/document.html?reference=EXPO_STU%282018%29603870.

Bouckaert, Peter Norbert. 1996. "Shutting Down the Death Factory: The Abolition of Capital Punishment in South Africa." *Stanford Journal of International Law* 32(2): 287–325.

Cole, Wade M. 2009. "Hard and Soft Commitments to Human Rights Treaties, 1966–20001." *Sociological Forum* 24(3): 563–588.

Elkins, Zachary, Tom Ginsburg, et al. 2013. "Getting to Rights: Treaty Ratification, Constitutional Convergence, and Human Rights Practice." *Harvard International Law Journal* 54(1): 61–95.

Elkins, Zachary, Tom Ginsburg, et al. 2014. "Characteristics of National Constitutions, Version 2.0." www.comparativeconstitutionsproject.org. (accessed December 28, 2016).

European Commission. 1997a. *Agenda 2000: Commission Opinion on Estonia's Application for Membership of the European Union*. July 15, 1997. http://ec.europa.eu/enlargement/archives/pdf/dwn/opinions/estonia/es-op_en.pdf (accessed May 24, 2007).

European Commission. 1997b. *Commission Opinion on Bulgaria's Application for Membership of the European Union*. July 15, 1997. http://ec.europa.eu/enlargement/archives/pdf/dwn/opinions/bulgaria/bu-op_en.pdf (accessed May 24, 2007).

European Commission. 1998. *1998 Regular Report from the Commission on Poland's Progress towards Accession*. November 4. http://ec.europa.eu/enlargement/archives/pdf/key_documents/1998/poland_en.pdf (accessed May 24, 2007).

European Commission. 1999. *Composite Paper: Reports on Progress towards Accession by Each of the Candidate Countries: Annex 3.* October 13, 1999. h ttp://ec.europa.eu/enlargement/archives/pdf/key_documents/1999/annex3_ en.pdf (accessed May 24, 2007).

European Commission. 2001. *Making a Success of Enlargement: Strategy Paper and Report of the European Commission on the Progress towards Accession by Each of the Candidate Countries.* November 13, 2001. http://ec.europa.eu/enlarge ment/archives/pdf/key_documents/2001/annexes_en.pdf (accessed July 9, 2007).

European Council. 1993. *European Council in Copenhagen 21–22 June 1993: Conclusions of the Presidency.* http://ue.eu.int/ueDocs/cms_Data/docs/press data/en/ec/72921.pdf (accessed May 24, 2007).

Evans, Richard J. 1996. *Rituals of Retribution: Capital Punishment in Germany 1600–1987.* Oxford: Oxford University Press.

Frankowski, Stanislaw. 1996. "Post-Communist Europe." Pp. 215–241 in *Capital Punishment: Global Issues and Prospects*, edited by Peter Hodgkinson and Andrew Rutherford. Winchester, UK: Waterside Press.

Garland, David. 2010. *Peculiar Institution : America's Death Penalty in an Age of Abolition.* Cambridge: Belknap Press of Harvard University Press.

Gottschalk, Marie, Alfred Blumstein, et al. 2006. *The Prison and the Gallows: The Politics of Mass Incarceration in America.* Cambridge: Cambridge University Press.

Halliday, Terence C., and Gregory Shaffer. 2015. "Transnational Legal Orders." Pp. 3–74 in *Transnational Legal Orders*, edited by Terence C. Halliday and Gregory Shaffer. Cambridge: Cambridge University Press.

Hodgkinson, Peter. 2000. "Europe – A Death Penalty Free Zone: Commentary and Critique of Abolitionist Strategies." *Ohio Northern University Law Review* 26: 625–663.

Hodgkinson, Peter, and Andrew Rutherford. 1996. *Capital Punishment: Global Issues and Prospects.* Winchester: Waterside Press.

Hood, Roger. 2002. *The Death Penalty: A Worldwide Perspective.* 3rd ed. Oxford: Oxford University Press.

Hood, Roger G., and Carolyn Hoyle. 2008. *The Death Penalty: A Worldwide Perspective*, 4th ed. Oxford: Oxford University Press.

Hood, Roger, and Carolyn Hoyle. 2009. "Abolishing the Death Penalty Worldwide: The Impact of a 'New Dynamic.'" *Crime and Justice* 38(1): 1–63.

Hood, Roger, and Carolyn Hoyle. 2015. *The Death Penalty: A Worldwide Perspective*, 5th ed. Oxford: Oxford University Press.

Jiang, Shanhe, Eric G. Lambert, et al. 2010. "Death Penalty Views in China, Japan and the U.S.: An Empirical Comparison." *Journal of Criminal Justice* 38(5): 862–869.

Johnson, David T. 2014. "Progress and Problems in Japanese Capital Punishment." Pp. 168–184 in *Confronting Capital Punishment in Asia:*

Human Rights, Politics, and Public Opinion, edited by Roger Hood and Surya Deva. Oxford: Oxford University Press.

Kim, Dongwook. 2016. "International Non-governmental Organizations and the Abolition of the Death Penalty." *European Journal of International Relations* 22(3): 596–621.

Law, David S., and Mila Versteeg. 2011. "The Evolution and Ideology of Global Constitutionalism." *California Law Review* 99: 1163–1257.

Meyer, John W., John Boli, et al. 1997. "World Society and the Nation-State." *American Journal of Sociology* 103(1): 144–181.

Neary, Ian. 2002. *Human Rights in Japan, South Korea, and Taiwan*. London: Routledge.

Neumayer, Eric. 2008. "Death Penalty: The Political Foundations of the Global Trend towards Abolition." *Human Rights Review* 9(2): 241–268.

Obara-Minnitt, Mika. 2016. *Japanese Moratorium on the Death Penalty*. New York: Palgrave Macmillan.

Organization of American States. 2018. *Signatures and Ratifications: Protocol to the American Convention on Human Rights to Abolish the Death Penalty*. Department of International Law. www.oas.org/juridico/english/sigs/a-53 .html (accessed May 20, 2018).

Organization for Security and Cooperation in Europe, Office for Democratic Institutions and Human Rights. 2003. *The Death Penalty in the OSCE Area*. October 2003. www.osce.org/documents/odihr/2003/10/771_en.pdf (accessed May 23, 2007).

Parliamentary Assembly of the Council of Europe. 1994. *Resolution 1044 (1994) on the Abolition of Capital Punishment*. http://assembly.coe.int/Docu ments/AdoptedText/ta96/ERES1097.HTM.

Parliamentary Assembly of the Council of Europe. 1996. *Resolution 1097 (1996) on the Abolition of the Death Penalty in Europe*. http://assembly .coe.int/Documents/AdoptedText/ta96/ERES1097.HTM.

Parliamentary Assembly of the Council of Europe. 2000. *Opinion No. 221 (2000): Armenia's Application for Membership of the Council of Europe*. June 28. http://assembly.coe.int/main.asp?Link=/documents/adoptedtext/t a00/eopi221.htm (accessed May 23, 2007).

Sandholtz, Wayne, and Stefanie Neumeier. 2019. "The Transnational Legal Ordering of the Death Penalty." *UCI Journal of International, Transnational, and Comparative Law* 4.

Sarat, Austin, and Jürgen Martschukat, eds. 2011. *Is the Death Penalty Dying? European and American Perspectives*. New York, Cambridge University Press.

Sato, Mai. 2014. *The Death Penalty in Japan: Will the Public Tolerate Abolition?* Wiesbaden: Springer.

Schabas, William A. 1997. *The Abolition of the Death Penalty in International Law*, 2nd edition. Cambridge: Cambridge University Press.

Sergeyeva, Viktoria, and Alla Pokras. 2012. *The Abolition of the Death Penalty and Its Alternative Sanction in Eastern Europe: Belarus, Russia and Ukraine*. London: Penal Reform International.

Shelton, Dinah. 2010. *Regional Protection of Human Rights*. Oxford: Oxford University Press.

Sloss, David, and Wayne Sandholtz. 2018. "Universal Human Rights and Constitutional Change." Manuscript. May 18, 2018. 52 pages.

Stack, Steven. 2004. "Public Opinion and the Death Penalty." *International Criminal Justice Review* 14(1): 69–98.

Steiker, Carol S. 2002. "Capital Punishment and American Exceptionalism." *Oregon Law Review* 81(1): 97–130.

Tsutsui, Kiyoteru, and Christine Min Wotipka. 2004. "Global Civil Society and the International Human Rights Movement: Citizen Participation in Human Rights International Nongovernmental Organizations." *Social Forces* 83(2): 587–620.

UN General Assembly. 1948. *Universal Declaration of Human Rights*. Resolution 217 A (III). December 10. www.unhchr.ch/udhr/lang/eng.htm (accessed April 29, 2018).

Unnever, James. 2010. "Global Support for the Death Penalty." *Punishment & Society* 12(4): 463–484.

Versteeg, Mila. 2015. "Law versus Norms: The Impact of Human Rights Treaties on National Bills of Rights." *Journal of Institutional and Theoretical Economics* 171(1): 87–111.

Wotipka, Christine Min, and Kiyoteru Tsutsui. 2008. "Global Human Rights and State Sovereignty: State Ratification of International Human Rights Treaties, 1965–2001." *Sociological Forum* 23(4): 724–754.

Zimring, Franklin E. 2003. *The Contradictions of American Capital Punishment*. Oxford: Oxford University Press.

CHAPTER ELEVEN

PERFORMANCE, POWER, AND TRANSNATIONAL LEGAL ORDERING

Addressing Sexual Violence as a Human Rights Concern

Ron Levi and Ioana Sendroiu

11.1   INTRODUCTION

Research on transnational legal orders provides a fundamentally global approach to understanding legal change. This research agenda effectively demonstrates that the dynamism of legal change is not fully captured by existing models within law, political science, sociology, or anthropology work (Halliday and Shaffer 2015). One of the key payoffs from research in transnational legal ordering is that we gain a deeply integrative theory of law. This stems from the capacious nature of the transnational legal ordering research enterprise: by understanding law as simultaneously the product of professional battles as well as diffusion and mimesis, and by cutting across levels so as to include the role of states, non-state organizations in both civil society and the private sector, international institutions, and moral entrepreneurs, transnational legal ordering provides a means of understanding global legal change.

In this chapter, we draw on two central insights of the transnational legal orders literature. The first is that the study of transnational legal ordering can extend beyond studies of legal diffusion through mimesis and isomorphism, to include in such models "much greater attention to *politics, material power, and agency*" across geographic contexts (Shaffer and Halliday 2016: 20; emphasis in original). The second insight is that the study of transnational legal ordering ought to incorporate international, transnational, and domestic legal influences, thereby emphasizing "the transnational production of legal norms and institutional forms in particular fields and their migration across borders, regardless of whether they address transnational activities or purely national ones" (Shaffer 2012: 234).

Our research adopts these insights of transnational legal ordering by focusing on human rights concerns over sexual violence within the Universal Periodic Review (UPR) system in the UN Human Rights Council. Beginning in 2008, every state's human rights performance is assessed by other countries on a rotating basis, through a peer review process. An analysis of the UPR process thus offers significant insights for transnational legal ordering. First, there has been universal partici-pation from all 193 UN Member States in the UPR process, offering a universal database for studying proposals for legal change. Second, the UPR process is conducted annually, which allows for the tracking of transnational legal ordering at the domestic level, both within and across countries over time (with each state reviewed approximately every four years). And third, although the UPR is formally a state-to-state process, this peer review also incorporates human rights reports from non-state actors, state peers, and international actors, thereby incorporating actors across levels in the analysis of domestic legal orders.

We thus focus on the transnational legal ordering of sexual violence when it is framed as a human rights concern. The study of sexual violence in the UPR process provides us with a unique opportunity to follow how a domestic criminal justice concern is ordered through a transnational legal conversation, across levels of actors, over time, and globally. The Universal Periodic Review is in many ways a ritual that – while taking place at the international level – is driven by national and local actors in response to human rights concerns occur-ring at the domestic level. In being held to account at the international level, national actors must interact over their legal positions, both in calling for reforms elsewhere, and in accepting or not accepting reform suggestions while being reviewed. Particularly in the field of criminal law, which is often said to be dominated by domestic law and its enforcement, we can benefit from extending the study of transnational legal ordering to the kind of globally developed, cross-level, and insti-tutionalized informality that the Universal Periodic Review offers.

Through this empirical case study of sexual violence and the Universal Periodic Review, this chapter also seeks to extend the ambit of transnational legal ordering by explicitly connecting it with insights from sociological field theory and cultural sociology (Conti

2016). As we discuss below, we do so by conceiving of the Universal Periodic Review as a diplomatic performance (Pouliot 2016), and we suggest that understanding these elements are important for grappling with some of the processes by which legal ordering occurs. We find that state actors take positions on human rights norms based on position-takings of the other states making or receiving these recommendations – so that the study of the UPR allows us to emphasize, through a study of all 193 member states, the field dynamics of positions and position-takings that underwrite legal ordering (Bourdieu 1986; Dezalay and Garth 2002; Hagan, Levi and Ferrales 2006; Pouliot 2016). This is further underscored by the UPR process itself being a multi-level ritual, in which states are communicating – to each other, to human rights actors, to donors, and to their domestic constituencies – their support or resistance for domestic legal change.

11.2 TRANSNATIONAL LEGAL ORDERS, FIELDS, AND PERFORMANCE

Sociological research on the internationalization of law has generally oscillated between two poles. The first, drawing on the new institutionalism, emphasizes mimesis, isomorphism, and the decoupling of words and deeds to explain the spread of legal norms (Boyle and Meyer 1998; Hafner-Burton 2012; Meyer et al. 1997). The second emphasizes the professional and social fields that lead to the importing and exporting of new legal models (Dezalay and Garth 2002; Hagan and Levi 2005), including the presence of individuals and organizations who interpret between local and international frames (Massoud 2011; Merry 2006). These approaches complement research in law and political science, which has often focused on the compelling character of some legal norms, and the success of transnational activists in persuading the public and powerful actors to adopt new legal approaches (Goodman and Jinks 2004; Keck and Sikkink 1998; Moravcsik 2000; Mackie 1996).

Transnational legal orders emphasize the institutions, ideas, and interactions through which legal globalization occurs. In this cross-disciplinary research endeavor, however, the research did not explicitly engage sociological field theory or cultural theory (Conti 2016). Understood as "a collection of formalized legal norms and associated organizations and actors that authoritatively order the understanding and practice of law across national jurisdictions," this perspective continues to include actors, institutions, and norms. In so doing, transnational legal ordering imagines legal authority as rooted in both power and reason, including economic and political power and "legal reasoning and process" (Halliday and Shaffer 2015: 2–3). Law is placed at the center of the analysis, along with an argument that law is a particularly salient normative battlefield for global change (Halliday and Shaffer 2015: 6).

The transnational legal ordering perspective also includes attention to the processes through which transnational legal orders may emerge or fail, and the relations that are embedded in those processes. Take, for example, the TLO hypotheses that "[i]f transnational legal norms are perceived to be instruments of imposition, coercion, surveillance, or control by stronger actors on weaker states or local actors, then the probability of resistance increases," or that "right-line rules or model laws may have a higher probability of adoption, because states can readily drop them into their statute books without much effort and cost" (Halliday and Shaffer 2015: 520). In each of these, we see how the emergence, rise, or resistance to transnational legal orders can impli-cate not only political power, but both positional and ritual dimensions. As we read this work, ritual compliance can allow TLOs to propagate, while perceptions, domestic and international audiences, and rela-tional dynamics between states or other actors can influence whether TLOs are accepted or resisted.

It is here that we seek to intervene, by connecting and expanding transnational legal ordering through field theory and cultural sociology. Others have noted the absence of explicit attention in transnational legal ordering to field-based approaches (Conti 2016) – which, indeed, would require fully attending to how the production of the legal is itself part of the production of the transnational itself. Yet through the TLO connections to processual, positional, and ritual-based aspects of order-ing, we see opportunities here for developing a field-based approach. Field-based approaches emphasize the positions and position-takings of different actors – in the context of the legal field, this includes a tacit understanding that these varied positions structure the normative debate, and that this underlies the unification of the field itself (Bourdieu 1986; 1996). There is thus, as Shaffer and Halliday (2016) echo within the transnational legal ordering model, a "bounded rela-tional space" for individuals, states, non-state actors, and international institutions through which normative change and lawmaking emerges (see also Hagan and Levi 2005).

We further argue that to properly combine attention to field sociology and transnational legal ordering also requires attending to performative aspects of authority. As Bourdieu indicates in his more recently published lectures *On the State* (2012, 2015 in English), "this set of institutions that we call 'the state' must theatricalize the official and the universal" (2015: 28). "It would be naive," Bourdieu (2015: 28) argues, "not to take seriously these acts of theatricalization of the official that have a real effect, even if the official is never more than the official, something that in all societies is established only to be transgressed." In other words, there are public rituals through which formal legal norms are developed, engaged, and transnationalized.

Integrating cultural sociology allows us to underscore the processes through which performances and rituals lead to apparent instances of agreement, norm acceptance, or resistance. In any sort of performance, including legal rituals, audiences may be swayed but they may also resist – or in cultural terms may not "fuse" with the performance (Alexander and Mast 2006; Sendroiu 2019). This fusion is required to make "culture structures," which would include legal norms "stick" (Alexander and Mast 2006: 4). Although not articulated in these conceptual terms, we believe this can speak to an open question in the transnational legal ordering literature. For TLOs, there is a question of how and when states and sub-national actors resist legal ideas. In the TLO model, this would largely occur in situations where states *perceive* that the relevant legal norm is an external imposition (Halliday and Shaffer 2015: 23). The TLO literature further hypothesizes that such resistance is ever more likely to occur where there is social distance between the different actors, generating a lack of will to engage in a transnational legal enterprise. Within cultural sociology, a similar outcome would be seen as a failure of performance, with a lack of fusion between the performer and the audience. In drawing these two literatures together, we are thus alerted by both to the differences in power positioning that is always part of transnational norms and institutions, the performativity of the choice to adopt or resist, and the potential implications of these for legal ordering.

11.3   THE UNIVERSAL PERIODIC REVIEW AND TRANSNATIONAL LEGAL ORDERING

Having begun in 2008, the Universal Periodic Review is a peer review of human rights records within the UN Human Rights Council. Each state undergoes a review process once per session. While three states are randomly chose to comment on the human rights behavior of each state under review, any state may choose to make a recommendation. The state under review then has to respond to each recommendation, either "accepting" or "noting" the recommendation, and consequently complete a final report. There have been two cycles of the UPR, with a third ongoing, meaning that every state has had its human rights record reviewed at least twice through the UPR process.

At first blush, the Universal Periodic Review may not appear to be an ideal case for studying transnational legal ordering. Transnational legal ordering insists on the importance of studying legal orders not simply internationally, but across scales – so that TLO research is explicitly driven by the study of normative consolidation and settlement at the transnational, national, and local levels. In addition, transnational legal ordering is focused on explicitly legal norms, rather than on the political or social norms that may influence legal actors. As Sally Merry (this volume) succinctly puts it, "[t]ransnational legal orders are challenging to study in practice," at least partly due to "the multi-sited, multi-organizational and multi-actor basis of most TLOs."

Yet on closer examination, we contend that the Universal Periodic Review provides a unique vantage point for understanding the process of transnational legal ordering. After all, while the Universal Periodic Review takes place in an international forum, it is by definition multi-scalar, with vertical and horizontal elements (Halliday and Shaffer 2015: 19). Each state under review provides a national report, but there is also a stakeholder report derived largely from local civil society actors – including civil society actors that do not have consultative status with the United Nations Economic and Social Council – and a UN report built from information across UN agencies. In contrast to other international lawmaking, the UPR is a *public* event rather than a closed-door diplomatic one, so that it is high-profile and visible to local, national, and transnational audiences (Cowan 2015; Milewicz and Goodin 2018). Furthermore, the Universal Periodic Review is not merely focused on treaty ratification and compliance – though it can include this as well – but on human rights concerns that occur at the domestic level, including local state practices, with capacity-building and technical support also available for implementation. As a peer review process through which domestic human rights records are considered and assessed in an interactive dialogue, rather than an international law-making body, the UPR is also distinct from the sort of international legal approach that characterizes regime theory, about which the transnational legal ordering project is skeptical (Milewicz and Goodin 2018). And indeed, while the UPR is not exclusively about explicitly legal norms, the human rights project is itself conceived of in legal terms – and given the wealth of available data, the UPR process in fact allows us to attend to the degree of explicit legality used in these human rights recommendations.

In other words, the UPR is driven by actors across scales, and focused on human rights concerns at the domestic level. Furthermore, that it occurs in a single forum makes the UPR a unique empirical site for a truly global study of transnational ordering. It includes reporting from all UN member states, local actors, and UN agencies, and with two sessions already complete allows for tracking over time for differently positioned states; and in contrast to other situations, states under review must respond in some way to each human rights recommendation raised, providing us with an explicit mapping of how human rights concerns are taken on board or resisted.

This is similarly highlighted by interview research we conducted in the UN Office of the High Commissioner for Human Rights. Some respondents were skeptical of the UPR as merely grandstanding; as one respondent noted, "it's very depressing what you see ... Nothing really happens. There is a lot of shoulder-patting, a lot of complacency." Yet others expressed that the UPR can make a difference particularly because it by crossing levels. As one notes, "I think UPR is creating numerous opportunities to promote and protect rights by different actors and at different levels," with another explicitly noting that

> the more I observe it and the more I think from the perspective of governments who are willing, from the perspective of civil society actors who are given an unprecedented voice in the process, from the perspective of the UN Country Team or even the government actors ... it's incredible the opportunities to engage dialogue on human rights issues that exist because of this commitment that they've made to implement UPR recommendations. ... Even if it's 10 percent, the dynamic that it creates at home will reap fruits in the future. You know, in many countries you had no dialogue between civil society and the government, and human rights was a no-go area. It's not all countries, but it's through the UPR process, through the notion of participation and inclusion and integration that dialogue is starting – talking to children about issues which used to be taboo.

Despite initial skepticism over the non-binding and peer-review nature of the UPR process, recent research highlights successes of the UPR in addressing human rights commitments across levels of actors. At the state level, this includes findings that states are induced by the UPR to agree to new human rights actions, that states with poor human rights records make faster progress on human rights recommendations between UPR cycles, and that the UPR process leads to increased treaty ratification (Collister 2015; De la Vega and Yamasaki 2015; Milewicz and Goodin 2018). The UPR also provides horizontal opportunities for collaboration across international agencies (Billaud 2015), and is a forum for states resistant to human rights reforms to more slowly engage and potentially adopt these norms (Bulto 2015; McMahon, Busia, and Ascherio 2013). Finally, accounts also suggest that though it comes with new obstacles, the UPR can provide NGOs and local media outlets with new opportunities for influencing human rights at home and internationally (Chauville 2015; Collister 2015; Joseph 2015; Schokman and Lynch 2015).

In contrast to other international mechanisms, the transnational UPR process also appears to have changed relations within domestic states. For NGOs, the UPR is now seen as "an integral part of domestic advocacy strategies, using it as a catalyst to set up national consultations to identify the human rights problems in a country, to generate coalitions and partnerships, and to coalesce strategies to follow-up on recommendations emanating from the UPR" (International Service for Human Rights 2011, as cited in Schokman and Lynch 2015: 144). And even within governments, "At every point – within the government, among the civil society organisations and during the consultations – there are disagreements and conflicts, and negotiations and compromises over what to include and exclude, and what to prioritise" (Cowan 2015: 56).

There is thus evidence that the UPR enjoys the sort of multi-scalar reach that is central to transnational legal ordering. This has led Charlesworth and Larking (2015) to argue that while the UPR is certainly a ritual, it is not doomed to be merely "ritualistic" as an endeavor. Yet others have suggested that this concern over ritualism may itself be misplaced. If anything, Cowan (2015) argues that the performance of the UPR – including the ritualism – is itself part of the power that the UPR offers. In her analysis of the UPR as a public audit ritual, she thus argues that by requiring states to account, the UPR requires a "performative demonstration," and that the UPR's power lies in requiring state officials to "speak and act in new ways" due to the peer-based nature of the activity (Cowan 2015: 50, 54, 58–59).

In what follows, we draw on this understanding of the UPR as a powerful performance to connect the analysis of transnational legal orders with field theory and with work in cultural sociology that understands law as social performance (Alexander 2006; Eyerman 2006; Halliday and Shaffer 2015: 518; Pouliot 2016). In so doing, we highlight how in this global setting, legal norms are recommended, accepted, and resisted in what sociologists think of as an "embattled stage" (Ermakoff 2008: 5). We thus analyze the ritual of the UPR by studying the scripts that are developed in this ritual, along with the performative effects that they have in gaining adherence or encountering resistance to human rights commitments.

11.4 SEXUAL VIOLENCE AS A HUMAN RIGHTS CONCERN

Sexual violence has, of course, been a central focus of national and international criminal law reforms for decades. The decades following the 1993 World Conference on Human Rights and the Declaration on the Elimination of Violence against Women have been particularly central to the understanding and articulation of sexual violence not only as a crime, but as a human rights concern (Merry 2006a).

This has led to investment in new measurements and analyses of sexual violence levels worldwide, through agencies such as the United Nations Office on Drugs and Crime to Interpol – though these measurements are of course also political and the subject of intense contestation (Devries et al. 2013; Merry 2012). Yet research suggests that there is some disconnect between the spread of anti-sexual violence norms from increased legal and policy attention to the problem. On the one hand, Pierotti (2013) demonstrates across twenty-six countries that women are increasingly likely to reject intimate partner violence, independently of other large societal changes, such as rising education or urbanization. Similarly, Russell et al. (2018) show that after 1993, textbooks from seventy-six countries have increasingly discussed the problem of gender-based violence *and* that these discussions are typically framed in the context of women's rights. Yet on the other hand, translating the fight against sexual violence from international norms to domestic practice has proven complicated (Merry 2006). Legal and policy measures against sexual violence have encountered considerable resistance, with successful implementation necessitating, according to Merry (2006), a reframing of human rights law to local terms and terminologies. For instance, women's human rights claims are implicated in marriage ceremonies in rural Bolivia (Goodale 2002), or in claims to land ownership in Kenya (Nyamu-Musembi 2002).

International legal standards have witnessed significant legal change when it comes to sexual violence. Sexual violence has also proven to be the most prominent focus of the international criminal law regime, with prosecutions of sexual violence as a war crime extolled as "monumental jurisprudence," including the concept of genocidal rape developed in the International Criminal Tribunal for Rwanda, often as a result of the advocacy of US-based lawyers and law students in these international settings (Askin 2001; Schoenfeld, Levi and Hagan 2007; Van Schaack 2008). Social science research has similarly come to emphasize the differences between war and peace for sexual violence (Wood 2014).

From the perspective of transnational legal ordering, we further note that these developments at the international level can also be mobilized for domestic, peace-time, reform of sexual violence laws. New international frameworks on gender violence, such as the Istanbul Convention on violence against women, are being cited by NGOs as part of attempts to change domestic policy (Błuś 2018). And a recent report by Amnesty International (2010), for instance, focuses on gaps in police and prosecution response to rape in the Nordic countries, largely relying on the definitions of consent and of sexual violence that have been developed in international criminal law cases and in the European Court of Human Rights, in order to advocate for legal change in Denmark, Finland, and Sweden. In other words, this definition, created for situations of armed conflict and reflecting US-based legal advocacy abroad (Van Schaack 2008) – now appears to be part of the repertoire for domestic law reform.

In what follows, we take up the issue of sexual violence and human rights by examining the recommendations on sexual violence that have been articulated in the Universal Periodic Review from 2008 to 2017. Given the wide scope of these data – recommendations to all UN member states, across two time periods – we rely on three quantitative techniques that, in our view, provide unique purchase on the process of transnational legal ordering. First, we rely on multiple correspondence analyses to geometrically map the relational, and performative, context in which recommendations are made to states during the Universal

Periodic Review – as well as whether these recommendations are accepted, or explicitly ignored, by the state under review. Second, to study the degree to which these recommendations reflect specifically *legal* transnational ordering, we rely on automated text analysis to develop scores across all recommendations for the degree to which law is contained in these proposals for reform. And finally, to be able to measure the pace and sequencing of transnational legal ordering, we include growth curve models from which we can analyze the processes of all states as they go through repeated Universal Periodic Reviews. Taken together, these techniques provide us with unique purchase on the transnational legal order of sexual violence as a human rights concern.

11.5   DATA AND METHODS

To focus on sexual violence recommendations in the Universal Periodic Review, we relied on a database of all UPR recommendations made available by UPR Info, an NGO that aims to create awareness of the process and empower civil society stakeholders to take part in UPR reviews. This database includes information about the recommendation itself, namely the text of the recommendation, whether the recommendation is "accepted" or "noted" by the state under review, as well as the level of specificity involved in the recommendation itself on a five-point scale from "minimal action," to "continuing action," "considering action," "general action," and "specific action."[1] For each recommendation, this database also includes data on the state actors directly involved, both the "state under review" and the "reviewing state," also providing information on any inter-governmental organizations to which they are party.

In our analysis, we included all recommendations to states that include the terms "gender-based violence," "rape," "sexual abuse," "sexual assault," "sexual violence," "violence against girls," and "violence against women." After removing duplicates, we produced a data set containing 3,049 unique recommendations, made from 2008 to 2017.

We have supplemented these data with several other variables for both the content of the recommendation and the relationship between

---

[1] Since the action variable was heavily right-skewed, creating multiple small cell size problems, we collapsed the first three categories and created a three-category variable.

states in the UPR process. To analyze the text of human rights recommendations, we built a new variable designed to capture whether the human rights recommendation focuses on the creation or revision of a legal mechanism, or whether the recommendation instead focuses on broader approaches to reform. We do so by relying on Linguistic Inquiry and Word Count (LIWC), an automated text analysis tool, which we describe in more detail in the next section. Building on prior work in political science and sociology (Simmons 2009), at the level of the state dyad involved with each recommendation we further include data on gross national GDP (World Bank 2018), freedom levels (Freedom House 2018), the repressiveness of state institutions (i.e., Polity 2 score from Polity IV), the proportion of women in parliament (Inter-Parliamentary Union 2018), number of international organizations headquartered in the state (Yearbook of International Organizations 2018), and trade balance within the recommendation state dyad (Correlates of War 2017).[2] While there are criticisms over some of these measures (Munck and Verkuilen 2002), following convention we include two measures of repression are the only two commonly used measures of repression available for the time period in question, for most of our sample (Zhou 2012). We therefore augment the more holistic Freedom House measure with a variable that accounts for the repressiveness of state institutions – the Polity 2 score from the Polity IV Project (see also Tsutsui and Wotipka 2004).

11.5.1 Measuring the Use of Law through LIWC

LIWC is a dictionary-based text analysis tool that has been broadly used and validated in social psychology to study topics ranging from deception (Semin and Fiedler 1998) to team-building (Sexton and Helmreich 2000). LIWC is built on the insight that "[t]he words we use in daily life reflect what we are paying attention to, what we are thinking about, what we are trying to avoid, how we are feeling, and how we are organizing and analyzing our worlds" (Tausczik and Pennebaker 2010: 30). Research consistently shows that LIWC measures socially meaningful categories such as gender (Newman, Groom, Handelman, and Pennebaker 2008), age (Pennebaker and Stone

---

[2] We also ran our models including each state's Gini coefficient, and found that coefficient direction and p-values stayed the same. However, due to the listwise deletion we employed in our statistical analyses, having Gini measures in the model removed roughly 30 percent of our sample. As a result, we decided to drop Gini measures from our analyses and employ the fuller range of our sample.

2003), and the closeness of relationships (Simmons, Chambless, and Gordon 2008).

Text is uploaded into LIWC, and each word in the text is sorted into one or more categories or dictionaries. For our analysis, we took advantage of an extension of the LIWC program that involves utilizing user-created dictionaries. After a systematic reading of 10 percent of recommendations, we created a list of words or word groupings that explicitly involves legal creation – a measure, in other words, that revolves around whether the recommendation asks for a change in law or the creation of a law (though note that this does not include implementing laws). Our law dictionary involved the words or word combinations: "abolish," "adopt," "amend," criminalize," "enact legislation," "enact penal code," "pass legislation," "pass penal code," "ratify," "repeal," "revise legislation," "revise penal code," "sign." Once uploaded to LIWC, the program computed the percentage of each text that fit one of the word combinations we specified and tagged them in the text. For instance, a code of "no law" is for recommendations such as "[t]ake measures to stop violence that has cost the lives of more than five thousand women, and caused more than 500,000 rapes in the last year." As a result, a code of "has law" was assigned to recommendations such as "[a]mend article 375 of the Penal Code, dealing with the crime of rape, in order to remove the exception for sexual intercourse by a man with his wife."

11.5.2 Analytic Strategy

In the first part of the analysis, we sought to map out the field of UPR recommendations, and so we turned to multiple correspondence analysis (MCA). Popularized by Pierre Bourdieu (e.g., Bourdieu 1986, 1996), MCA is a geometric method for mapping social spaces that produces a visualization of the relationship among both cases *and* variables in a sample.

Since multiple correspondence analysis is a geometric mapping technique, it analyzes the distance both among cases, but also among variable categories. As a result, for the MCA portion of our analysis, we recoded our continuous country variables such as GDP or proportion of women in parliament into tertiles. Each of these variables thus became a three-category variable divided into high, medium, and low values of the variable in question.

In the second part of the analysis, we turned to growth curve models (GCMs) in order to predict the determinants of recommendation acceptance, as well as shifts in acceptance over time. GCMs are multi-level models that estimate change within cases over time, and then compare change across individuals. Our GCMs thus nested measurements within a given case – or more precisely, a given country under review. Level one is thus a country's acceptance of recommendations in a particular time period, and level two is each particular country.

We ran multiple GCMs as part of our analysis. The first, unconditional GCM, involved modeling only change over time. Subsequent GCMs were conditional, meaning that they involved further independent variables in predicting recommendation acceptance. Finally, we used piecewise GCMs to more closely fit the model to our data – instead of predicting one curve for the entire period being studied, piecewise GCMs allow for multiple curve estimates over shorter time-periods. We thus used piecewise GCMs to estimate changes in acceptance year to year, both for the entire sample as well as subsamples selected based on state under review or recommending state levels of freedom.

11.6 FINDINGS

11.6.1 MCA Country and Recommendation Type Clusters

Our MCA visualization (Figure 11.1; see also stylized MCA in Figure 11.2) maps out the UPR process as a field (see Cowan 2015). We identify four distinct quadrants in the MCA, with the first and third quadrant containing two distinct country profiles of recommending states, and the second and fourth detailing two profiles of states under review. States under review thus fall into two groups: in the second quadrant are richer, free countries with many international organizations and women in parliament; meanwhile, the fourth quadrant has poorer, less free countries with fewer international organizations or women in parliament. Among recommending states, there is a similar, clear opposition between free states with high GDP, many international organizations, and more women in parliament in the first quadrant, and less free states with lower GDPs and fewer women in parliament or international organizations in the third quadrant. We see, therefore, that certain state characteristics tend to cluster together.

The MCA also provides insight into the characteristics of recommendations made by the two recommending state clusters. The wealthier, freer states of quadrant one are associated with more specific recommendations, as well as those involving law, in addition to recommendations that are "noted" rather than "supported." Turning to raw

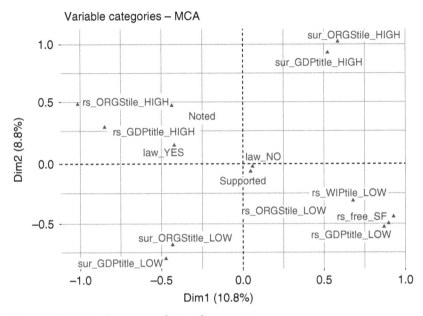

Figure 11.1 MCA of recommendation characteristics

High GDP, free recommending states ~ Difficult recommendations that involve law, are likely to be rejected	High GDP, free states under review
Low GDP, not free states under review	Low GDP, not free recommending states ~ Easy recommendations that do not involve law, and are likely to be supported

Figure 11.2 Stylized MCA

statistics from the data set, we see a strong correlation among these variables. The most specific recommendations are also the ones most likely to involve law: almost 33 percent of most specific recommendations are legal in nature, compared to roughly 10 percent of highly specific recommendations and dropping down to 0 percent of non-specific recommendations. In turn, acceptance drops when a recommendation is legal, from 87.6 percent to 76.3 percent, as well as when the recommending state is "free." In fact, almost 18 percent of a "free" states' recommendations are rejected, compared to only 7 percent of "somewhat free" or "not free" states' recommendations. Thus, returning to the MCA, the clustering of poorer, less free states in quadrant three alongside recommendations that are less specific, do not involve law, and/or are "accepted" underscores these raw data patterns.

At the same time, the MCA also highlights the lack of a relationship between our two clusters of states under review and the recommendation-level variables. For instance, descriptive statistics show that states under review are roughly equally distributed across the three levels of freedom. Instead, as we have described above, recommendation acceptance, use of law, and specificity are more closely related to the two recommending state clusters.

11.6.2 Predicting Recommendation Acceptance over Time

There have been sexual violence recommendations made every year of the UPR process, though we find that two-thirds of the sample is concentrated in the second UPR period (2012–2017) rather than the first (2008–2011). "Free" states have made roughly 70 percent of these recommendations, but yearly proportions have been decreasing, from a high of 87.5 percent in 2008 to a low of roughly 65 percent in both 2016 and 2017. Interestingly, there is a less clear pattern when it comes to the freedom level of states under review, whereby in some years – namely 2008, 2012, and 2017 – "free" states have received the majority of sexual violence recommendations, but proportions fluctuate over time. Overall, 44.3 percent of sexual violence recommendations have been aimed at "free" states, compared to 34.44 percent aimed at "somewhat free" states and 21.3 percent to "not free" states. Conditional and piecewise growth curve models allow us to track the effects of these variables on their own and over time on the likelihood of a recommendation being accepted.

A first, unconditional growth curve model shows that there is statistically significant, nonlinear change over time in the likelihood of recommendation acceptance (see Model A in Table 11.1). In other words, year-to-year differences do shape acceptance patterns, and as we will discuss later in the context of piecewise models, the overall

TABLE 11.1 Growth curve models of recommendation acceptance

	MODEL 1			MODEL 2			MODEL 3			MODEL 4		
	Value	Std. error	p-value	value	Std. error	p-value	value	Std. error	p-value	value	Std. error	p-value
Constant	0.66	0.04	***	0.71	0.04	***	1.26	0.19	***	1.19	0.19	***
Time												
Year	0.19	0.04	***	0.19	0.04	***	0.17	0.04	***	0.17	0.04	***
Year^2	-0.04	0.01	***	-0.04	0.01	***	-0.04	0.01	***	-0.04	0.01	***
Year^3	0.00	0.00	***	0.00	0.00	***	0.00	0.00	***	0.00	0.00	***
Recommendation content												
Medium specificity				-0.01	0.02		0.00	0.02		0.01	0.02	
High specificity				-0.11	0.02	***	-0.08	0.02	***	-0.08	0.02	***
Law				-0.08	0.02	***	-0.06	0.02	***	-0.06	0.02	***
State under review characteristics												
SUR Freedom							0.00	0.01		0.01	0.00	
SUR Polity2 score							0.00	0.00		-0.01	0.01	
SUR Log GDO							-0.01	0.01		0.00	0.00	
SUR Women in parliament							0.00	0.00		0.00		
SUR International Organizations							0.00	0.00	***	0.00	0.00	

TABLE 11.1 (cont.)

	MODEL 1			MODEL 2			MODEL 3			MODEL 4		
	Value	Std. error	p-value	Value	Std. error	p-value	Value	Std. error	p-value	Value	Std. error	p-value
Recommending state characteristics												
RS Freedom							-0.02	0.00	***			
RS Polity2 score							0.01	0.00		0.00	0.00	*
RS Log GDP							0.00	0.00		0.00	0.00	
RS Women in parliament							0.00	0.00		0.00	0.00	
RS International Organizations							0.00	0.00		0.00	0.00	***
Relational measures												
Trade										0.00	0.00	*
Free RS * Free SUR (frel2)										-0.06	0.04	
Not free RS * Free SUR (frel3)										0.00	0.04	
Free RS * Not free SUR (frel4)										-0.08	0.02	***
N	3049			3049			2573			2573		

Note: continuous freedom scores removed from model when relational freedom variables are added in Model 4, in order to reduce multicollinearity; ***p<.001; **p<.01; *p<.05.

predicted trend is one of increases in acceptance levels, though as we see the unconditional growth curve model, this is a largely nonlinear trend (time^2=–0.04, p<.001; time^3=0.003, p<.001).

Meanwhile, our first conditional growth curve model (i.e., a growth curve model with independent variables other than time) takes into account two variables regarding recommendation content, namely use of law and level of specificity. Here, we find that using law predicts a statistically significant drop in acceptance (–0.08, p<.001), as does the highest level of specificity (–0.11, p<.001). All time variables remain the same in this model.

In Model C, we add in country variables. For each state, whether recommending or under review, this includes: level of freedom, government repression, log GDP, the proportion of women in parliament, and the number of international organizations headquartered in that state. Among the variables indicating the characteristics of states under review, the only one that is statistically significant is the number of international organizations headquartered in that country, but the coefficient is almost equal to zero (–0.0001, p<.01). Meanwhile, turning to the variables describing a recommending state, see that freer countries' recommendations are associated with a large, statistically significant drop in acceptance (–0.02, p<.001). Therefore, in Model C, we see again the pattern from our MCA, namely that recommendations from "free" states are associated with a "noted" rather than "supported" response. Finally, the time and recommendation content variables maintain both the same significance and direction of effect seen in previous models.

Model D adds relational variables to the analysis. These include both a measure of trade between states that are under review or making recommendations, as well as the freedom level matching within the state dyad associated with each recommendation. In order to reduce collinearity due to the addition of the relational freedom variables, the continuous freedom variables are removed from this model. Here, we see that the effect of trade is statistically significant though minimal in size (0.00001; p<.05). Meanwhile, among the freedom level dyads, the only one that is significant is that of "free" states making recommendations to "not free" states, which Model D shows is associated with a predicted drop in the likelihood of acceptance (–0.08; p<.001). All other variables carried over from previous models maintain the same significance levels and effect direction.

11.6.3 Piecewise Growth Curve Acceptance Patterns

Model E in Table 11.2 shows the results of a piecewise growth curve model for the entire sample. Here, we see that each year is associated with a statistically significant increase in acceptance, with the largest predicted increase taking place in 2011 (0.31, p<.001) and the smallest in 2017 (0.19, p<.05). These large yearly predicted increases are also visible in Figure 11.3, which uses the yearly increases to estimate predicted acceptance per year.

Models F through I, meanwhile, similarly disentangle the growth curve into multiple, yearly curves, but show the predicted yearly increase according to freedom level, segregating the sample into "free" and "not free" states under review, as well as reviewing states. Throughout all four models, we again see yearly increases in predicted acceptance though interestingly, yearly increases are more pronounced (and consistently significant) for "not free" states. Thus, for states under review that are classified as free, the estimates of change for 2015 and 2017 are not statistically significant (0.12, p>.05; 0.14, p>.05), while the 2017 coefficient is not statistically significant for free recommending states (0.09, p>.05).

Estimates of change for "not free" states are consistently statistically significant, and as we see in Figures 11.4 and 11.5, the gaps between yearly estimates for "free" and "not free" states are increasing over time. Thus in Figure 11.4 we see that for the first two years of the analysis, "free" states under review have higher yearly estimates of acceptance. But the pattern then switches, and starting in 2010, "not free" states are those with more rapidly increasing estimates of acceptance, estimates that indeed outstrip those of "free" states. In Figure 11.5, we again see this pattern, but here recommendations from "free" states are only out-accepted in the first year of the analysis. After 2008, recommendations from "not free" states are more likely to be accepted, with the gap increasing every year.

11.6.4 Typologies of TLO Engagement

Our statistical models show four categories of state engagement with the UPR process. For states under review, the MCA shows that freer and richer countries cluster together, and vice versa. Similar country-level characteristics divide the recommending states, but here we see that the recommendations made by freer and richer countries differ significantly from those of their less free or economically developed peers. In particular, "free," economically developed countries are likely to make more specific

TABLE 11.2 Piecewise growth curve models of recommendation acceptance

	MODEL E: All cases			MODEL F: "Free" states under review			MODEL G: "Not free" states under review			MODEL H: "Free" recommending states			MODEL I: "Not free" recommending states		
	Estimate of change	Std. error	p-value	Estimate of change	Std. error	p-value	Estimate of change	Std. error	p-value	Estimate of change	Std. error	p-value	Estimate of change	Std. error	p-value
Intercept (2008)	0.62	0.05	0.00	0.67	0.06	0.00	0.51	0.09	0.00	0.62	0.06	0.00	0.58	0.08	0.00
2009	0.20	0.06	0.00	0.21	0.08	0.01	0.29	0.10	0.00	0.17	0.07	0.02	0.35	0.09	0.00
2010	0.27	0.06	0.00	0.21	0.07	0.00	0.38	0.09	0.00	0.24	0.07	0.00	0.36	0.09	0.00
2011	0.32	0.06	0.00	0.28	0.07	0.00	0.39	0.09	0.00	0.29	0.07	0.00	0.38	0.09	0.00
2012	0.25	0.05	0.00	0.19	0.07	0.00	0.36	0.09	0.00	0.24	0.06	0.00	0.31	0.09	0.00
2013	0.25	0.05	0.00	0.18	0.07	0.01	0.37	0.09	0.00	0.19	0.06	0.00	0.39	0.08	0.00
2014	0.23	0.06	0.00	0.25	0.08	0.00	0.30	0.09	0.00	0.19	0.07	0.00	0.37	0.08	0.00
2015	0.20	0.06	0.00	0.12	0.08	0.12	0.34	0.10	0.00	0.17	0.07	0.01	0.29	0.08	0.00
2016	0.24	0.06	0.00	0.19	0.08	0.02	0.34	0.10	0.00	0.21	0.07	0.00	0.35	0.08	0.00
2017	0.19	0.08	0.03	0.14	0.11	0.23	0.28	0.13	0.03	0.09	0.10	0.39	0.37	0.09	0.00

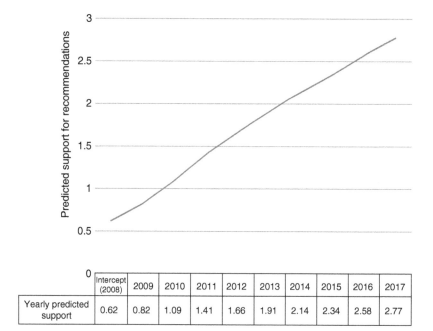

	Intercept (2008)	2009	2010	2011	2012	2013	2014	2015	2016	2017
Yearly predicted support	0.62	0.82	1.09	1.41	1.66	1.91	2.14	2.34	2.58	2.77

Year

Figure 11.3 Support for recommendations, predicted estimates per year based on piecewise Model E

recommendations, as well as recommendations that involve law, and will not be accepted. The growth curve models fill out this picture, showing that acceptance is less likely when recommendations are specific, involve law, or come from "free" recommending states. But importantly, the GCMs also point us in the direction of particular country dyads – a nexus between reviewing states and states under review – that drive acceptance. We thus see that it is when "free" states comment on the human rights record of "non-free" states that acceptance drops, suggesting that the interaction between audience and performer matters and indeed shapes audience behavior.

11.7 DISCUSSION AND CONCLUSION

The Universal Periodic Review offers a specific vantage point for studying transnational legal orders. While it itself does not provide evidence of whether legal norms will be acted upon at other scales, many of these

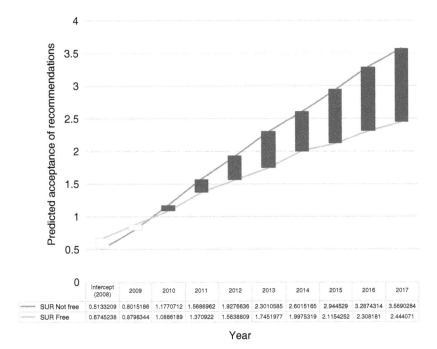

Figure 11.4 Support for recommendations by state under review level of freedom, predicted estimates per year based on piecewise Models F and G

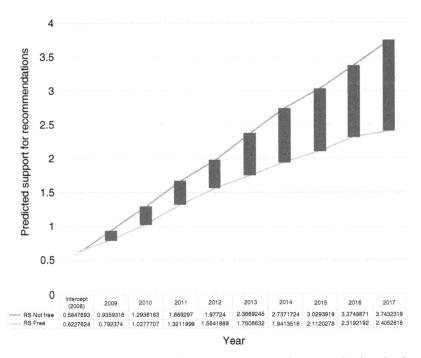

Figure 11.5 Support for recommendations by recommending state freedom level, predicted estimates per year based on piecewise Models H and I

scales are already nested within the UPR human rights process – which includes state reports, domestic civil society and other stakeholders, and information from a wide range of UN agencies. The latest social science evidence also suggests that there are effects of the UPR on behavior within states, and particularly among states with poor human rights records. It also reminds us that thousands of people watch the live webcast dialogues within the Universal Periodic Review, including "some 5,000 people in China, 6,000 in Malaysia and an astonishing 7,000 in tiny Vanuatu (almost 3 percent of its population). In some cases, citizens were seeing their rulers publicly account for their human rights practices for the first time" (Milewicz and Goodin 2018: 518). These findings are further reinforced by experiential accounts of NGOs and states, as well as our own interviews within the Office of the High Commissioner for Human Rights, that identify how the deliberative and engagement process of the Universal Periodic Review can lead to human rights changes at home.

Part of the reasons for these effects stem from the Universal Periodic Review being both a ritual and a public performance (Charlesworth and Larking 2015; Cowan 2015; Milewicz and Goodin 2018). We build on these insights to combine the transnational legal orders model with sociological field theory and the sociology of culture, to connect international ordering with diplomatic and state performance (Pouliot 2016). In so doing, we do not seek to imply that the state is a unitary object that speaks with one voice (Bourdieu 2015). Yet by conceiving of the interactions within the UPR process as performative state acts, we explore the dynamic of when states recommend human rights reforms on sexual violence concerns, the conditions under which states accept or simply note (and thus ignore) such recommendations, and indeed the very language of the recommendations being made and their explicit use of legal framing for human rights recommendations. Our statistical models thereby allow us to map the field of sexual violence recommendations in the Universal Periodic Review, including the positions of state actors and the degree to which these recommendations reflect explicitly legal concerns.

In her analysis of the UPR, Cowan (2015) suggests that the Universal Periodic Review can itself be thought of as a field of performance and position-takings. Our findings demonstrate that there is a distinct pattern to how states make sexual violence recommendations in the UPR. Relying on multiple correspondence analysis, we find that wealthier and "free" states tend to make more legally based recommendations in this UPR process, and that these recommendations are more likely to be rejected; on the other hand, poorer and "not free" states make simpler recommendations that are less likely to involve law, but are more likely to be supported by states under review. These preliminary findings are particularly important given that the Universal Periodic Review has received comparatively little empirical attention to date (Elizalde 2019).

This state mapping gives us some empirically robust insight into the structure and position-takings in this transnational legal order. We gain a great deal more about the ordering process, however, when we examine the growth curve models. To begin, we find that this transnational legal order is indeed growing and rising, with a general increase over time in acceptance of sexual violence recommendations. Yet we find that even in the context of TLO growth, the mapping of relative position matters a great deal (Halliday and Shaffer 2015: 20–21). Acceptance of sexual violence recommendations is growing at a faster rate among not free states – a finding that resonates with other research on UPR recommendations and human rights ratification (Hafner Burton 2012; Milewicz and Goodin 2018; Simmons 2009). While others explain similar findings through arguments about decoupling, ease of incremental human rights reforms in less free states, or reputational concerns, our analysis sheds light on the importance of performance. We find that state actors are most likely to resist these recommendations in situations of high divergence, namely when "free" states make recommendations to "not free" states, net of other factors regarding the recommendations or the attributes of these states.

Taken together, we find that the transnational legal order of sexual violence as a human rights concern is on the rise. Yet we show that overall, acceptance is more likely to be driven by recommendations made by not free states to other not free states. This dynamic suggests to us that there is a relational quality to legal norms that must be accounted for in our understanding of how transnational legal ordering grows or is resisted. These combined insights are particularly important, we argue, in the context of crime and violence, which is often said to be dominated by domestic legal regimes (Christensen and Levi 2018).

We gain further confidence in the centrality of our findings from recent work on the prosecution of wartime sexual violence, which demonstrates how the *narrative authority* of ending impunity shapes the spread of this norm – vertically and horizontally, across NGOs, academics, international organizations, and state diplomats (Houge and Lohne 2017). For transnational legal ordering in particular, we find that language matters a great deal. Net of other factors such as specificity or difficulty of the recommendation being made, the use of legal language – as measured across thousands of recommendations – leads to less acceptance of human rights recommendations. This raises several interesting possibilities within the TLO model. Is it the case that non-legal framing of recommendations could expand the audience, so that within this peer review forum an explicitly legal discourse is less able to gain traction (Halliday and Shaffer 2015: 8)? While we cannot definitively answer that question here, our finding alerts us to the possibility that, even within legal sites among official state actors, the explicit use of legal frames can itself signal different moral content and political cultures (Levi and Sendroiu 2019; Skotnicki 2019). In other words, the use of legal language may be part of state performance, both in the making of recommendations and in the willingness of state actors to appear to accept them. Though we here highlight relational performances, subsequent field analyses should further unpack these state acts through analyses of the specific agencies and actors involved in the UPR process, both at the international and domestic levels.

In developing this analysis of state performance, we explicitly refrain from identifying whether or not this transnational legal order is gaining compliance – or even normative acceptance – within states (Hafner-Burton 2012). The benefit of relying on a broad data set of thousands of sexual violence recommendation is that we are able to detect patterns in this performance, though we recognize that this is at the expense of nuanced and textured case studies of a small number of countries. We also recognize that broad state-level indicators such as Freedom House are single measures that can lack classificatory nuance (Halliday and Shaffer 2015: 20). That said, we do get some traction here because the Universal Periodic Review has been found in recent work to influence both state and NGO practice, and because by its design the Universal Periodic Review itself embeds the participation of a wide range of vertical and horizontal actors (see, for instance, Charlesworth and Larking 2015). Similarly, we combine Freedom House indicators with a wide array of other measures – including economic indicators, measures of democracy, indicators of gender equality and measures of international organizations – to provide some domestic context and greater analytical nuance.

In his analyses of the state, Bourdieu argues that official commissions must generate a performance of being unified in order to maintain state legitimacy. They must appear "as a commission of wise men, that is, above contingencies, interests, conflicts, ultimately outside the social space, because as soon as you are in the social space, you are a point, and therefore a viewpoint, that can be relativized" (Bourdieu 2015: 28). Through this analysis of the Universal Periodic Review, we argue that state performances in transnational legal contexts are potentially different. We find that in this global public forum, the rise in acceptance of sexual violence as a human rights concern is being driven by "not free" states, in situations that are not explicitly defined as "legal" – and in response to the human rights recommendations of peer states, rather than nominally "free" states that dominate classic models of spheres of influence (Bowling and Sheptycki 2012). In other words, this study reveals that in transnational legal ordering, official state performance can explicitly be about multiple position-takings in response to particular performers. The effect of these position-takings, in turn, is to expand a transnational order while also delineating its pace and pattern.

REFERENCES

Alexander, Jeffrey C. 2011. *Performative Revolution in Egypt: An Essay in Cultural Power*. London, New York: Bloomsbury Academic.

Alexander, Jeffrey C., and Jason L. Mast. 2006. "Introduction: Symbolic Action in Theory and Practice: The Cultural Pragmatics of Symbolic Action." Pp. 1–28 in *Social Performance: Symbolic Action, Cultural Pragmatics, and Ritual*, edited by J. C. Alexander, B. Giesen, and J. L. Mast. Cambridge: Cambridge University Press.

Amnesty International. 2010. *Case Closed: Rape and Human Rights in the Nordic Countries: Summary Report*. ACT 77/001/2010. Amnesty International.

Askin, Kelly. 2001. *Analysis: Foca's Monumental Jurisprudence*. 226. https://iwpr.net/global-voices/analysis-focas-monumental-jurisprudence.

Barbieri, Kathrine, and Omar M. G. Keshk. 2009. "'Trading Data': Evaluating Our Assumptions and Coding Rules." *Conflict Management and Peace Science* 26(5): 471–491.

Barbieri, Kathrine, and Omar M. G. Keshk. 2017. *Correlates of War Project Trade Data Set Codebook*, Version 4.0. https://correlatesofwar.org/.

Billaud, Julie. 2015. "The Universal Periodic Review as a Public Audit Ritual: An Anthropological Perspective on Emerging Practices in the Global Governance of Human Rights." Pp. 63–84 in *Human Rights and the Universal Periodic Review: Rituals and Ritualism*, edited by H. Charlesworth and E. Larking. Cambridge: Cambridge University Press.

Błuś, Anna. 2018. "Sex without Consent Is Rape. So Why Do Only Eight European Countries Recognise This?" *Amnesty International.* www .amnesty.org/en/latest/campaigns/2018/04/eu-sex-without-consent-is-rape/ (accessed February 25, 2019).

Bourdieu, Pierre. 1986. *Distinction: A Social Critique of the Judgement of Taste.* London: Routledge.

Bourdieu, Pierre. 1996. *The State Nobility: Elite Schools in the Field of Power.* Stanford: Stanford University Press.

Bourdieu, Pierre. 2012. *Sur l'État.* Paris: Seuil.

Bourdieu, Pierre. 2015. *On the State: Lectures at the College de France, 1989–1992.* Cambridge: Polity.

Boyle, Elizabeth Heger, and John W. Meyer. 1998. "Modern Law as a Secularized and Global Model: Implications for the Sociology of Law." *Soziale Welt* 49(3): 213–232.

Bulto, Takele Soboka. 2015. "Africa's Engagement with the Universal Periodic Review: Commitment or Capitulation?" Pp. 63–84 in *Human Rights and the Universal Periodic Review: Rituals and Ritualism*, edited by H. Charlesworth and E. Larking. Cambridge: Cambridge University Press.

Charlesworth, Hilary, and Emma Larking. 2015. "Introduction: The Regulatory Power of the Universal Periodic Review." Pp. 1–22 in *Human Rights and the Universal Periodic Review: Rituals and Ritualism*, edited by H. Charlesworth and E. Larking. Cambridge: Cambridge University Press.

Chauville, Roland. 2015. "The Universal Periodic Review's First Cycle: Successes and Failures." Pp. 87–108 in *Human Rights and the Universal Periodic Review: Rituals and Ritualism*, edited by H. Charlesworth and E. Larking. Cambridge: Cambridge University Press.

Christensen, Mikkel, and Ron Levi. 2018. "An Internationalized Criminal Justice: Paths of Law and Paths of Police." Pp. 1–14 in *International Practices of Criminal Justice: Social and Legal Perspectives*, edited by M. Christensen and R. Levi. London: Routledge.

Collister, Heather. 2015. "Rituals and Implementation in the Universal Periodic Review and the Human Rights Treaty Bodies." Pp. 235–255 in *Human Rights and the Universal Periodic Review: Rituals and Ritualism*, edited by H. Charlesworth and E. Larking. Cambridge: Cambridge University Press.

Conti, Joseph. 2016. "Legitimacy Chains: Legitimation of Compliance with International Courts Across Social Fields." *Law and Society Review* 50 (1):154–188.

Cowan, Jane. 2015. "The Universal Periodic Review as a Public Audit Ritual: An Anthropological Perspective on Emerging Practices in the Global Governance of Human Rights." Pp. 42–62 in *Human Rights and the Universal Periodic Review: Rituals and Ritualism*, edited by H. Charlesworth and E. Larking. Cambridge: Cambridge University Press.

De la Vega, Constance, and Cassandra Yamasaki. 2015. "The Effects of the Universal Periodic Review on Human Rights Practices in the United States." Pp. 213–234 in *Human Rights and the Universal Periodic Review: Rituals and Ritualism*, edited by H. Charlesworth and E. Larking. Cambridge: Cambridge University Press.

Devries, Karen M., Joelle Y. Mak, Loraine J. Bacchus, Jennifer C. Child, Gail Falder, Max Petzold, Jill Astbury, and Charlotte H. Watts. 2013. "Intimate Partner Violence and Incident Depressive Symptoms and Suicide Attempts: A Systematic Review of Longitudinal Studies." *PLOS Medicine* 10(5): e1001439.

Dezalay, Yves, and Bryant G. Garth. 2002. *The Internationalization of Palace Wars: Lawyers, Economists, and the Contest to Transform Latin American States*. Chicago: University Of Chicago Press.

Elizalde, Pilar. 2019. "A Horizontal Pathway to Impact? An Assessment of the Universal Periodic Review at 10." Pp. 83–106 in *Contesting Human Rights: Norms, Institutions, and Practice*. Cheltenham: Edward Elgar Publishing.

Ermakoff, Ivan. 2008. *Ruling Oneself Out: A Theory of Collective Abdications*. Durham: Duke University Press.

Eyerman, Ron. 2006. "Performing Opposition, or How Social Movements Move." Pp. 193–217 in *Social Performance: Symbolic Action, Cultural Pragmatics, and Ritual*, edited by J. C. Alexander, B. Giesen, and J. L. Mast. Cambridge: Cambridge University Press.

Freedom House. 2018. *Freedom in the World 2017*. New York: Freedom House.

Goffman, Erving. 1959. *The Presentation of Self in Everyday Life*, 1st ed. New York: Anchor.

Goffman, Erving. 1982. *Interaction Ritual: Essays on Face-to-Face Behavior*, 1st ed. New York: Pantheon.

Goodale, Mark. 2002. "Legal Ethnography in an Era of Globalization: The Arrival of Western Human Rights Discourse to Rural Bolivia." Pp. 50–72 in *Practicing Ethnography in Law: New Dialogues, Enduring Methods*, edited by J. Starr and M. Goodale. New York: Palgrave Macmillan.

Goodman, Ryan, and Derek Jinks. 2004. "How to Influence States: Socialization and International Human Rights Law." *Duke Law Journal* 54(3): 621–703.

Hafner-Burton, Emilie. 2012. "International Regimes for Human Rights." *Annual Review of Political Science* 15: 265–286.

Hafner-Burton, Emilie M., Laurence R. Helfer, and Christopher J. Fariss. 2011. "Emergency and Escape: Explaining Derogations from Human Rights Treaties." *International Organization* 65(4): 673–707.

Hafner-Burton, Emilie M., and Kiyoteru Tsutsui. 2005. "Human Rights in a Globalizing World: The Paradox of Empty Promises." *American Journal of Sociology* 110: 1373–1411.

Hafner-Burton, Emilie M., and Kiyoteru Tsutsui. 2007. "Justice Lost! The Failure of International Human Rights Law To Matter Where Needed Most." *Journal of Peace Research* 44(4): 407–425.

Hagan, John, and Ron Levi. 2005. "Crimes of War and the Force of Law." *Social Forces* 83(4): 1499–1534.

Hagan, John, Ron Levi, and Gabrielle Ferrales. 2006. "Swaying the Hand of Justice: The Internal and External Dynamics of Regime Change at the International Criminal Tribunal for the Former Yugoslavia." *Law and Social Inquiry* 31(3): 585–616.

Halliday, Terence C., and Gregory Shaffer. 2015. *Transnational Legal Orders.* Cambridge: Cambridge University Press.

Houge, Anette Bringedal, and Kjersti Lohne. 2017. "End Impunity! Reducing Conflict-Related Sexual Violence to a Problem of Law." *Law and Society Review* 51(4): 755–789.

Joseph, Sarah. 2015. "Global Media Coverage of the Universal Periodic Review Process." Pp. 147–166 in *Human Rights and the Universal Periodic Review: Rituals and Ritualism*, edited by H. Charlesworth and E. Larking. Cambridge: Cambridge University Press.

Keck, Margaret E., and Kathryn Sikkink. 1998. *Activists Beyond Borders: Advocacy Networks in International Politics*, 1st ed. Ithaca: Cornell University Press.

Levi, Ron, and Ioana Sendroiu. 2019. "Moral Claims and Redress after Atrocity: Economies of Worth across Political Cultures in the Holocaust Swiss Banks Litigation." *Poetics* 73:45–60.

Mackie, Gerry. 1996. "Ending Footbinding and Infibulation: A Convention Account." *American Sociological Review* 61(6): 999–1017.

Massoud, Mark Fathi. 2011. "Do Victims of War Need International Law? Human Rights Education Programs in Authoritarian Sudan." *Law and Society Review* 45(1): 1–32.

McMahon, Edward R., Kojo Busia, and Marta Ascherio. 2013. "Comparing Peer Reviews: The Universal Periodic Review of the UN Human Rights Council and the African Peer Review Mechanism." *African and Asian Studies* 12(3): 266–289.

Merry, Sally Engle. 2006a. *Human Rights and Gender Violence: Translating International Law into Local Justice.* Chicago: University of Chicago Press.

Merry, Sally Engle. 2006b. "Transnational Human Rights and Local Activism: Mapping the Middle." *American Anthropologist* 108(1): 38–51.

Merry, Sally Engle. 2012. "Measuring the World: Indicators, Human Rights, and Global Governance." *Current Anthropology* 52(S3): S83–S95.

Meyer, John W., John Boli, George M. Thomas, and Francisco O. Ramirez. 1997. "World Society and the Nation-State." *American Journal of Sociology* 103(1): 144–181.

Michaels, Ralf. 2016. "State Law as a Transnational Legal Order." *UC Irvine Journal of International, Transnational, and Comparative Law* 1: 141.

Milewicz, Karolina M., and Robert E. Goodin. 2018. "Deliberative Capacity Building through International Organizations: The Case of the Universal Periodic Review of Human Rights." *British Journal of Political Science* 48(2): 513–533.

Moravcsik, Andrew. 2000. "The Origins of Human Rights Regimes: Democratic Delegation in Postwar Europe." *International Organization* 54 (2): 217–252.

Munck, Gerardo L., and Jay Verkuilen. 2002. "Conceptualizing and Measuring Democracy: Evaluating Alternative Indices." *Comparative Political Studies* 35 (1): 5–34.

Newman, Matthew L., Carla J. Groom, Lori D. Handelman, and James W. Pennebaker. 2008. "Gender Differences in Language Use: An Analysis of 14,000 Text Samples." *Discourse Processes* 45(3): 211–236.

Newman, Matthew L., James W. Pennebaker, Diane S. Berry, and Jane M. Richards. 2003. "Lying Words: Predicting Deception from Linguistic Styles." *Personality and Social Psychology Bulletin* 29(5): 665–675.

Nyamu-Musembi, Celestine. 2002. "Are Local Norms and Practices Fences or Pathways? The Example of Women's Property Rights." Pp. 126–150 in *Cultural Transformation and Human Rights in Africa*. London: Zed Books.

Pennebaker, James W., and Lori D. Stone. 2003. "Words of Wisdom: Language Use over the Life Span." *Journal of Personality and Social Psychology* 85(2): 291–301.

Pierotti, Rachael S. 2013. "Increasing Rejection of Intimate Partner Violence: Evidence of Global Cultural Diffusion." *American Sociological Review* 78(2): 240–265.

Pouliot, Vincent. 2016. *International Pecking Orders: The Politics and Practice of Multilateral Diplomacy*. Cambridge: Cambridge University Press.

Russell, S. Garnett, Julia C. Lerch, and Christine Min Wotipka. 2018. "The Making of a Human Rights Issue: A Cross-National Analysis of Gender-Based Violence in Textbooks, 1950-2011." *Gender and Society* 32 (5): 713–738.

Schmidt, Averell, and Kathryn Sikkink. 2019. "Breaking the Ban? The Heterogeneous Impact of US Contestation of the Torture Norm." *Journal of Global Security Studies* 4(1): 105–122.

Schokman, Ben, and Phil Lynch. 2015. "Effective NGO Engagement with the Universal Periodic Review." Pp. 126–146 in *Human Rights and the Universal Periodic Review: Rituals and Ritualism*, edited by H. Charlesworth and E. Larking. Cambridge: Cambridge University Press.

Semin, Gün R., and Klaus Fiedler. 1988. "The Cognitive Functions of Linguistic Categories in Describing Persons: Social Cognition and Language." *Journal of Personality and Social Psychology* 54(4): 558–568.

Sendroiu, Ioana. 2019. "Human Rights as Uncertain Performance During the Arab Spring." *Poetics* 73: 32–44.

Sexton, J. B., E. J. Thomas, and R. L. Helmreich. 2000. "Error, Stress, and Teamwork in Medicine and Aviation: Cross Sectional Surveys." *BMJ (Clinical Research Ed.)* 320(7237): 745–749.

Shaffer, Gregory. 2012. "Transnational Legal Process and State Change." *Law and Social Inquiry* 37(2): 229–264.

Shaffer, Gregory. 2016. "Theorizing Transnational Legal Ordering." *Annual Review of Law and Social Science* 12(1): 231–253.

Shaffer, Gregory, ed. 2012. *Transnational Legal Ordering and State Change.* Cambridge: Cambridge University Press.

Shaffer, Gregory, and Terence Halliday. 2016. *With, Within, and Beyond the State: The Promise and Limits of Transnational Legal Ordering.* SSRN Scholarly Paper. ID 2882851. Rochester: Social Science Research Network.

Simmons, Beth A. 2009. *Mobilizing for Human Rights: International Law in Domestic Politics*, 1st ed. Cambridge: Cambridge University Press.

Simmons, Rachel A., Dianne L. Chambless, and Peter C. Gordon. 2008. "How Do Hostile and Emotionally Overinvolved Relatives View Relationships?: What Relatives' Pronoun Use Tells Us." *Family Process* 47(3): 405–419.

Skotnicki, Tad. 2019. "Unseen Suffering: Slow Violence and the Phenomenological Structure of Social Problems." *Theory and Society* 48: 299–323.

Tausczik, Yla R., and James W. Pennebaker. 2010. "The Psychological Meaning of Words: LIWC and Computerized Text Analysis Methods." *Journal of Language and Social Psychology* 29(1): 24–54.

Tsutsui, Kiyoteru, and Christine Min Wotipka. 2004. "Global Civil Society and the International Human Rights Movement: Citizen Participation in Human Rights International Nongovernmental Organizations." *Social Forces* 83(2):587–620.

Union of International Associations. 2018. "Yearbook of International Organizations" (accessed March 23, 2018).

Van Schaack, Beth. 2008. "Engendering Genocide: The Akayesu Case Before the International Criminal Tribunal for Rwanda." *Santa Clara Law Digital Commons.* https://digitalcommons.law.scu.edu/facpubs/629.

Vega, Constance, and Cassandra Yamasaki. 2015. "The Effects of the Universal Periodic Review on Human Rights Practices in the United States." Pp. 213–234 in *Human Rights and the Universal Periodic Review: Rituals and Ritualism*, edited by H. Charlesworth and E. Larking. Cambridge: Cambridge University Press.

Wood, Elisabeth Jean. 2014. "Conflict-Related Sexual Violence and the Policy Implications of Recent Research." *International Review of the Red Cross* 96(894): 457–478.

World Bank. 2018. "GDP (Current US$)."

Zhou, Min. 2012. "Participation in International Human Rights NGOs: The Effect of Democracy and State Capacity." *Social Science Research* 41 (5):1254–1274.

PART V

CONCLUSION

CHAPTER TWELVE

CONCLUSIONS

A Processual Approach to Transnational Legal Orders

Sally Engle Merry

The emergence of transnational criminal justice orders is a major development in our rapidly globalizing world. As problems such as money laundering, human trafficking, corruption, and drugs assume an international as well as transnational scale, the need to develop transnational mechanisms for ordering them clearly grows. Yet, we lack a centralized political or legal system capable of exerting the kinds of control found in nation-states. As the chapters in this book show, there has developed, in response to this situation, a series of what have been labeled transnational legal orders (TLOs). They differ in numerous ways, have various origins, are unevenly institutionalized, and rely on a range of forms of authority from those of national hegemons, such as the United States and Europe, to social pressure and the fragile authority of the United Nations and its treaties. They are newly emerging in a wide variety of areas and are a critically important feature of the new global system. Yet they are also forms of social ordering that are sufficiently diffuse and varied to render their analysis difficult. The concept of transnational legal orders offers a useful framework for thinking about the range of formal and informal, national and international, legal and reputational systems being mobilized in attempts to construct systems of ordering that stretch beyond the nation-state. This book uses the transnational legal orders framework to tackle the question of how such approaches have been mobilized to deal with criminal justice issues.

Although the concept of transnational legal orders is clearly an important contribution, developing theoretical principles to explain the operation of TLOs is challenging given the wide variation in their characteristics, histories, and social processes. TLOs are challenging to study in practice. They are constituted by myriad national, international, and nongovernmental organizations and actors who often have shifting and informal as well as formal relationships with each other. They differ significantly in power. Some parts are organized as institutions, but other parts are made up of diffuse and even inchoate social networks. Moreover, these mechanisms develop over time, sometimes solidifying and sometimes falling apart. They typically keep changing. Informal social practices gradually become bureaucratic routines, demands for more data and activity generate new bureaucratic offices, and acceptance by states and publics increase or dissipate over time. At the same time, TLOs may rise and fall as the need for the kind of ordering each one promises emerges then disappears, is replaced by another system, or is seen as ineffectual. Patterns of decay depend to some extent on the amount of institutionalization of the TLO. For example, the human rights system, which shares some of the characteristics of a transnational legal order, is criticized for failing to produce a more human-rights compliant world despite its institutionalization in UN agencies, treaties, and nongovernmental organizations, along with extensive informal networks of activists. Like many of the projects discussed in this book, such apparent failure has not led to the demise of human rights, at least not yet, but instead has inspired a demand for more resources and more activity.

Clearly, the first step in understanding the varied ways that transnational criminal justice orders function is identifying them. The concept of TLO is valuable in allowing researchers to identify them as distinct social phenomena. The chapters in this book show how various organizations that can be labeled TLOs work, focusing on the processes within national and transnational ordering projects. They map their practices, ideologies, and operating constraints. The contributors to this book have provided rich accounts of a range of transnational and national ordering practices within the criminal justice domain viewed broadly. Given the variety and volatility of these practices, the processual approach that most adopt seems the most promising approach to understanding transnational legal orders. TLO-type entities develop over time and sometimes coalesce into a coherent system, but how and why that happens is less clear. Given the multi-sited, multi-organizational, and multi-actor basis of most TLOs, it is hard to develop a systematic theory about how they work and when and why they arise and fall. But as this book shows, analyzing the dynamics of creation, transformation, and demise of these forms of social organization by the in-depth analysis of individual TLOs provides valuable insight into the TLO model developed by Halliday and Shaffer (2015). Once a TLO is identified, it can be analyzed in ways that recognize the variability and instability of TLOs. This volume makes a major contribution to that analysis.

This collection of studies offers a detailed examination of a wide variety of organizations that aspire to regulate criminal behavior transnationally. The authors in this collection have generally adopted an approach that examines individual TLOs empirically. In so doing, they focus on three important issues, although they are not always labeled as such: process, ideology, and infrastructure. They take a processual approach to understanding how TLOs operate, seeing them as developing and changing over time as norms settle or unsettle, competitors emerge or disappear, and conditions change or remain stable.

An analysis of the processes, practices, ideologies, and infrastructural and contextual conditions of particular TLOs helps build understanding of how TLOs work in transnational ordering, as the chapters in this book demonstrate. They focus on how a TLO develops over time, what makes it work or fail, and what institutional systems undergird it if it lasts. This requires a longitudinal and historical approach as well as an ethnographic examination of a TLO in practice. It involves attending to its context, culture, ideology, routines, bureaucracies, and the power dynamics among its constituent parts. As Radha Ivory insightfully observes in her chapter on a proposed Australian corporate foreign bribery offense, transnational law reform should be understood as a social process that emerges in particular places and times in the context of specific jurisdictional forms and prevailing issues. The chapters in this volume all show clearly the importance of this local specificity in understanding the emergence of transnational legal mechanisms.

One valuable way to develop a processual understanding of a TLO is to follow how it responds to particular events and crises. Such events are typically rooted in particular places, although similar events and crises may occur in a variety of places such as campaigns against migrants or worries about corruption. The analysis of practices, of everyday ways of doing things, also helps explain how TLOs work and what holds a TLO together. Studying the constituent formal and informal rules and the links between national and international sections of the TLO opens up the internal dynamics of the TLO mechanism. An examination of the overall ecology of the TLO provides further insight into the prevailing legal and social practices constituting the TLO. A focus on the particular values of a TLO is important, since some generate moral support, such as anti-trafficking projects or drug control, while others are more pragmatic, such as banking regulatory systems. The infrastructure of TLOs is another important consideration that warrants further attention, since they differ in size, resources, staffing, communication systems, and many other dimensions of their physical operation. In sum, the analysis of TLOs requires attention to process, ideology, and infrastructure.

Process dimensions of analysis include a focus on both internal and external processes. TLOs typically have a complicated internal organization in which various parts exercise different kinds and degrees of power so that making sense of how they work together requires tracing how they function over time and the power base of each part. A process analysis of a TLO includes an historical genealogy of its formation and vicissitudes. For example, in his chapter on the cannabis prohibition TLO, Ely Aaronson shows how cannabis prohibition, a problem typically handled at the national level, has become transnational. He describes the process by which this regime is established, highlighting the pressure imposed by the United States using the threat of withholding funds while pursuing a criminal justice approach. The approach parallels that of the US anti-trafficking initiative based in the US State Department, which generates the Trafficking in Persons Report (TIP Report). The trafficking initiative similarly adopted a criminal justice framework to the problem even though other countries took more socially supportive approaches. Thus, there is a tendency for one TLO reform approach to be replicated in tackling other, similar problems. However, in the cannabis control situation, as also in the anti-trafficking movement, local sites of resistance to the transnational TLO are beginning to weaken its control. Clearly, attention to the temporality of TLOs is essential.

Furthermore, once a system is established with personnel, offices, techniques of working, expertise, and funding support, it acquires its own inertia and may resist being dismantled. The infrastructural dimension of a TLO contributes to its ability to endure over time. There is an important degree of inertia in these transnational systems, so it is valuable to focus on the process of construction of such transnational systems and on the infrastructures they develop to manage flows of money, goods, and personnel. Such infrastructural features affect the way TLOs resist change. Indeed, my research on global indicators and the mechanisms established to create them suggests that once they are established with a clear ideology (such as combatting corruption or promoting freedom) and an infrastructure for counting and representing information along with experts and expertise, they have considerable inertia (Merry 2016). Part of the inertia is the desire to have comparable data over time while another part is the reliance on expertise developed in managing similar problems in the past. Even when TLOs emerge in the context of a particular crisis, once established they are hard to change even when the crisis changes. In many ways, inertia is in part the product of the infrastructure: of knowledge, personnel, bureaucracies, and resources. My look at global indicators – informational systems that are often produced by TLO-type organizations – shows that once a system is established, there is considerable inertia both in data and in expertise.

An infrastructural, contextual analysis highlights the role of powerful countries in supporting a TLO. For example, the US State Department's approach to trafficking includes a threat of US sanctions if a country refuses to pass laws and make other efforts to prevent trafficking or to provide information to the State Department about its trafficking situation. It also funds NGOs that take a criminal justice anti-trafficking approach rather than those that address issues such as marriage practices or poverty. These NGOs subsequently provide information to the State Department, which uses it to rank countries according to their efforts to control trafficking, sanctioning those who do poorly by withholding non-humanitarian aid. In so far as countries go along with the US approach, it may be the threat of sanctions embedded in the system and possibly the power of the ranking system itself.

Similarly, in their chapter on the Financial Action Task Force on Money Laundering FATF, Halliday, Levi, and Reuters describe a TLO under the leadership of the United States and Europe that has galvanized an enormous set of institutions and actors in a disciplinary project to control money laundering. In some ways, it is parallel to the anti-trafficking initiative created by the US government in 2000, in that both are designed to control behavior designated as criminal that is hard to pin down and count. Both invest substantial resources in pursuing a criminal justice approach to a problem seen as large and troubling with little clear data to support claims to its size and scope.

Similarly, success is virtually impossible to measure in both cases since the problem is itself largely underground and hidden. Both the anti-trafficking and anti-money laundering TLOs cases count proxies for success such as the number of laws passed instead of the number of violations averted.

The Halliday, Levi, and Reuters chapter provides a good analysis of the structure of the TLO and its ideology and suggests other fascinating questions about its process and infrastructure. How did the FATF get put together? Who was behind it? Who pays for the staff? How do shared rules develop and how are they adapted when new problems, such as terrorism, become more salient? How can an official, transnational body, which in places might be more like a network, coordinate its activities, develop shared rules, and enforce them? How did it expand to all states, when some are clearly targets rather than victims of these systems? What is the role of formal law versus other kinds of quasi-legal arrangements, and to what extent does the FATF rely on national law rather than international law? To what extent is the operation of the TLO based on reciprocity rather than law?

These questions are important in trying to explain the puzzle raised in the chapter: Why do states and citizens put up with the surveillance necessary to control money laundering? Again, parallel to the emergence of anti-trafficking networks engaging both civil society and state participation, there is cooperation on the side of a moral good, espoused by religious and secular reformers who are invested in eliminating organized crime. But it also satisfies conservatives and authoritarian leaders who want to control borders. There is clearly an ideological dimension to a system in both cases, which suggests that its major contribution could be symbolic.

Ideological dimensions are typically central to the operation of TLOs. They refer to the underlying moral purpose and framing of the problems the TLO is engaging. The ideology of a TLO matters. Values can shape a transnational initiative, even in the absence of explicit legal authority. For example, in his chapter, Dirk van Zyl Smit shows that there is an influential transnational set of legal standards for prisons, even though prisons are clearly under the control of states. In a similar vein, Stefanie Neumeier and Wayne Sandholtz demonstrate that even though the death penalty is legal and under the control of individual states, there has been a substantial curtailment of its legal use under the influence of a transnational movement supported by international human rights values, such as the right to life and the right to be free from cruel, inhuman, or degrading punishment. In both of these chapters, the authors show that a transnational ideology can be influential in shaping criminal justice policy, even without any transnational legal authority to regulate state behavior.

A focus on the ideology of a TLO can explain puzzling aspects of its operation. For example, as Halliday, Levi, and Reuters ask about the anti-money-laundering TLO, why does it persist despite its failure to control money laundering? Their answer considers the role of ideology. The FATF clearly offers a narrative of a world in which there are dark, nefarious activities that must be stopped, joining fear of the unknown and the criminal with the opportunity to be a rescuer. It promises to eliminate corruption – a widely appealing goal. Perhaps the answer to the puzzle the chapter raises about why so much effort and cost are being expended despite a lack of clarity about its accomplishments is that its real success is supporting this narrative of danger and the hope of an end to corruption. The trafficking narrative does similar ideological work in promising to end the exploitation of innocent young women. Thus both TLOs offer a comforting image that something is being done in the face of shadowy, evil, criminal actors when in practice such violations, whether with relation to money laundering or human trafficking, are virtually impossible to stop. Radha Ivory's chapter on a proposed Australian anti-corruption law similarly shows the importance of ideology, in this case of the threat of foreign bribery.

Of course, the anti-money-laundering TLO also provides valuable tools for national leaders seeking to extend their power. In her chapter, Prabha Kotiswaran notes that since the alleged crisis in trafficking is not matched by any firm numbers of victims, perpetrators, prosecutions, or convictions, the problem may be overblown. She argues that this is in part because the criminal justice model allows states to use more stringent, criminal-justice-focused techniques to police borders. As in the case of the FATF, the persistence of a TLO may have more to do with its collateral benefits to actors external to the system (such as governments) than to its ideological claims. Similarly, Vanessa Barker's analysis of the criminalization of migration focuses on the way criminal justice laws, personnel, practices, and ideologies are mobilized to expand and justify border control activities. Thus the ideology of a TLO may serve to increase public support, but its benefits may lie elsewhere. This collateral benefit in the case of trafficking is greater because of the uncertainty about what the term actually means, leaving more opportunity for others to mobilize the TLO in ways outside its core ideology. For example, does the term refer only to sex trafficking? Does it include labor trafficking? Does it require mobility? Is every sex worker by definition a trafficking victim? Is the central concern controlling women's sexuality or preventing exploitative forced labor? Clearly, the ideology of a TLO is central to its operation.

In many situations, there are alternative TLOs addressing the same issue but with different ideologies and strategies. Sometimes the alternative parts blend but often they contradict each other and are in competition, as is the case with some of the ideologies of anti-trafficking. For example, in the field of violence against women, there is considerable tension at the global level between organizations and projects that seek to diminish gender violence by promoting gender equality, a liberal and human rights approach, and those focused on gender complementarity. The latter position argues that men and women are fundamentally different but women can be safe if they are honored and respected. The first position tends to be a secular human rights one and the second a religious one, found in many religious traditions. While the secular human rights approach seems to have more widespread global support, the religious view is also widespread and often defended in the face of human rights critiques, supported by the argument that maintaining existing practices promotes social order and stability.

Tensions among alternative ideologies are particularly vivid in the case of the anti-trafficking movement. As Prabha Kotiswaran shows in her chapter, the anti-trafficking movement contains some parts that take a criminal justice approach of rescuing sex workers and punishing traffickers while other parts use a forced labor framework and focus on improving regulations on employers and reducing the opportunities for exploiting workers. There are distinct international regimes with different frames in this ideological space, some of which can be seen as competing TLOs. There are also TLOs that adopt more than one ideological stance. Several, such as the US TIP Report, Palermo Protocol, and the UN Office of Drugs and Crime promote a criminal justice model which, as Kotiswaran shows, strengthens surveillance and the control of borders and is popular with states. A second ideological space is the International Labour Organization (ILO) model, which sees trafficking as form of forced labor in some cases and seeks to improve the working conditions of forced workers (Kotiswaran 2017). A third has developed the modern-day slavery framework, such as NGOs like Walk Free with its Global Slavery Report and Index, a move also adopted by the US State Department *TIP Report.* As Kotiswaran notes, the current move to add trafficking to the Sustainable Development Goals (SDG) puts it into the development model, thus ideologically framing it in relation to underlying social and economic conditions rather than as the product of exceptional "bad apples" that traffic innocent girls. From this perspective, trafficking is a systemic economic problem as well as a matter of criminal individuals who need to be caught and punished.

As Kotiswaran argues, despite claims that there are a vast number of victims of trafficking or the more recent label, "modern-day slaves," with an estimate at 45.8 million slaves in a recent Global Slavery Index, and despite widespread state support of anti-trafficking, indicated by 170 ratifications for the global anti-trafficking convention (the Palermo Protocol), there are relatively few reported victims and perpetrators arrested and fewer convicted. How can we explain this disparity? As she says, trafficking may be an appealing framework for states to distract from or conceal their tolerance for bad labor practices and from seeing such abuse as systemic rather than individual and therefore a problem in which the state itself could be seen as complicit.

Joachim Savelsberg offers another example of the tensions between alternative ideologies of TLOs in his discussion of the conflicts between humanitarian, diplomatic, and justice frames for addressing human rights abuses. After describing the rise of an anti-impunity TLO based on international human rights law, he notes that in practice, this approach conflicts with those of humanitarian organizations, such as Doctors Without Borders, who seek to end suffering rather than enforce justice. Moreover, diplomats seeking to negotiate peace must sometimes focus on ending conflict rather than punishing violators. Clearly, the anti-impunity approach coexists with and contradicts other prevailing approaches to dealing with political and military conflict. Similarly, in efforts to overcome the decades of violence in Colombia, the desire for retribution conflicts with strategies of peacebuilding, as Manuel Iturralde clearly demonstrates.

Using a TLO framework helps to expose the diversity and incoherence of the anti-trafficking TLO(s). It highlights the quite different approaches overall as well as the limitations of the criminal justice framework with, as Kotiswaran says, its requirement that a specific offender must be identified rather than more general patterns of poverty, migration restrictions, or violence and coercion in family relationships. The possibility of moving the focus on human trafficking more onto labor questions and a conceptualizing it in a larger social and economic framework rather than that of the exceptional victim and criminal perpetrator construction through engagement with the SDGs is intriguing. It will be interesting to see how it develops.

Ron Levi and Ioana Sendroiu offer yet another perspective on the ideological and infrastructural dimensions of TLOs in their analysis of the TLO of sexual violence as a human rights concern. They examine human rights recommendations with regard to sexual violence in the Uniform Periodic Review (UPR) process of the UN Human Rights Council. They note that despite the universality of peer review of all nations' human rights performance and an egalitarian system of recommendations in which any country can recommend reforms to any other country, which it can accept or reject, there are many countries that reject some of the recommendations they receive. They see the UPR process as a performance engaged in with differing commitments by countries that vary according to their political orientation. Their empirical analysis shows that poorer and less free countries are less likely to accept recommendations for reform from richer, freer countries, which tend to be more specific and more law-based, than from poorer, not free countries, whose recommendations tend to be less specific and less legal. Their approach highlights the importance of a contextual and disaggregated analysis of TLO processes and ideologies, including the relations between countries. Their data shows the importance of the relationship between particular recommending countries and receiving countries, thus emphasizing the importance of position-taking by countries in public forums. By conceptualizing a TLO as a field, they are able to consider the relative power of countries, the relationships among them, and the significance of a public performance for countries with varying levels of freedom and affluence.

Moreover, this example also underscores the role of infrastructure, in this case the organization of the UN, the human rights system, the Human Rights Council, and the public nature of these deliberations as they are electronically available around the world. These infrastructural features help to perpetuate a TLO mechanism that, as Levi and Sendroiu point out, offers a powerful performance on an international stage despite some indications that its effectiveness is limited (Charlesworth and Larkin 2015).

As with any international system, TLOs such as the human rights approach to sexual violence are built on compromises among competing values and ideas of how to identify and solve problems. The founding texts are likely to be ambiguous and unsettled. A fundamental strategy of international discussions and documents is to paper over differences in complex and vague texts and agreements. This strategy emerges even in global indicator systems like the SDGs which are founded on broad and sometimes contradictory ideologies expressed vaguely in order to reach any agreement at all. The UPR system exhibits these tendencies. It seems likely that the emergence of vague and broad norms to cover up real differences in interest and ideology contributes to the ability of TLOs to become established and to the lack of compliance with them. This point also raises the issue of what norm settlement means. If the underlying norms are vague and contradictory, the norms are unlikely to settle except in a very general way. Some of the case studies reveal such a lack of settlement along with continuing contestation and lack of compliance. Yet TLOs persist despite this lack of agreement on more specific norms. Why this happens is an interesting question that has more to do with infrastructure and the interests of national political leaders than with the ideology promoted by a TLO. For example, we have seen the benefits to states of criminal interventions against drug trafficking and human trafficking that allow them to enhance control over migration and borders.

In sum, as scholars move toward understanding the practices within TLOs and their relationship to the wider society and other TLOs, it is clear that an empirical, ethnographic examination of processes, practices, ideology, and infrastructure are critical. TLOs work in social spaces where they compete with other ideological definitions of a problem and depend for their continued existence on resources, personnel, and other forms of infrastructure. Their endurance depends on articulating an ideological position which generates attention and support, building an effective organization of some kind, and constructing an infrastructure of bureaucrats, experts, techniques of doing things, and resources that will allow it to continue. Collateral benefits for others outside the TLO may be central to this process. This is clearly a rich terrain for further transnational research to which this collection has made a significant contribution.

REFERENCES

Charlesworth, Hilary, and Emma Larking, eds. 2015. *Human Rights and the Universal Periodic Review: Rituals and Ritualism*. Cambridge: Cambridge University Press.

Halliday, Terence C., and Gregory Shaffer, eds. 2015. *Transnational Legal Orders*. Cambridge: Cambridge University Press.

Kotiswaran, Prabha, ed. 2017. *Revisiting the Law and Governance of Trafficking, Forced Labor, and Modern Slavery*. Law and Society Series. Cambridge: Cambridge University Press.

Merry, Sally Engle. 2016. *The Seductions of Quantification: Measuring Human Rights, Gender Violence, and Sex Trafficking*. Chicago: University of Chicago Press.

INDEX

CAMBRIDGE STUDIES IN LAW AND SOCIETY